The Times and Life of Edward Robinson

SBL
SOCIETY OF BIBLICAL LITERATURE
Biblical Scholarship in North America

Thomas H. Olbricht
Volume Editor

Number 19
THE TIMES AND LIFE OF
EDWARD ROBINSON
Connecticut Yankee in
King Solomon's Court

Jay G. Williams

Jay G. Williams

THE TIMES AND LIFE OF EDWARD ROBINSON

Connecticut Yankee in King Solomon's Court

Society of Biblical Literature
Atlanta, Georgia

THE TIMES AND LIFE OF EDWARD ROBINSON

Connecticut Yankee in King Solomon's Court

Jay G. Williams

Copyright © 1999 by the Society of Biblical Literature

All rights reserved. No part of this work may be reproduced or transmitted in any form or by any means, electronic or mechanical, including photocopying and recording, or by means of any information storage or retrieval system, except as may be expressly permitted by the 1976 Copyright Act or in writing from the publisher. Requests for permission should be addressed in writing to the Rights and Permissions Office, Scholars Press, P.O. Box 15399, Atlanta, GA 30333-0399, USA.

Library of Congress Cataloging-in-Publication Data

Williams, Jay G., 1932–
   The times and life of Edward Robinson : Connecticut Yankee in King Solomon's court / Jay G. Williams.
     p. cm. —(Biblical scholarship in North America ; no. 19)
   Includes bibliographical references and indexes.
   ISBN 0-88414-012-1 (alk. paper)
   1. Robinson, Edward, 1794–1863. 2. Biblical scholars—United States—Biography. 3. Congregationalists—United States—Biography. I. Title. II. Series.

BX7260.R62 W55 1999
285.8'092—dc21
[B]

                                                                                                                      99-046803
                                                                                                                      CIP

08 07 06 05 04 03 02 01 00 99   5 4 3 2 1

Printed in the United States of America
on acid-free paper

To Edward and Janet Robinson

In great appreciation

TABLE OF CONTENTS

Introduction	1
Chapter One: A Connecticut Yankee	9
Chapter Two: Boyhood in Southington	37
Chapter Three: The Hamilton Years	55
Chapter Four: Andover Days	79
Chapter Five: European Interlude	113
Chapter Six: Andover and Boston	175
Chapter Seven: Palestine and the Book	207
Chapter Eight: New York, New York	263
Chapter Nine: The Last Years	307
Appendix	341
Bibliography	349
Indices	
Index of Persons	375
Index of Places	381

INTRODUCTION

Edward Robinson was, perhaps, America's greatest Biblical scholar of the ante-bellum period. He was a noted philologist and lexicographer who contributed monumentally to those precise and erudite disciplines. He made his name, however, as an explorer and traveler, a Biblical geographer who redrew the maps of ancient Israel and, in that way, founded the whole field of modern Biblical archaeology. Moreover, because of his wide ranging interests, he presided for years over the first American attempts to study the cultures of Asia and Africa as well as over the first efforts to develop the science of ethnology. As a friend of poets and novelists, of artists and editors and inventors, Edward Robinson's life was woven into the fabric of nineteenth century America in significant ways.

Before we proceed to a study of his life, however, we must stop to explain how this study came to be:

In 1967, immediately after the six day war, I worked on an archaeological excavation at Tel Arad in southern Israel. In the evening Immanuel Ben Dor, an archaeologist who had once served as a curator for the Rockefeller Museum in East Jerusalem, lectured on the history and nature of archaeology in *eretz* Israel. He began his series with a fascinating lecture devoted to the man whom he called the father of Biblical archaeology, Edward Robinson. Although I taught a course in the Hebrew Scriptures, I had never studied in depth the development of archaeology and had never heard of this man whom Professor Ben Dor praised so highly. I dutifully inscribed what he said in my notebook and thought little more about it.

That fall, while advising a student, my eye fell upon a line in the Hamilton College Catalogue which said that the college library contained a collection of books on Palestinian travel once owned by an Edward Robinson. Was this the same man? Why should Hamilton own such a collection? I was intrigued.

A brief exploration proved that it was the same person. Edward Robinson had graduated from Hamilton in 1816 as valedictorian of the college's first full graduating class. I was surprised not only that such a famous scholar had graduated from Hamilton but that I had not known about him earlier. At that time I considered the possibility of writing a short monograph about him. Further research, however, showed that, aside from the various short biographies already available, there was little new information to add. Even a trip to the Union Theological Seminary Library in New York City where he taught for many years failed to turn up anything very significant. Somewhat reluctantly, I set the project aside to pursue other matters.

Then, in 1992, quite "out of the blue" the college received in the mail some memorabilia from early Hamilton days—a one page "catalogue," a junior class program, etc.—from the Edward Robinsons of Franklin Park, New Jersey. Frank Lorenz, the Hamilton College archivist, wrote to thank the donors and invited them to the college. A few weeks later they arrived and in the course of conversation we discovered that the Robinsons possessed other letters and papers belonging to their famous ancestor. These items had been stored in a trunk for years. They asked whether we would like to see them and we, needless to say, said we would.

Some of the materials were subsequently sent to us by mail. Others my wife and I examined in New Jersey and brought home. It turned out to be a treasure trove of materials: some four hundred letters and papers all tied up neatly in bundles just as Edward Robinson had left them, the medal he was presented by the Royal Geographical Society, his pipe, a book he had given to his sister, etc. Some items, like the records of various real estate transactions in and around Clinton, are of mainly local historical interest. Other things are of sentimental value at best. Most of the collection, however, is a priceless window into nineteenth century America and into the life of Robinson himself. There are autographs from General Lafayette, John Quincy Adams, Henry Wadsworth Longfellow, Edward Everett, and George Bancroft as well as from the many scholars he met in Europe. There are references to his relationships with many other famous figures of the time. Suddenly, into my hands was placed what I had looked for and failed to find decades before: unknown material shedding light on the great scholar. The task before me was clear.

And yet I hesitated. Although I once had taught the Hebrew Scriptures and published both books and articles in the field, that is not where my interests lie now. Instead my concentrated study today concerns

India, its Sutras and its Upanishads. I am not a trained American historian either, by any stretch of the imagination, and yet I could see that considerable knowledge of the history of our country would be necessary to understand Robinson's life and work. Should I not give over this task to someone more qualified? I was tempted to offer the whole project to someone else.

Still, our mutual connections with Hamilton, with Union Seminary, with Israel and things which Robinson would have described as "oriental" draw Robinson and me together. It is in the Hamilton Library where not only his collection of travel books but his own notebooks from Germany are housed. Anyone working on his life would have to come to Hamilton to do a significant portion of the research. Besides, I soon came to discover both Robinson and his times extraordinarily fascinating. And so I decided to plunge ahead.

Actually, however, much of the spade work was done not by me but by my wife, Hermine, to whom this book and I owe a great debt of gratitude. She not only organized all the materials of the Robinson collection chronologically and provided a catalogue for them; she also deciphered the scribbling which turned out to be a 400 page letter-journal of Robinson's study years in Europe. One cannot imagine the amount of time it took her to turn his illegibility into a readable document. Without her work very little could have been added to his life story.

As I began to read his printed works and his hand-written letters and notes, Robinson's own style of thinking began to emerge. He was a believer in the literal factuality of the Bible, but he also believed that the only way to understand the Biblical facts was to put them in their historical, geographical, and ethnographic context. Much of his life was spent accumulating information to illumine the context in which the Bible was written. It seemed to me appropriate, therefore, to do the same for him. Actually, a simple recording of the main facts of his life would take only a few pages and, indeed, has already been done, not only by others but by Robinson himself. Papers found in the New York Public Library indicate that E. R. wrote his own biography which is contained in the *Cyclopaedia of American Literature* of 1866. For the most part, my contributions to the basic outline of his life are to add various major and minor emendations and corrections to the old story. The broad outlines of Robinson's own and then Hitchcock's "life" remain intact. What I have tried to do in this work, then, is to see him in context, as a Connecticut Yankee moving on the ever-changing landscape of the nineteenth century. Hence, the title reads "The Times and Life of Edward Robinson."

Each chapter begins with "Headlines and Notices." These, as the reader shall see, include significant events of the day which may well have influenced and/or interested the subject of our discussion. He was, we know, an avid reader of newspapers. It was his daily habit. He was also an uncommonly patriotic American who believed whole-heartedly in the values of liberty and democracy. To understand his mind then is to understand that whole flow of history in which he lived.

Sometimes these headlines and notices are further discussed as the chapter goes on, sometimes not. They are there as a stimulation for "historical envisioning" and as a constant reminder that even the most arcane scholar does not exist in a vacuum. Around us all swirl those major and minor events which we cannot escape and which both subtly and overtly affect us. Robinson, himself, loved history and incorporated it frequently in the description of his explorations. Everything he saw, he interpreted within an historical context. I am sure he would like to be seen that way too.

When Robinson was born, Washington was still President. When he died, the Civil War was raging. Thus he lived through the most formative decades of the American Republic and saw the nation grow from a small band of rather isolated and under-populated states into a major nation of vast extent and potential influence. A major theme of this study then is America's development and expansion as a nation. To understand Robinson one needs to remember the Lewis and Clark expedition, which certainly excited him as a boy, and all those other explorations which made the United States a reality. Another major theme to dominate this portion of our history was the growing struggle over slavery. Therefore, although Robinson himself basically avoids public statements about the issue, it must be a theme of our study. The very fact that he, as a major Biblical scholar and theological professor, was largely silent about the issue is itself significant.

Still another question concerns what Edward Said has termed "Orientalism." Robinson was, quite clearly, one of the founding fathers of American Orientalism. He joined the American Oriental Society when it was first founded in 1842, remained a member for the rest of his life, and served as its President from 1846 to 1863. His major works concern his research in what was then thought of as the orient and they frequently express attitudes about the west Asian societies he visited. We must ask, then, what sort of orientalism he expresses. Does he or does he not conform to Said's paradigm?

Finally, Robinson lived through the beginnings of the Women's

Rights Movement. He was married to an important German intellectual who, though a woman in a very patriarchal society, achieved considerable eminence as a writer and scholar. Does he through attitude or writing express himself on what was considered the incendiary issue of womenís rights?

These, of course, are our questions which we must ask of the past. We must also attend to his questions. What did he aim to do? What genuine contributions did he make or attempt to make to the study of the Bible and the ancient Near East? Was Immanuel Ben Dor correct in calling him the "Father of Biblical Archaeology?" Was he really, as some have said, the most significant American Biblical scholar of the antebellum period?

I cannot close this introduction without mentioning a matter of considerable frustration. This concerns bibliography. My aim has been to produce as complete a bibliography of Robinson's works as possible. The problem, however, is that "completeness" seems to be in his case an ever-receding goal. He had the habit of publishing in a great variety of places, particularly in journals and newspapers. Oftentimes, he simply placed extracts from his other works, sometimes he offered something new or perhaps revised and supplemented.

In the obituary in the *Observer* the editor says, "We secured his contributions from week to week in the field of learning which was specially his own and in which he had no superior. He declined our offer of pecuniary compensation, but desired us to give the sum from time to time to such indigent theological students at the Seminary as he should send to receive the same." [*Observer* XLI, 6 (Feb. 5, 1863), 42.] Locating such contributions after the obvious spate of articles in 1840-41 is difficult. Although not included in the bibliography, "Scripture Illustrations" and "Scripture Sketches" found in The New-York Observer during February, March and April of 1854 may well be by him.

In any case, given the great number of newspapers both in New York and elsewhere at the time, the task of finding all those articles he wrote is endless. Undoubtedly there are unsigned articles which were from him. Some are probably to be found in newspaper and journal archives in England and Germany, for he occasionally published there as well. Nevertheless, I believe that the bibliography of his works here presented contains everything significant which can be attributed to him. Certainly if any reader is aware of other writings, I would be grateful to know about them.

Needless to say, no study of this sort is accomplished alone. I again want to express my great gratitude to the Edward Robinsons for making the

Robinson papers available to me and to my wife Hermine for cataloguing them and transcribing key documents. Thanks must also go to Dr. Frank Lorenz, Hamilton's archivist, for his unfailing support, to the Hamilton Library staff for considerable help, to Diane Yount and the Andover-Newton Theological School Library for assistance in locating and duplicating documents, to Dr. Milton Gatch and the reference staff at Union Theological Seminary for their help and support. I would also like to express my gratitude to Professor Joseph Malloy for assistance in rendering sometimes tricky German passages and Professor Douglas Ambrose for his willingness to peruse the manuscript. Most of all, I wish to extend my gratitude to Dr. Thomas Olbricht for his very helpful editorial suggestions which did so much to improve the manuscript and to Terri Viglietta for her excellent work proof-reading and formatting the document.

Finally, I would like to say just how much I have enjoyed working on this project and discovering anew what, I am sure, American historians have all known for a long time, that American history is endlessly fascinating and multidimensional. Robinson's view of life did not incorporate the great generalizations and abstractions of history—he disliked Hegel and his ilk—and neither does mine. It is essentially a "ground level" history which I seek to achieve. My hope is that readers will enjoy as much as I have seeing Robinson and his world from a very specific and human perspective.

JGW

Chapter One

A CONNECTICUT YANKEE

Headlines and Notices: 1794

January	Washington's second term in office has already begun. Political parties start to form around Alexander Hamilton, Secretary of the Treasury and proponent of rule by the elite (the Federalists) and Thomas Jefferson who favors a much more egalitarian, agricultural nation (the Republicans). Because of Jefferson's Deism, Connecticut people generally favor the Federalists.
February	Barbary pirates capture and enslave American seamen in Algiers. The result is eventually the formation of the U.S. Navy.
April 10	Born: **Edward, son of William and Elizabeth Norton Robinson, in Southington, Connecticut.**
April 11	Born: Edward Everett in Dorchester, Massachusetts. Everett became one of America's foremost orators and politicians. He served as U.S. Senator, Congressman, Secretary of State, Ambassador to England, President of Harvard University. It was he who orated for two hours before Lincoln's Gettysburg Address.

May	Tom Paine's *The Age of Reason* is published. For the Philadelphia edition Jefferson provides an introduction criticizing Hamilton.
May 27	Cornelius Vanderbilt is born on Staten Island, New York. He becomes, of course, one of the great transportation moguls of the United States, typifying America's industrialization and expansion.
July 28	Robespierre is guillotined in Paris, ending the monstrous Reign of Terror. It is this Jacobin terror which turns Americans against the revolutionary cause.
August 7	15,000 militia men are called out to put down the Whiskey Rebellion which is a reaction by "Westerners" (largely in Pennsylvania) to Hamilton's tax on whiskey.
August 20	"Mad" Anthony Wayne wins the battle of Fallen Timbers and removes the Indian (and British) threat to settlement north of the Ohio.
November 3	Born: William Cullen Bryant. As a poet, editor, man of letters, Bryant led Americans to more sophisticated tastes in the *belles lettres*.
November 19	The Treaty of London (Jay's Treaty) is signed preparing for the relinquishing of the northwest forts by the British and for rapid American expansion westward.
Near the end of the year	Citizen Genet, instead of returning to France marries Gov. Clinton's daughter and settles in Hudson Valley. Citizen Genet had stirred up much trouble in the United States as the French ambassador by making ludicrous demands and strongly encouraging Jacobin activity in America.

Chapter One

CONNECTICUT

Connecticut, that land of stable habits, was one of the earliest colonies established by Englishmen in the New World. During the 1630s, two colonies, Connecticut and New Haven, were founded, but the latter, partly in order to remain independent of New York, reluctantly merged with its eastern neighbor to form one colony. Tensions sometimes ran high between east and west, but ever after Connecticut remained one in government and in essential mood. Connecticut was a Puritan establishment, a beacon on the hill, aiming to follow the Lord's bidding in all its ways. Religion was as central in the minds of its inhabitants as the church steeple was to the village landscape.

It is difficult for modern Americans to imagine what a thin veneer of civilization Connecticut and the other colonies provided for the American continent. Even when Robinson was born, close to 90% of all Americans—excepting, of course, the so-called Indians—lived within fifty miles of tidewater. At the same time, this thin veneer had already developed a long history. When Edward Robinson was born, Connecticut was more than 150 years old and had been settled longer than many of our western cities have been in existence today. As we shall see, the Robinson family had already been in New England for five generations—Edward represents the sixth—and had probably lost all memory and contact with whatever family ties were left with England. For the citizens of the new Republic, the Pequod wars were also but a distant memory and the wild, aboriginal world which had been Connecticut was more of a dream than a reality. The not very productive land had been tamed, divided into farms, and worked laboriously. The countryside was dotted with villages and towns, each with its familiar Congregational Church steeple pointing heavenward.

Even in 1794 cities were tiny by modern standards, with Hartford and New Haven each numbering fewer than 5,000 souls. Southington, which lay between them, was but a tiny village. Manufacturing was present but unimpressive in output. There was some trade with the West Indies from Connecticut ports, but most commerce passed through either Boston or New York. The vast majority of citizens were farmers. Connecticut civilization was hard working, but rather slow and non-progressive. Its themes, to which we will return, were profoundly religious, even metaphysical.

Just a short distance to the west, not so many miles across the Hudson River, began a world of native Americans, of vast, unexplored valleys and plains, of wonders and fearsome threats which had scarcely been imagined, to say nothing of domesticated. There were forts and some tiny settlements and a few brave explorers who attempted to traverse the wilds, but, until almost the time of Edward's birth, European settlement had been confined very largely to the veneer. James Fenimore Cooper, writing much later, in the 1820s and 30s, portrays this world of native Americans and the few hardy palefaces who dared venture into it, quite vividly. *The Last of the Mohicans* is set but a few miles north of Albany, in the wilds of the southern Adirondacks.

While the Continent waited, 18th century Connecticuters indulged themselves in the affairs of the soul, in those endless disquisitions about free will and human depravity and eschatological hope. With a great empire yet to conquer, divines and laymen together pondered the atoning blood of Jesus and just how free humans are to save themselves. It was a Puritan dream-life.

The American Revolution, however, had begun to change all that. Connecticut Yankees, dissatisfied with the quality of their land (and, perhaps, the oppressiveness of their religiosity) and threatened by the population pressure brought about by large families, began to move. During the 18th century, they had headed north to populate western Massachusetts and what was to become Vermont. Now they headed west, to New York, to settle much of the central and western agricultural areas, and then to the Western Reserve in Ohio and on into Indiana and Illinois. As a result, despite a very high birth rate, Connecticut's population scarcely grew at all during the first decades of the 19th century, remaining during those years about 250,000. Instead of local population growth, much of the rest of America became Yankee. It is said that in 1837 one quarter of those in Congress, representing a variety of states, actually were born in Connecticut.

At home, however, conditions remained amazingly stable throughout the first half of the 19th century. Congregationalism was disestablished in 1818, but continued as the dominant religious tradition. There was little immigration so that, unlike New York, Connecticut had little experience of the challenge of new cultures and religions. Connecticut remained rural, Calvinistic, and to the mind of many others rather parochial. From the point of view of the inhabitants, what was important was to maintain a way of life and a religion which was being threatened or destroyed all around them. Connecticut was a state of mind.

The primary inspiration and authority for the religion of these Yankees was, of course, the Bible, as interpreted by Calvin and as reinterpreted by New England's greatest intellect, Jonathan Edwards (1703-1758). It was he who almost single-handedly wrested the momentum of the church from the Rationalists and Half-way Covenanters in order to stimulate a great awakening and revival in the churches of New England during the mid-eighteenth century. Although himself a ferocious intellect who placed tremendous emphasis upon right understanding as essential to faith, Edwards also knew that revival of religion is a matter of the heart. It is significant, if not paradoxical, that one of his greatest intellectual efforts involved an analysis of the importance and place of the affections in religion.

Edwards began and remained a Calvinist throughout his life. God is all in all; everything happens according to his will. Faith is not just a matter of free choice; it is a miracle wrought by God's Spirit working in the heart. Unlike Calvin, however, Edwards appealed not only to the Bible but to the new science—Newton *et al*—and the new philosophy—Locke and Berkeley in particular. Just beneath the surface of his thought was George Berkeley's essential insight: that the idea of matter and an independent world are superfluous. Reality is the human soul and the God who provides experience directly.

At the same time, Edwards was no apathetic stoic, for he saw that human beings can be God's instruments for bringing about his miracles. The preacher, in particular, can serve to transmit God's transforming power to his hearers. Moreover, although ultimately God is in charge of all things, Edwards allowed for a provisional free will. People do choose, though finally it is God who does the choosing through them.

Edwards, in a way, felt confirmed when he saw the effects which his own words caused among the church goers of Northampton, Massachusetts. When the fervor began to wane, it was rekindled by the visits of George Whitefield from England who stirred revivals all up and down the eastern seaboard.

Nevertheless, there was always the inevitable relapse. Eventually religious sentiments waned and people settled back into their routine. Then, only another period of revival could bring the Spirit back to the church. Thus Edwards, more than anyone else, set the rhythm of American Protestantism, a rhythm marked by periodic revivals separated by times of religious backsliding and the resultant torpor.

Revival inevitably seems to be followed by at least partial relapse and that, of course, is what happened after Edwards and his colleagues had done their work. The revival of one generation becomes the burden or the tedium or perhaps even the enemy of the next. Gradually, Connecticut would slip back into the humdrum, routine religious patterns of the unawakened. Such backsliding in the late 18th century had been augmented both by the American Revolution with its disruption of normal patterns of life and by the growth of free, more rationalistic thought.

Edwards was not just a preacher and reviver. Like many other clergymen in New England he served as mentor for numbers of young men who lived with him and learned from him the science and art of pastoring. Two of his most famous and influential students were Samuel Hopkins (1721-1803) and Joseph Bellamy (1719-1790) who, in turn, became the founders of the two basic branches or variations of Edwardseanism. Although there were old Calvinists around who disliked the whole idea of revival, Hopkins and Bellamy, through their own teaching and writing, gradually won over the majority of Connecticut Congregational clergy.

By the 1790's much of the Church, particularly the rural Church, was under the sway of these men and was ready for new revival. I say, "the Church" because, in fact, Congregationalism was the established religious organization of Connecticut, still supported by tax money and central to the whole civilization. Catholicism, at the time, was virtually non-existent within the State, while Methodists, Baptists, and Anglicans constituted quite small minorities.

Congregationalism prided itself on the preeminence of the individual congregation and its lack of hierarchy. Its ministers, however, were bound together by a uniformity of thought scarcely imaginable today. The "schools of the prophets" which gathered around those gifted clergy who taught young clergy-to-be theology produced committed, personally trained successors who were often related to their teacher through marriage to one of his daughters. Schools of thought there were: some followed Hopkins and some Bellamy, but the differences were actually very slight, for nearly everyone traced his theological ancestry back to Edwards.

By the 1790s, particularly in the rural churches, the rumblings of new revival were starting to be heard. In the face of a world beginning to run amuck, the pastors, supplemented by some effective itinerant evangelists, began to call their congregations to severe repentance for their hard-heartedness. In a sense, however, it was not so much the preachers as it was the people who produced the awakening. Some ministers, without dramatic effect, had been preaching evangelical sermons for years. Now, however, the tide turned and people began to listen and repent.[1] It was a matter of spiritual rhythm.

From our point of view, it seems almost ludicrous to call to repentance such hard-working and essentially pious people. Connecticut was hardly a land of free-thinking and dissipation. Nevertheless, there were dark clouds on the horizon. At the outset, American Protestants had cheered on the French revolutionaries. After all, the common enemy was old European despotism and, of course, the Roman Catholic Church. There was even some little hope expressed that France might become like Connecticut: sober, pious, and Protestant. As the French Revolution wore on, however, its excesses became manifold and obvious. The fruits of free-thinking led to the most horrible uses of the guillotine and to frightening social chaos. The year 1794 experienced the rule of the Jacobins and the reign of terror in which hundreds were unjustly killed.

For many it appeared that there was a danger that the bitter fruits of free-thought might spread to America. In 1787, proto-Unitarianism came to birth in Massachusetts; the unity of the bold Puritan experiment came under severe threat. Moreover, Thomas Paine published his *Age of Reason* in 1794 and there were those who were attracted by his heretical rationalism and his attack upon Christianity. Citizen Genet had travelled around the country founding Jacobin Clubs and was not unsuccessful in locating those who agreed with the radical French revolutionaries. At Yale College, interest in religion seemed slight as undergraduates enjoyed the tastes of worldly

---

[1] Richard D. Shiels, "The Second Great Awakening in Connecticut: Critique of the Traditional Interpretation," *Church History* 49, no. 4 (Dec. 1980), 401-415. See also: Richard Birdsall, "The Second Awakening and the New England Social Order," *Church History* 39 (1970), 345-364.

pleasure and the temptations of free thought. Young men went around addressing each other as "Citizen Voltaire" or "Citizen Diderot." Although it would hardly have appeared so to an outsider visiting the villages and towns of the state, the ministers sensed the danger of collapse.

Most of the Edwardseans were Yale graduates and feared the worst for their alma mater. The appointment of one of their own, Timothy Dwight, to the presidency of Yale in 1795, therefore, was heartening to them. Dwight began his career as President of Yale with a student body of little more than one hundred and a college church which had almost collapsed. During his tenure, however, the college more than doubled in size and the student body itself was revived religiously. It is often said that Dwight, himself, was largely instrumental in the renewed religious vigor not only at Yale, but in the state as a whole. Although there is some truth in this, it should also be noted that revivals were well underway before Dwight's influence became pronounced. If the people had not wanted revival, Dwight could never have had the influence which he exerted.

It may be that Yale, particularly through its theologian Nathaniel Taylor, eventually adopted a somewhat "softer" theology which the more orthodox Edwardseans regarded as flirting with Arminianism. Nevertheless, in the late 1790s and early 1800s Yale College, through the person of President Timothy Dwight, was the manifestation in the revival of the faith throughout New England. Since many Connecticuters migrated to New York during this period, Dwight's influence was important there as well. As we shall see, Hamilton College, Robinson's alma mater, was clearly under the influence of Dwight, who recommended to its trustees most of the faculty.

One should not think that the revivals which overtook Yale were what they later became in New York: emotional outbursts, full of weeping and writhing. The second Great Awakening began with strong emphasis upon the intellect and theology. Sermons, by modern standards, spoke very much to the understanding rather than just to the emotions. In fact, there were many meetings in which the minister at the end spoke very quietly and personally to each individual. If there was weeping for sins, it was the silent sobbing of the heart. Congregations were expected to leave in silence, considering deeply the nature of their sins and the promise of the gospel.

When, in the 1820s, Connecticuters heard of the new measures of Charles Finney which were, of course, designed for the rough and ready folk of the frontier, they generally took offense. Lyman Beecher, in one of his more famous sayings, proclaimed that he would stop Finney at the border and if he entered Connecticut would fight him at every stop, and if he got to Boston would stay and fight him there. Of course, eventually it was Beecher who invited Finney to Boston.

Although not nearly as dramatic or emotional as Finney's techniques, the methods of the Connecticut evangelists were very effective, producing "great movement of the Spirit." Hundreds were converted—or rather more accurately recommitted—and the rolls of many country churches swelled enormously. Young Edward grew up with the signs of revival all around him.

Out of this invigoration of the Spirit grew a whole host of new developments in church life. According to Connecticut law, each family in the state was expected to own a Bible. In fact, however, there was a shortage of Bibles and many citizens had no access to one. Therefore, church people united to form the Connecticut Bible Society which sought to supply Bibles to the destitute and, indeed, to anyone who lacked the good book. The movement was patterned after similar organizations in England, but had there been no revival, it would have at least been delayed in its development.

The use of tracts, apparently, was initiated by Voltaire in France in order to popularize his anticlerical stance, but was appropriated by the churches to get straightforward, earnest, moral and spiritual messages before saint and sinner alike. Tract societies appeared and delivered their trenchant messages not only to churches but also to schools and drinking establishments as well.

Both domestic and foreign missionary work now began to grow in importance in the minds of church people. Again, the Yankees followed the lead of the English. Few foreigners came to Connecticut, but Connecticut Yankees began to carry their theological message to many foreign climes. Some missionaries were sent west to serve the unchurched people on the frontiers and to carry the gospel message to the "Indian" nations. At first established pastors were relieved temporarily of their responsibilities at home to travel to the newly established communities in the west. When this proved an unworkable arrangement, regular missionaries were sent forth.[2]

---

[2] For a good discussion of American Protestant missions see: William R. Hutchison, *Errand to the World* (Chicago: University of Chicago Press, 1987).

Before long, missionaries were being sent to much more distant lands, such as Africa and India and in 1820 to the Sandwich Islands. So began one of the characteristic features of 19th century Christianity: the impulse to convert the world to the faith. In retrospect, there was something wonderfully (and hatefully) naive about the venture. Connecticut Yankees had been peculiarly (though, of course, never completely) isolated from foreign influence for a century and a half. What exactly did they know about the realities of non-Christian life? Did they really want non-whites to join the Connecticut tribe? They desired conversion, but when two native American converts studying at a mission school in Cornwall expressed their plans to marry a couple of nice Connecticut girls, there was a great explosion of hatred. Charles Keller writes:

> Finally, two marriages between Indian students and Cornwall girls roused much opposition to the school. The second of these marriages, between Harriet Gold, daughter of one of Cornwall's leading citizens, and Elias Boudinot, a Cherokee, created a considerable stir. An angry mob demonstrated against the marriage on the Cornwall Green, the exasperated agents of the school took a firm stand against the union, and Isaiah Bunce, the vigorous editor of Litchfield's *American Eagle*, gave the matter much attention.[3]

Faith in Christ apparently did little to erase the not so subtle racism quite evident in the society.

It is significant that among the first and most important foreign mission sites for New Englanders was the Sandwich Islands, a place which, because of peculiar social conditions in the islands, was ripe for conversion. Contact with the West had brought a precipitous collapse of the indigenous faith. The islanders desperately needed to find a new religious tradition to replace their old one. Thus Yankee missionaries arrived at the right place and the right time. Success on the islands, however, encouraged them to think that converting all the heathen was not only quite possible, but even easy. If Polynesians accept the gospel so readily, why not the Chinese and the Indians? It took more than one hundred years before the church began genuinely to wake up to the realities and difficulties of intercultural communication and the real dangers of converting people not only to another

---

[3] Charles Roy Keller, *The Second Great Awakening in Connecticut* (New Haven: Yale University Press, 1942), 104.

religion but to another culture. It took perhaps even longer to recognize that many other societies have religious and philosophical traditions at least as sophisticated and thoughtful as the West's and that it is spiritually damaging and maybe ultimately impossible, for people to give up one culture for another.

In any event, the early decades of the 19th century saw the rise of foreign missions and that meant that Yankees began to get news back from all corners of the globe. Readers of the *Panoplist* or the *Connecticut Evangelist and Religious Intelligencer* regularly were introduced to what was going on in missions around the world: in Palestine, Bombay, or South Africa. The world became bigger and more fascinating. There were dreams of travel and adventure—all in the service of the Lord, of course—in strange lands around the world.

To be sure, what they read and heard about the world outside was doubly reflected in a Yankee mirror. The missionaries themselves were "there," but only partially understood what they saw. Little victories were seen as major events; local resistance, the work of the devil. The heathen were most frequently pictured as dirty, ignorant and given to horrible religious practices; the missionaries, as heroic and beyond reproach. One story printed in 1805 in *The Panoplist* will help to convey the mood:

> These wild people (the Hottentots) have no idea whatever of the Supreme Being, consequently they practice no kind of worship . . . Their manner of life is extremely wretched and disgusting. They delight to smear their bodies with the fat of animals, mingled with a powder which makes it shine. They are utter strangers to cleanliness, as they never wash their bodies, but suffer the dirt to accumulate, so that it will hang a considerable length from their elbows. Their huts are formed by digging a hole in the earth about three feet deep, and then making a roof of reeds, which is however insufficient to keep off the rains. Here they lie close together like pigs in a stye. They are extremely lazy, so that nothing will rouse them to action, but excessive hunger. . . . They are total strangers to domestic happiness. The men have several wives, but conjugal affection is little known. They take no great care of their children, and never correct them except in a fit of rage, when they almost kill them with severe usage.[4]

---

[4] *The Panoplist or the Christian's Armory I, no. 1* (July 1805), 29. Parentheses my own.

That there might be something prejudiced about this description or entirely wrong-headed about the whole project occurred to few. If one can revive Connecticut, why not the world? Perhaps, eventually, the world will become Connecticut.

Of course, the expansion of churches, new social projects, and foreign and domestic missions meant that there was greater and greater demand for trained clergy. Until this point, ministers were educated by other ministers in their homes or studied further, after graduation from college, with a professor of the college who was, of course, a clergyman too. With the increased demand for clergy and the awareness that some professors, particularly at Harvard, had strayed into the proto-Unitarian camp, a great need was felt for a regular institution of theological learning to prepare future generations of clergy in New England.

After an attempt to establish such an institution in West Hartford failed, Andover Theological Seminary was founded in 1808 in Andover, Massachusetts. The location placed the institution close to New England's largest city (and that citadel of heresy, Harvard), and not far from New Hampshire and Maine, but the faculty, with such men as Edwin D. Griffin, Ebenezer Porter, and Moses Stuart, was very heavily from Connecticut. It was not until 1822 that Connecticut established its own theological school at Yale. Yale Theological Seminary, even then, remained small, producing only about nine graduates annually, over a forty year period.

The development of theological schools, of course, also stimulated new sorts of scholarly activity. Earlier theological education usually involved the study of a whole list of theological questions and answers under the direction of the clergy-tutor. The Bible, of course, was the ultimate source, but there was little systematic study of the setting, history, and meaning of Biblical books. That is, the Bible tended to be treated as a series of proof-texts rather than as literature. The need to teach the Bible systematically, however, led to its formal study and exposition. Thus Moses Stuart, of whom we will hear much later, was one of the first Americans to treat the Bible as an object of study in and for itself.

The Great Awakening also had its effects upon many other aspects of society as well. When public education was weaned away from the church's immediate influence, churches responded with the Sunday School, an institution not invented but greatly enlarged and developed by the Great

Awakening. Here children learned Bible verses and hymns, stimulated in their learning by prizes and awards.

Eighteenth century Connecticut not only countenanced but enjoyed the widespread use of alcoholic beverages, particularly "ardent spirits " (i.e. hard liquors). They were served everywhere, even at ordination parties and meetings of the clergy. If a clergyman came to call it was expected that he would be served rum or some other strong drink. Dancing was also a part of life. Children took dancing lessons and there were even ordination balls.

The Awakening changed all that as preachers began to warn about the obvious dangers of alcohol and promote temperance in society. Clergy associations agreed to forego the alcohol once freely served at their meetings. At the same time, dancing came to be regarded as frivolous, perhaps licentious, and not in keeping with the serious life of the pious Christian. It was not until the very end of the 18th and beginning of the 19th century, therefore, that the puritans became what we think of as puritanical.

All of this is to say that Edward Robinson, the subject of our study was born at a dramatic watershed in human history. Although one can make too much of the exact date, 1794 stands as a very good marker between one age and the next.

Before that time, rationalism in religion had been on the rise as had the quest for equality and liberty in political life. Nathan Hale, an American patriot who graduated from Yale with Edward's father, in 1773, stated the new creed most succinctly when he said, "I only regret that I have but one life to give for my country." His emphasis was not upon dying for Christ but for the newly declared nation which was to become the United States. By the same token, Patrick Henry's choice between liberty and death emphasized political rather than spiritual freedom. This attitude led to great support for the French who desired the same. The Reign of Terror dampened such enthusiasm, however, and turned Yankee Puritans back to a more religious quest. Robinson as a child must have heard much about both the horrors of the French Revolution and, to ward off such difficulties, revival, temperance, foreign missions, and Federalism.

At the same time, the world of America was no longer a thin veneer on a vast wilderness. Connecticuters were moving West in great numbers, not only to New York State but beyond. Wayne's victory at Fallen Timbers coupled with the Treaty of London negotiated by John Jay opened vast reaches of America to new settlement. The success of Lewis and Clark in their expedition across the country in 1804-06 stimulated even more the quest for new land and new settlements. One can well imagine what a profound effect the opening of the American continent had upon the imagination of a boy growing up during that era. Edward tells us, in fact, that he could not get enough of books on travel and exploration.

Moreover, this opening of America was coupled with a steady stream of at least pseudo-news from that growing band of missionaries sent first from England and then from America to convert the ignorant, idolatrous, and darkened in mind. Suddenly, the world seemed so much larger, so much stranger than the earlier Connecticut imagination had allowed. A child could pick up one of those pious magazines dedicated to the conversion of the heathen and read of people with the strangest ideas and customs.

Before the 1790s the world of the Bible seemed like a far off dream, something that happened centuries ago, on another landscape. Few imagined actually walking where Jesus walked or seeing the real Sea of Galilee. But now young Edward **could** dream, for he read about missionaries who actually lived in such places, who walked the streets of Damascus and Jerusalem. Of course, we do not know certainly how his interest began, but one can imagine the young Edward developing his thirst for travel and adventure from all the news, both domestic and foreign which swirled about him.

What is particularly interesting is that Edward Robinson, though surrounded by all the fruits and demands of the Great Awakening, never succumbed to the pressure to conform but went his own way. It is that way which will be the subject of our investigation. Before we proceed to examine the facts and direction of his life, it will be good to look first at where he came from, that is, at his family.

THE FAMILY

In 1859, Edward Robinson privately published a memoir of his father, William Robinson, together with an exposition of his family's genealogy. In many respects the volume, which was meant primarily for family and friends, is an excellent example of that period's renewed concern for family history, particularly such history as extended back to the founding of American society. It parallels, though in a far less gloomy fashion, the generations represented in Hawthorne's *The House of Seven Gables*. To my knowledge, Robinson never explored where his ancestors came from in England or whether there was recoverable family history there. It was enough that the first William Robinson in America arrived in about 1636; the Robinsons were, by that very fact, distinguished as one of America's oldest families. In a world like New York City which groaned with new immigrants in the 1850s, that may have been important to make clear. Certainly, for him his genealogy was a significant part of his person; we cannot speak of him without reviewing his family from the beginning.

Characteristically, Edward went about his task with impressive energy and diligence, corresponding with librarians, visiting cemeteries, uncovering old family documents. Although his family history was to him a matter of great pride, he was equally proud of his ability to distinguish fiction and fact, even when that distinction lessened to a certain extent the luster of the family tree. For instance, his distant cousin, Col. John Trumbull, the artist, began his autobiography by tracing his ancestry back to John Robinson of Leyden, the original minister to the Separatists from Scrooby, England who eventually landed at Plymouth Rock.[5] Edward takes considerable pains to show that Trumbull was wrong and that his ancestor was not John Robinson of Leyden but William Robinson, a much less prestigious immigrant, who arrived in Massachusetts Bay in about 1636 and proceeded to settle in Dorchester, about four miles distant from Boston itself.

Indeed, it should be noted that there is nothing particularly distinguished about the various representatives of the Robinson line whom he describes. Except for John Alden and Jonathan Trumbull, the Governor of Connecticut, who were both related to the Robinsons by marriage, there are no famous people in the genealogy.[6] Nevertheless, each generation represents an interesting era of Americana and another link connecting Edward to the very earliest American settlement. Perhaps, collectively, they reveal something of his own character.

---

[5] John Trumbull, *The Autobiography of Colonel John Trumbull, patriot-artist (1756-1843)*, ed. Theodore Sizer (New Haven: Yale University Press, 1953) p. 2.

[6] Through marriage Robinson was also related to John Trumbull, the artist, and to Benjamin Silliman, the well-known lecturer and professor of Chemistry at Yale.

The First Generation

Dorchester, Massachusetts was the Bay Colony's first settlement, having been founded by John White in 1630, before William Brewster had even arrived in the New World. By the time William Robinson landed six years later, however, many of the inhabitants of Dorchester had already left, moving to better land in Windsor, Connecticut. The new colonists of 1636, therefore, moved into an already settled area which afforded them unoccupied housing and cleared pasturage.

Because the resident minister, the Rev. Mr. Warham, had moved with his congregation to Connecticut and his co-pastor, The Rev. Mr. Maverick had died, there was need for a new minister to come in and, for all intents and purposes, gather a new church. Significantly, the new settled pastor was to be none other than Richard Mather, the father of Increase and grandfather of Cotton Mather. From the beginning, then, the Robinsons were near the center of the grand Puritan experiment.

The experiment in Dorchester, however, did not begin very auspiciously, for when Mather attempted to form a church the General Council turned the request down. According to their judgment, only two of the seven founding members were truly regenerated Christians. Mather had to spend considerable time and energy after that first failure educating his new potential flock in the ways of acceptable theology and religious experience before the ecclesiastics who oversaw such matters would officially approve the founding of the church and the settlement of Mather as minister.

William Robinson was not one of the initial founding members of the Dorchester congregation but his position near the top of the membership list means that he must have joined soon after it was established. Undoubtedly he, like most other immigrants, was a convinced Puritan when he arrived in the colony, and, like Mather, a victim of the repressive policies of Charles I and William Laud. Therefore he would very likely have joined the church soon after his arrival. His vocation, however, was secular and not sacred. Eventually he became the owner of a tide mill (one of two such mills in Dorchester) and, it would appear, was reasonably prosperous. That mill, known as Tilotson's Mill was still in existence when Edward wrote the memoir.

While William established himself as a modest entrepreneur, grinding corn and tilling the soil for a living, the events of the day, so significant for the history of New England, swirled around him. It is interesting to note that the very year of his arrival Harvard College was founded as an institution to train clergy for the church; a new era of education was begun. During the same year, the Ann Hutchison affair boiled over and she was exiled from the colony for her excessive religious claims. Roger Williams also left for Providence and the founding of a colony based on quite a different philosophy from that of Massachusetts.

Mather, who represented in many respects the quintessence of the Massachusetts Bay religiosity, fulminated repeatedly in his sermons against the antinomianism represented by Hutchison while defending the almost absolute authority of the clergy in the life of the church and society. Since Mather considered himself the "religious expert," he also would have thought a man like William Robinson to be an uneducated peasant whose role was to accept the wisdom and admonitions of the clerical caste. Mather was **not** the founder of American egalitarianism.

The very next year, war broke out in Connecticut between the settlers and the Pequods. The settlers eventually "won," wiping out a major segment of the Pequod tribe but the struggle was a harbinger of things to come. Although at times relations between the English settlers and native Americans were friendly, many of the tribes began to feel the pressure of colonial expansion. Eventually this erupted into the King Philip's War of the 1670s which came so close to absolute disaster for the whole colony. Many of the outlying settlements like Northampton were virtually destroyed and hundreds of the settlers were killed before the native American tribes were defeated in the bloody Great Swamp Fight.

Although the Puritans may not have quite realized it, their very attempt to found a new, more perfect Christian society was flawed from the outset. It is true that John Eliot, minister at nearby Roxbury, worked to convert the Indians to Christianity and was, in part, successful. There were several communities of "praying Indians" established in the colony. Nevertheless, to create this beacon on the hill, the colonists had to beg, borrow, or steal (the so-called Indians had no concept of buying) native

American land and that by implication brought them into conflict not only with the natives but with their own good book. The Puritans, of course, appealed to the example of Joshua and saw America as like the promised land—to be taken as Joshua took the country promised to the patriarchs from the Canaanites. Had they paid more attention to Jesus' teachings about violence, however, they might have felt much more uneasy. To found a Christian state through the use of violence and/or stealing is, in fact, a major contradiction at the very core of the enterprise. We must ask, before we are through, whether this implicit attitude toward "others," so characteristic of the Puritan mind, had its effects upon America's and Edward Robinson's view of the "oriental" to which he turned so much of his attention.

William Robinson, like many of his male descendents, was married several times. His first wife, Prudence, gave birth to his four children, Samuel, Increase, Prudence, and Waiting. Subsequently he married in succession Margaret and then Ursula, who survived him. William died in 1668 and his will was recorded in the Probate Court of Boston. It is from John Eliot, the famous minister of nearby Roxbury, however, that we learn that he met his death by being pulled through the cogwheels of his own mill.

The Second Generation

Samuel, the eldest, was born in 1640 and inherited the major portion of the estate of his father. He became a prosperous landholder, acquiring much additional property. He served as a rater, a selectman, and finally as a representative to the General Court in 1701 and 1702 before he died in 1718.

It is unfortunate that we do not know more about the life of Samuel Robinson, for he lived through a crucial period of the colony's history. Not only did he experience first-hand the King Philip's War through which the native tribes sought to extirpate the whole colony. He also lived through the period of the Salem witch trials and all the spiritual pain which that era entailed as well. Then there was the revocation of the colony's charter in 1684, and the merger of the Bay and Plymouth colonies to form the Dominion of New England.

This latter event took place as a result of the restoration of the Stuart monarchy in England and the attempt of that regime to bring its recalcitrant

Puritan colony to heel. To do this the crown appointed Sir Edmund Andros, a most autocratic governor, to keep the colonists in line. The colony seethed with discontent until the Glorious Revolution of William and Mary. When word that the Stuarts had been overthrown reached New England, the colonists took matters into their own hands and deposed the hated Andros. Whether Samuel took part in this, the first American revolution, is but a matter of speculation.

Under William and Mary a new charter was granted to New England in 1691. Maine and Plymouth were legally joined to Massachusetts Bay colony to become simply "Massachusetts." The governor was to be appointed by the crown but the power to levy taxes resided in the legislature, i.e. the General Court. The requirement of church membership for voting was abolished, thus ending officially the theocracy.

In any event, Samuel Robinson, as a member of the General Court, was in a position of considerable influence for the colony. Because all expenses, including the Governor's salary were paid out of the taxes levied by the Court, the legislative body had genuine power. The arrangement also, of course, prompted frequent conflict between the legislative and executive branches of government, a conflict which would ultimately lead to revolution.

Samuel married Mary Baker of Dorchester and had three children: Samuel, Jr. (1666-1734), Mary (1668), and John (1671-1745). Although no record of John's birth or baptism is extant, Edward demonstrates quite conclusively that John was indeed a member of that family. It is through him that the line descends to Edward.

The Third Generation

John Robinson was the first of the New England Robinsons to enter the clergy. He attended Harvard, graduating in 1695. It seems probable that he spent the next few years apprenticed to a clergyman, but we have no information in that regard. In 1698, in any event, with the blessing of, among others, both Increase and Cotton Mather, he traveled to Newcastle, Pennsylvania as a missionary. Whether this was a very small village near Pottsville as Edward Robinson believed or Newcastle, Delaware which was then a part of Pennsylvania is difficult to tell. My guess is that Edward was wrong on this point, for Pottsville and that general area were largely unsettled territory in 1698. In any event, either this was meant to be a short-term appointment or the venture turned out disappointingly, for the next year he returned to Dorchester where he was accepted into full communion in the church there. After several more years and apparently considerable discussion of salary, John Robinson became the settled minister in Duxbury, Massachusetts in 1700. His ordination, however, did not take place until 1702.

While Dorchester was originally a part of the Massachusetts Bay Colony, Duxbury was connected to the separatist establishment at Plymouth. Across the bay from the original settlement, Duxbury became, early on, the settlement of choice for Miles Standish, John Alden, and many others. From the point of view of history, no pulpit in the area could have been more distinguished. History, however, does not pay salaries and from the beginning, it would seem, John Robinson was concerned about the size of his stipend and the irregularity with which it was paid. After some initial disagreement, however, he became the settled minister of the church in 1702, remaining there until his dismission in 1738.

In many ways, John was the most noted member of Edward's direct Robinson lineage, for he was the only college-educated, ordained clergyman in the direct line of descent until Edward's father William went to Yale. Edward does little to glorify John, however. Instead, he describes him as

> a man of great eccentricity of character, which manifested itself on many occasions. He was impetuous, sometimes violent, and not always polished in his modes of expression. It is related, that he always appeared in the pulpit in a short jacket; and in consequence irreverently spoken of as "Master Jack." It is said also, that he never wore an outside garment.[7]

Edward had in his possession a number of John Robinson's sermons, particularly those preached for special occasions. Of his preaching he writes:

> As a preacher he was sound in discourse, and sentitious in his arguments. His sermons were usually written out in full, a tolerably legible hand . . .

---

[7] Edward Robinson, *Memoir of the Rev. William Robinson* (New York: John F. Trow, printer, 1959), 31.

> Some of them are very long, forming almost a treatise upon a single text. These probably occupied several Sabbaths in delivery . . . He was remarkable for his occasional sermons and text; and the occurrence of great events or unusual phenomena afforded themes to his liking, which he would treat in a manner as eccentric as characteristic.[8]

Unfortunately, although Edward was careful in preserving documents of importance and left behind in neat bundles many of his own papers, these sermons apparently no longer exist.

One of the lost sermons was preached upon the occasion of the fateful death in 1722 of John's wife and daughter while on a "coaster" sailing to Boston. The storm capsized the boat and all were lost at sea. Indeed, his wife's body was not recovered for sometime and then at a distant point on Cape Cod. Robinson also includes in his memoir a poem written by the Rev. Nathaniel Pitcher of nearby Scituate, Massachusetts commemorating the death of John's wife Hannah and eldest daughter Mary.

Hannah was the daughter of the Rev. Ichabod Wiswall, John Robinson's predecessor at the Duxbury Church. Since Mr. Wiswall's wife (and Hannah's mother) was a direct descendant of the John and Priscilla Alden made famous in Longfellow's *The Courtship of Miles Standish* (1858), Edward lingers over this direct relationship, explaining at some length Hannah's, and therefore his own, pedigree.

In the light of these connections with the most legendary roots of America, John Robinson's eccentricities do not matter much and Edward delights in telling some rather droll tales about his great grandfather. He even hints that his dismission from the Duxbury pulpit in 1738 may have resulted from more than a simple fight over salary. It is likely that John's moodiness and somewhat violent and eccentric nature, made his ministry less than wholly satisfying for the congregation. The official reasons for dismission were given as simply age and bodily infirmities, but the documents which Edward quotes about the rather lengthy negotiations before dismission indicate that many people were not unhappy to see him go.

---

[8] *Ibid.,* 30-31.

The Fourth Generation

By the time John Robinson left Duxbury for Connecticut his children were already adults. Of the seven children who reached maturity, Faith was doubtless the most famous because of her marriage to Jonathan Trumbull, the very successful and significant Governor of Connecticut who held office before, during, and after the Revolution. One of his greatest and most applauded contributions to his country was the providing of provisions for General Washington's army during the Revolutionary War. Faith also became of mother of Col. John Trumbull, already referred to, whose well-known paintings are still to be seen in the nation's capitol. One of her daughters, also named Faith, was the grandmother of the first wife of the Rev. Eli Smith who will later figure prominently in Edward Robinson's own story since Smith accompanied him on his famous trips to Palestine.

John's daughter Alethea also married into the important Stiles family and in so doing became the aunt of Ezra Stiles, long-time President of Yale College, with whom William, Edward's father was well acquainted. Edward Robinson, however, descended from John's youngest son, Ichabod, named undoubtedly for his grandfather, Ichabod Wiswall.

After his dismissal, John left Duxbury and moved to Lebanon, Connecticut to be with his children Betty, John, and Faith who all lived by this time in or near Lebanon. It should be noted in passing that Lebanon was also the site of Eleazar Wheelock's famous school for native Americans and settlers which Samuel Kirkland, the missionary to the Oneidas and founder of Hamilton College, attended. We will return to Kirkland later in our discussion, for Edward married his youngest daughter. Ichabod, John's youngest child, born in 1720, just two years before the drowning death of his mother, accompanied his father to their new home.

For most of his adult life Ichabod ran a small country store, carrying both Boston-made and imported goods. Due to the influence of his brother-in-law Jonathan Trumbull who was at that time judge of probate for the district of Windham, Ichabod was appointed clerk of the court, a position he continued to hold until 1768. Unfortunately, in later life he had a falling out with the Trumbulls and did not benefit much from that important political and social connection.

He married twice, but only his second wife, Lydia, bore his children. Three sons and two daughters lived until their adult years. All were baptized by the Rev. Solomon Williams, famous for the fact that he was one of the signers of the Declaration of Independence. Lydia died in 1778 at the age of 58, leaving Ichabod a widower for almost thirty years.

Although Ichabod had no higher education, Edward remembered his extensive library of modern works of high caliber and the fact that he subscribed to the *Spectator* and *The Gentleman's Magazine* for years. Clearly he was an unusual shopkeeper. It is also unusual that such a man, who never owned many of the world's goods, was willing and able to send two of his sons to Yale. At the same time, it would appear that he inherited a considerable portion of his father's eccentricities. Edward writes:

> He is still remembered by many in Lebanon, after the lapse of half a century, as a man respected indeed, but not beloved; of a disposition inclined to be peevish and irritable; of good intentions, but in some respects eccentric. My father used to say of him, that he was prone to despondency, and always looked on the dark side of things while his wife preferred to look at the bright side. In my visits as a boy, I have no recollection of a single kind word or look from him.[9]

William used to visit him semi-annually, often accompanied by Edward, but the father never visited the son in Southington. Ichabod lived until 1809, having experienced, among other things, the first Great Awakening, the French and Indian War, and the monumental changes which constituted the American Revolution.

The Fifth Generation

William was Ichabod's second son. Joseph, his eldest, never married but remained on the family homestead as a farmer. Mary died of "an unusual sore throat" at the age of 24. Lydia, the second daughter, like Joseph remained unmarried and suffered from what appears to have been some sort of psychological problem. John, the third son, went to Yale and studied

---

[9] *Ibid.*, 53-54.

theology. He served as a pastor in Westborough, Massachusetts from 1789 until his dismissal in 1807. He then returned to the homestead and worked, apparently as a farmer until his death in 1832. He was married twice and had two children. Aside from William, therefore, none of that generation of Robinsons appears particularly distinguished.

William, the second son and Edward's father, was born in Lebanon, Connecticut in 1754. According to the *Memoir*, he resembled in personality and habit his mother, Lydia, rather than his father.[10] He received his education at the famous Grammar School of Master Tisdale in Lebanon and then, beginning in 1770, at Yale College. Among his classmates were James Hillhouse and Benjamin Tallmadge, who later became members of Congress, and Nathan Hale, America's martyr spy. As a part of the graduation in 1773 Robinson participated with Hale, Tallmadge, and his good friend Ezra Sampson in a forensic debate on the subject, "Whether the Education of Daughters be not, without any just reason, more neglected than that of Sons?"

William seems to have been a very successful student, winning the Berkeley prize for declamation and thereby serving as "Scholar of the House" for one year that he was in residence. After teaching school for two years in Windsor, Connecticut he returned to study theology, probably under President Daggett. He was licensed to preach in 1776 and delivered his first sermon at the Goshen parish in Lebanon that same year. The next several years were spent in occasional preaching and then as tutor at Yale. It was in that capacity that he became a close acquaintance of Timothy Dwight and Joseph Buckminster and came to meet his primary theological mentor, Joseph Bellamy.

In 1777, a committee of the Ecclesiastical Society of Northampton, Massachusetts invited William Robinson to preach in that famous pulpit once regularly occupied by Jonathan Edwards with the idea that if the response were favorable he would be invited to be settled there as minister. Robinson, however, turned the offer down and instead returned to Yale as a tutor. In 1779 he became Senior Tutor and it appeared that he might find a career in academia.

Instead, however, he received a call to become settled minister of the Congregational Church in Southington, Connecticut, a small village midway

---

[10] *Ibid.*, 66.

between Hartford and New Haven. He eventually accepted that call and was ordained in that church in January 1780. One month later he married Naomi Wolcott whom he had met while teaching in Windsor, Connecticut.

Ms. Wolcott was from an old and distinguished family, her uncle Oliver having been one of the signers of the Declaration of Independence and her cousin Oliver, the successor of Alexander Hamilton as Secretary of the Treasury. Subsequently, he became Governor of Connecticut from 1817 until 1827. Her own father, who held the rank of Major, had fought in the French and Indian War.

After some little delay, she joined her husband in a newly rented house in Southington and began housekeeping. It is perhaps significant that Edward Robinson, writing in 1859 on the eve of America's most violent upheaval, included the following comment:

> Mrs. Robinson brought with her to Southington, as a domestic, a coloured girl, named Mercy. She was a slave; and married, a few years later, Antony, a coloured man in the family of Joshua Porter; where she spent the rest of her life. She had one son, Peter; who, having been born after March 1, 1784, was by law not a slave, but was held to service as an apprentice, until the age of twenty-five years. This service belonged to Mr. Robinson.[11]

One might have thought the author, sensitive to the highly-charged feelings of the day, would have either omitted any reference to slave-holding by his family or offered some sort of lament for the moral blindness of his father. That he does neither strikes the modern reader as at least unusual.

In April 1781, Naomi gave birth to her first son, but he died after only four days of life. Even more tragic, Naomi herself contracted smallpox through a faulty inoculation and died in 1782 from the medical treatment which was supposed to protect her. The days of domestic tragedy for William were beginning.

In September 1783 he married again, this time to Sophia Mosely of Westfield, Massachusetts. Less than a year later she also gave birth to a William Robinson. Before the year was out, however, Sophia was dead of "quick consumption" at age 25. Her son, William, survived childhood and followed in his father's footsteps, graduating from Yale in 1804.

---

[11] *Ibid.*, 94-95.

Unfortunately, however, he too died of consumption in November of the same year.

Two and one half years passed after the death of his second wife before Robinson again married. This time he took as his bride Annie Mills of Simsbury. She came from a whole family of clergymen, among whom was her cousin Samuel J. Mills Jr., noted as one of the first to awaken the church to an interest in foreign missions. In May of 1788, she gave birth to Robinson's first daughter, named Naomi Sophia after, one might suppose, his first two wives. Naomi lived into her sixties, residing with her husband James Woodruff much of her life in Catskill, New York, but her mother contracted the measles in 1789 and, after giving birth to a dead infant, expired at age 28 after less than two years of marriage.

So, in less than nine years, William Robinson had lost not only two infant children but also three young wives. It is not surprising that he was attracted to the Calvinistic emphasis upon the inscrutability of God's will. It is also quite probable that his own suffering made him a pastor who was exceptionally sensitive to the sufferings of others.

None of these personal losses, however, caused William to retreat from the world. Indeed, it was exactly during this time that he laid the groundwork for his secular, worldly success. Like many other ministers of the church, he found his yearly salary small and often in arrears. Therefore, he supported himself, in part, by farming. For most ministers, this was a marginal enterprise at best, a matter of survival, not material gain.

William Robinson, however, was an astute man and before long he had acquired property and cattle which provided more than mere subsistence. He owned hives of bees which he often rented out. The same was true of milk cows. He bought a sawmill which functioned, apparently, as a reasonably lucrative enterprise. Before many years passed, he had become one of the wealthier clergy of Connecticut as well as a man who adopted the newest and most successful agricultural methods. His properties were models for agricultural life in the area.

By modern standards one could hardly pronounce him rich, but he surely was successful according to the measure of his own day. Just how he managed all his enterprises and also served satisfactorily as the minister of the Southington Church is a matter largely left unexplained. Clearly, he attended to his ecclesiastical business with vigor and discernment, for he remained the settled pastor in Southington for forty-one years. Perhaps, in fact, his parishioners rather liked the fact that he was wealthy enough so that he did not have to complain repeatedly about his modest clerical livelihood.

Edward describes him as a rather large man who arose early to study and do the work of the church in the morning while managing and inspecting his various holdings in the afternoon. His sons, as they grew up, joined him in agricultural labor. In 1790 Ezra Stiles listed him as one of the wealthy ministers of the state.[12]

That same year he married his fourth wife, Miss Elizabeth Norton (b. 1761) of Farmington. This marriage, like the preceding ones, brought him into relation with other long-standing, Connecticut families. John Norton, the patriarch of the family, arrived in the town of Branford in 1646, in Farmington in about 1661. Elizabeth was a fourth generation Connecticuter, the daughter of Col. Ichabod Norton and Ruth Strong. Her father had served in the Continental Army and, after the war, represented Farmington in the state legislature for every year but one from 1785 until 1791.[13] He also served for many years as justice of the peace. His wife, Ruth, also came from an old Connecticut family which included quite a number of clergy, including the Rev. Cyprian Strong, among its members.

Elizabeth, William's new wife, had three sisters and five brothers. Ruth married Mark Hopkins of Clinton, N.Y. Ashael was called to be the settled minister of the Congregational Church in Clinton, while Seth served as Principal of the Hamilton-Oneida Academy and then as a founding faculty member of Hamilton College also in Clinton. Her brother Thomas, a goldsmith by trade, also lived in Clinton for some time before moving to Morrisville N.Y. In 1802, William and Elizabeth, on one of the few extended trips they ever took, journeyed to Clinton to visit her family there.

Thus the Nortons illustrate well the post-revolutionary war penchant of Connecticuters to move west. Clinton, N.Y. was, in fact, a heavily Connecticut Yankee town, as any visit to the old cemetery in that village will demonstrate. Edward's own decision to turn from Yale toward the wide-open west for his education was simply another example of this phenomenon.

---

[12] *Ibid.*, 106.
[13] *Ibid.*, 208.

Happily, the marriage of William and Elizabeth was not cut short by sudden tragedy. She died only a few months before he did. They were to have, during the course of their marriage, five children. **John** (1791) died in infancy. **Edward** (1794) is the subject of our story. **George** (1796) died before he reached his third birthday. **George II** (1798) became a merchant in New Haven and Northampton and then a clerk in the comptroller's office in Hartford. **Charles** (1801) graduated from Yale and became a lawyer in New Haven. **Elizabeth** (1803) never married and lived in New Haven most of her life. It is she who was the recipient of many of Edward's most important letters.

In some ways, it must have been difficult for Edward to break away from all those Connecticut connections represented by both his genealogy and his immediate family. What this little foray into Edward's family tree illustrates is that, in fact, his family relations in the state were extensive, almost overwhelming. Although I am sure this is a gross exaggeration, one gets the feeling that if one followed out the interconnections of all the Robinsons and those they married since William arrived in 1636, one could say that somehow, Edward was related to most of the people in the state. Although he traveled to New York for his education and to Palestine for his most important research, he remained to the end a thoroughly Connecticut Yankee.

Chapter Two

BOYHOOD IN SOUTHINGTON

Headlines and Notices: 1794-1811

1795   James K. Polk is born. As U.S. President he led the nation to acquire through conflict vast areas of land from Mexico in order to achieve the country's "Manifest Destiny."
France is ruled by the Directory. Had the five-man Directory been less corrupt and ineffective, Europe might have avoided the Napoleonic wars.
John Keats is born. Romanticism, begun by Wordsworth *et al*, continues to flourish.

1796   Washington gives his famous Farewell Address.
Tennessee is admitted as a state.

1797   John Adams is elected President as Federalists triumph.
Kant publishes his *Metaphysics of Morals*.
Charles Hodge, theological defender of conservative, Old School theology is born.

1798 Napoleon begins his Egyptian expedition in which the Rosetta Stone is discovered.
Thomas Malthus publishes "The Essay on Population."
Eugene Delacroix, the great French romantic painter, is born.

1799 George Washington dies.
Napoleon captures Joppa and shells Acre.
Frederick Scheiermacher publishes *Speeches on Religion to its Cultured Despisers.*

1800 *The Lyrical Ballads,* this time with the famous preface, is published by Wordsworth and Coleridge.
Jefferson is inaugurated as President and the Federalists believe the worst is upon them. When disaster does not occur, the Federalists begin to crumble.

1801 Thomas Cole, the founder of the Hudson River School of painting, is born in England. In many respects, the Hudson River School's view of nature and geography provides an important parallel to Robinson's own views.

1802 Ohio admitted as a state.
Horace Bushnell, one of America's greatest theological thinkers, is born.
Cuneiform writing is first deciphered by George Frederick Grotefend.

1803 In a surprise move which will change America forever, the Jefferson administration successfully completes the Louisiana Purchase from France.
Ralph Waldo Emerson is born.

Chapter Two

1804   Lewis and Clark begin their expedition to the Pacific.
Napoleon crowns himself Emperor of France.
Alexander Hamilton, sometime darling of the Federalists, is killed in a duel by Aaron Burr.

1805   In the Battle of Trafalgar Britain virtually destroys the French Navy.
Napoleon wins an important victory at Austerlitz.
Joseph Smith is born.

1806   Beethoven's Symphony #3 (The Eroica) is published. The original title was, apparently, "Napoleon."

1807   Fulton's steamboat, the Clermont, steams up the Hudson to Albany.
Gas lights are introduced in London for the first time.
Robert E. Lee, Longfellow, and Whittier are born.

1808   African Slave trade is prohibited.
Jefferson Davis is born.
Goethe publishes *Faust I.*

1809   James Madison is elected President.
Abraham Lincoln, Edgar Allen Poe, and Cyrus McCormick are born.

1810   Sir Walter Scott publishes *The Lady of the Lake.* Not surprisingly, Scott seems to have been one of Robinson's favorite authors.

1811   William Henry Harrison wins the battle of Tippecanoe.
John Humphreys Noyes, Harriet Beecher Stowe, and Horace Greeley are born.

    The world that Edward Robinson entered in April of 1794 was busy, productive, and yet somehow particularly secluded. In an age of revolution and vast social change, Connecticut remained an island of unusual stability.

Second Great Awakening Protestantism provided the metaphysical, moral, and psychological matrix in which people thought and worked. Federalism, though not in all respects consistent with that religious perspective, provided the political ideology to which nearly all clergy and most of their constituents subscribed. The great enemy was fast becoming French free thinking, i.e. Deism, and its American incarnation, Thomas Jefferson. Connecticuters, almost to a person regarded him as the *bête noire* who, if elected to the Presidency, would surely destroy all that they (and America at its best) stood for by radicalizing the country and tearing down the religious fabric they held so dear. Doubtless Robinson imbibed such an attitude even before he had any idea what any of it meant. Although his father did not preach politics from the pulpit, he was an ardent Federalist.

William Robinson, born in August of 1754, was almost forty when Edward was born. He had been the settled minister of the Southington Church since 1780, that is, for fourteen years, and had endured, as we have noted, the sudden death of three wives, three infant children, and a favorite sister, Mary. It is not surprising that his relation to Edward seems to have been somewhat "reserved," as though he did not wish, because of the fragility of life, to become too emotionally attached to anyone. Perhaps, however, that is reading much too much into the slender evidence. Clearly, Edward thought highly of his father throughout his life, for he even went so far as to write a memorial about him and print it at his own expense.

William himself was a large, vigorous man, six feet two inches in height and weighing 250 lbs., who was equally at home in the pulpit and on his horse. Edward emphasizes his strong intellectual abilities and laments that he never quite fulfilled his role as a theological leader. Much of his memoir is devoted to what could have been had life taken a slightly different course. As it was, low pay as a clergyman and some very practical interests combined to produce a clergyman farmer who succeeded in agricultural pursuits beyond any ordinary expectations.

Ezra Stiles, the President of Yale who preached at his ordination, describes his success:

> The Rev. Mr. Robinson settled at Southington in 1780, worth nothing. Now, 1790, he is possessed of a good two-story house, and farm of one hundred and fifty acres. This year he has about a dozen acres of Indian corn, perhaps as many of English grain. He has forty hives of bees. He has

stock, about a hundred cows, let out in different parts of his parish, and six or eight pair of oxen; beside two pair oxen he keeps himself. He hires two men and sons; and will sow this fall twenty-three acres of wheat; from which is expected four hundred bushels next year.[1]

To these holdings he was to add, over the years, 150 more acres of land, a gristmill, a sawmill, and more cattle.

Clearly William Robinson was not only the village's pastor; he was also the community's leading entrepreneur. There was, undoubtedly, some resentment about his success; one can sense an undertone of that in Stiles' description. But at least, as has been said, it kept him from looking to increase his pitifully low salary, a fact that many parishioners doubtless appreciated. Moreover, he was very generous with his money and his expertise and set a fine example for other farmers who learned from him the latest agricultural methods.

According to Edward, his father was a very early riser and accomplished much of his ministerial preparation before others were even up and about. Happily for him, the tasks of the minister in those days were largely oratorical and perhaps, if Protestantism of the time would allow the word, liturgical. Programmatic outreach was largely non-existent; even family visitation was somewhat limited, though Edward insists that his father knew everyone by name and was well acquainted with their various problems. People who failed to attend church were very likely to hear from him the following day. Apparently, in any event, he was able to satisfy his parishioners with his ministrations, for he remained in that pulpit for forty-one years. Only infirmities of age and not his secular interests brought about, at his own request, his dismissal.

Ezra Stiles also describes William as one of those young "Luthers" who wish to bring about a new great awakening of the church. As an admirer of Edwards and Bellamy, he certainly fits that mold. Whether such evangelists as Asahel Nettleton, who was so effective in the stirring of the Spirit in Connecticut, ever conducted revivals in the Southington Church is not clear. Edward himself, says nothing about such events, though he does mention the growth of the congregation under his father's leadership. One has a sense that Edward was much too reserved to enter wholeheartedly into the revival spirit.

---

[1] *Ibid.*, 105.

He describes his father's preaching in the following way:

> The Preaching of Mr. Robinson was adapted, perhaps, rather to instruct, convince, and edify, than to awaken conviction of sin. He dwelt much upon the great doctrines of the Gospel, especially the absolute sovereignty and infinite holiness of God; and felt, in so doing, that he was following apostolic example . . . His general appearance and manner in the pulpit, while strikingly natural and unconstrained, were yet full of dignity and even majesty. To this his tall commanding figure, and the expression of his eyes and features, greatly contributed. He apparently made no use of his few notes while preaching; so that, except when reading the Bible, his eyes seemed to be fixed constantly upon his hearers. His manner and appearance were such as to secure, in an uncommon degree, the attention of his audience. If his sermons were doctrinal, there was often great tenderness and pathos in the application. He was himself not seldom affected even to tears, and his voice then faltered with emotion.[2]

Both the theological and the agricultural sides of his father's life were to affect Edward directly. Although he never became a settled minister, he certainly walked upon the theological landscape depicted by his father in his teaching and preaching. As far as one can determine, he never rebelled against or overthrew the essential creed of Connecticut Protestantism. That to him was orthodox religion, the Truth. Perhaps this is the reason why he showed so little interest in the metaphysical speculations of a Hegel or even a Schleiermacher.

William also expected his children to do their part "on the farm" and although Edward was a somewhat sickly child and worked in Mr. Wittelsey's store rather than entirely on the farm, he still experienced first hand some of the joys and trials of manual labor. This, it would seem, instilled in him a rather practical and pragmatic spirit. Hard physical work and the secular affairs of life were not something he shunned or despised. Roswell Hitchcock, who wrote the first biography of Robinson, includes the following description of Edward, apparently derived from his younger brother, Charles.

> He was early noted for his mechanical ingenuity. Many contrivances, for the facilitating of manual labor in the house and on the farm, attested at once his skill, and his care for the comfort and happiness of the family. He

---

[2] *Ibid.*, 152-53.

became an expert weaver; a beautiful blanket of his handiwork being still carefully preserved as a memento of his youthful industry . . . He was at this time remarkable chiefly for the kindliness of his disposition, the maturity of his practical judgment, the soundness of his moral principles, and the general propriety of his deportment. His brother is of the opinion, that he had no great mental precocity, and was not at first a remarkably bright scholar; but another member of the family has said, that his companions in the village school always considered him the first scholar among them. [3]

He retained something of this practicality and inventiveness throughout his life. When in Germany, he indulged himself in extraordinarily long walks on which he made many interesting observations about German agriculture. While other Biblical scholars were to spend their days in their studies poring over texts, Robinson, on horseback, viewed the sites that those texts so anciently described. He became, as it were, the quintessence of an American scholar: precise, but down to earth; literary, but observant and practical. There was little of the "Brahmin" caste about him. He was equally at home parsing Hebrew verbs and crawling through Hezekiah's tunnel on his belly.

Edward's mother, Elisabeth, was born in 1761 and thus was already 29 when she married William in 1790. In 1791 she gave birth to their first born, John, but he died after less than two months of life. Edward, then, was her first child to live beyond infancy. Edward says little about his mother but leaves the impression that she was soft-spoken and rather retiring, perhaps like her brother Asahel. Possibly he received something of his own shy and retiring nature from her. Even as an adult he felt some unease in social gatherings and had to "work at" light and casual conversation.

In any event, it was a good thing that she was more mature than William's previous wives, for she inherited a hornet's nest of activity. First of all, she became mother to William's two children by previous marriages: William who was, at the time of their marriage, almost six and Naomi Sophia who was two. Then there were the hired men and their boys who worked the farm and who, I am sure, had to be fed. And there were the ministerial visitors who would stop by, sometimes unannounced, on their

---

[3] Henry Boynton Smith and Roswell D. Hitchcock, *The Life, Writings and Character of Edward Robinson, D.D., LL..D.* (New York: Anson D. F. Randolph, 1863), 36-37.

way somewhere and the deacons from the church who were always welcomed at the house for theological discussion.

One must add to this group, of course, not only Edward, but George II who was born in 1798, Charles who was born in 1801, and Elisabeth who was born in 1803. With the six children, the workmen, and all the activity of the church, it was indeed a busy world. Not surprisingly, then, the Robinsons hired a "female domestic" named Clarissa Hitchcock—Miss Clara to the family—of whom Edward sings the praises:

> She proved to be a most valuable acquisition; and continued a member of the family until it was broken up by the death of Mr. Robinson . . . Her integrity and fidelity were never questioned. The affairs of the house, and also the children, were cared for as if they had been her own; and no amount of fatigue or watchfulness was ever spared or shunned. In her prime she was an excellent housekeeper, and always took the main charge of the household.[4]

She appears to have been to Edward almost a second mother, a favorite with all the children.

Surely there was plenty to keep two women busy. Although William received payment in cheese for the cows he rented out, all the butter was made at home. Furthermore,

> All the linen and woolen cloth needed in the family, for clothing and other purposes was spun, woven, and made up, at home. The spinning was mostly done by my mother and Miss Clara, already mentioned; and was carried on chiefly in the kitchen, which was also the common sitting room of the family. The busy hum of the spinning-wheels, both large and small, and the click of the loom in the wash-house, are among the indelible remembrances of my childhood. The first article of foreign broadcloth, that I remember in the family, was the coat of my brother William during his last year of college.[5]

Curiously, Edward says almost nothing about his early formal education. We do know that Southington, like virtually all Connecticut towns, had an elementary school. According to a 1650 Connecticut law,

---

[4] Robinson, *op. cit.*, 107.
[5] *Ibid.*, 114.

modeled after a Massachusetts law of 1647 and still in force after the Revolution, town officials were compelled to appoint teachers and establish schools.

> Every town of fifty families was to have a school in which reading and writing might be learned, and every town of one hundred families was compelled to provide a Latin grammar school, in both instances under penalty of a fine for non-compliance with the law.[6]

Although this law was sometimes honored in the breach, we know that in Southington's case the law prevailed, for William Robinson, as the town's minister, played an active role in the supervision of the school. Edward writes:

> Like most pastors in Connecticut in his day, he was annually appointed one of the school visitors. As such, he usually conducted the examination of the teachers; and regularly visited each school twice in every season. He laid great stress upon having the Westminster catechism taught in the schools; and once a year, for a long time, the children of all the schools were brought together in the meeting-house, where the pastor publicly examined them in the catechism.[7]

The education of children in Connecticut did not change very much over the years. The reading primer, for instance, was substantially like the primers used fifty or even one hundred years earlier. Probably young Edward began with a hornbook, a paddle shaped object with the letters of the alphabet and perhaps the Lord's Prayer written on it. It was covered with transparent horn to protect the letters from wear and tear.

One innovation which captured people's imagination during this era was the spelling book. Among the most popular was Noah Webster's *The American Spelling Book* which set Americans off on a craze for spelling bees and other forms of competition.[8] It is interesting that on more than one occasion Robinson comments about the value of good orthography. For

---

[6] Edward H. Reisner, *Nationalism and Education Since 1789* (New York: Macmillan Co., 1922), 346.
[7] Robinson, *op. cit.*, 151.
[8] James Bowen, *A History of Western Education* (New York: St. Martin's Press, 1981) III, 271.

those who desire to read his letters, however, one might wish that his schooling had placed at least equal emphasis upon penmanship. Frequently, because of his hand writing, it is virtually impossible to tell whether he is spelling a word correctly or not.

Pupils were, of course, expected to learn to write after a fashion, but the use of turkey or goose quills with student-carved points and self-mixed ink made the whole process, from a modern point of view, highly complex and often disastrous. There were no erasers, no blotting paper, only sand to dry the ink. One can imagine how many clumsy hands made a mess out of the whole process.

The third "R," 'rithmetic, was, of course, also taught at a very rudimentary level. Textbooks were few and largely ineffective instruments. Children did, however, use the abacus to do the simple arithmetic which was demanded of them.[9]

Despite Benjamin Rush's desire to use education to make of pupils "republican machines"[10] there seems less concern in the teaching materials for universal democratic values and much more concern for the dissemination of Calvinistic theology and Christian moral principles. As shocking as it may appear to modern sensibilities, there was no separation of religion and education in early 19th century Connecticut. Until 1818 the Congregational Church was established by law and supported by taxes. It was assumed that the role of education was to teach the beliefs and values of that institution. Ministers, as we have already seen, were expected to supervise the schools to assure that heresy did not creep into the curriculum. For most people, the central tenets of Calvinism were no more "theoretical" than the ideas of Einstein or Darwin are today. They were taught as "fact."

In some of the more advanced materials, as, for instance, in Noah Webster's *An American Selection of Lessons in Reading and Speaking*, there are readings which strongly commend patriotism and concern for the well-being of society. Both ancient and modern texts are included which speak eloquently of civic virtue. There are also, however, selections such as "Narrative of the Captivity of Mrs. Jemima Howe, taken by the Indians at

---

[9] *Ibid.*, 172.
[10] *Ibid.*, 266.

Hinsdale, New-Hampshire, July 27, 1755"[11] which teach dark lessons about the "hideous Indians" and the "bigoted" French Canadians. Although there is a counter-balancing story about the virtues of Pocahontas, the over-all impression is that native Americans are savages with few redeeming features and the French to the north are insufferable Catholics, beneath contempt. There seems to be little sense that native Americans had some reason to be angry with and harass white settlers or that Catholics might have some good reasons for their opinions.

Just how effective the teaching in Connecticut elementary schools was is a difficult question to answer. Many of the teachers were hardly through grammar school themselves and had no training whatsoever in the art of pedagogy. "Spare the rod and spoil the child" frequently was the only educational maxim known. Moreover, even though Connecticut had set aside a rather sizable fund from moneys gained from the sale of land in the Western Reserve of Ohio to support education, salaries were generally poor and such recompense did little to attract the most gifted into the teaching profession.

While there may have been many who benefited from their school years and looked back upon them with a certain nostalgia, there were undoubtedly just as many who endured the whole process as a great suffering. Learning disabilities were regarded as just "stupidity;" left-handedness had to be "corrected;" lack of enthusiasm for the opportunity to memorize spelling words, sheer laziness. And, of course, girls were often left out entirely as quite unfit for manly learning beyond the most rudimentary level. Well-to-do girls were frequently tutored in the basic skills and arts at home or were sent to a finishing school; poor girls often remained illiterate or virtually so.

After a very few years of education in these basics, which often involved little more than simple reading, writing, addition and subtraction, most children left school and went to work on the farm or in some commercial enterprise. Those with particular interest and ability went on to the Latin Grammar School where they began the arduous and, for many, irrelevant task of learning the rudiments of Latin and, perhaps, Greek. After starting, most frequently, with Comenius' *Orbis pictus,* an introduction to

---

[11] Noah Webster, *An American Selection, of Lessons in Reading and Speaking* (Utica, N.Y.: Ashahel Seward, 1806), 72-80.

the Latin language, they went on to Corderius' *Colloquia selecta* before plowing through Caesar, Ovid, Vergil, and Cicero.[12]

Thus the Latin Grammar School continued the tradition of the English public school in a world which seemed to have little need for the development of a literati caste. Clergymen and lawyers might use such classical training, but for the rest it was like frosting a piece of hard tack. It might be argued that even for the clergy this sort of education was often something of an albatross. The Methodists and Baptists soon taught Americans that the best preaching comes from the heart, not from Cicero and Vergil. While Congregationalists, Presbyterians, and Anglicans held forth with their usual high oratory in their established pulpits, the Methodists and Baptists were on horseback, meeting people where they were and winning, for their churches, the West.

At its best, the classical humanistic education led to a broad appreciation of literature, history, and life. It transported the angular, unsophisticated farm boy into an ancient world of eloquence, wisdom, and duty where he gained a more transcendent view of humanity. At its worst, however, it was a boring grind which resulted in a smattering of useless knowledge. There were many who endured the process only to end like Chaucer's Clerk, knowing "little Latin and less Greek."

Some Americans, of course, saw the folly of the Latin Grammar School and resolved to offer something more useful to American youth. Benjamin Franklin, for instance, devised a curriculum which included "writing, arithmetic, accounting, geometry, astronomy, English language, oratory, history, geography, chronology, morality, and natural history."[13] He also emphasized physical education as well as practical work and field excursions. Only those who so desired needed to study the classics.

It is notable, however, that Franklin's English language curriculum ultimately failed to attract students while the classical curriculum succeeded. This is doubtless in part because most universities and colleges continued to demand a knowledge of the classics for entrance. It was difficult to break from the old system without completely reforming it from top to bottom.

Given the nature of higher education, there were many Americans who saw no particular reason for education beyond the elementary level at

---

[12] Bowen, *op. cit.*, III, 273.
[13] *Ibid.*, 274.

all unless one wished to become a minister. William Robinson, in fact, thought that way. Edward describes the time when Timothy Dwight, the President of Yale, stopped to see them.

> The President, I recollect, putting his hand on my head, said to my father, "I suppose, Sir, you intend to send him to us by and by." The latter had no such intention, but gave an evasive reply.[14]

William's lack of intention probably stemmed from Edward's own lack of purpose to become a minister as well as his somewhat sickly nature. E. R. was not sure what his vocation would be for sometime and his father saw no reason for him to endure a classical education if the ministry was not the aim. This was the age when a Martin Van Buren, who had only the most rudimentary formal education, could become a lawyer simply by "reading law" and then, through sheer perseverance, achieve political success and eventually be elected President of the United States. American educational lock-step was not yet in place; dropping out was by no means frowned upon as disastrous. One wonders, in fact, whether it would be a disaster today if American commitment to credentialism were not so all-pervasive.

Edward did not go to a formal Latin Grammar School, but did receive something of a classical education nonetheless. Like his brother William who was "fitted for college with the Rev. Dr. Chapin of Rocky Hill,"[15] Edward at age fourteen began to study with a minister, the Rev. Mr. Woodward, in nearby Wolcott with several other boys.[16] Among them, according to Robinson, was James Gates Percival who was later to become a well-known poet.[17] Whether he had studied in a small group with a minister or at a larger school, the content was probably about the same: a rich dose of Latin grammar and a taste of the Latin classics in the original tongue. Grammar schools were, indeed, just that: grammar, grammar, grammar. Robinson was one of those who took to the subject with great enthusiasm and ability. He was among the few to benefit immensely from the rigors of

---

[14] Robinson, *op. cit.*, 150.
[15] *Ibid.*, 120.
[16] Hitchcock, *op. cit.*, 38.
[17] Evert A. Duyckinck and George L. Duyckinck, *Cyclopaedia of American Literature* (New York: Charles Scribner, 1866), p. 167. Since this article was written by Robinson himself it is reasonably reliable.

classicism. According to his own account, he studied English and Latin, but he does not mention Greek.[18] This he probably began during the summer before entering Hamilton.

Later he was to deplore the insufficiency of his early education, but he at least learned enough to matriculate at Hamilton College in 1812. One may guess that despite all their classical pretensions, standards even at Harvard and Yale were none too high. In that era boys of 14 or 15 who had mastered the essentials of classical grammar could and did enter college. Robinson, however, was much older than that, having taught school before proceeding to his higher education. Indeed, when he was not yet seventeen he taught pupils often older than himself in a district school in East Haven. Then he moved to another district school in Farmington where he taught for a year. Finally, he worked in a country store in the drug department—his father hoped he would become a partner in the business—before leaving for Hamilton. For us matriculation in a college at 18 is about normal, but this age made him one of the oldest in his class.

Although classical languages were forever to be important to Robinson, it may be other events outside the classroom which served to shape his life even more than his studies. In 1804, when Edward was ten, his older brother, long suffering from pulmonary distress, contracted "consumption," i.e. tuberculosis. He came home for the summer to rest and recuperate and even went on a journey

> to the mountainous southern part of Massachusetts, to a celebrated root doctor; and . . . returned, bringing . . . sundry jugs of tinctures prepared from roots and herbs, and the body of a rattlesnake, skinned and dressed, which was to be administered in some way.[19]

Nothing, however, worked and William II died shortly after his September graduation. Surely, this must have had profound effect upon Edward, for it was the first family death which he had personally experienced. Now, he was the eldest son, with all the responsibility which that implied. William had, it would appear, planned on a career in the ministry. Should Edward replace him in that role? Could he replace him in his father's heart?

---

[18] *Ibid.*
[19] Robinson, *op. cit.*, 120-21.

Then, in 1811 his elder sister Sophie was married, to James Woodruff. The couple then moved west, to Catskill, New York where James was to engage in a mercantile business. In so doing the Woodruffs followed a typical Yankee pattern of heading into New York State where there were more opportunities. The Hudson River had become an economic gateway, and Yankees were ready to take advantage of the possibilities for trade there. This made Edward's own decision to continue his education in "the west" seem even more natural.

There were also other, much greater events which were to influence Edward. One thinks, for instance, of the excitement generated by the Lewis and Clark expedition which concluded triumphantly when Edward was just twelve. Although in 1800 more than 80% of all Americans lived within 50 miles of tide-water, the West by 1806 had opened its doors. For William Robinson, the "Wild West" was Clinton, N.Y.; for Edward, it was the Dakotas and Montana.

All of this led to a sense of excitement about exploration and travel. He tells us he had an insatiable appetite for travel books when young. Exotic places were constantly in the news in the *Missionary Herald* to which William Robinson subscribed and in the secular journals which told of adventures in the West and in the Asian East. Napoleon's Egyptian campaign marked a significant new era, for that land of greatest antiquity had now been subdued by France's noted general and hero. And discoveries, for instance the Rosetta Stone, had been made which were to prove pivotal for a rediscovery and reinterpretation of antiquity. One can hardly doubt that all this had its impact upon young Edward as he thought about his future.

Clearly he did not initially plan to enter the ministry. If he had, his father would have been more enthusiastic about him going to Yale. Because William believed that higher education was useful primarily for those going into the clergy, he saw no particular reason to encourage Edward to continue his education. He could become a merchant, even a lawyer, without benefit of further conjugating and parsing. The choice of more education was Edward's and not his father's. Perhaps even at that time Edward had a sense that a career of exploration somehow was in the future. The question was how to get to that indefinite goal from where he was. He chose to begin in his father's Wild West, in Clinton, N.Y.

Edward, one can be sure, was quite unaware as a child that a new age, an age of Romanticism was dawning. He did not know yet that he was a contemporary of such great figures as John Keats, William Cullen Bryant, Eugene Delacroix, and Thomas Cole. I doubt very much that many people in Southington read the *Lyrical Ballads* or *Faust* until years passed and the critics proclaimed them classics. Nevertheless, the spirit of Romanticism was there, growing unannounced in the hearts of many.

Romanticism is notoriously difficult to define, perhaps because it is a human concept and human concepts never quite conform to reality. Nevertheless, we can say that the romantic prefers nature over civilization, Mont Saint Michel over the Pantheon, spirit over materialism, mystery over explanation. "Romanticism" comes from the word romance which refers particularly to those tales of love and adventure written in the vernacular which take the reader or hearer into a world of exotic imagination. King Arthur and his court are the stuff that romance is made of. So too are Don Juan and Sinbad and Don Quixote.

Surely there are ways in which Edward Robinson was totally out of step with the Romantic Age. He produced lexicons and word books, not odes; when he climbed Mt. Washington he used his compass to make careful sightings, not his pen to sketch the magnificent view. He was sober, cool, and rational. Nevertheless, beneath that aloof exterior which his classical education helped to shape was a strongly romantic streak.

He loved to travel and to explore. He journeyed to Palestine for many of the same reasons that Delacroix visited Morocco and Frederic Church reached Petra. Perhaps he crawled through Hezekiah's tunnel for the same reason that Lord Byron swam the Hellespont. He was, in a sense, the next generation's Childe Harold. He loved the exotic, the call of the unknown, the challenge. In many respects his whole life was like the experience of the hunter of *The Lady of the Lake* who finds himself plunging through the forest, chasing a stag, only to lose the prey but to discover that mysterious, unspeakable Other in a world which never quite fits with his own. His works on Palestine are like the husks of a kernel which can never be put into rational language.

But that is to leap ahead in our story. Edward, after some experience teaching children and then weighing out drugs, decided to pursue what his father thought was, for him, quite useless: a college education. For this, he followed, not his father's and brother's path to New Haven, but his uncle's footsteps to a brand new institution in Clinton, New York: Hamilton College. In June of 1812 he left Southington for his uncle's home in Clinton. There, presumably, he studied enough Greek during the summer to gain admission to the college in the fall.

Chapter Three

THE HAMILTON YEARS

Headlines and Notices: 1812-20

1812   Napoleon invades Russia.
        The War of 1812 begins.
        Louisiana is admitted as a state.

1813   Henry Ward Beecher is born.
        Perry wins the naval battle on Lake Erie.

1814   Louis XVIII returns to power in France.
        The Hartford Convention considers secession from the Union by New England.
        MacDonough wins the naval battle of Plattsburg on Lake Champlain.
        Washington D.C. is burned by the British.
        The Treaty of Ghent officially ends the War of 1812.

1815   Napoleon returns from exile for the "Hundred Days."
       Napoleon loses the battle of Waterloo.
       Andrew Jackson wins the battle of New Orleans.
       Henry Boynton Smith is born; so too are Karl Marx and Soren Kierkegaard.

1816   Regular transatlantic service using fast sailing ships is begun between New York and Liverpool.
       Indiana is admitted to the Union.

1817   James Monroe is elected President.
       Henry David Thoreau is born.

1818   Illinois is admitted to the Union.
       Auburn Theological Seminary is founded.

1819   The first steamer crosses the Atlantic to Liverpool.
       Florida is ceded to United States; Alabama is admitted to the Union.
       Philip Schaff, Herman Melville, Queen Victoria, Walt Whitman, and Abner Doubleday are born.

1820   Maine and Missouri are admitted to the Union as a part of the Missouri Compromise.
       Susan B. Anthony is born.

The year 1812 was not a very happy one for Connecticut and its Federalists. New England had, during the first decade of the century, benefited greatly from trade with both sides of the European conflict. It is true that there were many examples of harassment and the impressment of seamen by both the English and the French, but, over all, trade had increased enormously and the New England merchants resented and resisted any attempt to curtail their businesses.

It was for that reason that they despised Jefferson's Embargo Act, which, it could be rightly argued, worked only to suppress legitimate commerce and to benefit smugglers. It was also for this reason that they were very critical of the war talk which dominated many conversations during the beginning of the second decade. And the saber rattling was serious. For some, the main reason for considering armed conflict was the fact that the British were seizing American vessels and impressing seamen who the British believed were His Majesty's subjects. They claimed the seamen had fled to America for better maritime jobs but still, from the British point of view, owed allegiance to the crown. Many Americans indignantly disagreed.

Those who lived in the west, however, were more concerned about British support for Tecumseh and the native American resistance to westward expansion. For Henry Clay and the other Warhawks a war would end British meddling by the defeat and annexation of Canada. This would, in turn, open the rest of the continent for American settlement. In the south there were also hopes that war could lead to the annexation of Florida.

Therefore, on June 1, 1812, despite a sizable negative vote, the Congress of the United States declared war on Great Britain. Immediately, there was trouble. The American navy was woefully weak and the Congress made no provision to strengthen it. The army was undermanned and never did reach the size approved by Congress. Military leadership was fumbling and inept. Congress found it difficult to finance the war by loans because the wealthiest merchants from New England lacked enthusiasm for the enterprise. The only saving grace was that Britain was quite occupied with its war with France and did not have, until Napoleon's defeat in 1814, sufficient resources to devote to the American war.

Because of simple unpreparedness and poor leadership, what should have been a fairly easy victory over Canada for the United States became a quagmire of defeats. Instead of increasing the territory of the nation, Americans found the British occupying Fort Niagara and Detroit and Fort Dearborn (Chicago). The British navy harassed the Atlantic coast and, despite some major losses in naval battles, was able to bottle up the small United States navy in coastal ports for much of the war. Eventually, the American nation had to endure the indignity of seeing the public buildings of Washington, D. C. burned by forces which met with little or no opposition.

All of this must have been of particular concern to Edward Robinson as he began to study in central New York, for after initial American failures to take Canada, the British began to threaten both western and northern

New York State. The Americans, as a consequence, built a road from Albany to Sackett's Harbor (it is still called the "Military Road") to transport men and equipment to an area of possible conflict. Although no foreign armies marched through the central region of the state, the danger was certainly there that the British, after burning Buffalo and occupying Fort Niagara, might move eastward and turn the area into a new Canadian province. The British also penetrated to Plattsburgh in the north and might have sailed right into the heart of the state had not MacDonough won the naval battle on Lake Champlain and forced the British to retreat.

It is not wholly surprising that New Englanders, fed up with American diplomatic and military ineptitude, called a convention in Hartford to, among other things, consider secession. That this drastic step was never taken was due in part to the monumental nature of its implications and to the fact that as the war progressed America began slowly to turn defeat into at least a face-saving, though hardly a victorious, result. When the Treaty of Ghent was signed in December of 1814, the United States could scarcely say it won much, but then it did not lose much either. Andrew Jackson's decisive victory at New Orleans actually came after the Treaty was signed but served as excellent frosting on an otherwise very bland and tasteless cake.

Nevertheless, most Americans rejoiced that somehow their nation had been able to tweak the tail of the British lion and get away relatively unscathed. Mr. Madison's war had not been so bad after all. Tecumseh was dead and what was then thought of as the northwest was now open to settlement. The British dream of a vast native American realm to be left untouched by white settlers was dissipated. Moreover, with the defeat of Napoleon and the end of hostilities in Europe, a new era of good feelings began and commerce ever dear to New England's heart returned to normal once more.

Parenthetically, this result also meant the virtual end of the Federalist Party which had fought so vigorously against Madison and all he stood for. The Federalists were elitists who, though forsaking the notion of titled aristocracy, still believed in rule by "the best" (which included in New England the clergy) rather than by the masses. America, however, no longer looked to Boston Brahmins and the ordained clergy for all the answers. Although neither blacks nor women would have noticed any improvement, the world had become slightly more egalitarian; the frontier spirit began to prevail over the metaphysical dreams of New England. In 1818 the Congregational Church was disestablished in Connecticut. The era of Andrew Jackson was not far away.

Hamilton College opened its doors for the first time as an institution of higher learning—the third college in New York State—in the fall of 1812, as the storm clouds of war rumbled. Its history, however, long antedated its official opening. Hamilton's so-called founder was Samuel Kirkland, a Connecticut man who had attended Eleazar Wheelock's school for native Americans and colonist children in Lebanon, Connecticut.[1] There he caught the vision of an educational program in which Caucasians and native Americans learned, and hence developed a common culture, together.

From Lebanon he went to Princeton College but, even before graduating with an A. B. degree, set out for the wilds of New York State to minister to the Iroquois. He began among the Senecas, but soon moved eastward to live with the somewhat less warlike Oneidas in what is now Oneida Castle. Originally, the idea was that he would send promising young Oneidas back to Wheelock's school in Connecticut, but it proved really impossible to convince young tribesmen to journey so far away from their tribal lands. Hence, Kirkland began setting up schools in Oneida territory with the idea that native Americans in that age had to be educated in the basic ways of the white settler if they were going to survive.

His big dream was to cap off this fledgling educational system with an institution of higher learning in which native Americans and settlers would learn together not so much Latin and Greek as more practical subjects of use in an agricultural and commercial world. "Diffusing useful knowledge" is the way he phrased his aim. This dream began to come to fruition through the foundation of the Hamilton-Oneida Academy.

Kirkland was, by any estimate, an amazing man. Although he is usually pictured in the finery of a Congregational domine, he, in fact, "went native" while living among the Oneidas, adopting their language, style of dress and food. He also endured the rigors of their way of life which brought him on more than one occasion close to death. Although there undoubtedly were those who felt otherwise, it would appear that the

---

[1] Wheelock, of course, later became the founder of Dartmouth College, another institution which in origin was meant for native American education.

Oneidas really loved him and, for that reason, remained neutral during the Revolutionary War. It was this fact which won Kirkland such appreciation from Washington and Hamilton.

Although Kirkland, during much of his career, lived as an Oneida, he also retained linkage with the colonial world, serving as a chaplain at Fort Stanwix (now Rome, New York) and for General Scott's vituperative campaign against the native peoples of south-central and western New York. He traveled to Philadelphia and New York on missions of diplomacy and in so doing came to know Washington and Hamilton quite well.

As a consequence, he was not only able to gain moral support for his scheme to found a native American-settler school; he also convinced the Congress to provide a small $1500 yearly grant for the establishment of the school and Alexander Hamilton to lend his name to the enterprise. It is doubtful whether Hamilton ever gave more than his name to the new institution, but that, in fact, was a great deal. Central New York was being settled in the 1780s and 1790s by New England Yankees for whom the evocation of Hamilton's name would have been very attractive. Although Hamilton never got on well with their other great political leader, John Adams, he nevertheless represented their intellectual views and was a name of which New York Federalists were particularly proud. Perhaps had Hamilton lived, he would have provided more than nominal support. As it was, the college which was to bear his name was not chartered until eight years after he was killed in a duel with Aaron Burr.

In the meantime, the Hamilton-Oneida Academy began very modestly in 1793, in a small, one room school building near Kirkland's log cabin.[2] In gratitude for his work among them, the Oneida nation had given to Kirkland a tract of land of 4760 acres on the eastern edge of their territory. This grant included not only an attractive farming area along the Oriskany Creek but a considerable holding in the hill country to the west. Eventually, Kirkland donated to the institution a major tract of land on the hill from his patent. This has remained, with some additions, the college campus to this day.

---

[2] Clearly, the small building which today stands on the Hamilton campus, was not, as the sign on it says, Kirkland's home, for we know that he lived with his family in a log cabin before moving into what was called the Kirkland mansion in 1795. Probably what is called the Kirkland cottage is, in fact, the school building constructed after the first one burned.

Kirkland began in the valley, opening his school for Oneidas and white settlers within walking distance of the newly founded village of Clinton. From the outset, the school attracted many more settlers than Oneidas—only four Indian youth attended. The latter, for obvious reasons, resisted the notion of paying tuition with money they did not possess for an education they were not even sure they needed. Moreover, the settlers apparently wanted a "Grammar School" education and the Oneidas seemed quite clear that Latin verbs were not for them.

Kirkland was, to say the least, a rather unusual founder. He, of course, did not do the teaching. One Eleazar Caukins, who had been very successful teaching native Americans in Oneida Castle, was chosen as school master. But Kirkland did not serve on the Board of Trustees either, leaving that work to the local leaders like Asahel Norton, one of Edward Robinson's uncles, and the brothers, Eli and Joel Bristol, progenitors of the many Bristols[3] who have served the college so well over the decades. Somehow he seemed to know that his dream of a multicultural college was doomed from the start and therefore let others take over the substitute institution. It is also true that ill health may have prohibited him from taking the active role he might have wished for during his latter years.

In any event, the first, experimental phase of the institution did not go well. After less than a year of operation, the original building, along with all the books and supplies, burned and instruction was temporarily suspended. A new building was constructed—is it the Kirkland Cottage which now exists on the Hamilton campus?—but only one Oneida returned to study there. In the fall Caulkins himself went back to Oneida Castle to teach and the school "temporarily" suspended operation.

The local trustees, in the meantime, were dreaming bigger dreams and in 1794 the cornerstone (which was actually a brick) was laid for a much larger structure up on what is now "College Hill." The ceremony was impressive with a troop of militia under the command of Samuel Kirkland's son George Whitfield Kirkland leading the parade and many local townsfolk in attendance. The actual cornerstone laying was done by Baron Frederick von Steuben, drill master of the Revolution, who owned property given him by the State north of Utica and hence was a "neighbor."

---

[3] The Bristol-Meyers Pharmaceutical Company originated in Clinton.

The building planned was to be much more impressive than the tiny original structure. It was to have three floors and many rooms and facilities. Construction to turn dream into reality began, but the trustees soon ran out of money. There the frame of the building stood until 1798, while foxes burrowed under the foundation, the sheriff threatened foreclosure, and Oneida interest in the enterprise almost completely disappeared. When the school finally reopened as what appears to have been a typical Latin Grammar School, no native Americans were in attendance. During its history after 1798 apparently only three Oneidas ever matriculated. Kirkland's dream of a practical multicultural education, a dream probably curricularly like Ben Franklin's vision, had largely vanished. Although some practical subjects were introduced and not all followed the Latin and Greek course, a sizable percentage of the children spent their time parsing, parsing, parsing.

The first preceptor, John Niles, came from Connecticut with the strong recommendation of Timothy Dwight himself, under whom he had studied theology. Niles brought with him James Murdock, also a Yale graduate who eventually was to serve with Edward Robinson on the faculty of Andover Theological Seminary. There he caused no little stir before his dismissal for theological "improprieties." At the academy he seems to have been less controversial, serving as teacher for the female students who numbered about twenty.[4] Murdock was let go after a year because of financial considerations, but he stayed on in Clinton to study theology with Asahel Norton.

In 1801 Niles also left and was replaced by Robert Porter from Framingham, Connecticut who had graduated from Yale in 1795. He stayed until 1806 when he was succeeded by Asahel Norton's brother, Seth. After a year Seth left to become a tutor at Yale but returned the following season to head the institution until it was transformed into a college in 1812 by New York State Charter.

After a few years running at a deficit the academy began to prosper. With more than one hundred students, it was able to pay its bills and even add modestly to its campus. By 1805, therefore, the trustees began the

---

[4] It is ironic that while the Hamilton-Oneida Academy was coeducational, the successor college remained an all-male institution until 1978.

process of petitioning for a college charter from the State. This seems to have been, in fact, their intent from the beginning.

There are many reasons why the charter should have been granted easily. New York State, at the time, had only two undergraduate institutions of higher learning: Columbia College in New York City and Union College in Schenectady. Many settlers had flooded into central and western New York and it seemed necessary to provide education which did not demand travel to such distant, eastern locations. Utica was a boom town, a major center for transportation, and many believed it would become one of the nation's largest cities. Clinton, located only a few miles to the west just off the Great Western Turnpike, looked like an ideal location.

Nevertheless, there were problems. Academies in Kingston and Fairfield, N.Y. vied for the right to be chartered too and there was strong political pressure from many communities to found a college in their locale. Most important, the Board of Regents believed that no college should be chartered which did not have assets of at least $50,000 in ready cash. None of the contenders had that much money behind them.

It took a great deal of political maneuvering and pleading, with many false starts and refused petitions, before the Charter was granted in 1812. By this time Samuel Kirkland had already been dead for four years. To call him "founder," therefore, is something of a misnomer. To be honest, that honor ought to go, not to one man but to the whole group of new settlers who as trustees worked to make the Hamilton dream a reality. Robinson regarded his uncle Seth as the most "effective founder."

In any event, when Edward Robinson arrived, after what must have been a long and demanding journey over the Great Western Turnpike to Clinton, he found an institution which, though new, was also, physically, several years old. The main academic building had been a building since 1798 and though now usable in part was still not complete. In it were to be found not only classrooms but a chapel and living accommodations for students. To the south of that edifice stood a wood frame building which had served the Academy as a dining hall but which would shortly become the President's house. Today it still exists in a somewhat different location as the Azel Backus House, a faculty club. Although not complete in the fall of 1812, a new refectory, today Buttrick Hall, was under construction and would begin serving students the following spring. Aside from the privies and horse barns, these three buildings were to constitute the whole of the original campus.

Today, Hamilton's campus is well manicured and affords numerous amenities. In 1812, the virgin forest had been felled, but the grounds, then surrounded by a board fence, still revealed the stumps of the original trees. The road up College Hill was no longer an Indian trail. It had been widened and then beautified by tree planting supervised by Kirkland's daughter Eliza of whom we shall hear more later. Like most of the roads of the area, however, it was muddy and virtually impassable during the rainy season which often lasts, in Clinton, from about the beginning of April until the end of March. If Clinton, with its stately homes, village green, and white spired Congregational church, was already quite reminiscent of old Connecticut, the college still intimated the rigors of the frontier. Only gradually did the clearing become a civilized campus.

Edmund Wetmore, in his Fifty Year Annalist letter, recalls the absolutely frigid early morning chapel services in which the preacher—usually President Backus—had to wear overcoat and mittens to survive. He also remembers his room:

> I was sent to a room with one chum. Our beds were in a shallow recess formed by the jutting of the chimney. There was a large dark closet intended for a bedroom, but that was occupied by rats who furiously disputed possession with all comers. We yielded at once. They made nightly incursions, in military array, into our premises, carefully examining our beds and our clothing, especially our boots and shoes, hovering around the fireplace and having a good time generally.[5]

The conditions, one might say, were spartan. The drafty, uninsulated rooms and the primitive conditions generally must have been particularly hard on Edward who seems to have suffered repeatedly from upper respiratory disorders. Later he was to attain attestations from local physicians about his physical problems so that he would be exempted from military service.[6] Edward tells us in the Memoir that during a summer's visit with his sister Sophie in Catskill, he very nearly died from the same disorder. He also says

---

[5] Edmund Wetmore, "Letter of 1867," in Clarence Aubrey Fetterly, *Fifty Years Ago* (Clinton, N.Y.: 1947), 24.
[6] Robinson Papers B.7. 1817.

repeatedly that he would have gotten much more out of college had he not been so ill.

Presiding temporarily over the new institution when Edward arrived was his uncle, Seth Norton, who also was the college's first professor of languages. That meant that he taught Latin and Greek, for no modern languages were to be offered at Hamilton for a number of years. About Seth Norton we know little, but those who mention him describe him as a well-educated, solid scholar and an effective teacher. Like many of the other early Hamilton faculty members he had gone to, and served as a tutor at Yale.

His rather sallow complexion and his jerky movements apparently did not diminish his popularity with students. He is said to have loved music and wrote several hymns. He also served as chorister, that is, choir director, at his brother's church, a position that the famous Thomas Hastings was later to hold. Some believe Seth Norton was very disappointed not to have been chosen the permanent president of the college, but if he had such aspirations, they apparently did not lead to major conflict with his superior. In fact, there was not a great deal of time for such tensions to surface. Azel Backus, the first president, was to die after only four years in office. Norton died but one year later, in 1818, at the age of 39.

The second professor was Josiah Noyes, a chemist who had been lured away from the rival Fairfield Academy by the possibility that the Hamilton-Oneida Academy would be turned into a medical school. The plan never materialized, but Noyes remained anyway to amuse students with his scientific demonstrations, particularly when they went awry. He had a little house down College Hill Road which served as a laboratory for his sometimes explosive experiments. One has a distinct feeling that Noyes was well-liked but did not teach students much hard science. Chemistry, in fact, was still in its infancy and hardly offered much more than somewhat disorganized speculations anyway. Noyes was also known for his over-indulgence in local drinking establishments and that did not enhance his work at the college either.

A month after the college opened, Theodore Strong, known as "Uncle Ted" to students, was appointed tutor. In 1816 he was named to the regular faculty to teach mathematics and natural philosophy. Undoubtedly the most distinguished member of the early faculty, he made a fine reputation as a mathematician and eventually was lured away by Queens College (later Rutgers) in New Brunswick, N. J.[7] Like Seth Norton he came from Yale and was recommended for appointment by Timothy Dwight. Parenthetically, it should also be noted that Strong and Norton (and thus Robinson) were distantly related for they were all direct descendants of Elder John Strong, one of the first colonialists of Massachusetts.[8]

Finally, there was the President, the Rev. Azel Backus, a well-known Connecticut clergyman who arrived in November of 1812, a few days after the opening of the college. He was a somewhat portly man with a keen appetite and a wonderful sense of humor, often injecting witticisms into his sermons and lectures. He was a strong Federalist, as witnessed by the fact that he was once arraigned in court for saying some critical things about Jefferson from the pulpit. Before coming to Hamilton, Backus had been the settled minister in Bethlehem, Connecticut where he had succeeded the famous theologian, Joseph Bellamy. There he had a school which gained considerable fame. Among his students was Nathaniel Taylor who was to become one of Yale's greatest theological teachers. Backus' abilities in the pulpit were already widely recognized, for he had been invited to preach at a number of important occasions around Connecticut.

At Hamilton, Backus taught rhetoric and what might be called philosophical ethics and theology, particularly to seniors. That he seems to have been much beloved is attested to by a letter from Stephen Taylor, later President of Madison (later Colgate) University, to Robinson describing his death.[9] Backus expired after nursing a tutor, Josiah Spalding, who had contracted typhoid fever, back to health. Spalding recovered but Backus caught the fever and his demise came very suddenly. He was only fifty-one when he died.

Beside these few faculty members, there were other tutors who usually stayed at the college no more than a year or two or three. They were in charge of conducting recitations which began after chapel and breakfast—at 7 o'clock in the morning. Little remains to tell us exactly what

---

[7] In 1813 he published an essay in which he made a demonstration of Matthew Stewart's propositions regarding the circle; this made a name for him as a mathematician.
[8] See Benjamin W. Dwight, *The History of the Descendents of Elder John Strong of Northampton, Mass.* 2 Vols. (Albany, N.Y.: J. Munsell, 1871) I, 290-291.
[9] See Robinson Papers B.5.

the curriculum was like, but it seems obvious that offerings were very limited. There was no modern history, literature, or language. There was nothing resembling social science. Latin, Greek, basic mathematics, moral and natural philosophy all flavored with a strong dash of Congregational piety—the "Connecticut" nature of the institution is obvious—were the order of the day. One student commented that "our time was occupied chiefly in the study of Greek and Latin languages, and mathematics."[10]

And then, of course, there were the students. Edward's class numbered some 24 or 25 to begin, but by Commencement had dwindled to only 17. Classes before him were, of course, smaller, for the college was just founded and any upper class students were transfers or came from the preceding academy. Classes behind him were of about comparable size to his. The college catalogue of the day, one sheet listing of faculty and students, reveals that most came from the central New York region, though there were some, like Robinson, from New England and a few from the frontier in western New York.

David Baker, in his recollections of the class of 1816, offers a description of the class which is none too complimentary:

> They were as much diversified in appearance, manner, tastes and character of their minds as any like number usually found in one class of its size of equally learned "pundits." Some of them looked upon the studying of their lessons as a menial and degrading business, and proof positive of the deficiency of intellect. These passed most of their time, while in their rooms, in light reading—in fact, reading anything rather than the prescribed studies—and never learned anything properly and thoroughly. Some studied hard and didn't learn; nor did they know or care whether they could learn or not; at least, they did not seem to try to find out. Some by faithful and persevering application mastered their lessons, and had time to spare for miscellaneous reading. Some learned well in spite of obstacles and impediments; others learned but little and ever seemed afraid to engage in the battle of human life, and were never happy.[11]

---

[10] Walter Pilkington, *Hamilton College 1812/1962* (Clinton, N.Y.: Hamilton College, 1962), 74.
[11] George Bristol, "Letter of 1865" in Fetterly, *op. cit.*, 8-9.

Clearly Edward was a notch above the rest, for Baker singles him out for particular notice:

> EDWARD ROBINSON, though suffering from ill health, steadily pursued his studies, got his lessons well, and more probed to the bottom of whatever he undertook to learn than any other member of the class. He exhibited not original thoughts so much as ability to follow out what others had well begun, and to discover and to possess himself of that which others had known before. He was unremitting and persevering in whatever he undertook and left nothing, on which he fastened his attention, only half learned or unfinished. Neither he nor Philo Gridley ever joined in the amusements or merrymakings of their fellow students whose manners, if not repulsive, were not winning.[12]

Gerrit Smith, the famous abolitionist and friend of Robinson, who also graduated from Hamilton, put it more succinctly:

> The only remarkable scholar amongst the students of the College, during the years of our class, was Edward Robinson. That he came to stand amongst the eminent scholars of the world is not surprising to us, who saw with what great facility he acquired varied learning in his youth.[13]

Given his serious attitude and native intelligence, it is not surprising that Edward graduated first in his class. Clearly, in a college which was struggling to maintain serious standards, he stood very much alone. In defense of the new institution, however, one must add that descriptions of student life at Harvard and Yale in those days hardly reveal much more seriousness. Although the rigors of Latin and Greek were the official diet, many students preferred the intellectual pose, the social *entre nous*, the moneyed show to hard learning.

All of this, of course, flew in the face of the basically religious and moral objectives of the education. Each student to enter was expected to

---

[12] *Ibid.,* 10.
[13] *Ibid.,* 32. Gerrit Smith and Robinson apparently kept in touch after graduation, for a letter is preserved from Smith to E. R. dated June 18, 1860 in which Smith recommends to him Louis Jamanque, a person with extraordinary knowledge of European languages. Robinson Papers K. 3.

"produce satisfactory evidence of a blameless life and conversation."[14] While at college all were expected to attend chapel twice a day and conform to the college's moral strictures:

> "Students were forbidden under penalty of expulsion, to blaspheme, rob, fornicate, steal, forge, duel, or assault, wound or strike the president or members of the faculty. Fighting, quarreling, challenging, the uttering of turbulent words or behavior, fraud, lying, defamation or any such like crimes, were punishable by fine, admonition or in other ways, Billiards, cards, dice, backgammon and drinking within two miles of the campus were unlawful; violators became subject to rustication, suspension or being sent home."[15]

In any event, although there seems to have been a large gap between expectation and reality, what the students rebelled against is clear. The faculty intended to support and maintain the values of the past and hence did little to shake or question those basic beliefs which characterized so much of Yankee piety. There was no gap between the academic and the religious. The whole education was designed to inculcate rather than destroy the beliefs of Congregational Christendom. For many this was the first step into the ministerial life.

It is clear, however, that Robinson had not yet decided upon a career in either the ministry or in academia. After graduation he spent a year with James Strong of Hudson, New York, another very distant relative on his mother's side, reading law. Actually, the law would have suited Robinson very well. As he reveals repeatedly, he was meticulous in his study, judicious in his opinions, and reserved in his expression. Although one doubts that he had the charisma to follow Strong into politics—his mentor was to serve in the House of Representatives for several terms—he would have made an excellent judge.

Such, however, was not to be, for Robinson received and accepted an invitation to return to his alma mater as junior tutor. He never explains in any of his writings his motivation for the return. Perhaps he discovered that the law really was not for him; perhaps he found that the academic world

---

[14] Pilkington, *op.cit.*, 74.
[15] *Ibid.*, 76.

suited him best. In any event, he returned to drill students in both Greek and mathematics and to become again a part of the Hamilton community.

His reentry into academic life, however, illustrates very well the ancient saying that one cannot step into the same river twice. In the December following Robinson's graduation, Hamilton's president, Azel Backus, caught typhoid and died. When Robinson returned, Seth Norton was again momentarily in charge, but was soon to be replaced by the somber and somewhat old-fashioned Henry Davis who, while President at Middlebury, actually was offered the Presidencies of both Yale and Hamilton. Initially he refused both but then, when difficulties at Middlebury had cleared, chose to accept Hamilton's renewed invitation.

Unhappy with the situation he saw when he arrived and regarding Norton's attitudes as too lenient, he worked quickly to "bring back discipline" to the college. In so doing he ruffled many feathers and helped to bring about what he himself was to call "the decline and embarrassment of Hamilton College." Unlike Backus who was sometimes accused of being too droll, Davis was severe, a Calvinist of the decidedly old school. In the 1820s he was to fight hard against the new measures revivalism represented in the area by Charles Granison Finney. Many students left Hamilton because they believed that Finney should have been allowed to conduct revivals at the college. In any event, one can well imagine that Robinson might have found the new regime, which was critical of his uncle, not to his liking.

Moreover, 1818 marked the year of Seth Norton's death at the age of 39. The relationship which had probably lured Robinson to Hamilton in the first place was no more. We do not know the reason for his sudden demise, but his passing must have been a great blow to the college, for he represented continuity with the past and well-seasoned leadership.

And finally, there was the annoyance of his fellow tutor, the Rev. Mr. Barstow who loved to "pull rank" and argue that he should be given priority because he was also "chaplain." Robinson, apparently, accepted these pretensions without great reaction, but was clearly uncomfortable with the relationship. This may have been the straw that broke the camel's back and convinced him to stay as tutor for but one year.

Robinson did not leave the area, however, for in September of 1818 he married Eliza Kirkland, the youngest daughter of Hamilton's founder.

Eliza (Elizabeth, Betsy) had grown up with her mother, Jerusha, and her siblings in Stockbridge, Massachusetts. While her father ministered to the Oneidas, traveled to Philadelphia and New York on diplomatic missions, and made an occasional stop in Stockbridge to father yet one more child, his family eked out a meager existence, living in a house formerly occupied by Stockbridge Indians who had moved, ironically enough, to Oneida territory, just west of the Kirkland Patent.

Jerusha, whom Samuel had married in 1769 and who was a niece of his teacher Eleazar Wheelock, however, died in 1788 and, as a consequence, Kirkland in 1791 brought his children and their nanny, Mary Donnelly, to Clinton. Even then he was not in town to greet them when they arrived. His son, John, and Mary Donnelly had to do the honors of settling them in the not yet completely enlarged log cabin. At that time, John and George, his twin boys were 22, Jerusha was about 16, Sarah 14, and Eliza probably 12. Little Samuel, who died before reaching manhood, was 9 or 10.

The family was not really together for long, however, for Jerusha soon went to finishing school in Connecticut while Sarah and Eliza were educated at the Moravian Female Seminary in Bethlehem, Pennsylvania. John was already at Harvard and George was a student at Dartmouth.

In any event, it was Eliza, the youngest daughter, who maintained the closest relation with the Clinton area. Her father eventually married the housekeeper, Mary Donnelly, and when he died Eliza remained to live with her in the big mansion which her father had built. Mary and Eliza together inherited Samuel's property. Although Samuel had had to sell off much of his patent to pay his son George's debts,[16] Eliza still inherited considerable land, particularly along the Oriskany Creek. Unfortunately, the estate had many liens and encumbrances and even when Robinson married her, there were still so many problems that her brother John described her as moneyless and felt compelled to send her payments of fifty dollars on a regular basis.

---

[16] While John Thornton Kirkland eventually distinguished himself as a notable President of Harvard University, George Whitfield Kirkland was constantly in debt and in trouble with the law. He died as a soldier of fortune in the Caribbean.

Eliza was, from contemporary reports, a beautiful woman with lovely long hair.[17] That she had attracted in the past other suitors is attested to by a New Year's note from none other than the famous Edward Everett[18] written in 1812:

> To Miss E. Kirkland
>
> I wish, dear friend, that this new year
> With spirits and with health may come
> (And if the time must be so near)
> May bear you safely home,
> There, with your friends, may every day
> In some new form of joy appear.
> That so your happiness repay
> The sorrow of your absence here.
> A painful void behind you'll leave,
> And, when you bid us here farewell,
> There is, who less may speak than grieve,
> And feel, what words would fail to tell.
> Then, ere we take our mournful leave,
> Which, ere the homeward stage appear,
> My little new year's gift receive,
> And then my new year's wishes hear:
> Long happy years that you may see,
> And each in joy the past exceed,
> That all you ask your friends may be,
> And all you pray that God concede:
> This, from my heart I wish for you,
> And for myself, I only pray.

---

[17] There is an account which claims that when her body was exhumed and moved to the college cemetery several decades after her death, her hair was still as beautiful as when she was buried.

[18] Edward Everett served as Governor of Massachusetts, President of Harvard University, Ambassador to Great Britain, Secretary of State, etc. Known as a great orator, he held forth at Gettysburg for two hours before Abraham Lincoln offered his famous Gettysburg Address. It was he who, in 1842, received for Robinson the Gold Medal given to him by the Royal Geographical Society of London.

That soon your visit you'd renew
And when you come again, you'd stay.

Dorchester, Jan.1, 1812   Edward Everett[19]

How seriously Everett meant all this, is something we shall never know, but it appears that he found Eliza much to his liking. Perhaps their difference in age—he was the same age as Robinson—may have created a barrier.

Despite her beauty and her property, Robinson's marriage to Eliza seems a little surprising, for in 1818 he was only 24 and she was already 39, the same age as his uncle Seth. Apparently Eliza had some serious questions about the relationship, for she wrote to her brother John, who was already President of Harvard, for his advice. His response is revealing:

Cambridge 5 Aug. 1818

My dear Sister,

You said I was to come after you this autumn. Will you not make up your mind one way or another upon one subject. I am too old and too unenterprising to undertake to advise you upon such a matter . . . If you think concurrence best, I will be present; if you consider it advisable I shall be at your wedding . . . .Suppose I was dead and gone. You would not make any imprudent desperate match on that account or say it was not worthwhile to have a plan of life. If you think it will promote your happiness, do you form this Annexation. It will be (as they say) a nine days wonder. But if you think it will not, do not be induced by the wishes of your excellent young friend, because the evil of defeat in his purpose will certainly be transient, whilst the evil of the other side may be durable. I am sure that absolute hopelessness in the case can be a speedy remedy for him; at least an important alleviation—not that I would doubt the depth of his attachment or deny the inconsolable quality of the wounds which you inflict. It is certain there is a witchery irresistible in you and that nothing but the passage of time on your person will bring any of your lovers to a tolerable state. Then the remembrances of charms passed away and the attractions of the mind, character, and manners remaining will be

---

[19] Robinson papers C.5.

> sufficient to cause disquietude. I have thought that the uncertainties about the claims on your estate and the disputes to be adjusted might be some inducement to marry. Now really that should not weigh because we can get those matters settled, you and I, that is, as I believe . . .[20]

It is obvious from Kirkland's remarks that it was young Edward who was strongly pressing the suit and that Eliza still had (or had had) serious doubts. It would appear, however, that she had already made up her mind by the time she received her brother's letter, for the couple was married in September.

Clearly Edward was smitten with love for Eliza and had fewer doubts than she. It may also be that he had learned from his father's tragic losses that it is dangerous to marry a young and hence not very robust bride. At 39 years of age, Eliza had proved that she could survive the harsh realities of communicable diseases and Clinton winters. If that was his reasoning, he was to be sorely disappointed, for by July of 1819 Eliza was dead—her nephew Samuel Kirkland Lothrop says in childbirth. In reminiscences collected by his son, Lothrop was to remember,

> While she (Aunt Amory) was there, news came that my Aunt Eliza, who in the August *(sic)* previous (1818) had married Edward Robinson, professor in Hamilton College, had suddenly died, and her new-born baby with her; and this news had to be concealed from Mrs. Kirkland lest the shock should be fatal to her.[21]

Robinson was left with a sense of tragic loss of both wife and child and responsibility for a rather considerable but confusingly unsettled estate. Eliza was buried by Asahel Norton next to her father and Oneida Chief Skenandoah near the family mansion. Later, her body was exhumed and moved to the Hamilton College cemetery, but no mention has ever been made of a newborn infant with her. From the letters of condolence received, it is clear that Robinson took the sudden loss very hard and fell for a time into deep depression. One of the few letters we have from his father

---

[20] *Ibid.,* C.1. Aug. 5, 1818.
[21] Thorton Kirkland Lothrop, ed. *Some Reminiscences of the Life of Samuel Kirkland Lothrop* (Cambridge: John Wilson and Son, University Press, 1888), 76.

extends to his son deep sympathy from a man who had experienced exactly what Edward felt. Apparently, Edward had written a second letter expressing his profound depression to his father. His father replies:

Southington July 26th 1819

My son,

Yours of 12th July was rec'd by last mail. No doubt you will say "Clouds and darkness are round about God" in his Providential dealings with me. But is it so "that you have no motive for exertion in life." Have you not many friends, and among them affectionate parents who are anxious to see you rising above your trials, & being useful in the world? Are you not God's Contract? Is not righteousness and judgment still the habitation of his throne? Is not he commanding you to perform many duties? Will you, because he has seen fit, in infinite wisdom, to remove from you one of the many blessings which he had lent you, therefore say that all which are continued are of no estimation? Had not God a right to do as he has done? Will you say to him "why dost thou thus and so?" . . . I notice an expression which you certainly ought not to use, unless you have an absolute and full assurance of your good estate, nor indeed then. It is "every morning when I wake, it is to wish that I had awoke no more." The person who is sure of the power of God may doubtless truly say as Paul, "for me to die is gain" but how fearful, how tremendous a thing it is for others to fall into the hands of an angry God for judgment? . . .

The event of this has shown you what was the will of God respecting your dear friend. It came indeed suddenly & by surprise to you—but think it was anything new or unexpected to God, who says "my counsel shall stand, and I will do all my pleasure." Thus be still and know that he is God. Be thankful to him that he gave her to you, and that he continued her to you so long as was his counsel . . . Raise yourself from your dull, desponding frame. Such a frame will not remove your difficulties—it will increase them. Difficulties call not for despair, but for exertion. Act the Man in the service of God, for the comfort and happiness of your friends...[22]

---

[22] Robinson Papers, C.3. b. July 26, 1819.

How long it took Robinson to recover from his depression we do not know, but recover he did. During the rest of 1819 until 1821 he busied himself with the affairs of the estate and with a literary project: the preparation of a new edition of several books of the Iliad for use in schools and colleges.

Robinson had begun the difficult task of putting the affairs of the estate in order almost immediately after his wedding. He seems to have bought out John Thornton Kirkland[23] and Mary Kirkland,[24] though the latter was accorded the right to two rooms in the mansion and certain other amenities as long as she lived. He hired Stephen Farr to run the farm and negotiated both sales and leases of land. When Eliza died, he became sole executor of the estate.

It is not clear how much he profited from all this, but it seems evident that he gained enough to feel confident about leaving Clinton for further study and to consider very soon study abroad. In the fall of 1821 Robinson wrote to J. T. Kirkland for advice, both about book publication and further study. Kirkland replied on December 1:

> ... In regard to a place for studying divinity, I think on account of the prejudice respecting our theology and the distrust expressed toward our candidates in advance, it would be much better to issue forth from N. Haven. At the same time, I should be much pleased if you should think it eligible to study with us; and perhaps if you take a proper portion of time at Yale, you might without much disadvantage take a part of your preparatory inquiries here. You might reside and study here without belonging absolutely to the school. Andover is a good plan for you on many accounts. You see Dr. Popkin thinks that if you execute your edition of Homer it would be important to be here. I enclose you his letter on your proposal. You observe his last intimation that as we wish 9 or 12 books you might publish the six books for other colleges—and add more for ours and bind them accordingly . . .[25]

By the time Robinson received this letter, he had already made up his mind. Although he still owned much of the original property inherited

---

[23] *Ibid.,* A.2. Sept. 17, 1818.
[24] *Ibid.,* A.3. May 15, 17, 1819.
[25] *Ibid.,* C.4. a Dec. 1, 1821.

through Eliza, he left Clinton, forever.[26] After a brief stay in Southington, to which Kirkland had directed his letter, he set forth for Andover and the next stage of his career. It was Andover and its professor of Bible, Moses Stewart, which would fix securely Robinson's purposes in life.

---

[26] He did return the next summer to sign some papers, but never lived in the area after he left for Andover.

Chapter Four

ANDOVER DAYS

Headlines and Notices: 1820-1826

1821-30   The Greek War of Independence is fought.

1820   Washington Irving publishes his famous *Sketchbook*.

1821   Mary Baker Eddy and Clara Barton are born.
          Jean-François Champollion deciphers Egyptian cuneiform using the Rosetta Stone.

1822   Ulysses S. Grant and Albrecht Ritschl are born.
          Yellow fever kills 400 in New York City.
          U.S. recognizes Mexico's independence.

1823   The Monroe Doctrine is proclaimed.
          James Fenimore Cooper publishes *The Pioneers*.

1824   Presidential election ends inconclusively, with no candidate receiving a majority of the electoral votes. Early in 1825 John Quincy Adams is elected by the House.
LaFayette tours America.
The American Sunday School Union established in Philadelphia.
Josiah Gibbs publishes his translation of Gesenius' 1815 Hebrew Lexicon.

1825   The Erie Canal officially opens with a great celebration in New York harbor.
Thomas Cole is "discovered" as a promising young landscape artist.
Archibald Alexander of Princeton publishes *The Brief Outline of Evidences of the Christian Religion*, revealing the influence of Scottish Common Sense philosophy.
Samuel Taylor Coleridge publishes his influential *Aids to Reflection*.

1826   James Fenimore Cooper publishes *The Last of the Mohicans*.
Anti-Masonic Party is formed.
Charles Granison Finney revivals begin in earnest.
Thomas Jefferson and John Adams both die on July 4th.

The Era of Good Feelings engendered by the end of the War of 1812 and the consequent improvement of relations with England and Canada did not last very long. Federalism, once so popular in New England, died a rather sudden death when Madison and Monroe adopted as their own key features of their rival's agenda. Monroe was one vote shy of a unanimous electoral vote in 1821. Almost immediately, however, the party of Jefferson and his Virginian followers began to splinter as political life in America reconfigured itself. John Quincy Adams, Monroe's Secretary of State, was elected in 1825, after an indecisive three way race, by the House of Representatives, but the military hero Andrew Jackson actually received more votes and needed to wait only four more years before his eventual triumph.

One of the factors which led to this reconfiguration of American politics was the Panic of 1819 which lasted longer and was more severe in the rapidly growing western states. The East versus West feeling which emerged was then deepened and made more complex by the struggle over Missouri's statehood. In 1819 the states were divided evenly between those which were slave and those which were free. The proposal that Missouri should upset that balance by being admitted as a slave state led to the opening of an acrimonious debate which was to end so tragically in the 1860s with the Civil War. The momentary solution to the conflict was to admit Missouri as a slave state but to balance that act by the admission to the union of Maine, newly separated from Massachusetts. There was also an important proviso that no other state should be admitted as a slave state north of Missouri's southern boundary.

Clearly, the debate surrounding the Missouri Compromise placed the question of slavery near the top of America's moral agenda. Although many (for instance, the famous Edwardsean, Samuel Hopkins) had, in earlier decades, inveighed against this national stain, the majority had managed to sweep the whole matter under the rug. Now that was no longer quite possible. For a growing number of citizens the ending of slavery took top priority as a national issue.

When Robinson left Clinton, New York in 1821 change was also in the wind there. The Erie Canal had been started in 1817 and already promised to the whole area new growth and industrialization. Finished in 1825 it was to link much of the West with eastern tidewater, thus stimulating trade and national growth. Although painfully slow by modern standards, Clinton's Ditch was a much speedier way to ship cargo and to travel than the rutted and bumpy turnpikes had been. Central New York, only a few decades earlier a rough frontier, was now a series of significant stops on America's relentless thrust to the West.

Religious changes were also in the offing. Many of the people who settled in central and western New York had come from Connecticut and Massachusetts, not only to find better land but to escape the stifling blue laws and rather rigid social standards of Puritan New England. What developed, therefore, was a hard drinking, unchurched society—not exactly lawless, but tending toward excess. Already in 1818, Christians in western New York sensed the need for religious leaders who could speak to this world of hard working, hard drinking, hard partying folk. Those ministers trained among the carriage trade in Boston, New York, and Philadelphia would not do. Therefore, Presbyterians founded a theological seminary in Auburn, New York with the distinct purpose of training ministers who were not afraid to rough it in order to live and work among their parishioners. The gospel message may have, in essence, remained the same, but the style was radically altered to fit the circumstance.

In 1821, the very year Robinson headed east to renew his studies, another, at the time little heralded, event occurred which was to rock the area. In the far northern part of the state, in Adams, worked a young lawyer, just two years older than Robinson. As a boy he had grown up not far from Clinton in a hamlet then called Hanover. There is no indisputable evidence, but it is possible that he may have gone to the Hamilton-Oneida Academy and studied with Seth Norton, Robinson's uncle. In any event, he did not go to college, but taught himself the law and became a barrister in the small upstate village of Adams.

Charles Granison Finney (1792-1875), however, was not to remain in the legal profession, for in 1821 he experienced a profound conversion experience. Up until that time he had had little interest in religion. He was critical of sermonizing and only went to church because he loved to sing and to play his bass fiddle. All that changed, however, with his conversion, for he was to become one of America's great and most successful evangelists, a prototype for all those tent meeting preachers who would follow. After a short period of evangelical effort in his own area, he was invited to work in central New York, first in Westernville and then in Rome, Utica, Rochester, and beyond.

His revivals were roughhewn and crude by Connecticut standards, though they were certainly less emotional than the Methodist revivals then going on in many parts of the United States. Indeed, most of what he did was not new but had been common practice among Methodists and Baptists for some time.[1] Nevertheless, it was new to most Presbyterians and

---

[1] Richard Carawardine, "The Second Great Awakening in the Urban Center: An Examination of Methodist and the New Measures," *Journal of American History* 59, no. 1 (June 1972), 327-340.

Congregationalists. Lyman Beecher and many of his New England colleagues resisted his dramatic and sometimes disturbing "new measures."[2] For the people of central and western New York, however, Finney was a master preacher and motivator. He did not read carefully contrived literary homilies. He did not bore his listeners with abstruse theological disquisitions. He did not much care whether or not he was an Arminian or whether the presbytery approved of his theology. He spoke from the heart, to their hearts about the real dangers of hell and its fires, about the demands of the gospel upon their lives, about change, transformation, kneeling in prayer before the Lord. Before long he was preaching about radical social change as well.

Thousands flocked to hear him; hundreds were converted. Some clergy—like President Davis at Hamilton College—resisted Finney and would not have him in their institutions, but many more saw the power of his message and the fruits of his labors and invited him to preach for them. People listened; churches grew; a faltering Christianity, racked by Enlightenment rationalism and the freedom of the frontier, was rejuvenated. Upstate New York would never be the same again. It came to be called, because of the many revivals, the Burned Over District.

Edward Robinson did not stay to witness this radical transformation of religion upstate. Instead, he headed east, to climb a mountain, to visit his parents, and to begin a new phase of his education. In June of 1821, his real estate affairs not fully settled and his Iliad text still not published, Robinson decided to relax. He traveled to Andover, Massachusetts and from there northward with some friends to climb Mt. Washington. After returning to Clinton to settle some business affairs, he journeyed to Southington to visit his now aging parents. As far as we know, he never returned to stay in Clinton again. From that time on, his sights were set on things eastward, always eastward.

We would never know of Robinson's journey through New Hampshire had it not been that his little, almost illegible diary was preserved among some old and little used Robinson family cookbooks. Almost discarded with other old rubbish, it remains one of the first accounts of a

---

[2] For an account of their reconciliation with Finney see: Howard Alexander Morrison, "The Finney Takeover of the Second Great Awakening during the Oneida Revivals of 1825-1827," *New York State History* 8, no. 1 (Jan. 1978), 27-54.

journey up the highest peak of the northeast. Although the descriptions are rife with typical Robinson understatement, it should be remembered that the trek took place before there was even a proper trail up the mountain. As in Palestine, Robinson was in the vanguard of that host of tourists who would almost immediately follow after.

His entries are cryptic and obviously meant only for his own eyes, but they are intriguing nonetheless, for they reveal Robinson the traveler and observer at a fairly early age. The traits which we find in this little diary are those which were to serve him so well when he recorded his trip to the Holy Land for the world to read. He approaches the journey with keen and objective eyes. He is interested in natural formations, flora and fauna, compass readings. He is open to the impact of romantic vistas and picturesqueness, but he does not linger over these matters. Although he is a firm believer in Christianity, he does not pontificate about the beauties of God's creation. When he arrives at the summit, he sings no hymns. Rather, he takes readings with his compass of the other mountains he can see.

Robinson left Andover on June 18 in the company of three others identified only as Rev. I. E. D., H. E. D., and R. C. M. They arrived at Massabesic Lake the first night and camped near an inlet called the Spectacle where Robinson complained of a violent headache, a problem he had frequently throughout his life. He rested—his usual cure—while the others went fishing. By the 19th they had arrived at Louden; by the 20th at the Shaker Village at Canterbury, New Hampshire.

> June 20 Thursday. 5 miles to Shaker village in Canterbury. fine granite reservoir at foot of hill—always full, never oerflowing. Kind reception—excellent breakfast—visit all the [illegible]—tannery—threshing machine similar to Engl. except spikes instead of beaters— cooper shoppe—cider mill—much like Mr. Gay's of Fra.—press—use little straw—kind of box made by slats 1/2 inch or more apart within a strong frame. Cider 5 years old & finest I ever saw—no peculiar process—but extreme mixture—use Rum Hpt—distilled & add 1 gallon brandy to hpt let over night. (Rack twice—in Dec. and March.— . . . later in Nov.)—Dairy, milk cellar—smoke of lamp carried off by funnel.
>
> 3 families, 220 or 30 members. 2000 Acres. 100 h. stock, 20 horses. barn 200 ft. fine garden 3 1/2 acres. Stream made by draining marshes.

Chapter Four

Such a description is typical of the diary. The author spends no time really reflecting about the religion of the Shakers nor does he seem to worry about their unorthodoxy. He is interested in their equipment, their organization and how they make their cider. There is something wonderfully American in all this. Although he surely held strong religious opinions and often reflected about matters of life and death, his pragmatic side is always in evidence. He is less concerned about their belief in Mother Ann Lee as the Messiah and more interested in their agricultural pursuits and innovations.

Later in life Edward and his German wife Therese would return to visit Shaker communities on several occasions. In fact, she wrote a rather long article about her experience with the Shakers for a German journal. While she could be rather sharply critical about some of their beliefs and customs, Robinson himself seems less worried about the idiosyncrasies of Shaker theology. But the cider was wonderful.

On Friday, June 21 the party traveled 13 more miles to Center Harbor and Lake "Winnipis-og-ee" which Robinson much admired. June 22 saw them proceed through Moultonborough to Tamworth where views of various mountains were plentiful. They stayed "very pleasantly" at McMillan's establishment which he describes as intelligent and accommodating both Saturday and Sunday, for, of course, they would not travel on the Sabbath.

The next day it rained, but they sent for the horses which they had planned to leave behind and were able to arrive at Abel Crawfords where they stayed before proceeding to the famous Crawford Notch[3] and the ascent of Mt. Washington.

> 25. Left Crawfords and came up the notch & up the white mountains. Vide infra. The mountains contract on each side as we advance westward & become more lofty. Notch house picturesque —steep mountain in front 1000 or more high—or still higher behind—small meadow 6 acres, 20 once cleared. At 8 miles from Abel Crawford's pass the notch— passage just sufficient for Saco— here a small brook which comes from a marsh beyond—winds part of way under road. Narrowest part 320 feet— overhanging rocks 40 feet or more with mountain above. Passage discovered by Nash and Sawyer about 1770 . . .

---

[3] Thomas Cole was to paint an oil painting of *The Notch of the White Mountains* in 1840. By this time the climb to the summit had become very popular.

The climb, without road or trail, was an all day venture. They left at 8:20 in the morning, arrived at the summit of Mt. Pleasant at 3 p.m., and set foot on the summit of Mt. Washington at 6:15. He writes:

> Summit of Mt. W. mild and pleasant. Soon, however, light fleecy clouds began to fly around us and breaking away at intervals, gave additional interest to the most magnificent prospect I ever expected to behold. That from the Catskills is not to be named with it. To E. and S.E., it is lost in the ocean of the sky; on the N. & S. & W., splendid piles of mountains are dimly seen at the distance of 100 miles or more—to have been an ocean & in the midst of some raging tempest, where the waves were running to the heavens, to have been suddenly fixed in solid masses— of all I saw sun set, near 1/2 hour later than in the world below.—mighty monarch assumed his misty crown. At sunset in valley of Ammonoosuc, Littleton. W. Mts. tops tinged with golden hues, & clouds, like golden crowns suspended over them.

Their views were brief, however, for clouds moved in rather suddenly. Most of the party went back down the mountain about 1/2 mile, but Robinson and "Mr. M." "crept into a hole in the rock" just below the summit and spent the night, hoping for good views in the morning.

In the morning the fog was very dense and the two descended with some difficulty to find the others. The weather looked more and more like rain, so the guides suggested descending about a mile to make camp.

> We accordingly went down almost a perpendicular story, along the little stream tumbling along its precipitous bed in falls of 10-20-30 -50 feet (now hidden by the rocks and sliding over their surface . . . The amphitheater as we descended the latter was grand beyond description. Behind it was Mt. W. hiding his summit in the clouds at the distance of 3000 feet above us. On the S. the ridge which we had descended 2/3 as high and on the N. as similar one—Before the mists dispersed & {before} reaching the camp, we found we had made the whole descent of Mt. Washington.

Rev. I. E. D. and H. E. D decided they had had enough, but not Robinson. At 1 a.m. he and "M" and Crawford, the guide, started back up.

> Crawford carried a torch of birch bark, which gave strong and brilliant light. This ascent from the camp was generally very steep, hands useful in climbing— road perfectly discernible by torch light . . . (This walk by torchlight, through thick woods & m[ountain] wilds was romantic in the extreme.)

Again fog settled around the mountain and they were forced to stop, build a fire, sleep, and have breakfast. By ten o'clock the fog had departed once more and they obtained the summit and a glorious view. This time, compass in hand, he enumerates all the various peaks he can see.

Although there is nothing highly unusual about the climb or Robinson's response to it, it illustrates wonderfully many features of his personality. First of all, he is a man of dogged determination. Others give up; he not only endures the rigors of the climb, but finds the whole experience highly romantic. This is very much the same man who, a few years later, would set off for Mt. Sinai on camelback across the Egyptian desert.

Second, although he greatly appreciates the beauties of nature and illustrates well the attitudes and passions captured by the Hudson River School of Art, he also is a careful observer, providing regularly data concerning how long, how far, in which direction. This trait also foreshadows his meticulous descriptions of his journey through the Holy Land. The romantic in him always allows room for plenty of measurements and quantitative observations.

Finally, although Robinson is about to enter a very conservative, Calvinistic establishment, Andover Theological Seminary, he does not wear his religious feelings on his sleeve. One looks in vain for any remarks about "the works of the Creator." Many of his age might have used the occasion to remind themselves that all of creation reflects the love and power of the Almighty. Robinson does not. This will be true of his writing throughout his life. Only on rare occasion in his travel books does he reflect theologically upon what he sees. If he has deep religious feelings—and he certainly does—he keeps them very much to himself.

The party remained at Crawfords on June 28th, apparently resting after their strenuous venture. Robinson describes briefly a visit to a beautiful flume as well as the sighting of various forms of animal life: a hedgehog, partridge with young, rabbits, a nightingale, red squirrels, etc. By 4 in the afternoon they were on their way again, traveling about sixteen miles before arriving and dining at one Col. Whipple's.

On the 29th, after a breakfast of trout they set off for Lancaster where they spent the night and presumably the Sabbath with "Mr. Willard & family." From there, they proceeded by stages down the Connecticut River valley. Although Robinson found his visit to Dartmouth and its medical school worth noting, it is clear he was ready to go home. Notes are few and quite cryptic. They proceeded through Walpole and Keene back to Andover where they arrived on July 9.

Apparently Edward returned to Clinton that summer for we have a document signed there by Amanda Norton, Seth's widow, and him. By fall, however, he was off to visit his parents in Southington. The reason seems obvious. His father had been in poor health for some time and had, more than once, asked his church for help in the form of an associate. The church agreed, but, in fact, no associate was hired. Meanwhile, William's legs and feet continued to swell and he found it very difficult to walk or to stand long in the pulpit.[4] Finally in March of 1821, he requested that he be dismissed as minister. That request was approved in April and by fall a new minister, David Ogden, was settled in his place.

His father continued to care for his garden and ride around in his wagon to call on friends, but his years of labor were over. His second son, George, returned home from college to look after the farm and Edward too returned, presumably to be sure that his father and mother were well cared for. It would be his last extended stay with his parents. In 1824 his mother, who had never enjoyed very good health, became increasingly feeble. She died on December 20th at the age of 63. His father, now feeling very alone, was to last only one more year, dying in August of 1825 at the age of 71. Edward carefully gives the details of both deaths in his memoir.

The Andover years, therefore, mark a radical turning point in the life of Edward Robinson. The older generation passes away and that cloud of parental authority is lifted. By the time he leaves Andover he not only has lost both parents but has gained a fairly sizable inheritance which will be instrumental in supporting his travel and his future study.

---

[4] Edward Robinson, *Memoir of the Rev. William Robinson* (New York: John F. Throw, 1859), 128.

Edward came to Andover in January of 1822, not to matriculate but to get advice about the publication of his first book. Already he was probably older than most of the institution's students. He was to become twenty-eight in April. According to his own account, he began to study Hebrew "but without connecting himself with the seminary."[5] After studying for a year with Moses Stuart, who became his primary mentor, he was asked to correct proofs for the second edition of Stuart's Hebrew Grammar and then to serve as his substitute during a period of illness. In the autumn he was hired as an assistant instructor of Hebrew and remained in that position until 1826.

With what sort of institution was Robinson, who was still unclear about his vocational plans and who hardly seems to qualify as a fervent evangelical, associating? Andover had been founded in 1808 by two different types of Calvinists in response to the growing threat of proto-Unitarianism. Already most of the churches of Boston and vicinity had been "converted" to this new, heterodox position.[6] When Henry Ware, an avowed "liberal," was elected to the Hollis Professorship of Divinity at Harvard in 1805, the Calvinists reacted vigorously with a counter-offensive. The fruit of that effort was Andover Theological School.

The struggle between the Unitarians and the Calvinists has often been portrayed as a fight between rationalists and believers in revelation, but such a characterization is much too simplified. In fact, virtually all Calvinists of the time could be described as "supernatural rationalists." That is to say, Leonard Woods, that ardent champion of Calvinism from Andover, would have agreed with Henry Ware that through reason one can know of both the existence and many of the properties of the divine. God, for most 18th and early 19th century theologians, was knowable through reason. Moreover, Calvinists and Unitarians of the time also agreed that there are many other aspects of God which remain hidden from human understanding. Some of these—the ones essential for human salvation—have been revealed through Holy Scripture.

The debate, then, was not about reason exactly but about what Holy Scripture really reveals. It should also be noted that reason, in fact, was used

---

[5] Duyckinck, op. cit., 167.
[6] The American Unitarian Association was not founded until 1825, so it may be anachronistic to speak of Unitarianism before that time. Nevertheless, the essential ingredients of this tradition were already in the making in the 1780s.

as much by the Calvinists as by the Unitarians in interpreting what it is that Scripture says. The position of the latter was set forth with great eloquence in an ordination sermon in Baltimore by William Ellery Channing in 1819. In that classic, often quoted address, Channing makes clear he believes in Holy Scripture and in its revelation. It is just that he does not, after careful study, believe that Scripture teaches what the Calvinists, indeed virtually all Christians, have asserted. How can Jesus be God, a Person of the so-called Holy Trinity, when he is regularly portrayed as praying to God and as being completely subordinate to the will of the Almighty? Channing concludes that Jesus was a man, albeit one with divine powers, and that the doctrine of the Trinity (and hence a whole host of other teachings) was a mistake.

This was no minor question, for if the Unitarians were correct, if Jesus should not be thought of as God, then the whole of traditional Christian theology would fall to the ground. Leonard Woods, in response to Channing's well-thrown gauntlet, goes to great length to reassert not only the basic tenets of Calvinism but of Christendom in general.[7] He is, on the whole, restrained, rational, and scholarly as he seeks to show the error of Channing's position and to restate what Christians have always affirmed to be true: that Jesus is God. Behind this apparent calmness, lies a great deal of anxiety and alarm, for the Unitarians cut at the heart of everything the orthodox believed.

The whole Unitarian controversy was very upsetting for the Congregationalists, for it showed a decided weakness in their system. In a few brief years the ardently Calvinistic churches of Boston had been converted to a theological position so abhorrent to Calvinists that it was really outside the pale. And there was danger that that viewpoint would spread throughout the churches of New England and beyond, with the blessing of the great university which in the past had been the source of such well-honed orthodoxy. Because the churches were congregational and recognized no higher ecclesiastical authority, there was no bishop to halt such a plunge into heresy. Unitarianism became a genuine crisis for the whole church.

Some church leaders began to see that part of the problem lay in the process by which young men were trained as clergy for the church. Up until

---

[7] Leonard Woods, *Letters to Unitarians and Reply to Dr. Ware* (Andover: Mark Newman, 1822).

this time, candidates preparing for the ministry usually apprenticed themselves to an active minister and learned from him the essentials of theology and the arts of pastoral care and parish administration. The other possibility was to return to a university like Harvard or Yale for further private study with a professor, most often with the president. This was a somewhat more academic route, for it often involved serving as a tutor at the college, but had the disadvantage that it involved little instruction in the day to day leadership of a congregation. In neither case, was there much control over what was taught or how much a student really learned. It was all left to the good graces of the particular teacher involved.

Because Greek was taught in secondary schools and in colleges, mastery of that Biblical language was not a problem, but Hebrew, by and large, was neglected. Certainly few clergy had the time or inclination or ability to teach Hebrew independently at home. Church history was also a much neglected area of inquiry, for that subject demands a greater library and expertise than most individual teachers could muster. Ministerial education then was almost entirely theological. It was a matter of learning, catechetical style, the essentials of (Calvinistic) theology. True Biblical study involving literary and historical analysis of texts, the study of Hebrew and Aramaic languages, church history and the history of doctrine were largely overlooked.

As long as the teachers remained orthodox, things worked tolerably well. Everything was seen through the colored glasses of Calvin-Edwards and then, for the most part, Hopkins or Bellamy. When teachers changed, however, and no longer hewed the party line, there was no apparently easy way to prevent a monumental theological upheaval.

Two groups resolved upon a solution at approximately the same time. One group was centered in Andover itself which had been graced by Phillips Academy since its founding in 1778 by John and Samuel Phillips. The Academy, though not an institution of higher learning, had as part of its purpose the education of students in Scripture and Christian theology. There were also scholarships for young men destined for the ministry to study theology privately with a clergyman.

Eliphalet Pearson, former headmaster at Andover and then professor at Harvard, returned to Andover, quite concerned about the liberalism of that university. He began drawing up plans to found a new institution at Andover to defend orthodoxy against the growing tide of what he believed to be infidelity. To his cause he enlisted the aid of the Phillips, Samuel Abbott, a wealthy citizen who had made his money in the mercantile business in Boston, and Samuel Farrar. The Phillips promised a building which would house sixty students as well as a library and classrooms. The project was under way.

About twenty miles away in Newburyport, another group of concerned churchmen was developing similar ideas. The leader was Samuel Spring, a well-known clergyman.[8] With him stood Leonard Woods, a young pastor of that town. Both were ardent followers of the Hopkinsian school of Calvinism. They enlisted the help of William Bartlet, Moses Brown, and John Norris, who were to support the venture financially.

Before either group finalized its plans, they learned of each other and began a process of negotiation. Although it was clear that it would be counterproductive to have two theological schools so close together, the negotiations were not easy. The problems were in large measure theological. The Andover group was itself largely made up of Old Calvinists who were not enthusiastic about revivals or about some of the extreme views held by the Hopkinsians. The Newburyport group, on the other hand, was definitely of the Hopkinsian school and believed it most important to insist upon those radical principles and revival methods which Hopkins had made so popular, especially in Connecticut.

The talks between the two parties came close to breaking down at several points, but it was also in the interest of both parties to reach an agreement, so eventually reason prevailed. Before the two sides came together, however, the Andover group drew up a charter which contained the regulation that every seminary professor must

> be a man of sound and orthodox principles in divinity according to that form of sound words or system of evangelical doctrines, drawn from the Scriptures, and denominated the Westminster

---

[8] Samuel was the father of Gardiner Spring, the eminent pastor of Brick Presbyterian Church in N.Y.C. during the middle decades of the century. One brief letter from the latter is found among the Robinson Papers.

Assembly's Shorter Catechism, and more concisely delineated in the Constitution of Phillips Academy.[9]

The Hopkinsians insisted on more, a creed with articles clearly delineating their brand of Calvinism to be subscribed to as well. The Old Calvinists hesitated, but the Newburyport men came armed, not only with their creed, but with an offer of some $30,000 in financial support. The monetary considerations eventually took precedence; the Old Calvinists swallowed their pride; and a new institution, the first American theological seminary was founded.[10] It should be noted that the $30,000 was only the tip of the iceberg. During his long association with Andover, William Bartlet, who did not even belong to a church, gave an astounding $100,000 to the Seminary. Others contributed amazingly sizable amounts for those days as well. The foundation of the seminary was not only theologically hard rock but it was financially well-grounded too.

The first appointment to the faculty was Eliphalet Pearson, a leader of the Andover group. By 1808, however, he was already rather feeble and had to forego his opening address to the assembled throng. Second to be appointed was Leonard Woods, a much younger and more vigorous man, who was to serve as a chief spokesman for Andover for decades. At the opening convocation in September of 1808, Dr. Timothy Dwight, the President of Yale, preached and Dr. Spring of Newburyport and the Rev. Jonathan French of Andover offered prayers. Dr. Pearson read the Constitution and Jedediah Morse, one of the most doughty defenders of Calvinism as well as America's "first geographer," read the Hopkinsian "Additional Statutes."[11] Leonard Woods pulled out all his oratorical stops in offering a sermon, *On the Glory and Excellency of the Gospel*. It was, over all, an extraordinary day for the Calvinists.

The liberals in Boston did not like the development very much and there was much complaint and vituperation. After all, the pledge every

---

[9] As quoted in Henry K. Rowe, *History of Andover Theological Seminary* (Newton, Mass.: 1933), 13-14.

[10] Princetonians might debate this claim, for Princeton Theological Seminary also began about this time and also claims first place.

[11] Morse was the father of Samuel F. B. Morse, the inventor of the telegraph and well known artist, and Sidney and Richard Morse, the editors and publishers of *The New-York Observer*.

professor at Andover had to reaffirm every five years lumped Unitarians and Universalists with Jews, Mahommetans (sic), Arians, Pelagians, etc. as opposed to the Gospel of Christ and hazardous to the souls of men.[12] What is ironic, of course, is that it was the Unitarians who, in fact, prompted this theological reaction. In order to make sure that the Unitarians would never take over Andover, the founders made theological standards for professors particularly rigorous, thus insuring that radical Calvinism would last longer in New England than its normal life expectancy would have admitted.

When Robinson arrived at Andover in January of 1822, the institution was already a little more than 13 years old. Student enrollments had greatly exceeded all expectations from the classes during the first eight years averaging about 50. The entering class in 1819, however, numbered more than 100.[13] Because of the popularity of Andover, Phillips Hall soon proved to be too small. William Bartlet, ever the generous donor, provided both Bartlet Chapel, which housed much more than a place of worship and Bartlet Hall to round out the Brick Row which was to constitute the Andover campus for several decades. Beside these academic and dormitory buildings there were faculty residences[14] and a building which housed the Mechanical Association.[15] The last was a student organization which made, among other things, caskets to sell for a profit.

In fact, by 1822, the student body was quite well organized. Beside the Mechanical Association there was a literary society called the Bartlet Atheneum, the Porter Rhetorical Society, which fostered skills in oratory and debate, and the Lockhardt Society for Improvement in Sacred Music. Most students were graduates of New England colleges, especially Yale, Harvard, and Middlebury, though Union and Hamilton from New York also provided some matriculants. Many studied for a while, but dropped out before finishing three years of work, for the institution did not give an official "degree" and, in any case, ordination could be obtained without one.

The curriculum was organized around its three professors each of whom, in effect, taught a class:

---

[12] *Ibid.,* 14.
[13] *Ibid.,* 25.
[14] The Moses Stuart house still stands in Andover.
[15] Bartlet Hall and Bartlet Chapel still stand on the campus of Phillips Andover Academy. The Mechanical Arts building later became the residence of Calvin and Harriet Beecher Stowe and still exists as the "Harriet Beecher Stowe House."

The first year, which was devoted to Biblical study, was under the tutelage of Moses Stuart, appointed in 1810 to replace Eliphalet Pearson who resigned the year the seminary opened. Stuart was very much a Connecticut man, having been born in Wilton, Connecticut, educated in the Academy of Norwalk and then at Yale College. He taught school after college and then prepared himself for a career in the law. He was admitted to the bar but instead of pursuing that work, accepted the position of tutor at Yale where he studied theology under Timothy Dwight himself. In 1806 he became pastor of that most prestigious church, the First Congregational Church of New Haven. It was there that Dr. Samuel Spring heard him preach and decided that he would be a fit appointment at Andover.

Fit indeed he was, but, in fact, he came to Andover with little knowledge of Hebrew and no knowledge of German, the language of modern Biblical study. Stuart was something of a grammatical genius, however, and quickly set to work learning both languages. So thoroughly did he learn them that he not only became one of the first American scholars to be well-versed in German Biblical scholarship;[16] he also produced a Hebrew grammar which was to be used in both America and Britain for generations.

Stuart was much more than a grammarian, however, for he also wrote commentaries on books from both the Old and New Testaments as well as many articles on significant theological and textual questions. Most important, he was an extraordinary teacher who captured the imagination and commitment of his students. Generations of Andover graduates tended to read the Scriptures through his eyes. For many American theologians and preachers he remained the eminent authority in Biblical studies until the time of his death in 1852. Clearly Stuart also caught the imagination of Edward Robinson. Under his spell E. R. found direction and, once directed, never looked back again.

During the first year, Andover students studied under him:

> "Stuart's Hebrew Grammar, Chrestomathy; written exercises, including translations from English into Hebrew; study of the Hebrew Bible; the principles of Hermeneutics; New Testament Greek and exegesis of the Four Gospels; lectures preparatory to the study of theology; natural theology; evidences of Revelation;

---

[16] Joseph Buckminster preceded Stuart in studying the German scholars. Unlike Stuart he actually studied in Germany.

inspiration of the Scriptures; Hebrew exegesis; Greek; Pauline epistles twice a week; criticism and exegetical compositions."[17]

Given the fact that there were as many as 100 in the Junior (first year) class, Stuart must have been extraordinarily busy. It is no wonder that he looked for someone to assist him in the presentation of all this.

The professor for the Middler (second) year was Professor Woods, for this year was devoted to the study of Christian theology. Woods was born in 1774 in Princeton, Massachusetts. He prepared for college at Leicester Academy and then attended Harvard University. His post-graduate theological education, however, was with Charles Backus of Somers, Connecticut. Thus, although connected with the Massachusetts old Calvinists, he also had direct relations with the Connecticut Hopkinsians. He was the perfect bridge between these two parties whose differences threatened to split the church in New England. When the two groups sought to form separate seminaries, each chose Woods as their professor of theology. It was Woods, more than anyone else, therefore, who fused the two groups at Andover Theological Seminary and who provided through the years a strongly Calvinistic, yet moderating influence.

During the second year, students were introduced to all the major doctrines of Christian theology. There was some little attention paid to Christian church history, but for the most part the emphasis was upon the essential beliefs of the church. This was what any New England minister was expected to hold forth about on Sunday morning. Most important was the ability to avoid the pitfalls of heterodoxy, pitfalls which the Unitarians had, from Woods' point of view, so completely misjudged. By the time Edward Robinson arrived at Andover, the third year of study was the province of Ebenezer Porter who held the professorship of Sacred Rhetoric. Born in 1772 in Cornwall, Connecticut, he was educated at Dartmouth and then, after some time teaching school, prepared for the ministry under John Smalley of Berlin, Connecticut. Like Woods, he was a Calvinist with an Edwardsean flavor. After serving a church in Washington, Conn. for thirteen years, he was called to Andover in 1812. There he remained, as teacher of rhetoric and, after 1827, as President, until his retirement. Porter was to

---

[17] *Ibid.,* 59-60.

influence several generations of preachers through both his classes and his many writings on homiletics.

Edward must have felt right at home among both the students and the professors. Doubtless, the faculty were all acquainted with his father's ministry in Southington and welcomed him as one of their own. He, in turn, had been raised with just the sort of theology being taught and probably knew many of the arguments and positions just as well as they did from having listened so often to his father and to Azel Backus at Hamilton. When his book, a text of six books of the Iliad, with notes, was published in the spring, he must have seemed to the faculty more like a colleague than a student. In fact, as we have said, that is what he soon became. In the catalogue of 1823 appear the names of not only Porter, Woods, and Stuart, but also of resident licentiates, Edward Robinson, Leonard Bacon, and Dana Boardman. Robinson is identified as "assistant instructor in the department of sacred literature."[18]

Also added to the faculty by this time was James Murdoch, the first incumbent of the chair of ecclesiastical history established by Moses Brown of Newburyport. His professorship was described as one dealing with virtually the whole scope of Christian history and its relation with Judaism and Islam. In truth, however, he was required to teach primarily sacred rhetoric for the first five years of his stay at Andover. Murdoch was a graduate of Yale who had also received an honorary D. D. from Harvard. For a short time he served at the Hamilton-Oneida Academy in Clinton. He was characterized as "a dry little man with a large elastic brain and nerves like catgut."[19]

Although Murdoch was very bright, he was also quite contentious and thus soon ran into trouble. Some of the founding fathers, especially Mr. Spring, questioned his orthodoxy. This unhappiness with his theology was exacerbated by an article he wrote on the nature of atonement which drew upon the writings of Grotius, a well-known Arminian. Murdoch, in turn, complained that he was not being allowed to teach what he had come to Andover to offer. For several years a struggle ensued which left many unhappy. Murdoch finally was forced out, but the attempt to keep the

---

[18] *Ibid.,* 68.
[19] *Ibid.,* 69.

institution theologically pure as well as the personality conflicts involved, left some black stains which did not wash out easily.

Just how Robinson was able to master the intricacies of Hebrew in such a short time is difficult to say. We do know from his experiences in Europe that he was able to pick up languages very quickly and had, like his mentor, Moses Stuart, a gift for grammatical studies. Perhaps, too, both he and Stuart decided that the best way to learn something is to teach it. However he did it, by 1823, he was an assistant to Stuart, already introducing graduate students to the intricacies of Biblical studies.

Robinson's sights, however, were set on even more far reaching goals. In April of 1822, he received a letter from his uncle, Ashael Norton, to whom he had sent a copy of his "Iliad." Norton replied, complimenting Edward on the new work, which he describes as very finely printed, and commenting upon his nephew's plans to study in Europe! Perhaps already Stuart had told him that anyone wishing to pursue the study of the Bible really had to spend some time with the great German scholars. Perhaps he had already learned of Edward Everett's experiences there. In any event, four years before he actually left for Europe, he was already planning his next educational venture. This is typical of his whole career. We will discover that his trip to the Holy Land was no spur of the moment lark but had been on his mind for several years.

In the meantime, Robinson was exceedingly busy, teaching, working with Stuart on various publications, and preparing to be licensed to preach. The last venture was necessary if Robinson were to teach at Andover at all. In fact, it was a rule that only those who were ordained and who had served a congregation could teach at Andover. Since this was a preparation for the ministry, it was logical that only ministers could be appointed to professorships there. For the moment, Robinson could be licensed and hence serve as a licentiate, but in the future this was to be a barrier to him. It may be a major reason why, eventually, he left the faculty of Andover.

In the fall of 1822, after just one semester at the seminary, Robinson prepared to be licensed to preach. The nature and extent of the examination is unrecorded, but we do have the original text of his trial sermon which he preached before the "H. S. Association at Middletown, New Hampshire" on October 1. He was to offer probably an abbreviated version of the same sermon at Kensington, Connecticut on October 6. The text is particularly important, for it is one of the few documents extant in which he expresses himself very fully theologically.

He took as his text II Peter 1:21. "For the prophecy came not in the old time by the will of man; but holy men of God spake as they were moved by the Holy Ghost." No text could have been more appropriate for him to demonstrate his orthodoxy, a task which was most necessary, given the very present threat of Unitarianism. Robinson set about quite methodically and at some considerable length to demonstrate that Holy Scripture, which provides us with knowledge beyond the reach of reason, has been inspired throughout by the Holy Ghost. For him, as for most Calvinists of the time, many ideas and values can be known without the benefit of Scripture by reason alone. One does not need revelation to know that God exists or that murder is evil. What Scripture provides is a system of doctrine which further extends our knowledge of God's will and his way to salvation.

How do we know that Scripture is inspired? In the first place, the writers of Scripture testify to their own inspiration and that testimony is corroborated by the many miracles which accompany the inspiration. Moreover, there are innumerable fulfilled prophecies, such as, for instance, the prophecies of the fall of Babylon which had just been rediscovered.

> It (that is Babylon) has as you are probably aware, has been recently explored by an English traveler Mr. Rich. & the description which (he) has given would almost support the assertion that the prophesy has been accomplished, even to the literal fulfillment of the figurative language of Oriental imagery.[20]

He does caution that Christians should wait humbly and patiently for unfulfilled prophecies rather than applying human conjecture to the Word. At the same time, he is willing to admit that some prophecies might point to the present times,

> That the great events of our own age *may have* been fit subjects of prophecy can admit of no reasonable doubt. We have seen a power gigantic & vast. in comparison of which the mightiest empires of the Eastern world,—surrounded as they are by the splendid apparatus of prophecy, dwindle into insignificance.[21]

---

[20] Robinson papers E.1. folio 18. Parenthesis added.
[21] *Ibid.,* f. 19.

Robinson does not press the matter, however, for he is interested in the clear and undebatable teachings of Scripture, not human conjectures about obscure passages.

For him, Scripture, though by many authors and from many eras, presents one consistent and unified system of thought. Whatever apparent inconsistencies there are can be explained by scribal error or, perhaps, a misunderstanding of ancient Jewish custom or expression. That system of thought is, of course, captured in the New England brand of Calvinism to which Robinson had been exposed since childhood.

Finally, the young preacher turns to a comparison of the Hebrews and that other civilization which all educated Americans knew so well: Greece. The Greeks he depicts as highly sophisticated, literary, and philosophical. They were in touch with the world and learned from the Egyptians and many others. The Jews, on the other hand, he depicts as backward and isolated, the butt of everyone's derision.

> Confined within their own land, from the river of Egypt to the great river of the Euphrates,— & more immediately between the river Jordan & the coast of the Mediterranean— they had no connexions with other countries. To the neighboring nations they were objects of ridicule and contempt, & were seldom visited by them except for the purposes of conquest.[22]

One of the proofs of inspiration that he offers is that while the Greeks were polytheists, the isolated Hebrews developed a glorious monotheism which is obviously superior to anything the Greeks had to offer. How could this have come to pass if there were not the miracle of revelation? Of course, what he does not see is that the people of Israel were never as isolated as he suggests but lived along some of the major trade routes of the ancient Near East. Their subjugation by various invaders also brought them into direct contact with the prevailing currents of opinion. In this assertion of Hebrew isolation, Robinson continues a longstanding misunderstanding which created the "Holy Land" as a place apart, unaffected by the world, rather than the eye of that hurricane called history.

---

[22] *Ibid.*, f. 22.

In any event, Robinson at this point reveals little interest in those questions of critical scholarship which were bothering Germans like Eichhorn and DeWette and which were eventually to explode traditional Biblical scholarship. For him, the Bible is true because it is inspired and because it is inspired there is little point in considering questions which concern the individual author's point of view or the literary composition of the text. At the same time, he is quite impatient with those who wish to offer conjectural interpretations. What he does not see is that the whole of Calvinism is but one, rather rationalistic, way to read Scripture. Without the use of reason and its conjectures, there is no one clear system of doctrine.

Along the way, during his discourse, Robinson reveals some of his fundamental prejudices. For instance, he does not like enthusiasts, i.e. people who claim some sort of divine revelation for themselves.

> There are in every age instances of persons who consider themselves as fitted by the Holy Ghost & sent as the messengers of God to men. But have these persons ever done any sign or wonder to support the credibility of their mission? That they have pretended to do so is granted, but where is the evidence of any real miracle . . . But in all these things Christ and his Apostles stand absolutely opposed to enthusiasm. Their system is pure and faultless,—it is attested by miracles,—& there is not discernible upon the face of it, or their writings the remotest trace of enthusiasm.[23]

In other words, the apostles were just like the New England divines: sober, systematic, and not prone to emotional outburst. They were also much simpler in expression than those Christians who were to follow them.

> While the writers of the N.T. are distinguished for their simplicity, their brevity & in most instances their clearness & precision & energy,—the fathers on the other hand are remarkable only for the opposite qualities,—their refinements, their distinctions without a difference, their prolixity, their obscurity & their feebleness. Involving themselves in the mazes of metaphysical disquisition, they have groped in a labyrinth of contradictory & inconsistent opinions.[24]

---

[23] *Ibid.*, f. 12-13.
[24] *Ibid.*, f. 33.

"Metaphysical" seems to be a very negative word for Robinson. It is not surprising, then, that he also reveals himself to have little love for Greek philosophy or speculation.

> Plato and Xenophon in their delineations of the character of their master Socrates, have given their ideas of an upright and moral man—correct and worthy of imitation in all his conduct. But this man, so perfect and pure, who affords so noble and example of all that is virtuous and praiseworthy—this man, were he to appear at this day in any country of Christendom,—would be spurned from society as a corrupter of youth,—a destroyer of purity—a loathsome excrescence on the fair frame of society.[25]

It is amazing to the modern reader that the author does not see the devastating irony of such a statement. What he actually proves is that modern Christendom is no more enlightened than ancient Athens and that all the classical education he received failed to communicate Socrates' point.

Further marks of bias are also worth noting as we consider the life of one of America's first orientalists. Again he writes,

> We will pursue this comparison no further. It has thus far been confined chiefly to the Greeks . . . But pursue it, if you please, among the Romans, who were but imitators of the Greeks,—among the inhabitants of Hindustan with their 33,000 gods and all their abominations,—among the followers of Mahomet with their life of beastliness and their paradise of lust,—you will arrive at last at the irresistible conclusion,—that the God of the Hebrews is the only God, the only true and proper object of worship,—& and that the poor, humble and despised Jesus is the Savior of the world, & the God of the whole earth.[26]

All of this is to remind ourselves that Edward Robinson was very much an American of the early 19th century and expressed throughout his life ideas which were then commonly accepted. He had read since childhood all those missionary reports which depicted the rest of the world as ignorant and heathen and naturally accepted them as fact. One may suspect that

---

[25] *Ibid.*, f. 30.
[26] *Ibid.*, f. 31.

neither his collegial nor his theological education did much to disabuse him of these prejudices. What is interesting is not that he held such ideas but what happened when he actually entered an Islamic country and met some real Muslims. For this we will have to wait.

After his licensing, Robinson began to preach widely around Massachusetts and Connecticut. Of the five complete sermons which he preserved, all were composed in 1822 but were then repeated in various places until 1825.[27] The one preached most frequently by him during this period took as its text Hebrews 2:3 and dealt with the whole theology of salvation under four headings: I. What is the salvation spoken of? II. Why is it called great? III. What is it to neglect salvation? IV. The consequences of neglect. In it he treats of sin, atonement through the blood of Christ, what the gospel demands, and the eternal punishment if the call to repentance and faith is not heeded.

Clearly, as a preacher he followed very much the theological teachings of his seminary and the Calvinists in his church. There is certainly no sign of Unitarianism or any other form of heterodoxy here. What is a little surprising, given the few signs of religiosity in his life thus far, is the fervency of his rhetoric. Although he is no Charles Grannison Finney, there is a powerful urgency about his message which one might not have quite expected from someone who nearly went into the law and who more recently had been spending much of his time editing the Iliad. The first airing of the sermon was at Southington on October 4, 1822. It was subsequently repeated three more times that year, four times in 1823, twice in 1824, and once in 1825. Clearly it represents the heart of what the young preacher believed.

The very next week, on October 13, he offered another sermon based on another text from Hebrews (12:1-2) which he entitled "Christian Race." Its subject really encompasses what he thinks to be the essence of Christian living. The race we run, he says, has as its goal eternal life. Therefore, we must not be distracted by the things of this world but must proceed with diligence and patience toward the goal which is Christ. We must forsake all worldly desires and pleasures for the sake of the gospel. Idleness must be avoided as we run the race for Christ. Again, his fervency and the depth of

---

[27] On the front page of each sermon, he carefully lists the dates and locations of each sermon.

his commitment shines through. He is not here the objective and aloof scholar. Robinson's legendary "coolness" is missing. For him the Christian life has deep significance and importance. He ends with these words:

> Do this, & you shall live forever. Do this, & the congregation of God's people on earth will embrace you with the warmest affection. Do this, & the redeemed in heaven will welcome you:—angels will tune their golden harps & rejoice over one more repenting sinner. Then will you meet the approving smile of the savior;—then will you gain a title and immortal joys at the right hand of God on high. Amen.[28]

This sermon was repeated once more in 1822, six times in 1823, four times in 1824, and twice in 1825. Since travel was slow in those days, much time must have been spent reaching such places as New Haven, Boston, Kensington, and Southington, Connecticut, etc. to preach. It is noteworthy, that as time went on his pace apparently slowed, for he seems to have preached these sermons only four times in 1824 and only twice in 1825. Whether there were other sermons which he delivered and then discarded, we do not know.

The fourth sermon which has been preserved for us is based upon Matthew 16:26, "For what is a man profited, if he shall gain the whole world & lose his own soul? or what shall a man give in exchange for his soul?" His central question is: what is a soul worth anyway? Interestingly enough in this sermon Robinson takes a much more philosophical approach, and in so doing reveals his and his society's dependence upon Scottish Common Sense Philosophy.[29] He begins with a rather worldly view of the soul, discussing how humans differ from animals, how our reason functions, and how the soul's abilities have led to the tremendous scientific and cultural advances which humans have made.

> This faculty of acquiring knowledge,—this propensity to improvement forms an important distinguishing characteristic of the human soul. It is this which calls into exercise, & gives a

---

[28] Robinson Papers E. Sermon: Hebrews 12:1-2, f. 21.
[29] For a very interesting study of Scottish Common Sense Philosophy and its influence on American Presbyterians see: T. D. Bozeman, *Protestants in an Age of Science* (Chapel Hill, N. C.: University of North Carolina Press), 1977.

spring to all the other faculties,—which causes man never to rest satisfied with his present attainments,—but to go on exploring the hidden things of nature, & grasping in his desires the past, present, & the future. It is indeed a power, which lifts him up from the earth, and leads him to his God;—take it away, & you reduce him almost to a level with the brutes.[30]

Thus Robinson, like many post-Cartesians, assumed that the soul is characterized by reason and is our conscious, willing ego. And because the soul is characterized by this ability and desire to explore, science is very much an expression of our God-given human nature. Hence, also, Robinson's own desire to explore is not only justified but is one expression of God's will for humankind.

The preacher, of course, does not leave the matter there, for he goes on to emphasize that this "scientific self" which ever creates history and progress is also immortal. He speaks briefly about the Greek philosophers and their teachings about immortality and wrestles with the fact that the Hebrew Bible seems much less clear about life after death than Plato. For him, however, there is ultimately no problem, for the New Testament settles the issue once and for all: human souls are immortal and will spend eternity in either heaven or hell.

He addresses the idea that perhaps life in hell is of more limited duration than life in heaven, but will have none of it. The same word is used to describe life in both heaven and hell. If you think heavenly life is eternal, then you must characterize hell the same way. What he does not address is how this soul, so intrigued by exploration and so driven to create new things, will fare in an eternity which is changeless and bodiless. Perhaps that is asking too much of the young Edward Robinson. He seems content to merge American ways of conceiving the self with both Platonic ideas of the soul and Biblical notions of the resurrection of the body. None of it quite fits together, but, it would appear, nobody in the church seemed to notice. The mixture was a commonplace.

The fifth and final sermon was preached first on Thanksgiving Day at the Essex Street Congregational Church of Boston. E. R. took as his text Proverbs 3:6 and essentially developed in it the doctrine of God. God, he describes as Creator, Sustainer, Governor, and Redeemer. Although he

---

[30] Robinson Papers E. Sermon Matt 16:26. f. 12.

develops no tight philosophical arguments, he rather assumes that knowledge of God as creator can be had by anyone, without benefit of revelation. Indeed, it is only when he turns to God as redeemer that he appeals directly to inspiration. The fact that there is a force which creates, sustains, and governs us can be known by anyone sensitive to the world around us. Redemption, of course, is known through the Bible, but here he places particular emphasis upon the inworking of the Holy Spirit which inspires from within. Faith is not just accepting theological propositions, but is the work of an inward spiritual force which makes trust in God possible.

Robinson concluded his sermon with a brief disquisition about all those things for which Americans should be thankful. When he preached the sermon again, at Andover, he removed this last section and added another conclusion concerning what we owe to the God who has created all.

Whether it be by happenstance or by design, what Robinson preserved for us in these five sermons is an outline of his early theology: I. Scripture and the nature of inspiration. II. The Doctrine of God. III. The whole epic of salvation. IV. The Christian life. V. The soul and its destiny: the last things. Now in none of this is there anything particularly new. If there had been, Robinson probably would not have remained at Andover for long. Sermons were not expected to say new things but to repeat the old in fresh but acceptable ways. Robinson certainly does this.

It should be noted, however, that in these seminal sermons, he does avoid mention of double predestination or being damned for the glory of God. There is little of the more radical forms of revivalism. In the last two sermons, in particular, one has the feeling that although he remains an ardent Calvinist, he also is an American, intrigued with scientific discovery, exploration, and human progress. Although God remains ultimately sovereign, he also allows a place in his plan for human initiative and development. The fact that Robinson only preached the sermon about the soul four times—at Andover Chapel; South Parish, Andover; Southington; and New Haven—may mean that he did not feel comfortable preaching it to unknown audiences. One could imagine that some more conservative Calvinists might find the "scientific soul" not to their liking. Certainly, it is ironic that this view of the soul was eventually to produce a great religious conflict, for as humans continued to explore the hidden mysteries of nature they came more and more into conflict with theological opinions drawn from the Bible.

Robinson, of course, was involved in much more than preaching during these years. His main occupation was teaching and apparently he was very good at this chosen profession. In a letter dated by the authors September 14, 1824 but which Robinson dates in 1825, a committee of the Junior class at Andover thanked him for the quality of his instruction:

> Respected Sir:
>
> We, the undersigned, have been appointed a Committee, to express to you, in the name of the Junior Class, the gratitude, affection, and respect, which we cherish towards you as a Teacher, and as a man. And we are happy to assure you, Sir, that altho' our connection with you has been short and interrupted, it has been to us, most interesting and profitable. When we review the course, through which you have conducted us, we feel that we cannot appreciate too highly your ordered labours, nor possess too abundantly the Spirit, with which you have executed them. If we have not become thoroughly acquainted with whatever you have attempted to teach us, it is not because knowledge, or skill, or faithfulness, has been wanting in you. You have led us into those minute particulars, which are of the first importance to us, but which from their very familiarity must have been uninteresting, and tedious to yourself: and yet you have done it, with a patience and a pleasure, which nothing but the strongest desire for our improvement, and the highest sense of duty could sustain. In all your intercourse with us, you have manifested the tenderest regard to our feelings, as men, and the most sincere and ardent desire for our usefulness as Christian ministers . . . be pleased to receive this expression of our feelings—not as the obsequious language of a single individual, or even of our Committee, but believe it to be, Sir, as it really is, the sincere and unanimous voice of the Junior Class. . .[31]

The language is a little flowery, but one cannot help but believe that this was not simply a *pro forma* exercise. Students at Andover, like students later in New York, really liked Robinson as a teacher even when he, as they felicitiously say, "led them into minute particulars."

As a teacher and a scholar he was throughout a "minute particulars" person. He reveled in both grammatical and geographical exactness. His

---

[31] Robinson Papers f.7.

works are objective, factual, and free of vapid generalizations. Theology he seemed to accept as "given." What mattered was whether the letter was a *yod* or a *waw*, whether the city was five or six miles distant. Some students, I am sure, would have preferred a broad sweep to his narrow focus, but it is the latter which made him the great scholar which he was to become.

During this time, Moses Stuart, who came to admire Robinson a great deal, continued to involve him in new scholarly work. In 1825 they together produced a translation from the German of Georg Benedikt Winer's (1789-1858) *A Greek Grammar of the New Testament*. This was a significant work, for it addressed the question of the Hebraic nature of New Testament Greek. As Lechter says,

> It is Winer's imperishable service, that he put an end forever to the vague suppositions respecting the hebraistic language of the Greek New Testament, and to the unending arbitrariness of an exposition, which, through decades of use, had become a system, and claimed a scientific character. He brought this great victory about by proving the truly Greek usage in the New Testament, both in grammatical forms and in style.[32]

Just how much "translation" Robinson could have done is an interesting question since he had never studied German and only really learned it thoroughly after traveling to Germany. One would expect that he would have done Stuart's "leg work," checking references, Greek spellings, etc., while Stuart did the actual translation. In the introduction, however, the translation of the last half of the work is ascribed to Robinson. Since this is a Greek grammar, the German would, in a sense, have been fairly straightforward, for the Greek would have been readable, even to the non-German speaker. Even so, it must have taken Robinson much time consulting a German dictionary to determine what the author meant. Given the fact that it was undoubtedly Stuart's project to begin with, it was very thoughtful and generous for the mature scholar to allow Robinson's name on the title page and to give him his second publication. It is also announced in the preface that the younger scholar would also be producing soon a

---

[32] G. Lechler, "Winer, Georg Benedikt." *A Religious Encyclopedia or Dictionary of Biblical, Historical, Doctrinal, and Practical Theology,* ed. Philip Schaff (New York: Christian Literature Company, 1888), III, 2539-2540. See also Giltner, *op. cit.* 84-85.

translation of Christian Abraham Wahl's *Clavis Philologia*, an advertisement prefigured in Robinson's own prospectus of 1823. This work was published in Andover in 1825 under the title *A Greek and English Lexicon of the New Testament,* and was to become one of Robinson's most successful contributions to Biblical scholarship,[33] at least until he prepared his own Greek-English lexicon. The latter was periodically reprinted throughout his life, was thoroughly revised in 1850, and even after his death saw new editions. In any event, by the time he left for Europe for further study, he already had three publications to his credit and was hence a scholar to be noted. It should also be added that in July of 1826, just after he had left America, an unsigned article on the lexicography of the New Testament appeared in the *North American Review*. Only when he republished it in 1831 in an expanded form was it acknowledged to be by him.

Along with his teaching and scholarship, of course, Robinson had to deal with the practical affairs of life, for he was not only a scholar but a land owner whose obligations would not go away. As early as January of 1822 he sent a letter to his brother Charles who apparently went to Clinton to attend to some of his affairs. Robinson instructs him about the disposal of the possessions he had left behind in the Kirkland homestead and into whose hands he should place the care of the property which he owned. Apparently he had left behind several books which he wanted retained. On a separate piece of paper, Charles lists those volumes which he failed to find. Among them were Byron's *Childe Harold* and Wordsworth's poems, indications that Robinson was reading the contemporary romantic writers. One may guess that a traveler like Robinson would have found Byron's own travel poem of considerable interest.

At the conclusion of the letter, Robinson adds an amusing comment.

> Lady Di is in good health & spirits & attracts a good deal of attention, for this is not a country of fine horses.[34]

In this he reminds us that although he devoted his life to scholarship and teaching, he, like other people of the period, was much more closely connected with the land and animals than most of us today. Care of a horse

---

[33] Robinson tells us the book sold about 1500 copies, a considerable number considering the nature of the topic.
[34] Robinson Papers f. 1. a.

is constant and demanding. One marvels at the accomplishments of all those great writers of the time who traveled so much more slowly and with so much more physical exertion than we and yet who accomplished so much.

Worldly involvement did not disappear as time went on. On April 1st of 1826, Othniel Williams, Robinson's lawyer and agent in Clinton sent a long letter explaining many of the details of the operation of Robinson's property. There were fences to be constructed and buildings to be renovated. Wheat had to be stored because prices were low; hay also sold for very little. As for selling the property, prospects seemed dim.

> I find no chance to sell the farm as yet; several have *talked* of buying but would do nothing else. Real estate in this place is very dull, and fear is to remain so for sometime. Mr. Wait has sold all but about 16 acres of his farm for $35 per acre. The buildings are reserved. This is about the only sale for a long time in this immediate vicinity. The Kellogg Farm was sold some years ago for a trifle under $40 per acre. The value of your land depends much upon the prosperity of our college. Institutions of this kind are becoming too numerous among us to have any one arrive at a high degree of reputation. The Trustees however seem determined to have buildings in readiness to accommodate students *if they come*.[35]

Clearly, Clinton, New York was experiencing bad times and Robinson was deriving very little from his extensive property there. In fact, rents seemed barely to cover expenses. This was undoubtedly due, not only to the difficult times the college was going through—at one point the student body dwindled to nine—but because the Erie Canal had opened up the west and made vast amounts of cheap and very good land available. Although the canal eventually brought prosperity to the region and was, over all, a very positive factor in the developing of the Empire State, its initial impact had a decided down-side which Robinson himself experienced.

Of far more positive influence, financially, was the legacy left to Edward by his father. The amount came to a little more than $10,000, a considerable sum in those days. There was, beside this, some land in Twinsburg, Ohio to which his father had staked claim which eventually produced a little more revenue. All this meant that Robinson had the

---

[35] Robinson Papers f. 2. a.

wherewithal to travel to Europe and support himself without difficulty. Eventually sale of the property in Clinton would also add to his financial security, but as of 1826, it was his father who made the scholarly life possible. So, he was able to fulfill at least part one of his academic dream: study in Germany.

Chapter Five

EUROPEAN INTERLUDE

Headlines and Notices: 1826-1830

1826   Stephen Foster and Frederic Church are born.
James Fenimore Cooper publishes *The Last of the Mohicans*.

1827   Ludwig von Beethoven dies.
James Audubon publishes the first part of his *Birds of America*.

1828   Andrew Jackson elected President of the United States.
Wellington becomes Prime Minister of Great Britain.
Russia declares war on the Ottoman Empire.
Noah Webster publishes his *American Dictionary of the English Language*.
Washington Irving publishes *History of the Life and Voyages of Columbus*.

1829   William Cullen Bryant becomes editor of New York's *Evening Post*.
Goethe completes *Wilhelm Meisters Wanderjahre*.

1830   The year of revolution:
Bourbons overthrown in France; Louis Philippe assumes the throne.
Revolutions break out in Poland, Belgium, Italy.
The Book of Mormon is published.

The election of 1824 signaled a radical change in American politics, for Andrew Jackson, supported by Western states, won a plurality but not a majority of the vote. John Quincy Adams became President only because Henry Clay, an ardent critic of Jackson, extended to Adams his electoral votes. Jackson supporters cried foul, particularly when Clay was appointed Secretary of State, and made life miserable for the victor. It was clear the Eastern elite establishment was on its way out and a new era of the common man was beginning.

To the old guard, Jackson was simply unfit. He had had little experience in government and certainly did not have the manners which befitted such high office. His followers tended to be rough-hewn and, to the eastern high brows, coarse. Adams had a pedigree, the eldest son of the second President, and a wealth of experience both in and out of government. Still, his Presidency seems largely a failure; Jackson's, largely a success. Despite his ill-health and his muddy boots, Jackson had the gusto and the common touch which Adams lacked. He would be elected for a second term in 1832.

Add to Jackson the shirt sleeves evangelism of Finney which was now sweeping the East and one has a picture of an America no longer under the sway of the gentry. Old hierarchical patterns were breaking down; the people were discovering democracy. Even slavery, that most insidious of institutions, felt the mounting pressure of a growingly egalitarian society.

Nothing could have contrasted more with the American scene than the Europe to which Robinson was to go. Still exhausted by the French Revolution and the Napoleonic Wars which had only concluded eleven years before Robinson arrived, Europeans had retreated to the old securities and fantasies of kings and their divine rights. The reason of the philosophes, which had ended in such a horrible bloodbath, had given way to the medieval dreams of the Romantics. "Of the people, by the people, for the people." was replaced by "of the king, by the king, for the king." Thus Novalis could write:

> The King is the pure life-principle of the state; he is, therefore, precisely what the sun is to the planets. Above all, there generates about the life-principle here within the highest life of the state, an atmosphere of light . . . The appearance of citizens in the King's proximity becomes lustrous, and as poetic as possible, so that they utter expressions of the highest animation and there the highest animation takes place.[1]

It is true that with the re-formation of the German peoples due to the Napoleonic era, many of the old nobility lost their positions of petty power. A number of the smaller fiefdoms had disappeared, swallowed up in the fewer, but still numerous principalities which made up the German Confederation. Nevertheless, old aristocratic ritual and hierarchy were maintained in the fractured world called the Holy Roman Empire. German unification was still a long way off. The noble families continued to enjoy great privileges while the ordinary peasant lived a life reminiscent of the Middle Ages.

Robinson, in his own way, is amused by this. He is excited, for instance, to see the king of France, Charles X, proceeding to Notre Dame in Paris. The pageantry and pomp has its appeal. Still he voices his reservations:

> The King came in a carriage with two horses, preceded by 15 or 20 horse guards & followed by perhaps twice that number. The sides of the coach were all glass, & the middle one was drawn so that I had a fair & full view of him for some time. He sat on the right, rather a fine looking man, and bears few marks of 70 years. He is not so thin as I had been led to suppose from his portraits. On his left was the Duchess of A., not handsome, but highly painted, & looking 30 years, although 49. The Duke, her husband, rode backwards—a very insignificant and silly looking man, with bad teeth,—so much for royalty.[2]

---

[1] Novalis, *Pollen and Fragments: Selected Poetry and Prose of Novalis.* trans. with an introductory essay by Arthur Versluis (Grand Rapids: Phanes Press, 1989),43.
[2] Robinson, *Journal*, Tuesday, August 15, 1821.

One wonders, however, whether any American of the time, born and bred in a nation without real aristocracy, could have understood the European mind. This may be the reason why Edward has so little to say about the political scene in his letters. While America seemed headed toward a more and more egalitarian future, at least for white males, Europe appeared to proceed backward into a ritualized and traditional past that probably never was. Samuel Clemens, later in the century, puts into the mouth of another Connecticut Yankee, the usual American reaction:

> It was pitiful for a person born in a wholesome free atmosphere to listen to their humble outpourings of loyalty toward their king and Church and nobility; as if they had any more occasion to love and honor king and Church and noble than a slave has to love and honor the lash, or a dog has to love and honor the stranger that kicks him! Why, dear me, *any* kind of royalty, howsoever modified, *any* kind of aristocracy, however pruned, is rightly an insult; but if you are born and brought up under that sort of arrangement you probably never find it out for yourself, and don't believe it when somebody else tells you. [3]

European adulation of kings and nobility was not, of course, to last forever. By 1830 the pot began to boil and a rash of revolutions spread across the continent, in a way prefiguring the greater conflicts which were to occur in 1848. Europe was both more conservative and more radical than America. In 1826, the romantics dreamed of the mystical powers of the king and his God-given role as ruler of the *Volk*. This vision of splendor, which tended only to hide the genuine abuses of petty tyrants, gave way to and, in fact, engendered the radical critiques of men like Feuerbach and Marx.

It was a dialectic for which a Calvinist like Robinson could have had little appreciation. In a world of knights and ladies, he worried about the proper observance of the Sabbath and whether the theologians he met were truly orthodox. One wonders what Europeans thought of this tall, obviously bright and well educated Yankee who seemed so taciturn and distant, so down to earth and non-metaphysical.

Robinson left for Europe from New York on June 1, 1826. He had been in New York at least once before, to participate in the celebration of the

---

[3] Mark Twain (Samuel L. Clemens), *A Connecticut Yankee in King Arthur's Court* (New York: Harper and Brothers, 1889), 65.

opening of the Erie Canal. Perhaps he had also sailed from Connecticut down the Long Island Sound and then, after disembarking in New York, up the Hudson and the Mohawk to Utica. This was the first time, however, that he had actually boarded an ocean-going vessel to commence a voyage of such magnitude. Although he was certainly not the first, he was one of really only a handful of Americans who had as yet gone to Europe to study. In colonial days, many, of course, had returned to their Mother country, but very, very few had gone to France or Germany. In this respect, he was once more virtually a pioneer.

Happily Robinson knew the significance of what he was doing and therefore wrote regular letters to his sister Elizabeth describing in detail what he saw and did. These letters were later to be sewn together in a two volume journal which, when transcribed, constitutes about 400 typed pages. Robinson wrote other personal letters to his sister and others but these are excluded from the journal. Although he specifically said that he did not want the journal published, he did intend it to chronicle as completely as possible his experiences.

This journal certainly does give us a lively picture of his life in Europe, but we must be careful to understand its context. First, he was writing to his younger sister who, though quite bright and knowledgeable about many things, had not received any higher education. Robinson, therefore, says little about the technicalities of the theology he was studying or about his intellectual reactions to the many scholars he met. Also, because there was censorship at the time and great concern about student revolts and protests, he may have consciously avoided any explicit political comments. Certainly it is the case that expression of his reaction to the German political scene is almost nonexistent in the letters. For the most part, then, his descriptions are free of either theological or political reflection.

There is, however, a great deal contained in the 400 pages of letters written between 1826 and 1830. It is fascinating to see 19th century Europe from ground level, without all those political abstractions which crowd together in history books and, in so doing, discern what an intelligent Yankee so long circumscribed by the mind-set of Connecticut could and did understand.

The venture began with Robinson and his brother taking a packet boat from the shore to the sailing vessel in the harbor beyond Staten Island. On the packet boat with them were "the American Author" Mr. Cooper and his family. As we know, James Fenimore Cooper was to spend some time in Europe, writing for an American audience about various places he stayed. Cooper was already well known as perhaps America's most important writer, but his travel books fell flat and never did make money for either the author or the publisher. Since Robinson was to visit many of the same places, it is interesting to compare Cooper's literary efforts and Robinson's much briefer, but nonetheless still valuable accounts.

After bidding farewell, his brother George[4] took the packet boat back to New York while Edward settled in for the most important journey of his life thus far. The sea voyage itself was a long one, lasting until late on July 3, some 33 days in crossing to Le Havre. There were few serious storms to threaten the *Don Quixote*, a rather small sailing ship accommodating at most ten passengers, but she was becalmed on several occasions and then faced frustrating head winds which prevented what looked at first to be a rapid crossing.

There were only eight passengers on board: seven Catholics and Robinson. Even though there was, in fact, a bishop from Louisiana and a priest from Kentucky, no Sabbath day services were conducted, much to the consternation of our traveler. Occasionally he makes a remark about their dependence upon the Almighty for safe crossing, but there is little said of particular theological interest beyond his concern for the Sabbath rest. Apparently he had planned to study on board, but could not quite find the energy to do so. Instead he seems to have occupied himself with learning to read a sextant and determine latitude and longitude. He did practice his French with some of his fellow travelers to get ready for a stay in Paris. Like most Americans, he found it difficult to distinguish

> the words of the language when spoken. They speak so fast, & run the words so much together, that it can be only by practice, which will enable a foreigner to follow them readily. I am encouraged, however, by finding that every day adds something to my power in this respect.[5]

---

[4] See Robinson, *Journal*, Saturday, May 19, 1826.
[5] *Ibid.*, Friday, June 16.

His determination and his phenomenal linguistic abilities, however, soon paid off. Within a very short time after landing he was attending lectures by noted scholars and getting the gist, if not all the details, of what they had to say.

After disembarking in Le Havre and going through a rather casual customs inspection, Robinson spent the night and then headed off to the great capital of the Franks. This was the age of the stage coach in America, so he was particularly intrigued by the "diligence," a set of three coaches in tandem pulled by one team of horses. Like many other Americans, he also marveled at the huge boots worn by the postillions. On the way, he praised the beautifully verdant countryside while deploring the outmoded agricultural methods of the Europeans. Throughout his trip, this is his common observation. It was probably not just national loyalty which led him to believe American practices and equipment to be much more advanced and fruitful than those of France and Germany. Since he had had long experience with American agriculture, the chances are great that he knew what he was talking about.

Once in Paris and settled at the Hotel de Montmorency on the Rue St. Marc, a popular spot for English speaking travelers, he set about immediately to learn the French language, hiring a tutor and spending long hours on his exercises. His diligence seems to have paid off, for within a few days, really, he was listening to, and claiming to understand, lectures on a variety of subjects in French. Among the most important lecturers whom he sought out was Alexander von Humboldt (1769-1859), who was residing in Paris at the time, writing and lecturing about his many scientific discoveries made during his trip to Central and South America in 1799-1803.

Humboldt, though a rather indifferent student as a child, became the scientific genius of the age contributing enormously to the fields of botany, zoology, geology, oceanography, and archaeology. His *Voyages aux regions equinoctiales du noveau continent,* published in 30 volumes between 1807 and 1833, is a gold mine of information gleaned from his trip into the wilds of the Americas and made his reputation as a man of science. Another expedition to Siberia in 1829 also yielded much information about that vast, largely unexplored region. He spent the last years of his life writing *Kosmos*, an attempt to integrate all scientific knowledge into one synoptic whole.

One can understand Robinson's attraction for Humboldt, for he was a man after his own heart. He was an adventurer, a geographer, an acute observer of this world with all its manifold curiosities. Perhaps, he did, as Robert Ingersoll was later to insist[6], emphasize Law at the expense of God, but at this time the warfare between science and religion was not intense. At least a good Calvinist like Robinson could, with a large dose of Scottish Common Sense Philosophy, not only accept but relish the findings of scientific exploration. Humboldt whetted his appetite to combine his interest in the Bible with his yen for scientific exploration. In a sense, Robinson was to become the Humboldt of Biblical studies.

Among the other lecturers whose presentations he attended was Claude-Servais Matthais Pouillet (1791-1868), a noted young physicist who had written and was to write on a great variety of subjects. Robinson explains:

> I then went over the river to call on Dr. McKean, & also to deliver my letter to Mr. De Sacy, but found Dr. McKean just going to the lecture of M. Pouillet at the Sorbonne, & accompanied him. Mons. P. is one of the best lecturers in Paris. The room was full-having not less than 500 or 600 persons. We were obliged to go half an hour earlier in order to obtain seats. When Mr. P. appeared there was a clapping of hands & also when he ended. The subject was optics, particularly refraction, as exhibited in the construction of microscopes. He spoke rapidly, but articulated well, so that I could follow him without great difficulty. The course which he is giving properly belongs to Guy Lustac.[7]

Robinson also attended a lecture by one Mr. Arago at the observatory. Whether this was Jacques Arago, a noted traveler who wrote about his journeys around the world, or his older brother Dominique-François is an open question. Because the site was the observatory, it was the probably the latter, for he was much more directly involved with astronomy and physics than his brother. In fact, however, it did not matter much to Robinson, for the room echoed so badly that he did not hear much of the lecture anyway.

---

[6] Robert G. Ingersoll, *The Works of Robert G. Ingersoll* in 12 vols. (New York: Dresden Publishing Co., 1908), I, 93-117.
[7] Robinson, *Journal*, Saturday, July 22, 1826.

What is interesting, at any rate, is his perpetual interest in things scientific rather than philosophical or literary.

He did, of course, express his religious interests by regular attendance at Sabbath day services. In fact, he was invited to preach at some services himself and found the congregation uncommonly attentive. He also must have spent some time thinking about the religious situation in France, for on July 27 he sent a letter to the American Board of Commissioners for Foreign Missions which was subsequently published in *The Missionary Herald*. In this letter he reports about the Biblical Society of Paris, the Evangelical Missionary Society of Paris and the work of Baron de Sacy.[8] For the first time, however, he had the sense that his brand of religion, so prevalent in Connecticut, was in the minority in this great city.

> As I stood looking down upon the great city of which I had heard and read so much, the focus of fashion & pleasure & where the God of this world has erected his chosen throne, I could barely realize that this was Paris, & could not but reflect how differently the Sabbath dawn was then breaking upon the happy villages of my own native land! There "life & immortality are brought to light" on this holy day; but here, of the many hundred thousands, perhaps not one thousand worship God in Spirit and in truth.[9]

Robinson is clearly developing a love-hate relation with the great city. On the one hand, he enjoys the parks, the tree-lined streets, the wonderful French coffee, the intellectual and scientific aura. But he still cannot quite bring himself to appreciate Gothic architecture or the religion carried on within it. He knows that the God of the world rules here, but the magical singing at the opera **is captivating.**

> This evening I have been with Mr. Porter to the Italian opera to hear the singing of Madlle.*(sic)* Sonntag, a German young lady who already rivals & bids fair to surpass Mad. Catalani. The throng is so great that we were obliged to go at or before 7, in order to secure a seat, tho' the curtain does not rise until 8. I had leisure therefore to look about & admire the building. It is small but superbly decorated, & as seen by the dim light of the immense

---

[8] "France: State of Protestant Religion," *The Missionary Herald* XXII, no. 10 (Oct. 1826), 322-323.
[9] *Ibid.*, Sunday July 8 (sic), 1826.

> chandelier with shaded lamps. It was superb. But when the curtain rose, & Madl. Sonntag began to sing, I lost all perception of every thing besides. Her figure is small & delicate with a very sweet & expressive face, but the music which she uttered—it is beyond description! I had never conceived of a voice so sweet, so flexible, & of such compass. No instrument could vie with it in the softness & rapidity of its transitions—its sweetness was nearest the thrilling tones of the Aeolian harp. Some of the other singers were very well, but Made. Sonnetag—if she & I remain here long, I fear she will rob me of a good many francs, The play was meager enough, & in Italian, but as we had it with a French translation by the side, I could follow the singers very well. The music is by Rossini, the most celebrated living composer. I know not whether I have even—yes I do know that I have *never* been thus impressed with the power of the female voice.[10]

This was probably the first opera he had ever heard, for America's so-called opera houses featured everything but grand opera. In 1825 a European troop did perform Rossini in New York, but there was no opera house there until 1833. Although founded by DaPonte, Mozart's librettist, it was a financial disaster. In 1839 it burned to the ground and was not replaced for sometime. Opera was, for decades, a European art form which sometimes was displayed in America but did not grow there naturally.

This was not just because the United States was still a rough, frontier nation without time or inclination for the arts. It was also because Puritan America generally took a dim view of the stage as sinful and therefore did not encourage serious theatrical productions.

Although the movement is gradual, we can see Robinson, in his journal, moving from being a rather restricted and provincial Connecticut Yankee to become a more sophisticated world citizen. As the document progresses we hear less and less about Sabbaths and sermons and more about European arts and civilization. Rossini is an opening through which Robinson passes during his transformation.

Like most nineteenth century travelers, Edward carried with him a whole sheaf of letters of introduction which he used to meet many of the great men of Europe. If his experience is typical, well known people must have spent an enormous amount of time simply entertaining guests who

---

[10] *Ibid.,* Thursday, July 13, 1826. Madam Sonntag was later to perform in America in the 1850s to enthusiastic audiences.

somehow had obtained an introductory letter. Among those whom Robinson visited or attempted to visit was General LaFayette, the great hero of the Americans who was still to play a political role in France. Robinson had already met him at Andover during LaFayette's grand and triumphant tour of America. There he had shown him a letter which he, LaFayette, had written to Samuel Kirkland years before in order to obtain an Oneida boy as a valet. So, in a sense, the two were already acquainted. Still, the visit was a mere ceremony, like visiting a Parisian landmark just to say that you have seen it. One doubts that the two had much to communicate to each other once formalities were past.

Of more substance was his visit with Baron Silvestre de Sacy (1758-1838), one of the great orientalists of the age. Unlike Alexander Von Humboldt, De Sacy was not a traveler, having left Paris only once to do research in Geneva during his entire lifetime. Nevertheless, he filled the Chair of Arabic for 43 years at the Sorbonne and was well-known as the decipherer of Sassanid Persian inscriptions. He also wrote one of the earliest and best articles on the Rosetta Stone. Finally, he was unable to solve that mystery, though he did provide certain ideas as to how to go about the task. The great decipherment, which occurred when it was discovered that hieroglyphs were mainly phonetic symbols rather than ideograms, was eventually performed by his pupil, Jean-François Champollion in 1824.[11]

Robinson describes his visit to de Sacy in the following way:

> Returning I called on the Baron de Sacy. He is a venerable man of more than 70, small, somewhat shriveled, & of a dark sallow complexion. He does not understand English, but speaks French very distinctly so that I got along with him very well. After satisfying all my inquiries with great politeness, as I rose to come away, he gave me several pamphlets which he has recently published on Arabic literature. On my remarking that I should send them to Prof. Stuart, he immediately gave me duplicates. His appearance, room, books & all, had much more the air of those of a severe & patient student, than I have yet seen.[12]

---

[11] Maurice Pope, *The Story of Decipherment* (London: Thames and Hudson, 1975), 60-84.
[12] Robinson, *Journal,* Thursday, July 27, 1826.

It is unfortunate that Robinson does not describe his questions or de Sacy's answers, but perhaps they were really of little importance any way. What seems to have been significant to him is that he had seen and talked with another great scholar. The fact of the meeting was more important than the substance. Later de Sacy very kindly went out of his way to provide him with more books and pamphlets to send back to America as well as with letters of introduction to other scholars.

As his education in Europe progresses, we find Robinson speaking of himself more as an orientalist and student of the ancient Near East and less as a Biblical theologian. This is the age of new discovery, of exploration and decipherment. Suddenly the world is becoming smaller; old mysteries are being dispelled. Although much of Robinson's work had been and would continue to be the fruit of arduous and painstaking editing and translation, he yearned for something different, for ground-breaking exploration. It would be ten years, however, before his dreams would become reality.

Among those other people whom he met in Paris was a young man still largely unknown to the world:

> I dined at 5 o'clock with Mr. Longfellow of Portland, whom I met at Prof. Sicknor's (?) in Boston. He is young, is a poet, & has some expectation of going to Germany. Mad. Portel with whom he lives keeps a boarding house for Americans, chiefly medical students and is famous for her kind motherly attention. [13]

Apparently, Longfellow and Robinson kept in touch over the years and, though not close friends, knew and admired each other. Robinson also says that he planned to call on Mr. Cooper in Paris, but whether he ever did so he does not say.

Finally, on August 18, he left Paris for Basel, Switzerland. The month and a half spent in Paris had been a good introduction to European culture. Old prejudices, particularly about the Church of Rome, remained, but there had been an opening and softening of the Yankee spirit. The opera, the Tuilleries, the delicious French coffee, the great savants had opened his mind. Robinson may still idealize the "happy villages of America and their Sabbaths" but he has become much less averse to European culture. The playbills accumulate; the museums are attended more closely. When he goes

---

[13] *Ibid.*, Wednesday, July 26, 1826.

to the great Parisian scientific museums he can even see the advantage of Royal patronage over democracy. He comments that the American government would never support science in the way the French king does.

Although the trip to Basel through Belfort and Mulhouse was 475 miles long and occupied three full days and nights of constant traveling, our traveler says that he survived the rigors of the journey quite well. The next day he was ready to make contact with Christian Gottlieb Blumhardt (1779-1838) for whom he had a letter of introduction. Blumhardt, a south German pietist had been instrumental in the founding of a school for missionaries in Basel in 1816. Influenced by the religious awakening in England, he worked closely with other groups in Holland and England to further Christian missions in west Africa, India, and Islamic countries. It is therefore not surprising that someone from Andover, one of the centers for missionary education in America, would have had correspondence with him and would have provided for E. R. a letter of introduction. As a result of this meeting, Robinson wrote a letter to *The Missionary Herald* about the Missionary Seminary in Basel and its work in preparing candidates for the mission field.[14]

It is through Blumhardt that Robinson made his first contact with a major Biblical scholar. In fact, one may guess that he went to Basel precisely because Wilhelm De Wette taught in the university there. "University," of course, conjures up to us a vast educational establishment with numerous faculties and graduate programs. We must remember, however, that the whole city of Basel had a population of only 15,000 and that the famous University of Berlin had, at the time, approximately 1,800 students. The University of Basel, in fact, boasted a student body of about 100.

For Wilhelm De Wette, Basel constituted something of an academic exile. He had been educated at the famous University of Jena and became noted almost immediately for his doctoral dissertation which identified the Biblical book of Deuteronomy with that scroll found in the Jerusalem temple at the time of Josiah. Thus De Wette discovered one of the cornerstones of the higher criticism of the Old Testament and undermined, in so doing, the traditional ascription of the Torah to Moses. It is not surprising that he became, before long, a member of the faculty of the new and very

---

[14] "State of Missionary Exertions," *The Missionary Herald* XII, no. 11 (Nov. 1826), 361-362.

prestigious University of Berlin where such notables as Hegel, Schleiermacher, and Schopenhauer were to teach. In effect, he was to Biblical studies what Schleiermacher was to theology, the scholar on the cutting edge of the new age.

Unfortunately, there were those who opposed anything liberal or radical in Biblical studies who would have preferred De Wette to go elsewhere. And then there was the Kotzebue incident. August de Kotzebue was a writer of minor importance, a reactionary journalist who was sent by the Russian Tsar to observe and report back on the academic and literary situation in Germany. Liberal students were incensed by what they believed to be an infringement of academic and intellectual freedoms and staged protests. Finally a deranged student, Karl Sand, murdered Kotzebue in Mannheim in 1819.

The result was a reaction against liberalism in the form of the Carlstadt Decrees which provided for tighter control over the universities, strict censorship of publications, and the investigation of all secret societies. De Wette, after the incident, wrote a letter to Sands' mother seeming to commend him for his revolutionary act. Unfortunately, this letter became known to the authorities and De Wette was removed from his position. Because of his fame as a scholar he was able to find a position at Basel, but he was ever after a little out of the mainstream of German intellectual life.

De Wette was not just a "higher critic," who dealt with theories of composition, for he attempted to ground his study of the Bible in a philosophical understanding of humanity and religious feeling. He begins his famous *Biblische Dogmatik: Alten und Neuen Testaments* in the following way:

> Da die Religion der Gegenstand der Dogmatik ist so ist nothwendige Vorbereitung erforderlich, uns mit der innern Natur derselben bekannt zu machen; da sie aber unter die Erscheinungen des geistigen Menschenlebens, und zwar zunächst des innern, gehört: so wird dieses nicht besser von Statten gehen, als wenn wir zuerst eine Übersicht von der innern Organisation des menschlichen Geistes überhaupt zu erlangen suchen. So werden wir der Religion ihre eigenthümliche Stelle in unserm Innern anweisen, und uns sowohl vor den Verwechselungen und Missverständnissen, welche bisher die meisten Untersuchungen über die Religion verwirrt haben, als auch vor den leeren und

todten Begriffsklärungen, mit denen man sich gewöhnlich getragen hat bewahren. Zugleich aber müssen wir auch Gesetze und Bedingungen erforschen, unter welchen die innere Erscheinung der Religion zur äussern wird, und eine religiöse Gemeinschaft unter den menschen entsteht.[15]

De Wette sought to provide this philosophical understanding of humanity by employing the philosophy of Jacob Frederick Fries, a Neo-Kantian and a former colleague from Jena.[16] Central to his philosophy is the concept of *Ahnung* (longing) which De Wette employs to explicate the religious feelings and ideas of the ancient Hebrew people. In other words, he seeks to replace the arid rationalism of the 18th century with a more appropriately philosophical basis for hermeneutics.

Thus, De Wette goes about his task of interpreting the Bible in ways quite foreign to many American Protestants. First of all, while Americans still sought a special place for the Bible, free from critical speculation, he assumes that the Bible should be subjected to the critical analysis due any other book. Furthermore, he assumes that in order to understand the voices which speak in the Bible, one must develop a useful philosophical hermeneutic. That means for him being particularly aware of the place of symbols in the text and those feelings which they can evoke which are not, literally, in the text.

---

[15] "Since religion is the object of dogmatics, some necessary preparation is required to make us familiar with its inner nature; since it belongs among the phenomena of the human spiritual life, and, indeed, to the interior side of that life, there is no better place to begin than initially to seek to reach an overview of the internal organization of the human spirit itself. Thus we will give to religion its peculiar place in our inner selves and protect ourselves from the confusion and misunderstanding which have confounded most prior investigations of religion and from the empty and deadly explanation of terms with which it has usually been saddled. At the same time, however, we must also research the laws and conditions under which the inner phenomenon of religion seeks to express itself and under which a religious community among human beings arises." Wilhelm Martin Leberrecht de Wette, *Biblische Dogmatik Alten und Neuen Testaments Oder kritische Darstellung der religionslehre des Hebraismus, des Judenthums und Urchristenthums*, third edition (Berlin: G. Reimer, 1831), 1.
[16] Perhaps the best modern work on Fries is Rudolph Otto, *The Philosophy of Religion Based on Kant and Fries,* trans. E.B. Dicker (London: Williams and Norgate, 1931). Otto, himself, used Fries' philosophy as a basis for developing an approach to theology and comparative religion.

De Wette was one of those German scholars whom Moses Stuart read and absorbed but did not really follow. The Calvinists of New England were just not ready for higher criticism nor for any interpretation of revelation based upon the universal structure of the human self. For them clear eyes (i.e. common sense) and the Holy Spirit were enough of a hermeneutic. Stuart knew De Wette's significance; he may have even been attracted to some of his arguments. But there was no chance, given the Andover creed and the Andover mood, that Stuart could adopt De Wette's radical proposals as his own.

In many ways, it is unfortunate that Robinson visited De Wette so early in his stay, when he had not as yet mastered the German language. His description of their meeting seems, quite frankly, superficial and disappointing:

> Tuesday, August 22. At 8 this morning Prof. De Wette sent one of his pupils who speaks French to conduct me to his lecture room. The building now occupied by the university is very old & was formerly a monastery. The benches, desks or counters, & indeed the whole appearance of the room was very plain, resembling more than anything some of our old country schoolhouses. In one corner, in a little rough desk, sat De Wette, one of the best & most celebrated writers of Germany. The audience was 25. He has a mild, quiet, & rather dejected look—his manner is slow, still, & almost stammering. His mode of lecturing differs not much from ours at Andover.[17]

That's all. Robinson talks with several others in Basel: Herr Stier, a teacher of Hebrew and friend of August Tholuck, Herr Isselen, who lectured on hermeneutics, and, of course, Blumhardt, but it would have been so much more gratifying had he talked in more depth with the great scholar. At this point, however, he could grasp but the "outlines" of what Germans were talking about. Only after several months of experience does he begin to feel confident with the language.

After a few days in Basel, Robinson sets out for Germany. He had planned to proceed through Tübigen, but the diligence only ran that way once a week, so he decided to proceed almost directly north, through

---

[17] Robinson, *Journal*, Tuesday, August 22, 1826.

Freiburg and Carlstadt to Heidelberg. As usual, he expresses mixed reaction to the scene:

> The plain of the Rhine is indeed a beautiful country. Its fertility seems inexhaustible, & it is everywhere cultivated. . .It is also well watered; the Rhine meanders through the middle, while brooks and streams and rivers descend from the mountains and cross the traveller's path in every mile. But the towns & villages are mean & dirty, & agriculture is very miserable & the crops are probably not half of what the soil would produce with proper attention. The country is a paradise, but it is inhabited by anything but angels or happy spirits.[18]

After two days and nights and a modest bit of sightseeing at stops on the way, he arrived at Heidelberg, quite exhausted from the steady traveling. After a little rest, however, he presented his letters as usual to some of the well-known scholars of Heidelberg and met Professors Schwartz, Umbreit, and Schlosser, the last distinguished as an important historian. More important, Professor Schlosser introduced him to Heinrich Eberhard Paulus (1761-1851), whom he describes as "a man very distinguished for his sagacity, his learning, & his heterodoxy. He is old, but has most keen and piercing eyes, & a countenance full of expression & intelligence."[19]

Certainly Robinson, from his point of view, is correct about Paulus' heterodoxy. Known as "the Rationalist," Paulus had for several years applied the principles of the enlightenment, i.e. Reason, to the study of the Bible and in so doing had called into question many of those phenomena—miracles *et al*—which Robinson a few years earlier had made central as evidences of the Bible's truth. Paulus' *Leben Jesu* discarded all references to the supernatural, to miracles, angels, demons, and the like in favor of a thoroughly rational and naturalistic understanding.

Paulus' position, however, was already becoming passé as men like De Wette sought to go beyond the rationalistic strictures of the 18th century to a fuller understanding of the feelings and symbols which make religion what it is. In other words, Romanticism had left Paulus behind so that even though he was to live until mid-century he was regarded only as a "period piece" by many. For Robinson, however, his arguments were still to be fully

---

[18] *Ibid.*, Sunday, August 27, 1826.
[19] *Ibid.*

absorbed and transformed. At least, if he continued to believe in his licensing sermon, his attitudes were pre-rationalist rather than romantic.

For Robinson, Paulus' work had more than theological interest. In fact, Paulus regarded himself as an orientalist rather than just a Biblical scholar and had compiled and published a collection of accounts of travel in the "orient" under the title *Sammlung der werkwurdigsten Reisen in den Orient*.[20] Doubtless, Robinson would refer to this work on many occasions in the future, for he became not only the great traveler but the great expert on other travelers in the Near East.

After paying brief respects to the savants of Heidelberg, Robinson took the diligence once more, this time to Göttingen for a much longer stay. On the way he makes one little aside which may be of significance. He says that he regrets not being able to stop in Darmstadt, for he has a letter of introduction for Professor Leander Van Ess. Who provided the letter is unknown. What we do believe is that at a later date, Robinson was to negotiate for New York (that is Union) Theological Seminary the purchase of several thousand books from Van Ess. These books, acquired for $5,000, became the core of Union Theological Seminary's famous research library.[21] In any event, it seems clear that even at this date, Robinson knew of Van Ess' reputation as a collector of rare and ancient books and might, in fact, have had some thought of acquiring some items for the Andover Library. As we shall see, Moses Stuart was most anxious that Robinson procure volumes which the Andover library lacked. When Robinson returned to America, he became, among other things, Andover's librarian.

The trip from Heidelberg took Robinson to Frankfort and then, after an unexpected delay, through Hesse. Our traveler definitely was not impressed by what he saw there.

> The appearance of the towns in Hesse Cassel & of the people is the most squalid and filthy imaginable. They are far worse than anything I have before seen. The towns & villages are built of framework fitted up with mud or unburnt bricks: & men, women, children, pigs, chickens, horses, cattle, sheep, goats & a thousand

---

[20] H. E. G. Paulus, *Sammulung der werwurdigsten Reisen in den Orient* (Jena: Christ. Heine Cuno's Erden, 1792).
[21] The name of New York Theological Seminary was changed to Union Theological Seminary by the Board of Regents when it was first chartered.

other creatures(?), all dwell under the same roof. The women have the same gownless dress, but are disgustingly squalid & ragged; & the children at the doors & in the streets are half naked and filthy. There is a look of greater stolidity than I have before met. When the English employed the Hessians to fight their battles in America, they could not have found a people less likely to question the purposes for which they were sent.[22]

Finally, on Friday, the first of September, he arrived in Göttingen where he would stay several weeks. Some biographical accounts have said that he studied at the university there, but such was not the case. In fact, the university was closed for vacation and for more than a month, Robinson lived in the university town with little to do except learn German. That, indeed, was his goal. He hired a "poor student" as a tutor and set about immersing himself in the language so that by the time he arrived at his scholarly destination, the University of Halle, he would be at least passably fluent. The student arrived every morning at 7 a.m. to go over his exercises, drill him in various matters, and then take long walks with him around the countryside so that Robinson could carry on a natural conversation and learn from him the names of the various objects they would see. Slowly but surely, his German improved, though he admitted that he was not really ready to understand in depth German lectures on scholarly subjects.

One impediment to the acquisition of German were the number of American acquaintances who seem to have gravitated to Göttingen that summer. Unfortunately, Robinson has the habit of mentioning people only by their last names, so that some of his friends remain unidentified but there are some of whom we can be fairly certain.

"Mr. Cunningham," who also had decided to study in Halle and became quite a close friend, is still not identifiable, but "Mr. Kirkland" is surely William Kirkland, the grand nephew of the founder of Hamilton. He graduated from Hamilton just two years after Robinson and like him became a tutor of the college. His father was Gen. Joseph Kirkland who was for a time chairman of Hamilton's Board of Trustees. Because of William's support of "the rules," he was less than popular with the students and this led to a very unfortunate incident. One night students carried a cannon up to the door of his living quarters in Hamilton Hall and fired it. The shot tore

---

[22] Robinson, *Journal,* Tuesday, August 29, 1826.

through the room, put holes in roof, wall and floor and generally caused amazing destruction to his belongings and to the building. William survived but was permanently deafened by the blast.

In 1827 Kirkland was to marry Caroline Stansbury, a remarkable woman who wrote quite popular novels about life in the West and who also was a well-known editor. After the tragic death of William by drowning she lived in a house on the William Cullen Bryant estate on Long Island and became a very good friend of Robinson and his wife. Edgar Allen Poe was to say of her:

> Unquestionably, she is one of our best writers, has a province of her own, and in that province has few equals. Her most notable trait is a certain freshness of style, seemingly drawn, as her subjects, in general, from the west.[23]

Another American abroad whom E. R. saw in Göttingen was "Mr. Dwight" who was most certainly Sereno Dwight (1786-1850), the fifth son of Timothy Dwight, the President of Yale and friend of Robinson's father. Sereno was a man of great ability—tall, handsome, eloquent—but fell victim to a "lung fever" and to the mercury treatment which was applied to cure it. He had been minister of Park Street Church, Boston from 1817 until 1824. That year, however, he decided to travel to Europe in a vain search for a cure for his very painful malady. Robinson describes him as quite feeble: "He is very unwell, more so than I expected to have found him."[24]

Somehow he apparently recovered a little, for in 1833 Dwight was called to be president of Robinson's alma mater, an institution on the brink of financial ruin. Even though his own brother Benjamin was treasurer of Hamilton, Sereno seems not to have been aware that the situation was so grim. In any event, Dwight was able to raise a considerable sum of money for the college's support—about $50,000—but the debts remained. Eventually, he resigned his Presidency when the trustees refused to move the campus into nearby Utica to attract more financial support.

Still another American in Göttingen was a "Mr. Amory of Boston."

---

[23] Edgar Allen Poe, *The Complete Works of Edgar Allen Poe,* ed. James Harrison (New York: AMS Press, 1965), XV, 86. Poe has a section on William Kirkland too but does not speak of him in quite such glowing terms.
[24] Robinson, *Journal,* Friday, September 1, 1826.

Although there is no conclusive evidence, it is probable that this was, in fact, Frank Amory, Robinson's brother-in-law, the husband of Eliza Kirkland Robinson's sister Sally. Since Sally was somewhat older than Eliza and had already married and moved to Boston before Eliza's marriage, it is likely that Edward did not know her husband intimately, but the fact that he later compares Sally and the woman he would eventually marry reveals that he knew his sister-in-law fairly well. In 1829, John Kirkland would write to Robinson, informing him of the sudden death of his sister-in-law, an event which must have conjured up all those old memories and sadness about his own wife's passing.

In any event, it was, even then, a very small world. Robinson headed off on a European adventure only to discover that friends and relations were already there. Happily for him, most of them were in Göttingen only briefly during his stay there—he never does meet Kirkland—so that he could give nearly full attention to speaking German rather than English.

Unlike Paris, Göttingen in the summer offered few lectures or musical events. Still, Robinson used his letters of introduction to good advantage, calling almost immediately upon:

> Prof. Blumenbach, the celebrate physiologist. He is 75 years old & as great a curiosity as any in his own collection. He had on his little black cap, stoops very much, rolls his eyes, and writhes his face in innumerable contortions, & accompanies his bad English with a sort of puff or exclamatory expiration every few words. Yet his conversation was interesting, & and he received us with great kindness. As Russell says of him, no one would suspect him to be the first physiologist of Europe.[25]

Again, the next day, he took the opportunity to go with Mr. Cunningham to a lecture by "the younger Plauck."

> It was on 1 Cor. xiv. His writings indicate him to be one of the most acute & profound philologists in Germany but in his personal appearance he is the most heavy, stupid, frowsy looking German I have ever seen. He is short & thick, the top of his head perfectly flat, his face is square & somewhat bloated, eyes black & fine when open, but shut most of the time. His manner is bad, indeed

---

[25] *Ibid.*

> every thing about him makes a most unfavorable impression. Beside this, he is subject to epileptic fits, which have probably given him in part this fatuity of expression.[26]

Parenthetically, it should be noted that some of Robinson's biographers have thought him to have been subject to epilepsy too.[27] It is difficult to believe, however, that if this were the case he would have spoken of Plauck's malady as he did. There are several times when he complains of various pulmonary problems, but never of epileptic seizures.

Cunningham and Robinson also visit:

> Dr. Bialloblotzky, who is what they call here a *privatlehrer*, or private teacher; they are connected with the university & give private lessons to those who wish. He has just returned from England & is the only orthodox man here. He wishes to continue the study of English, and I shall probably change works with him, i.e. aid him in English while he assists me in German.[28]

The next day he goes to hear Bialloblotsky preach. He writes:

> There are 7 or 8 churches in Göttingen, but there is only 1 service on the Sabbath, in the morning. I went to one where Dr. Bialloblotsky preached. He seemed to have a good deal of fervor. His figure is bad & his hair & complexion are sandy. They accuse him here of being a fanatic. For aught I can see, the Sabbath is quite as lightly esteemed here as at Paris.[29]

Rather quickly now, we find Robinson waking up to the realities of Protestant Germany. The Sabbath is not taken very seriously; in this major university town only one man can be thought of as orthodox! Although he himself continues to make an occasional remark about someone's orthodoxy, we hear much less about the Sabbath or even about sermons. In spite of his own best intentions, he seems to be sliding into a different attitude toward religion and its expression.

---

[26] *Ibid.,* Saturday, September 2, 1826.
[27] Daniel G. Reid, "Edward Robinson (1794-1863)," in *Dictionary of Christianity in America*, ed. D.G. Reid (Downers' Grove, Ill.: Intervarsity Press, 1990).
[28] Robinson, *Journal,* Sept. 2, 1826.
[29] *Ibid.*

He does, at least momentarily, align himself with Bialloblotsky, going with him to visit a variety of country ministers in the villages surrounding Göttingen. The association is as much to learn German as anything else, for each visit gives him the chance to listen to the German language and try out his own spoken German.

There was but one other major contact made, but this was of some significance:

> I have had but one new acquaintance, a Prof. Eichhorn, an old man of 75, very polite & affable in his manners. He begins to fail, & is gradually giving up his lectures. During the summer he has had but one course, whereas he had often 3 or 4.[30]

Later, on October 9, he visits him again, this time to converse in German rather than French. One wishes he had recorded his conversation, for Joachim Eichhorn was the grand old man of German Biblical studies, famed for his introductions to the Old Testament. One wonders whether Robinson told him the amusing story of how Moses Stuart had outbid Edward Everett at the auction of Joseph Buckminster's library and thus obtained a copy of Eichhorn's *Einleitung ins Alte Testament*.[31] He might also have gone on to explain that Stuart's interest in German Biblical scholarship—in Eichhorn in particular—had earned him considerable suspicion on the part of his Andover colleagues.

Eichhorn, however, was not nearly as radical as those who were to follow him. He did believe that the Bible should be subjected to the same literary scrutiny that one would apply to any human book and saw that Genesis, for instance, is not a seamless robe but is composed of several strands of tradition. Nevertheless, he also believed that it was Moses who took these strands and wove them together in one narrative and thus accepted the traditional ascription to Mosaic authorship. Still, conservatives were, from their own point of view, correct in their negative assessment, for his insight into the various strands of Genesis was picked up and developed by others and this led to, among other things, the creation of the famous documentary hypothesis which so radically altered Protestant views of

---

[30] *Ibid.*, Wednesday, September 6, 1826.
[31] Jerry Wayne Brown, *The Rise of Biblical Criticism in America, 1800-1870: the New England Scholars* (Middletown, Conn.: Weleyan University Press, 1969), 36.

scripture. One really cannot subject Biblical texts to the same scrutiny as other literary works and remain true to the Andover creed.

After five weeks in Göttingen Robinson was ready to move on, so early on the morning of the 11th of October he climbed aboard an *Einspannung*, a carriage drawn by one horse, and headed toward the Prussian border. The journey took him through Nordhausen and Sangerhausen and then on to Eisleben, the birthplace of Luther. Here he visited the church of St. Andrew while the horses were feeding and stood for a moment in the pulpit once occupied by the great reformer, sensing as he did so profound religious feelings. The poignant experience, however, was brief. By 8 p.m. they had traveled fifty English miles farther and had arrived at Halle, where Robinson was to spend the next several months.

HALLE

People have been living in and around Halle since the Paleolithic era, probably because the area is both fertile and rich in minerals, particularly in rock salts and coal. In fact the name Halle means "salt works." From the 9th century onward, there was a castle there to guard the crossing of the Saale River and the salt mines. In 981 Otto, the Holy Roman Emperor, chartered Halle as a city and it remained a thriving market town throughout the Medieval period. It was, from 1281 until 1478, a member of the Hanseatic League. Throughout the Middles Ages, however, the city was at odds with its overlord, the archbishop of Magdeburg, and so, partly as a consequence, accepted the Lutheran Reformation as its own in 1522. A building still stands where Luther stayed when he visited the city.

The University of Halle was founded in 1694, in part through the influence of the noted Pietist Philipp Jakob Spener (1635-1705). The more immediate cause was the fact that the famous jurist Christian Thomasius was driven from Leipzig by irate theologians who did not like his somewhat liberal and rationalistic views. With a large number of students following, he came to Halle, about twenty miles from Leipzig, where the elector of Brandenburg was in the process of founding a university of his own. His presence gave the University immediate standing. Also important was the arrival of August Hermann Francke (1663-1727), another one of Germany's greatest Pietists. It is he who made Halle the center of Pietism until his death. He established a series of schools including a Latin school for poor boys as well as his famous orphanage.[32] Halle became the center for heart-felt, experiential religion and vigorous social action. Out of Pietism was also to come the first Protestant missionary movement.

Although the University of Halle was inspired by Pietism and hence embodied in its early days that earnest form of German religiosity, it was also the first modern university. Instruction took place in German, not Latin; more important, the university was free from ecclesiastical control and fostered independent, scientific, critical thought. The old study of canonical texts was replaced by lectures and seminars. There were even electives. Professors were given the freedom to think and research for themselves. There was no adherence to a creedal statement required. Therefore when Francke died and Pietism waned, Halle followed the tendencies of the age into rationalism. By the time Robinson arrived, the age of Pietism had long since passed, though there was still a struggle between the rationalists, now the old guard, and the somewhat more heart-felt, romantic thinkers represented by August Tholuck.

The Napoleonic era, of course, had had profound effects upon the university. In fact, Napoleon had closed it twice, in 1806 and 1813. In 1813, the city of Halle was also shelled by the French and badly damaged. On one of their many walks, Wilhelm Gesenius took Robinson to the place where he stood to watch the conflict and explained the struggle at some length. For Germans, the Napoleonic era was still a recent and traumatic memory.

The University was reestablished in 1815, but with a vital difference. The Elector of Prussia decided that Prussia could not support two universities and so in 1817 merged the universities of Halle and Wittenburg. Actually, Wittenberg was the older and in some ways the more historic of the two institutions. Founded in 1502 by Elector Frederick II of Saxony, it became most famous because Martin Luther arrived to teach there in 1508 and from there began his reformation of the Church. Philip Melancthon also taught at Wittenburg, making it the storm center for Lutheran theology. So, the moving of that university to Halle led to particularly bad feelings. As a sop to the "losers," a graduate program in theology was continued in

---

[32] Several of Francke's buildings still exist in Halle today.

Wittenberg, but it did not amount to much. Few students came and the professors, according to Robinson, tended to sleep out their last days there.

In any event, beneath the surface of the university there was still bad feeling about the merger, especially since, one year later, Prussia opened the University of Berlin, proving that the state could support two universities after all. While the University of Berlin now prospered, using some palaces for its campus, Halle still had little by way of facilities. The King granted $40,000 (Rix) for a new edifice, but nothing had been started, even after Robinson had returned to America. Robinson reports that in 1829 the University had some 1330 students of which 944 were in theology, 239 in law, 58 in medicine and 89 in philosophy. The library, which had its own building, housed 40,000 volumes.[33]

Robinson says little about the actual buildings of the university, but he was not very impressed with the city which housed it:

> The town is old & ill built & dirty, though better than many I have seen. The streets are narrow, crooked, & badly paved, & without sidewalks. It contains about 26,000 inhabitants. About the center is an open place in squares, where the market is held; in the middle of it rises a lofty tower or steeple, standing alone. On the W. is a large old church with 4 steeples; & on the E. Side the town house, a clumsy old building, & another still worse belonging to the University, in which some of the Professors read their lectures. The library occupies a separate building in another part of town. There are also salt springs & large works which I have not yet seen. I think Halle would not be an unpleasant summer residence,—for the winter season the prospect is rather gloomy.[34]

While he was in Göttingen he had received a letter from Wilhelm Gesenius, welcoming him to Halle and offering him a room in his house. Robinson expressed to his sister some concern about this, because he really was going to Halle to study with their new professor, August Tholuck, and he knew Gesenius and Tholuck hardly saw eye to eye theologically. Nevertheless, when he arrived in Halle he called upon Professor Gesenius:

---

[33] Edward Robinson, *The Biblical Repository,* Vol. I, January 1831, 30.
[34] Robinson, *Journal,* Thursday, October 19, 1826. It should be noted that the tower, now a tourist office, and the church still exist, but the old university building is gone.

> This morning about 9 I waited on Prof. Gesenius. I found him at work in his study; he received me very kindly & said he had reserved a room for me in his house. He is some 42 or 44, rather small in stature, with a pale round face, strongly marked by small pox, very lively & spirited in his manner, speaking English very little, but German pretty distinctly.[35]

In many respects, Gesenius was a man after Robinson's own heart, for Gesenius was interested in philology and the history of language and not in metaphysics, etc. Much of his best work was lexigraphical. In fact, his lexicon of the Hebrew language, which Robinson was later to translate, became the basis for most subsequent Protestant Hebrew study, in both Europe and America. Still, Gesenius had little interest in Protestant piety or in the maintenance of orthodoxy. Known as a rationalist who was critical of supernatural claims, he was the sort of German scholar of which Andover men were more than a little suspicious. One can be sure that beneath the surface, Robinson was feeling theological qualms.

Gesenius, however, was very pleasant and so Robinson made the best of what must have been a somewhat awkward situation.

> At 8 o'clock I went to Gesenius' room by apptm. & was introduced to his lady, & supped with them. I say supped because according to custom, the table exhibited chicken, etc. & wine, but no tea. He is very lively in conversation, animated, and uses much gesture,—Has small, grey, piercing eyes, and a round good humored face. He is quite a gentleman in his manner, as I have always heard. He is 40 years old. His lady is 29, not beautiful, has projecting teeth, etc. but seems amiable & perhaps well informed. He was very affable, spoke much & well, & the time passed very agreeably till the present hour.[36]

Truth to tell, Gesenius was not as much of an enemy as many of the other German scholars. Cheyne writes:

> That he was disrespectful to orthodox explanations of Old Testament problems, and that he indulged in mirth-provoking sallies in his lectures on Church history, is certain. On the other hand, he never sought to inculcate rationalistic doctrines, or to foist

---

[35] *Ibid.*, October 11, 1826.
[36] *Ibid.*

them upon the Biblical writers, and it appears that what the best students of that generation craved was, not a mere revived orthodoxy, but a theology which could adjust itself to a more rational and critical view of the Bible.[37]

One problem that Robinson faced immediately was that the room reserved for him was cramped and not really very attractive. He puts the best face on the matter, saying that his quarters are probably as good as the average room in Halle, but clearly he is dissatisfied and rather discouraged. He diagnoses himself as having a "sinking of spirits." One may guess that he sensed a return of that despondency he felt when his first wife died.

Letters from home cheer him somewhat, but also produce a bout with home-sickness. As tears flow "unbidden" down his face, the usually cool and objective Edward Robinson reveals very briefly his inner emotions—but only for a moment. Before long he is back to himself, particularly after he is able to negotiate for himself a much more attractive room in the same house. For the first few days, Gesenius attends to the needs and interests of his new roomers—"Mr." Cunningham is there too. He takes them on walks showing them a few of the sights, etc. But then, after a little, Edward comments that he does not see Gesenius much any more. In Germany there is a barrier between teacher and student. Each goes his own way. Outside the classroom communication is very limited.

This was not so true of August Tholuck, the new Halle professor with whom Robinson apparently came to study, for he was known for his friendly relations with students and for his long, philosophical walks with them. When first Robinson dined with him, however, Professor Tholuck "seemed unwell, & was somewhat cold in his manner, & did not speak English half as well as before."[38] Before long, however, his impression changed. "This evening I have been to drink tea with Tholuck, & have found him pleasant & amiable. His acquaintance promises to be more valuable to me in a moral & religious point of view, than any other I am likely to find in Halle."[39] Whether this turned out to be the case, however, is unclear. It would appear

---

[37] T.K. Cheyne, *Founders of Old Testament Criticism*, (London: Methuen & Co., 1893), 56-57.
[38] *Ibid.*, Sunday, October 15, 1826.
[39] *Ibid.*, Thursday, October 19, 1826.

that, after all, Gesenius became the preferred professor because of his adept philological skills.

Soon Robinson's routine as a student became fixed and his communications with Elizabeth less frequent simply because he had little new to tell her. He describes his daily life in the following way:

> A sketch of a day will give you the history of a week, for all the weekdays are alike. I rise at 5, or till 5 1/2, & go to work in my *Schlafrock,* a stuffed quilted morning gown, which are here common, & about 7 I take coffee & a small roll, which are brot *(sic)* to my room, & thus lose no time in breakfast. About 8 I make my toilette etc, & go out for 10 or 15 minutes, but study again until 11, when I go to Gesenius' lecture on Ch.(urch) Hist.(ory) Soon after 12 my dinner is brot *(sic)* to my room & is quite tolerable, for 75 cents the week. Till two I lounge, or do odd things, etc. At 2, Gesenius lectures on the Psalms or Isaiah, at 3 I have an hour's instruction in Arabic, at 4 another in German, at 5 go to walk, at 6 have my tea in my room, and then work till 10. My mornings I devote at present chiefly to Arabic, the evenings to reading and writing German. All the lectures and instruction use, of course, many exercises in German, so that I may be said to hear & read & write & speak German at least 4 or 8 hours every day. I am now able to go into society & understand the ordinary conversation, & to express myself in ordinary topics without difficulty—tho' my cache of words is yet small.[40]

As we shall see a little later on, not everything in Robinson's life was devoted to academic labors, but, for the most part, it was all business. It is noteworthy that he seems to have spent so much of his time learning Arabic, a language certainly not essential for Biblical studies. There are signs, however, that already he was thinking of himself, not simply as a traditional Biblical scholar, but as an orientalist with Biblical interests.

In the same letter, Robinson also provides a vivid description of the *Sitz im leben* of German higher education:

> The room in which several of the professors lecture (at different hours of the day) is in a building on the E. side of the Square & is very ordinary & even mean. At Göttingen the professors furnish their own rooms & so in many instances here. One description

---

[40] *Ibid.,* November 11, 1826.

> suffices for all. The little desk, or box, of the professor is as near the door as possible, & in front are seats for writing, the plainest possible. All are very punctual—the students arrive first, & amuse themselves with whistling till the professor comes. On his appearance, he is saluted with a general hiss; this, in fact, is not meant for him, but is a token for silence. The moment he steps into his box, he begins to speak, & every pen is in motion & the utmost attention & silence prevail. When he wishes to add illustrations, he breaks off in a more rapid strain, & the pens rest. If in his dictation, he goes faster than they can write, they hiss, & he repeats. He generally begins about 5 m. after the hour & stops 2 or 3 before the clock strikes, whisks rapidly out, & the students follow, to repair to a similar scene . . . Some students attend 6 or 7 lectures every day, their notes they retain & afterwards study, as it would seem in general without much original investigation.[41]

During the first classes, Robinson took his notes in English, but thereafter his German was good enough so he simply wrote down what his instructors said in that language. In his usual methodical way, he brought the notes back to America and had them bound in leather. All that his teachers—Gesenius, Tholuck, Neander, etc.—had to say, therefore, is still available if one can decipher Robinson's quite legible but now arcane German script.[42] Volumes one and two are, at least, in English and though his English hand is difficult, it is, with effort, decipherable.

Gesenius' lectures on the Psalms began on October 25 with a brief *Einleitung* to Hebrew poetry. It was brief because, as he explains, he had covered much of the subject in his introduction to the Old Testament and in another course specifically devoted to Hebrew poetry. He opens by characterizing Hebrew poetry as mainly lyrical and subjective, that is, as dealing with inner feelings rather than outward events as an epic might do. He describes the poetry's diction and rhythm and the types of parallelism used. He examines the types of Psalms, and deals with the ascriptions and authorship of the Psalms.

---

[41] *Ibid.*

[42] Cheyne laments the fact that we have no direct record of Gesenius' fascinating lectures, but, in fact, thanks to Robinson such a record does exist and has been buried in the Hamilton College archives since shortly after Robinson's death when the College bought a large portion of his library. See Cheyne, *op.cit.*, 59.

Here is where Robinson might have disagreed, for he seems, earlier, to have accepted all the traditional Biblical ascriptions, but Gesenius argues in such a reasonable way, pointing to the references to the exile as precluding Davidic authorship, that it is difficult to believe that an intelligent auditor could have taken much issue. Robinson might have also been very disturbed by his remark that the "Messianic psalms are nearly exploded," for prophecy of Christ in the Old Testament was still held up by Andover Calvinists as a proof of Scripture's validity. Gesenius' remarks, however, are so matter-of-fact and so based upon German scholarly consensus, that it would have, again, been difficult to argue with him.

Throughout the lectures, Gesenius refers to other scholars, particularly De Wette, in order to bolster his position or to show other conflicting opinions. He also makes good references to poetry in traditional and modern German poetry, from *die Meistersingers* to Klopstock. In other words, the lectures of Gesenius seem very modern, the sort of presentation which would still *mutatis mutandi* be heard in the halls of academia.

After his introduction, Gesenius turns to a considerable number—about two-thirds—of the Psalms in particular. His method is simply to review each psalm under consideration by focusing on specific word and grammatical form study. The main thrust of these lectures, therefore, is not theoretical or theological. There is no attempt to give a big picture theologically or to read the lecturer's own rationalism into the Psalms. Again, the presentation seems very modern, objective, and, though a little dull, eminently useful. One cannot but believe that Robinson would have found the lectures informative and basically much to his liking.

The other course of lectures which Robinson attended his first semester in Halle was also given by Gesenius, this time on Church History from its onset until Gregory the VII. This was probably a fairly new subject for Robinson, for Andover scarcely offered anything in the area. It was also extraordinarily important, for it introduced him to the German historical method. After providing a definition of the church and comparing it with civil communities, the lecturer turns to the question of history and how an historian should proceed. Important for a writer of history, he says, are critical skills and discrimination. One must distinguish what actually happened from what is said to have happened. The historian must develop the power to comprehend, judge, and rightly estimate events and transactions to be narrated. The historian must be able to distinguish between the important and the insignificant and order the facts in a judicious and comprehensible manner.

Above all, the historian must aim at impartiality and have truth as his or her great object. This is particularly important because many past histories of the church have been characterized by accounts of the fabulous, springing often from either superstition or pious fraud, and partiality, motivated by a desire to prove other interpretations of Christianity false. Indeed, from Eusebius onward histories of the church have been marked by a polemical style used to argue for a particular point of view.

The historian, according to Gesenius, must forswear all such attempts to skew the evidence in favor of the orthodox and simply search for the truth wherever it is to be found. Because of the nature of history the investigator can never arrive at complete certainty but must always remain content with the probable. Nevertheless, by careful investigation many false and misleading ideas can be discarded; through skillful historical critique, "much may still be won."

This skillful technique begins by examining the genuineness and reliability of the sources under consideration, looking to distinguish pious fraud and later interpolations from the best sources. One must also, he says, look at the character of the author and ask about his intentions and penchants.

In order to understand the history of the church within its context, one must also have a wide background in the history of political life, literature and science, philosophy, and religion in general in order to assess the history of the church in any given period. Command of the requisite languages, particularly ecclesiastical Greek and Latin, ecclesiastical chronology, geography and statistics, paleography, and canon law is also important.

Above all, one must not follow fads. A few years ago, Gesenius says, nothing from the Middle Ages was worth anything. People wrote about the period only to show its superstition and stupidity. Today, all that is changed as people now see everything medieval as wonderful and necessary. Even Neander, the great modern church historian, Gesenius sees as "looking too much on the bright side." For Gesenius, however, the medieval period is neither good nor bad, but an era to be examined with open eyes. Doubtless there was superstition and stupidity, but there were also good things too.

Gesenius never quite tells us how anyone can gain the transcendent perspective he endorses. The post-modern reader suspects that he too carries a great deal of intellectual baggage which he imposes upon the objects of his investigation. For instance, children of the Enlightenment found (and find) it difficult to accept miracles and marvels as anything more than pious fraud. Therefore, they cast such reports aside as spurious even though in every age there are reliable sources which report that miracles have occurred. In a sense, an impartial account of church history can only be offered by someone who stands outside the church and therefore takes another partial stance.

Nevertheless, this methodology of clear-eyed honesty was a great solvent for dissolving all that legendary material which had constituted so much of church history. It was of particular importance for Robinson, for when he went to Palestine he employed it to question all those old legends which clung to traditional Biblical sites. While guide books even today tend to repeat old, legendary stories for the tourist, Robinson's *magnum opus* does not. That is because he went to Palestine with the historical weapons provided by Gesenius, weapons which would cut through centuries of legend and myth to ask, "Where really was the city? Why did they build the tunnel? What was the route across the desert?"

Gesenius, however, actually went further than Robinson, applying modern historiographical methods to the Bible itself. The Christian church, of course, finds its beginning with Jesus, so Gesenius, to begin his historical analysis of the church, starts with a brief examination of what we can know about Jesus. He examines sources, evaluates reliability, and points out some of the numerous contradictions among the gospels themselves. Because this is a course surveying several centuries, he cannot conduct a full scale quest for the historical Jesus, but it is clear he has located many of the problems which still perplex modern interpreters of the Bible.

Robinson, as a son of Andover, never quite accepted the modern historical methodology as one which could be applied to Scripture itself. For him the truth of the Bible is a rock which should not be moved. Therefore, although he saw, for instance, that the notion of two million Israelites marching through the Sinai desert raises many logistical problems—where did all those people find enough water to drink?—he looked for a plausible solution rather than considering whether the numbers offered by the Bible might be wrong. By and large, Robinson tried to avoid the problem entirely, by concentrating upon what can be known about the land and its people. For "ordinary history," he accepted Gesenius' historiography as his own, but when it came to the Biblical stories themselves, he tended to leave the historical (and therefore skeptical) analysis to others.

During the semester, Robinson seems to have kept very close to a serious academic schedule, but happily there were vacations to escape the regular academic routine. Christmas not only introduced him to German practices of gift-giving and special celebration—as yet America had not become inebriated with the festival; it also gave him the chance to do a little traveling, this time to nearby Leipzig. As usual, he took along plenty of letters of introduction. He was frustrated in his attempts to visit people, however, for Weber's new, but posthumous, opera, *Oberon*, was being premiered and all the literati were in attendance. He was, however, able to make contact with various booksellers and discover how they operated.

Robinson, in fact, had been commissioned by Andover to purchase books for the divinity school library, and he needed to find out how to purchase them at the lowest prices. To this end he called on Herr Jauchnitz, one of the biggest book sellers in Leipzig.

> Herr Jauchnitz insisted on my staying & spending the evening with him & telling him about America. This I was glad to do, as he gave me much insight into the book trade and other objects on which I made inquiry, & spoke of the battle etc. of 1814.[43]

Although they had just met, Jauchnitz invited him to an "elegant" evening meal. Robinson stayed and chatted with him until 9 p.m. What must impress us today is the very relaxed and personal mode of life which existed then. Leipzig was, in fact, a small town of only about 33,000[44] and everything moved at a leisurely pace. An American visitor was something of a rarity and so doors opened, meals were spread out, and contacts were made which doubtless lasted a lifetime.

The next day, Robinson spent time with other booksellers making inquiries into the book trade and learning about discounts, etc. All of this became very important for him, because he was eventually appointed the

---

[43] Robinson, *Journal*, January 1, 1827.
[44] *Ibid.*

librarian first at Andover and then at Union Theological Seminary. Each institution benefited greatly from his knowledge of books, for more than anyone else, he established for each impressive research library holdings. In a way, therefore, the time he spent with book sellers, particularly at the Leipzig book fair, was as significant as his study of German historiography.

Although his major coup was the eventual purchase of the Van Ess collection for New York (Union) Theological Seminary, he also was continually prompted by letters from Moses Stuart to search for this book or that for the Andover collection. It is interesting that Stuart looked not only for commentaries and the like but works by various orientalists like De Sacy and Champillion and above all, "Maps, Maps, Maps." Stuart not only desired maps for himself, but encouraged Robinson's apparently expressed desire to study and write about Palestinian geography. Clearly his eventual trip to Palestine was not a sudden venture, but had been long in the planning.

During the spring vacation in late April and early May Robinson took a much more adventuresome "trip," a 180 mile walking tour through Cothen, Dessau, Wittenberg, Torgau, Oschaz, Wurzen, and Leipzig! Although public conveyances were certainly available, he chose to walk, in part because he loved to observe the land and its people more closely. On the way he would stop under a tree and jot down observations which became his journal entries. He writes of German education, particularly on the secondary level, agriculture, gardens, and the friendly people he meets. As usual he went armed with letters of introduction so that wherever he stopped he found people with whom to converse.

Among the people he visited on the way was Christian Abraham Wahl whose book he had only recently translated into English.

> I waited on Wahl, who is Pastor and Superintendent here, and was received with great joy and 3 kisses, & immediately presented to his wife & daughter, & also his children were called in to see the American, & be presented to him. Wahl is a small man of 54, quite active & sprightly, but I should think not very social & would in the end be rather a dull companion. His learning lies most in what he knows of the N(ew).T(estament).—beyond that he does not seem to have very much & can never be a man of great personal influence . . . W. has the vanity of all German writers, speaks of his

> writings, plans, etc., & was the first to tell me that the Univ. of Leipzig had just sent him the diploma of Doct. of Theology.[45]

Clearly, Robinson was not impressed. He himself seldom spoke about his own work or accomplishments to others and was always annoyed when others did so.

Far more inspiring to him was his visit to Wittenberg.

> April 30. This has been a very busy & a very interesting & pleasant day of my life. I find myself here in the cradle of the Reformation, for as Jerusalem was the seat of Christianity, so was Wittenberg the seat of Protestant Christianity. From this little spot have gone forth thoughts & principles, which have literally operated to the ends of the earth, the effect of which will never cease as long as time endures, which have determined the character of nations & of millions of individuals, both for time & eternity. I have today stood over the ashes of Luther and Melancthon, have walked where they walked, have sat where they were wont to sit, & have lived surrounded by the same objects, on which their eyes were used to rest. Here is Luther's room, just as he left it, & yet Luther lived & acted, & the Reformation was effected — 1517— a century before our fathers first set foot on the soil of New England. Of them scarce a trace remains, while here all is as fresh as it was then.[46]

Although most people like to visit historic places as Robinson does, to feel intimately the reality of history, I think our traveler was especially attuned to being in the real place and seeing the real artifacts. This is why he found his trip to Palestine so exciting and why, in a sense, he worked so hard to rediscover ancient sites. There were many German Biblical scholars with the means and the opportunity to have done so, but it was Robinson and not they who actually traveled to the Holy Land to see what the *eretz* of the Bible really looked and felt like. While Eichhorn and De Wette point forward to Von Rad and Eichrodt, Robinson is the predecessor of the Americans, W. F. Albright, G. Ernest Wright, and Nelson Glueck. Thus while the history of higher Biblical criticism has always been largely a German story, the history of Biblical exploration has been dominated by the Americans and English and now, of course, by the Israelis themselves.

---

[45] Robinson, *Journal*, May 3, 1837.
[46] *Ibid.,* April 30, 1827.

The last stop on Robinson's long walk was Leipzig, full of tourists and merchants because of the Easter fair. He finally had to take a room on the fourth floor, in order to find lodgings.

> Monday morning, May 7. Leipzig is indeed very full, in every street almost is a row of booths, & every open place is covered with them, & also every room, cellar & even gangway is occupied by the foreign dealers. Signs of every shape & in every language thrust themselves upon one's notice & the great variety of costumes, which one meets, announce that here is a concourse of many nations. One sign is in German, Hebrew, Mod. Greek, & Russian, others combine English, French, Italian, etc. etc. etc. One meets in the streets citizens of all these countries & also Turks, Greeks, Russians, Hungarians, Tyrolese, etc. But the most striking class are the Polish Jews, with their beards, high fur caps, & Black gowns. I should think there must be several 1000s of them now here. The bustle and display of wares of every sort & kind is much like some of the most busy parts of Paris, but there it is permanent, here it continues only 3 weeks . . . The booksellers exchange opens tomorrow. With them it is rather a coming together to settle accounts than to purchase books.[47]

Robinson spent the next few days visiting the fair and seeing some of the sights in Leipzig connected with the great battle there against Napoleon. After satisfying himself that he had seen enough, he walked the twenty miles back to Halle.

Classes resumed on May 17th and he elected to take Gesenius' course on Job as well as continuing Arabic and "Chaldee." The course, he says, is known to be Gesenius' best and will probably be attended by more than 400 students. As he settles into his studies, letters momentarily become fewer and less informative. Of Arabic verbs there is little to write.

I should not imply that all was solitary work during the university year. In the first place there were many contacts with his fellow students, a circle which soon came to include Charles Hodge of Princeton. It is interesting that Robinson and Hodge, who was to become famous as the Princetonian defender of Old School Presbyterianism and the perpetuation of slavery in the South, became close friends. Indeed, Robinson comments that it was good to be with someone with whom he agreed theologically!

---

[47] *Ibid.,* May 7, 1827.

Whether they continued to agree as the Civil War approached in America is a question we will have to ask later on.

In any event, we learn from Hodge that Robinson was the reason why he was studying in Halle rather than elsewhere. In December 21, 1826 he wrote to his wife Sarah,

> I wrote to Mr. Robinson (Rev. Dr. Edward Robinson) of Andover, now in Germany, to ascertain which university offered the greatest advantages, and the expenses of living, &c. I have received a very full and satisfactory answer from him. He tells me that for the purposes for which I have come hither there is no comparison between any other university at present and Halle. That the advice of every person he consulted directed him to that place, and the result of his own observation, after spending six weeks in Göttingen, and then proceeding to Halle, confirmed him in the correctness of all he had previously heard. There is one very important consideration, that one of its leading theological professors (Tholuck) is a very pious man, the like of which is not to be found elsewhere.[48]

Robinson and Hodge spent much time together and describe in their respective journals many events they shared in common. Clearly Hodge liked Robinson, but also had mixed feelings:

> Mr. Robinson I think you saw in Princeton. He is reserved and cold, but at the same time he appears to be really kind, and puts himself to more trouble to be of service than many whose feelings lead them to a more warm and cordial expression of good will.[49]

There were, for both Robinson and Hodge, many formal and informal social occasions with members of faculty, particularly August Tholuck, who often invited students for tea and conversation. Somewhat more burdensome for Robinson were the "state" occasions particularly with Chancellor Niemeyer. Robinson admits that he has always been bashful and often finds it difficult to make small talk at these parties. As his German improves he discovers himself somewhat more at ease, but even then would have stayed

---

[48] A. A. Hodge, *The Life of Charles Hodge, D.D. LL.D.*, (New York: Charles Scribners' Sons, 1880), 110.
[49] *Ibid.*, 115.

in his quarters and studied had not the social pressure to attend been so great. Clearly, what Hodge saw as coldness was to Robinson an almost morbid shyness with people he did not know well.

It is interesting that even though the temperance movement was beginning in America and, in fact, found one of its centers in Andover, Robinson seems to have had no trouble with the fact that wine was served and drunk very freely. In fact, he often comments on the fine quality of the wine proffered. He is, however, somewhat surprised to see theologians dancing and does not seem to have taken a very active role, until one night Schiller's daughter persuades him to join in. Over all, he finds the German theologians livelier and a little louder than their rather straight-laced American counterparts, but he makes no value judgment about this and, truth to tell, seems to enjoy the partying despite his initial protestations.

Perhaps the most important of the parties he attended was for the Jubilee celebration for Chancellor Niemuller.

> He led us along into other rooms, where we found ourselves in the midst of Bishops & Superintendents & Professors & officers of State, comprising some of the most distinguished men of Germany. . . Professor Schleiermacher of Berlin was there, who stands very high as a man of talent, tho' his personal appearance is bad; he is diminutive, with a head large in proportion, & his shoulders seem somewhat distorted, apparently from rickets.[50]

This was the first of several occasions when Robinson has the opportunity to meet perhaps the most famous theologian of Germany. The next night at a dinner party for the Jubilee, he sees him again:

> There were very many men, whom at home I had been accustomed to regard with respect and reverence, & to see them now, to mingle with them in their social hours, to witness & enjoy the simplicity and openness of their characters & manners, was deeply interesting. The learned men here have much less reserve & stiffness than with us. In conversing with them, they immediately put you at ease, & you speak to them as with familiar friends. I was amused in looking at Schleiermacher; he is the most distinguished preacher in Germany & is also very eminent as a philosopher & as a man of uncommon talents—he sat between two young ladies &

---

[50] Robinson, *Journal*, April 18, 1827.

seemed to be the happiest man in the room. His appearance reminds me much of old Bell, the crazy clergyman at the West,— but he is not so tall.[51]

Robinson would meet Schleiermacher again in Berlin, but never studied with him. This is perhaps, unfortunate, for Germany's greatest theologian was in the process of preparing a famous and quite sophisticated set of lectures on the life of Jesus. In them he discusses many of the pitfalls and problems which surround the quest for the historical Jesus and lays the groundwork, not only for Strauss but for Schweitzer. As far as we know, however, Robinson's contact with him was purely social and never reached anything like a theological level.

Of far greater importance for Robinson was a chance meeting with a man named Jacob whom he met as he rode into Halle for the first time. They shared a carriage together and, because it was late, Jacob invited him to stay with him the first night, before E. R. went to see Gesenius. We do not know Herr Jacob's first name, but we do know that two days later he invited Robinson to go with him to a "relative's" for tea. The relative turned out to be Ludwig Heinrich von Jacob, a professor at the University of Halle who, in the decade before his death, served as the Dean of the Faculty of Philosophy.

Ludwig Jacob was a political economist, a follower of Adam Smith, who was well-known on both sides of the Atlantic for his books and articles. During the Napoleonic era, he had fled Halle with his family to live, first in Kharkov in the Ukraine where he taught, and then in St. Petersburg where he served as a member of the legislative Commission and was given accordingly the title of "Staatsrath." It is by this title that Robinson usually refers to him.

It was not the Staatsrath, however, who intrigued Robinson but his daughter, Therese. He writes in his journal, "I was more interested in the conversation of his daughter, who exhibited more intellect and vivacity than I have lately met with."[52] He was certainly correct about her intellect. Therese, in fact, was a linguistic prodigy, already the master of several languages, including a number of Slavic tongues. This, in part, was due to

---

[51] *Ibid.,* April 20, 1827.
[52] *Ibid.,* October 14, 1826.

the fact that she had stayed with her father in Russia and had had the opportunity to learn Russian there. But she also was capable of mastering languages quite on her own in a very short space of time.

The fact that her father was a well-known intellectual who could introduce her to the most important German-speaking intellectuals such as Goethe and Grillparzer was also very important. In any event, Therese, intrigued by remarks that Jacob Grimm made about Serbo-Croatian poetry, decided to try her hand at translation. She consulted with Goethe, offering some sample translations and, after receiving from him and from Jacob Grimm great encouragement, eventually published a highly acclaimed two-volume edition of *Volkslieder der Serben* in 1825 and 1826. Even before this time she had published several critical essays, some poetry, and translations of two of Sir Walter Scott's novels!

To say the very least, Therese von Jacob, known to the world through her acronym, TALVJ (Therese Albertina Louisa von Jacob), was already one of the leading women of letters of Germany. She was a regular correspondent with both Goethe and Jacob Grimm and had a reputation for excellence which still exists to this day. Beside her work, the publications of Edward Robinson at the time seem slight by comparison.

It is very much to E. R.'s credit that he was honored and not rebuffed by her abilities and never seems to have tried, in patriarchal fashion, to stifle her initiatives. From the very beginning there was great appreciation for her intellectual life and her amazing capacities. One might almost accuse our Connecticut Puritan divine of more than a touch of feminism. Therese was to write to Jacob Grimm.

> Fortunately, Robinson belongs to those few men who know how to respect a lively interest in art and knowledge, even among women, and he would rather encourage me than hold me back in my literary work.[53]

In any event, it is clear from the beginning that Robinson was immediately drawn to the diminutive Therese and she too was attracted to this tall stranger from America. Almost immediately they arranged for regular meetings, for her to drill him in German and for him to help her with

---

[53] Reinhold Steig, "Briefwechsel zwischen Jacob Grimm und Therese von Jacob," *Preussische Jahrbücher* 76 (April-June 1894), 357.

English pronunciation. Few language drill sessions have been more delightful.

> I have one female acquaintance—Fräulein Jacob—who gives me much gratification. She reads English fluently, but needs to perfect her pronunciation of the language. She therefore proposed that I should read English with her and in return she would help me with German. This I was glad to do and it has thus far been very pleasant.[54]

This relationship continued on a regular basis until Therese went with the family to Berlin for two weeks. It was then that Edward realized how much their relationship meant to him and how much he missed her. When summer time came, the Jacobs moved to a summer home about two miles from town. There Robinson would go by foot to spend his evenings with Therese, often walking in the garden or along the Saale River. For both of them nature was exceedingly important. Although a good Calvinist he writes, "the world of nature . . . affords a temper in which my devotion kindles with a far holier flame than in the precincts of a gloomy German church."[55] Therese, the poetess and protégé of Goethe, doubtless agreed fully.

Only hints of the development of their relationship are to be found in the journal itself. This may be because he wrote other more personal letters home to his sister which were not designed to be included in the journal but which contained the more personal developments in his life. In any event, during the three month period, from January to the end of March in 1828, Robinson studied in Berlin and wrote home regularly about his experiences there. During that whole time he says nothing about Therese. Then on the very day he returns to Halle, he writes this:

> . . . and at 12 had the pleasure of meeting my *Braut*. How pleasant it is to be once more in a species of home and receive the kind offices of affection. I have a room in the house and spend every evening with the family.[56]

---

[54] Robinson, *Journal,* November 4, 1826.
[55] *Ibid.,* June 5, 1827.
[56] *Ibid.,* March 28, 1828.

As the word *Braut* reveals, sometime during this period Edward and Therese had become engaged! By August of 1828 they were married and ready for a most extensive honeymoon.

But that is to get ahead of ourselves. Before the wedding became a reality, Robinson had much traveling to do without her. Near the end of May, he received a letter from one Mr. Chauncy of New Haven who planned to travel through the northern part of Germany and invited him to go along. Robinson decided to do so, though it is doubtful that Gesenius had finished his course on Job by June 15. Either the summer course was short, or Robinson was able to copy the notes from the lectures from someone else. In either event, we somehow have his transcription of the full course.

Chauncy did not come directly to Halle, so Robinson went to meet him, partly on foot, partly by Schnellpost, in Magdeberg. Chauncy had arrived from Göttingen the day before, carrying the sad news of Eichhorn's death. Together they traveled to Brunswick, Hanover, Bremen, and Hamburg, enjoying the scenery and historical monuments. Then they proceeded to Denmark and Copenhagen, through southern Sweden, and then back to Germany and Stettin, Berlin, etc. It was in Stettin that Edward received the very sad news that Therese's father had died suddenly. Interestingly, Robinson did not end his journey to return to the side of his bereaved sweetheart. Instead, he continued his sight-seeing.

Characteristically, Robinson deplores the poverty of some areas and exults in the beauty of others. He loves the art museums, the castle of some ruling monarch, famous sites of history. As usual he goes armed with letters of introduction which he uses regularly. He never fails to comment about libraries and their organization. Perhaps most interesting to the modern reader are the population figures which he gives:

> Magdeburg 38,000
> Brunswick 37,000
> Hannover 27,500
> Bremen 38,000
> Hamburg 110,000
> etc.

Berlin and Vienna, of course, were somewhat larger, but on the whole the famous European cities were still small towns or at most, to us, medium sized cities. Intellectuals knew each other; the practice of stopping by to visit a famous writer, quite common. In thinking about the intellectual and social history of the West scale and intimacy must not be forgotten. Mass society had not yet really come into existence. Many of the kingdoms of Germany contained fewer than 100,000 people.

Robinson spent a few days in Berlin enjoying what he believed one of the finest cities of Europe. Then, he returned to Halle about August 5 after having attended church.

> This morning I went to hear Schleiermacher, who is considered the most eloquent preacher of Germany. He is not strictly an orthodox man, but has a philosophical system of his own;—wide however of Rationalism. His manner is pleasant, but not striking, & his sermon was more like one of our New England preachments than I have usually heard in Germany. The church was crowded.[57]

When he arrived home, of course, he found Therese and her mother in mourning. "They are, as I expected to find them, much bowed down, & I am glad if my attentions have at all served to occupy their minds, & thus soothe for a moment their sorrows."[58]

Robinson did not linger long, however, to share their grief. On August 16th he and Chauncy set out again, this time for an extended tour of southern Germany, Prague, the Tyrol, and Vienna. On this trip, much more than in the north, he exults in the beautiful scenery which he describes in some detail and in the art and architecture of the southern cities. He loves the Danube but not its boats, Viennese culture, but not the politics. Because of censorship, he waits until he has left Austria to say,

> The great object of government seems at present to crush the will of the people; they seem to feel the truth of the maxim that "knowledge is power," & to be determined to prevent the people from acquiring this power. All education is in the hands of the priests; the press is entirely under their censure; no newspaper in the empire (& there are very few) dares to print a single article

---

[57] *Ibid.,* August 5, 1827.
[58] *Ibid.,* August 15, 1827.

> relative to politics or political intelligence which has not already appeared in the Observer, the government paper in Vienna . . . The government seems determined that the good people shall only learn at home, just what the govt chooses; they may not even go abroad to learn. . .[59]

This is a significant passage, because Robinson very seldom speaks in his letters of things political, at least not in a negative way. Perhaps the reason why he does not do so in Halle, is precisely the same reason why he does not do so in Austria. He is not at all interested in the trouble that the censors might cause if he really speaks his mind. It is only when he returns to America that he writes in *The Biblical Repository* about the petty tyrants of Germany and their many short-comings.

In any event, Robinson does not return to Halle for any length of time until about October 18th, long after, one would suspect, the semester had started. Somehow we do have complete notes from Tholuk on Dogmatic Theology, Ethics, and an "Encyclopedia" of Theology, but one is not sure quite how they were taken. In fact, there are very few letters between that time and January when Robinson left Halle to study in Berlin.

> Monday Morn., Dec. 17. My poor journal seems indeed to pine away for want of sustenance. Nearly 3 weeks are gone since the preceding lines were written, & in that time almost nothing has taken place worth writing down. The chief thing is that I have decided to go to Berlin at New Year's. The reasons are grounded principally in my letters from Andover from which it would seem that there is a possibility that I may be called to return next autumn; in this case I shall have to leave Germany early in the spring,—& as I wish to spend some time at any rate in Berlin, it is better to make sure of it now.[60]

Probably Robinson is referring to the possibility that Professor Murdoch would be relieved of his duties and that Stuart wanted E. R. appointed in his stead. In fact, the Murdoch case dragged on for some time and no appointment was made. When Murdoch was finally forced out, the trustees decided to follow their own rules and appoint someone who had served in the pastorate. Therefore, the arrangement at Andover never

---

[59] *Ibid.,* October 17, 1827.
[60] *Ibid.,* December 17, 1827.

materialized and Robinson had no need to return so soon to America. Nevertheless, the choice was a good one, for the period in Berlin was probably more productive than another semester in Halle would have been despite his separation from Therese.

He arrived in Berlin on New Year's Day 1828 along with his friends, Cunningham and Hodge. Although to us relatively small, Berlin is described by Robinson as a large city of 220,000 souls.[61] Compared with Halle (25,000), Boston (40,000) or Hartford (5,000), Berlin was a large metropolis, particularly because it was the center for the Prussian court and hence had many elegant and impressive buildings. While Halle was a small, middle-class city, Berlin was the home of the rich and famous. Robinson saw the advantages and disadvantages in his new surroundings. Although he participated somewhat in polite society, he was generally repelled by the superciliousness of many of the elite and "talk for talk's sake."

The University of Berlin had only been founded in 1810, but it had become, very quickly, Germany's finest university, particularly for medicine, law, and philosophy. The King wanted the best and was quite willing to pay for the most outstanding intellects to teach in his establishment. Even today the reputation of that university in the early 19th century is well known. What most people do not realize, however, is how small the institution really was. It had about 100 professors and a little more than 1800 students.[62] Hence it was of the size of what today would be described as a small college. Here Hegel and Schopenhauer, Schleiermacher and von Humboldt held forth. Here the very best courses in medicine and jurisprudence were offered. Robinson had come to the heartland of German intellectuality.

Almost immediately he began attending two sets of lectures being given by Alexander von Humboldt on physical geography and astronomy. One set was for the general public and was attended by the elite, including the King and many of the nobility. The second course of lectures was on the same subject but was meant to be far more academic. Edward, it appears, attended both. Of Humboldt he writes:

---

[61] *The Biblical Repository*, I, 19.
[62] *Ibid.*, I, 21-22.

> He lectures twice a week at 12 in the university, & once, in the S . . . academie, a large music salon; the last is thronged by ladies, officers, etc. Humboldt is about 54 years old, & very social in his manner,— tho' having lost some of front teeth, his enunciation is not very distinct, & his voice makes him seem older than his looks. He is unmarried & keeps no house, but resides here at the request of the king, with whom he often dines. . .[63]

E. R. also made contact with Wilhelm von Humboldt, Alexander's older brother, who was a famous philologist and professor at the University of Berlin. He took no courses with him, however. Eventually, he paid him a formal visit and received from Wilhelm certain privileges to use material usually reserved for the professoriate.

All of his regular university courses were taken with Joachim Neander, perhaps the most important church historian of the age. Like many church historians of the time, however, he also taught what we would conceive as Biblical subjects. Robinson heard him lecture on Ephesians and the Johannine letters, on the epistles to the Corinthians, and on the Apostolic Age. He writes,

> The man who interests me most, however, as a literary man & as a Christian, is Neander. He is by birth a Jew, & has all the characteristical national features in his outer man; but his inner man is truly Christian kindness, meekness, & love. He lives only in his study, the walls of which are filled with books; at a little table in one corner you find him sitting with a book open before him & half a dozen more lying by his side on the floor. he receives you kindly, but awkwardly, having no external polish of manner,—but takes his seat, & you see his little sharp black Jewish eyes ever in motion & twinkling out at you from under his black brows. [64]

Academically, then, Robinson's time in Berlin was spent attending lectures by Humboldt and Neander and continuing his study of Syriac and Arabic. Of course, he also devoted some time to improving his German and reading Hebrew.

Perhaps more important for his career were the various contacts he made during his three months stay there. Among the people he met while

---

[63] Robinson, *Journal,* January 29, 1828.
[64] *Ibid.*

attending conversations with Neander was Professor Ernest Wilhelm Hengstenberg (1802-1869) some of whose work he was later to translate and publish. Robinson, however, was not initially impressed.

> Tholuck always spoke of him in the highest terms, but I have been disappointed in him;—he is only 23 or 24 years old, & has undoubtedly talent & learning, but his manner is so dogmatical, positive, & flippant, that he makes on me no good impression. He seems also to be narrow minded & inclined to intolerance. Neander on the contrary has liberal and expanded views and is remarkably candid.[65]

It is somewhat amusing for us to think of a Puritan Connecticut Yankee such as Robinson as regarding someone else as dogmatical and narrow minded, but, in fact, Americans—Calvinists, free thinkers, or social reformers—have seldom been as doctrinaire as their European counterparts. Robinson, in particular, had already experienced the broadening effect of another culture and had become much less ready to condemn opinions which differed from his own. Yes, he was a Biblicist and a Sabbatarian, but there was also a strong republican and pragmatic streak in him which rebelled against both political and ecclesiastical authoritarianism. It is also interesting that when he refers to his own "field" he describes it as "oriental literature in reference to that of the Bible,"[66] a designation which in itself seems to point to a broader, more liberal view.

During his stay in Berlin, he also became much better acquainted with Frederick Schleiermacher:

> Schleiermacher I have called on several times, & have spent an evening at his house. His lady is a very genteel & intellectual woman, & there are 5 daughters, young ladies of pleasing manners, but without anything particularly striking. Schleiermacher himself I have formerly described, as being very small & deformed, but he is considered as one of the profoundest thinkers in Germany. His manner in society is very simple, almost childlike, but he has no flow of conversation,—his sentences are short & his manner interrupted. I have not yet attended any of his lectures, but shall go once or twice. As a preacher he is considered one of their most

---

[65] *Ibid.*
[66] *Ibid.*

> distinguished,—he is far from rationalism, without being strictly orthodox, & it may be doubted whether he is a man of genuine piety, tho' Tholuck seems to consider him so.[67]

There is a tendency today to confine intellectual history to both discipline and geographical area. Thus Biblical Studies is separated from Theology and American Church History from that of the Continent. What Robinson reminds us of is that none of these boundaries were nor are very firm. American religious thought is not an insular phenomenon, for not only Robinson but Charles Hodge and a host of other Americans studied with and were influenced by German intellectuals and in turn had their own effects upon the European scene. In many cases, contact and influence continued for decades.

Whether Schleiermacher had any specific intellectual influence on Robinson is a moot question. Given the latter's lack of metaphysical interest, probably not. But their very meeting in itself could not help but inform Robinson about the "personhood" of German theology. Once one knows a person, the significance of theology changes. Robinson was more ready to listen.

Of course, it was also inevitable that eventually Robinson would hear Hegel, the greatest jewel in the faculty of Berlin's crown. And it was equally inevitable, given Robinson's attitudes, that the results would not be positive:

> I went today to hear Hegel, who makes a great noise at present in Germany as a philosopher who broaches an unintelligible system. He is rising of 60 years of age, & his mode of lecturing is the most unpleasant possible—he is nearsighted & bends his head down quite to the table, while he speaks low & thick & muttering like an old woman, repeating his words twice over, & often three times.[68]

That is all he says, but in those few words summarizes the attitude of more than one Anglo-American thinker: Hegel is but an unintelligible mutterer. Later, in his article on German education he explains this German penchant for metaphysical abstractions by noting how utterly impractical German civilization and education are. Business and industry, he observes, take second place to all the petty tyrants and their courts. If only, he says in

---

[67] *Ibid.*
[68] *Ibid.*, February 29, 1828.

effect, the Germans could devote themselves to more practical pursuits they would not spend so much time "wool gathering." It is doubtful that Robinson would have believed what Germany became in the twentieth century.

There were, of course, other more practical academics at Berlin. One of them was the famous geographer, Carl Ritter, who Robinson heard not long before leaving Berlin.

> I went the other day to hear Ritter, the celebrated Geographer,—he is a very interesting man, more than 60, tall & slender with a noble head & forehead, but old fashioned & plain in his dress & appearance, & reminding much of some venerable old New England clergyman. I regret not having found him out sooner, as I should have been much pleased to have made his personal acquaintance. He is also a pious man, tho' he is so much devoted to his scientific pursuits, that some of them complain here than he is not open and pious enough.[69]

Robinson would later carry on a lively correspondence with Ritter, for the latter was much interested in the geography of the east Mediterranean littoral, but it is clear that E. R. was never his student. Whether he was as much of an influence on Robinson as William Albright suggests is very difficult to determine.[70] It is interesting to note, parenthetically, that geography was an area of study in which the evangelicals seemed to thrive. Jedidiah Morse, an important spokesman for New England's conservative theology and co-founder of Andover Theological School, also produced one of America's first geographies. One might add that his son, Samuel, a noted artist, transformed geographical distance by inventing the telegraph and, of course, the Morse Code.

All of this is to say that, particularly with Calvinistic Protestants, the line between science and religion was very blurred. Calvinism, as it developed, was practical, this-worldly, and inventive. In fact, under the influence of Nathaniel Taylor, New School Presbyterians and Congregationalists began to think of the moral law as at least as knowable as natural law. Thus alcohol was seen as an obvious evil which had to be

---

[69] *Ibid.,* March 21, 1828. The Hamilton Library contains his notes of this lecture.

[70] Duma Malone, ed., *Dictionary of American Biography,* (New York: Charles Scribners' Sons, 1935), XVI, 40.

suppressed. When the Bible seemed to disagree, Moses Stuart and others promoted the idea of two wines, one fermented the other not, to accommodate Biblical approval of wine drinking.[71]

In a way, it was not until Darwin drove a wedge into the Biblical doctrine of creation that evangelicals and scientists parted company. Even then, many Calvinists and post-Calvinists were able, through a modest sleight-of-hand to keep the two enterprises together. Robinson, as a pre-Darwinian thinker, has no difficulty at all holding together his theological and his practical, this-worldly interests. Indeed, he is the perfect blending of theological and scientific concerns. His works on Palestine were applauded as much by the scientific community as by the world of theology.

During his brief stay in Berlin, Robinson was also busy with many other things. He heard Mozart's *Don Giovanni* and Handel's *Alexander's Feast*. He visited the studio of Rauch, "the celebrated sculptor," and a new diorama, representing a mode of entertainment fast becoming the rage. He was invited to a literary circle at the home of Frau von Bardeleben and there met Frederick Schiller's daughter. On another occasion, at the home of General von Helwig, he met her again. She complained of the cold, so it was proposed that they dance.

> Miss S. was very polite, & asked all the gentlemen to dance with her in their turn,—& me among the rest!! In Germany this is a thing of course, every body, even grave professors of Theology, dance in their families & with their own children, so that my only wonder has been that I was never asked before. It was however a singular concurrence that for the first time in Europe, & I believe in my life, I should be invited to dance by the daughter of Schiller. Last eveng, the company was more numerous,—at first it was rather wearisome, but at last I contrived to edge my chair in by Miss Schiller & another Fraulein, & the rest of the evening passed off pleasantly.[72]

Despite the many contacts and the pleasant evenings, Robinson was not especially pleased with his stay in Berlin and yearned to go back to Halle.

---

[71] Leo P. Hirrel, *Children of Wrath: New School Calvinism and Antebellum Reform* (Lexington, Ky.: University Press of Kentucky, 1998), 117-133.
[72] Robinson, *Journal*, February 18, 1828.

> I have now been near 3 months in Berlin; I cannot say I leave it with much regret. The life here is much broken up! And then to make intercourse with society pleasant, one must (or at least I must) either be able to look forward to a long acquaintance in which the heart may take interest, or it must be but calls of a stranger. I have in Berlin had neither the one nor the other feeling, & therefore have enjoyed myself less than I should otherwise have done. I have sought less acquaintance & valued it less.[73]

Truth to tell, Edward missed Therese and the warmth of the Jacob family. Although he never tells us exactly when or how, sometime during the Berlin period, the two were engaged, for when he returns, as has been said, he calls her his *Braut* and even takes a room in her house. He returns to Halle, but now his mind is definitely on other things.

In fact, the University was on vacation by the time he arrived at the end of March. For a few days he was by himself, for Therese left for a stay in Dresden, but very soon he followed her there to enjoy the sights surrounding that city and then to set off with her on a quite extended tour of Bohemia and southern Germany. Letters date from Töplitz, Carlsbad, Baireuth, Erlangen, Nürenberg, Stuttgard, Heidelberg, Mainz, Bonn, Cologne, Göttingen, and Claustral on the Harz. On the way they stopped to see Professor Winer, whose New Testament Greek grammar E. R. had translated with Moses Stuart. He was not very impressed:

> I sent a billet to Prof. Winer, requesting to know when I might call upon him; he came immediately to me & sat for an hour, & at evening took me to walk in the garden & on the hill. He seems rising of 40 years old, with reddish hair & bad teeth, & altogether a very common physiognomy. He talks much & well, & is intelligent; but has not the air of a man of genius or influence ... I cannot bring myself to believe Winer a *great* man,—his countenance is too common, too inexpressive, & has rather an expression of meanness about it.[74]

Clearly, Robinson, throughout his life, depended very heavily upon the looks of persons to determine their true worth. Hence, whenever he meets

---

[73] *Ibid.,* March 18, 1828.
[74] *Ibid.,* July 5, 6, 1828.

someone he assesses not so much their intellectual position as what they look like.

On this trip he also visited, in Cassel, the distinguished grammarian, Grimm, a close acquaintance of Therese, but unfortunately he left the meeting and conversation undescribed. This is particularly unfortunate, for Therese was to have considerable correspondence with the Grimms who very much valued her work.

THERESE

Edward and Therese arrived back in Halle on August third, just in time for their wedding on the seventh.

> Therese with her mother & sister arrived on Wednesday last; her brother & his wife from Stettin are expected today. Our marriage is fixed for Thursday the 7th, & on the 10th, we are to set off for Switzerland. Mr. Yates will be the only one of my countrymen present, so I shall not be entirely alone. Beside him there will be none but relatives present, some 8 or 10 persons.[75]

Robinson's Journal contains no further description of the ceremony or the festivities that surrounded it. This is doubtless because he sent a much fuller account in a letter specifically not to be included in the "official" journal. "Mr. Yates" was undoubtedly the Rev. Dr. Andrew Yates who became Professor of Moral Philosophy at Union College in Schenectady[76] though E. R. does not even mention his first name. In any event, Robinson's days as a student are now over and he enters suddenly into a new and long-lasting phase of his life. It is clear that though he learned intellectually from Stuart and Gesenius and Neander, it was Therese who may have been the greatest intellectual influence upon his life. About the marriage Hodge wrote to his wife:

---

[75] *Ibid.,* August 4, 1828.
[76] George Prentiss Lewis, *The Union Theological Seminary in the City of New York: Historical and Biographical Sketches of its First Fifty Years* (New York: Anson D. F. Randolph and Co., 1889), 152.

> You will be surprised to hear that the sober Mr. Robinson has fallen in love. I received a note, a day or two age, written by him (as his modesty prevented a personal communication) with the official information that Fraülein Von Jacob has consented to accompany him to America as his wife, I have spoken to you, I believe of this lady and her family before in my letters. **Robinson has done well.** The lady is agreeable and very accomplished, speaking several languages, and acquainted with the literature of most European nations.[77]

Their honeymoon, which began on August 10, was no brief weekend at Niagara Falls. In fact, it lasted, really, until they departed for the United States in June of 1829. They did not return to Halle for 41 weeks!

The first destination was Switzerland, but on the way, they had to stop to see Therese's friend, and supporter, Johann Wolfgang von Goethe. He was not at home in Jena, so they traveled on to his summer home.

> In the afternoon we rode to Dornberg, & spent 1 1/2 hours with Goethe alone. He received us with exceeding kindness, ordered coffee, & led us round to all the windows & pointed out the fine points of view. He is now 79 years old, rather above middle stature, of a full figure, & dressed like a man of taste, so that his appearance is not different from that of a man of 65. He has great dignity of manner, & a certain something which keeps one always at a distance & forbids familiarity; this I had always heard of him. He is still at work on the new edition of his works, & studies regularly every morning, & till 2 o'clock P.M. The rest of the day he gives up to society, of which he of course has much; all strangers visit him of course. The day after we were there, he was visited by Sir Michael Clare and Lady from Jamaica.[78]

A few days later, in Heidelberg, they were also to meet and hear the famous German poet, Johann Ludwig Tieck (1773-1853).

> It so happened that Tiek *(sic)* of Dresden, one of the most distinguished living poets of Germany, was here, & was to read Hamlet before the company at the house of Schwartz. He is celebrated for his readings, & holds them 2 or 3 times a week at Dresden in his own house where Therese has several times been

---

[77] A. A. Hodge, *op. cit.,* 177.
[78] Robinson, *Journal,* August 20, 1828.

> present. His reading now left nothing to desire, & I was glad to have thus the opportunity of enjoying what is reckoned in Germany one of the highest intellectual treats. Tiek himself is now 55 years old, much broken down with rheumatism, & has an eye & expression of face which reminded me much of Mr. Stone.[79]

Soon, however, they were to leave Germany and spend a month touring Switzerland. Although it is fascinating that they traveled at about the same time to many of the same places which James Fenimore Cooper describes in his travel books, there is actually little here of particular interest to the modern reader. They saw the Matterhorn and Jungfrau, visited Switzerland's major cities, and marveled at the wild and the picturesque landscape. Apparently the Swiss had not yet achieved their fame as the hoteliers, however, for Robinson complains frequently of poor inns, mediocre food, and high prices. Roads were frequently bad, little more than horse trails, and travel was slow. Still, they seemed to enjoy themselves immensely before heading off to the next stage of their extended travels: Paris and France.

The sojourn in Paris is the least documented part of Robinson's sojourn in Europe. His first letter from "the capital of world" is dated October 14, 1828 but concerns largely the miserable trip they had had from Strasbourg to their destination. No further letter is included in the Journal until January 30, 1829, this time to complain about the cold of Paris that winter and of the very poor heating of the buildings. Therese was from all accounts very cold and unhappy.

Apparently Robinson did study while in Paris, but whether he actually took courses is left unexplained. Charles Hodge is said to have studied earlier with de Sacy and perhaps Robinson did too. We do know that he also devoted time to buying books for the Andover Library. Aside from that, there is little news. He did visit General LaFayette once again and saw the Royal Family dine at the Tuilleries. And there were operas and plays to be attended. In fact, however, it is clear that marriage greatly reduced his enthusiasm for the journal and that his offerings are now much less detailed and comprehensive. It could also be that since he had already described Paris once, he was this time less interested in the subject. In any event, they stayed in the city until February 14, when they left to begin a whirlwind tour of Italy.

---

[79] *Ibid.*

There was some question, however, whether they should go at all. Although Robinson never makes the problem explicit, it becomes evident that Therese was pregnant. At this point he only writes:

> As the health of Therese is now much better, and the weather has again become mild, we have decided to make our proposed tour to Italy, if Providence shall permit . . . We had for a time given up all idea of this journey; but both family physician in Halle, & Dr. Niles, an American Physician here, say that there is no hazard in making it, & advise to do it. We shall probably find many Americans along upon the road & at Rome, where we also expect to see Prof. Tholuck.[80]

The initial leg of the journey, however, must have been very hard on Therese, for a two day stopover in Lyons proved to be impossible because of the scheduling of the *dilgence.* Therefore, they arrived in Turin after 8 days and 7 nights of travel! Robinson had eased the pain a little, by paying extra money for more room:

> As I could not, of course, but feel solicitous respecting the effects of a journey of 300 miles day and night on Therese, I took the whole coupée, i.e. paying for three seats; at night, she laid herself upon the seat, & I curled down upon the bottom, so that we even slept tolerably.[81]

From Lyons onward, however, there were four more passengers inside, three men and a woman, so one wonders just how they slept at all. Therese seems, at any rate, to have been a woman of amazing energy and determination and for some time was set upon seeing and doing everything her husband did. Once in Italy, the sight-seeing became virtually nonstop.

It was not until they arrived in Naples that the rigors of the trip caught up with her.

> Therese was this morning unwell, but still determined to go to the Studio. This is a large royal establishment, like an academy of arts. . . .We spent two or 3 hours there in the room of statuary; but by this time Therese was so much more unwell that we were forced to

---

[80] *Ibid.,* January 30, 1829.
[81] *Ibid.,* February 27, 1829.

return to our lodgings. There she went immediately to bed, in excruciating pain; & then we could only wait for the return of Dr. Bingham. We knew not where he was, & in a city of 350,000 inhabitants, it was in vain to send in search of him, & we knew no other person. After a while too she was in less pain; toward evening, however, it returned again, & as he did not come, I determined to ascertain if there was not a German physician to be found. I had a letter from Tholuck to Dr. Bellermann, the chaplain of the embassy, & went to his house; he and his wife were both out, & not expected home till 11 o'clock. I then went directly to the Prussian ambassador 1 1/2 miles distant; he was also out, but I followed him and found him: he gave me the name and address of a German physician, & I went in search of him. It was now 9 o'clock, & there was no remedy but to wait till Bingham came; and this was 11 1/2 o'clock. He gave ─────.which relieved the pain, & the next day began a course of treatment which in a few days restored her. But that afternoon of anxiety & uncertainty & deferred hope I shall never forget.[82]

Robinson's anxiety must have been doubled by the fact that he had already lost one wife in childbirth and now, miles and miles from familiar surroundings, his new wife, pregnant with their first child, seemed to be having extraordinary problems. For several days, Therese remained in their lodgings with female companionship while Edward went off on ventures by himself to Vesuvius and the Heraculeum. Eventually, her strength was restored enough to travel again, but after this time she was more cautious, often staying in the hotel while Edward made the more strenuous climbs and hikes.

The Robinsons began their Italian journey in Turin and proceeded to Genoa, Pisa, Florence, and Rome. From there they went to Naples and Pompey and then back to Rome. They returned home via Florence, Bologna, Venice, Milan, and Lake Como, crossing the Eastern Alps through Liechtenstein. In general, the journal contains an account of the usual tourist sites—churches, museums, natural beauties—with only an occasional memorable moment. On the way they continued to bump into old friends—Gesenius and Tholuck, Cunningham and Yates—and often shared evenings together. One notable meeting took place in Genoa.

---

[82] *Ibid.,* March 30, 1829.

> In going thro' the rooms of this palace, I noticed a gentleman, whom I took for an Englishman, whose face I thought I had somewhere seen; ere long he came up to me, asked if my name was not Robinson and introduced himself as Mr. Cooper. He was residing at Florence,—has left his family there & is passing on his way to Paris for 2 or 3 months. He expects to spend the next winter at Rome, & the summer following in Germany. I spent an evening with him very pleasantly; he left yesterday on his way to Turin.[83]

The Robinsons were also in Italy during a very important moment, for a new Pope was being chosen while they were there. They decided, however, not to remain in Rome during the days of waiting for that puff of smoke from the Sistine Chapel, but traveled on to Naples instead. While they were there Cardinal Castiglioni was elected and crowned Pope Pius VIII. They did, however, return for Holy Week in Rome and went for the blessing of the Palms at the Sistine Chapel where they saw the new Pope in his sedan chair. Edward describes him as "a fine, noble looking old man, of a mild, intelligent countenance."[84]

Over all Robinson exhibits only modest interest in, but little antagonism toward, the Catholic Church and its religious practices. Many Connecticut Puritans would have been quick to find fault and condemn, but he does not. Sometimes he offers critical opinions, but seldom from an ideological vantage point. The Church of Rome is no whore of Babylon; it is a church with both positive and negative features. In this Robinson was much closer to Charles Hodge and the Old School Presbyterians than to the New School Calvinists who were, on the whole, rabidly anti-Catholic. For the New School, Catholics could hardly be considered even Christian. They regarded the corruption and idolatry of Catholicism as so obvious that anyone with the least amount of rationality could see it.[85] For some, the Coming of Christ would only occur after the demise of Catholicism.

Throughout the Italian tour, the Robinsons seem much more interested in art and architecture than in religion *per se*. It is Raphael,[86] whom he first came to love in Dresden, and Michelangelo, and the other Italian masters

---

[83] *Ibid.,* March 1, 1829.
[84] *Ibid.,* April 12, 1829.
[85] Hirrel, *op. cit.,* 93-116.
[86] It is interesting that Raphael was the favorite of many American Calvinists. See Diane Apostolos-Cappadona, *The Spirit and the Vision* (Atlanta: Scholars Press, 1995), 45ff.

who attract his attention. Other Calvinists might have been put off by pictures of the Virgin, but he is not. When he dislikes a painting of the Virgin, it is for aesthetic, not theological reasons.

All of this is to say that, whether he quite realized it or not, all of his travel and study had greatly liberalized and broadened him. Although he still speaks in terms of orthodoxy, changes in his thinking have taken place. When, for instance, he reports that two of every seven births in Paris were illegitimate in 1826, he ascribes this problem not to sin but to the effects of a big city upon people. Many of his fellow clergymen from New England surely would not have put it this way.[87]

The trip to Italy was simply the frosting on this liberalizing cake. He had now explored the remains of pre-Christian antiquity, savored beauties of the Italian Renaissance, and seen the Church of Roman dressed up in splendor. One cannot but imagine that when he finally returned to Andover, not only the town but the issues discussed in it, appeared to him much smaller and less consequential than they had seemed before he left. Surely his readjustment to the Andoverian evangelical landscape must have been enormously difficult.

His trip back to America, however, was not yet. Therese and Edward arrived back in Halle on May 24 after forty-one weeks of traveling. Edward, in fact, had not written his journal since March, so much of their trip was described long after the fact, presumably from notes he kept. There they stayed, awaiting the birth of their first child. Mary Augusta was born on June 25, 1829, only one month after their return. Although apparently all three suffered from various illnesses during the summer—Elizabeth mentions that in her letters to them—they all eventually recovered. Mary survived the perils of infancy, which took so many children at that time, and eventually traveled with them to the United States. In the meantime, her father engaged in more study at the University and began the translation of Buttmann's Greek grammar which he published after returning to America and which, through several editions, became a standard textbook in American colleges and universities.

Sea travel was long and dangerous, not the sort of experience a new mother with her new-born child could easily endure and so the Robinsons waited in Halle until the next year before venturing to sail to America. In the

---

[87] Hirrel, *op. cit.*, 155-169.

meantime, E. R. came to know Eugene Roediger who had come to teach at Halle and who became one of his close friends and coworkers. From remarks made by Moses Stuart in his letters to E. R., it appears Robinson had begun to think about a new project: a book on sacred geography which Stuart very much encouraged.

Four of Moses Stuart's letters, which he wrote to Edward during 1829, have been preserved for us. Essentially, all four concentrate upon the same thing: the books which Stuart wants Robinson to buy and Edward's prospects for work at Andover. Stuart's initial hope was that E. R. would be appointed to Murdoch's chair, but he was also aware that there were serious problems about that, for according to the constitution of Andover, all faculty should have had experience as pastors of a congregation before appointment. He writes:

> I regret now, most sincerely, that you were not back here some 18 months ago, & settled snugly down as the bishop of a little diocese; in which case your election would have been clear & certain . . . all concede that no man on whom they can fix has any claim of acquisitions, that compare with yours. The point of hesitation is that one above mentioned, connected with a kind of *hell-dunkle* feeling, that more fervency and engagedness in active, experiential piety is exceedingly desirable.[88]

Lest this should create too much anxiety for Edward he adds:

> But if your election should fail here, there is not the least hasard *(sic)* as to your finding literary state and employment, worthy of your acquisitions in some measure, in our rising, opening, rapidly advancing literary republic. The progress has been very great since you left us. You will be immediately snatched up, if we are foolish enough to pass by you; & you need have no apprehensions, whether you & your new and beloved companion are to find an adequate & honorable support.[89]

Clearly Stuart thinks that to pass up Robinson would be foolish indeed and is very exercised to find a way to keep him on the faculty. So apparently were others at Andover. In May Stuart writes again:

---

[88] Robinson Papers f.5 Letter from Moses Stuart: February 9, 1829.
[89] *Ibid.*

> There is one common feeling running through the whole band of Visitors, Trustees, & Professors, now & it is a great desideratum to have you connected with this Seminary. They would be exceedingly averse to having your talent and influence devoted to another place. Mr. Farrar proposes a professorship (new), with a *sui generis* provision wh. shall leave you some one half of your time for *authorship*, which is so much needed in this country. He wishes to have you Librarian—to instruct in Hebrew and Sept. Greek etc., so as to make up part, say half or more of the Salary; & then let you *publish* so as to make up the remainder; the Trustees securing the filling of it up, in case there should be a failure & you having the excess as your own, in case your income should overgo.—How wd. this do?—Of all things I shd. like this. I wd. jump at it, in a moment, now. I shd. much prefer it to an ordinary Professorship, with full duties and obligations. But I can not, of course, decide for you. It is too much a matter of *Gefühl* & taste to make a universal proposition or decision about it. You will not fail to look at it, & let me know how it looks soon as it shall be in your power.[90]

Apparently, Robinson agreed to this proposal, for this is precisely the arrangement he accepted when he returned to Andover in 1831. He became the librarian of the collection which he, himself, had helped shape through his purchases. He taught the ancient languages and he became editor of a new and important journal for Biblical studies. For sometime, however, the arrangement was not finalized, for the stumbling block of pastoral experience had to be overcome. Eventually, after much debate he was appointed a Professor Extraordinary—a position which may have circumvented the constitutional problem. There must have been some question, however, as to how permanent such an appointment was. Could Robinson ever expect, in that role, to have the security of appointment enjoyed by the other members of the faculty?

As for the literary aspect of the position, Stuart had some fairly definite plans about it as well. In August he wrote to Robinson:

> Mr. Prof. Hodge has dropped his *Biblical Repertory*, & taken up a kind of Rel. Magazine in its room. M. Stuart and C. E. Stowe have issued a prospectus for a *Biblical Inquirer*, to be devoted to the

---

[90] *Ibid.*, Letter from Moses Stuart: May 5, 1829.

> interpretation and literature of the Bible. *A propos*, this is done by me, only by way of anticipating your return. I hope that you will take up & stand under this affair.[91]

So upon his return, Robinson also had the responsibility for an already announced and advertised journal to attend to. As we shall see, in this task he acquitted himself exceedingly well. Doubtless, even before returning home he solicited from German scholars articles to be included in issues of this new and international publication. For reasons, unexplained, however, the journal came to be called, not the *Biblical Inquirer*, but *The Biblical Repository*.

The Robinsons seem to have been in no great hurry to leave for Andover. Perhaps it was because of Therese's mother's ill health, perhaps because of Mary's infancy. Certainly they did not relish a winter's crossing. In any event, they did not embark from Bremen until the beginning of May. According to Rheinhold Steig, they arrived in New York on July 2, 1830 after a very tedious and difficult journey.[92] A new chapter in Robinson's life had begun.

---

[91] *Ibid.*, Letter from Moses Stuart: August 21, 1829.
[92] Rheinhold Steig, "Briefwecksel zwischen Jacob Grimm und Therese von Jacob" *Preussische Jahrbücher,* Vol. 76 (Berlin: Verlag von Hermann Walther, 1894), 361.

Chapter Six

ANDOVER AND BOSTON

Headlines and Notices: 1830-1837

1830   Revolutions sweep France, Belgium, Poland and many German States.
The Bourbon line is overthrown and Louis Philippe is crowned king.
Congress passes the Indian Removal Act.
Berlioz' *Symphonie Fantastique* is performed for the first time. This is the era of the great romantic musicians: Berlioz, Chopin, Mendelssohn, Robert and Clara Schumann, Liszt.
Emily Dickinson is born.

1831   Alexis de Tocqueville tours the United States.
William Miller begins to preach in earnest about the end of the world.
Hegel dies.
Goethe completes Faust II. He dies the next year.

1832   Andrew Jackson is reelected.
Louisa May Alcott is born.
The Disciples of Christ, a movement which encouraged New Testament simplicity and Christian unity is founded.
Moses Stuart publishes his controversial commentary on Romans.

1833   Britain abolishes slavery in the colonies.
        South Carolina, in an act of nullification, declares U.S. tariff laws null and void. Jackson sends in troops.
        Oberlin College admits students of both sexes.

1834   James Whistler, Geronimo, and Sitting Bull are born.
        The reaper is patented by Cyrus McCormick.

1835   Nathaniel Hawthorne publishes "The Young Goodman Brown."
        Madison (Colgate) University is founded.
        D. F. Strauss publishes his *Leben Jesu*.
        A pioneer railroad is opened from Nuremberg to Fürth in Germany.
        DeTocqueville publishes *Democracy in America*.
        Samuel Clemens and Phillips Brooks are born.
        The Great New York City Fire destroys many buildings.

1836   Emerson publishes his "Essay on Nature."
        Samuel Colt patents the revolving pistol.
        Winslow Homer and Washington Gladden are born.
        Texas declares independence; the Battle of the Alamo is fought.
        Arkansas joins the union.
        New York (Union) Theological Seminary is founded.

By voyaging to America in May, the Robinsons missed the tremendous political and social disruption which swept through much of Europe in 1830. In France, the Bourbons were overthrown and replaced by a regime supported by LaFayette which promised to be more liberal. Unfortunately, the reality never quite lived up to the promise, a fact which prompted even more bloody outbursts eighteen years later. In some German states petty tyrants were replaced by more democratic forms of government. The Belgians freed themselves from what they regarded as the tyranny of the Protestant Dutch. In Italy there were demands for more freedom, but in general the Pope and the aristocracy turned a deaf ear and retained control for yet a few more years. In a way, this was a modest adjustment after the rather arbitrary Napoleonic settlements, but it was also a sign that the spirit of the French revolution was not yet dead and that the glorification of the aristocracy and the king was an anachronism which more and more people sought to eliminate. It was the first of a series of European cataclysms which were to last until the Second World War.

In America there had been a similar, though different shift in a new direction. In many respects, John Quincy Adams was the last "aristocratic" President, the last for many years to come from America's established elite. Andrew Jackson was an old soldier and a commoner and appealed to the common man. His tone was anti-intellectual, egalitarian (for white males), and chauvinistic. He was so much dedicated to the Union that he had little regard for abolitionists or those who pled for the rights of native Americans.[1] Everything was either black or white and he definitely sided with the white. He hated the Bank of America, French diplomats who would not pay up on reparations, or anyone who weakened the solidarity of the Union. Jackson had great dreams for the Western expansion of the nation and what would later be called America's manifest destiny, but he was willing to put even these dreams on hold for the sake of preserving the Union.

Against Jackson and the Jacksonians stood the Whigs who, in the face of a growingly secular America, dreamed of recovering a Christian nation in which Protestantism formed the basis for morality and decision making. In fact, in some parts of the country, like Massachusetts, this was more than a dream, for atheists were still ostracized and even Universalists were sometimes not allowed to testify in a court of law. This tendency toward moralism and thought control prompted many writers and intellectuals to leave their natural affiliation and join, however reluctantly, with the rough and ready Jacksonians who, although hardly intellectuals themselves, at least allowed for greater freedom of thought and expression. Thus George Bancroft, Nathaniel Hawthorne, James Fenimore Cooper, Washington Irving, and eventually Herman Melville all, in one way or another, were connected with the Democrats.

---

[1] John M. McFaul, "Expediency vs. Morality: Jacksonian Politics and Slavery," *Journal of American History* 62, no. 1 (June 1975), 24-39.

The longstanding debate which still haunts America became ever more central. Should the United States think of itself as "Christian" or essentially secular? And if the latter is chosen, on what basis are laws made and decisions implemented? Can a nation survive which is not bound together by a common religious faith? And if Christianity were to rule, what would that imply about the dark question of slavery?

While America debated these issues, great new events were occurring which made this an unusually exciting age. John Deere and Cyrus McCormick, Samuel F. B. Morse and Elias Howe, among others, showed how Yankee ingenuity could solve problems, create new machines, and make human life vital and productive. On every mill stream of New England, it seemed, new industries were starting up as technology transformed agricultural America into an industrial nation. America was in a boom period fueled by that American "can do" attitude and, quite frankly, a highly materialistic desire for money and a more comfortable life.

It was also the age of great oratory and political leadership. Henry Clay, Robert C. Calhoun, Daniel Webster, Martin Van Buren and, in his own way, John Quincy Adams were masters of the political arts and would be considered extraordinary in any age. It was a period, not of sound bites, but of platform oratory which over the course of several hours could entrance and move a whole sea of listeners to new levels of excitement and commitment.

There were also promising new writers; Hawthorne, Emerson, and Fitz-Greene Halleck were to join with earlier writers like Cooper and Irving and Bryant to create a national literature. Within a few years the Hudson River school would dominate the art scene and produce works rivaling those created in Europe. America marched westward and one-by-one those states which we have come to know and even take for granted were added to the Union.

Religion also burst the bounds of rationalism and stiff orthodoxy to assume new forms and functions. The Finney-type revival had become commonplace and through his influence there was a greater and greater emphasis upon human perfectibility and reform. Abolitionism, temperance, peace and pacifism, and women's suffrage movements all find their roots in the Jacksonian era. Andover became a center for temperance concerns and for a missionary movement which was to sweep the world with the gospel according to America. To a rough and ready frontier society, much of this was salutary and civilizing, though there is always a divisive down-side to moralistic crusades. It was the genius of Hawthorne to see through the glorification of goodness to this dark side of human nature. The young Goodman Brown, an ideal Puritan by day, slips away to the witches' coven at night.

Despite the piety and the gusto and high spirits of the age, Hawthorne perceived that all was not well. How right he was! The Indian Relocation Act of 1830 meant that the United States had again broken faith with its native population and despite the obvious immorality of its action and the cost of thousands of lives simply moved large populations westward across the Mississippi into a life of fruitlessness and despair.

Moreover, although Americans loved to speak of liberty, they offered little to the black men and women who were enslaved all across the South. These were years of great religiosity, but somehow, for the rank-and-file American, there seemed no inconsistency in claiming piety while holding, or countenancing the holding of slaves. There were, of course, many who protested against this great stain upon the Republic, but, by and large, Christians seemed more concerned with personal rather than public piety. Some, like Charles Hodge, began to defend slavery as allowed if not authorized and blessed by the God of the Bible. Jackson, himself, was a profound champion of the common man and of democracy. He wanted the people to decide. The problem was that the people were (and perhaps are) a bundle of prejudices and biases which stand in the way of genuine liberty and justice for all. Money and Union took precedence over the liberty and justice so loudly proclaimed.

Nor was there widespread sympathy for those brave women who dared to point out that there was something peculiar about a nation dedicated to liberty which, at the same time, denied to women even the simple right to vote. Many Christians believed woman's subordinate position to be simply a fact of nature.[2] The Women's Rights movement was getting under way; at last a college like Oberlin opened its door to women, but the battle was (and is) a long and fierce one. Liberty is wonderful as long as it is not for someone else!

---

[2] Hillier, *op. cit.*, 177.

In a sense, all the elements which have made America great and not so great were made explicit in the age of Jackson. There was a profound sense of equality and the irrelevance of the old elite. But there was also deep prejudice and hatred of various minorities. As immigration, largely from Ireland and Germany, expanded, Protestant prejudice against Catholics and Jews became ever more vocal and shrill. There was a great sense of humanitarian reform as citizens took up the cudgels to fight drunkenness, ignorance, irreligion and a host of other evils, but this was balanced by a growingly materialistic culture in which what counted was financial success. There were the inventions which sparked radical changes in society and industrialists who made fortunes while a growing segment of society supported their high life by barely surviving on subsistence wages. There were the great statesmen and legislators, the orators and the diplomats, but there was also the crassest form of mud slinging and political campaigning and vote buying. Hickory sticks to symbolize support for Old Hickory were in their own way rather cute, but the yellow journalism and the bald face lies told on behalf of candidates certainly were not. Politics had become very quickly raucous, dirty, and crude.

This was the world the Robinsons entered when they docked in New York in July of 1830, and one cannot help but wonder what a young intellectual woman like Therese, born and bred in the rich culture of Bach and Beethoven, of Schiller and Goethe thought about all this. New York City itself was a busy, buzzing confusion. Already the largest city of America, it boasted only one true restaurant and no opera house. The streets were muddy and pigs apparently roamed everywhere. The mood was anything but intellectual. Columbia University was there, but, until the Civil War, graduated each year on average only 25 students. New York University was not founded until 1832 and even then remained for many years quite small. People were in New York, not for the arts and culture, but for the one thing that mattered: making money. This was hardly the happy village life about which Edward had occasionally become nostalgic in his journal.

Although it seems rather unlikely, Reinhold Steig says that Edward and Therese stayed in New York for a month before proceeding to Connecticut. Why they would not go immediately to see his family for introductions and reunion is unclear. Certainly Elizabeth makes obvious in her letters that she is most anxious to see Edward again and to meet his new wife and baby. Moreover a stay in New York would have added needless expense to an already long and costly trip. The best guess then is that Steig (who gives no sources for his information) is incorrect and that they proceeded to New England almost immediately to stay with either George or Charles in New Haven. Perhaps E. R. accepted the invitation from the Rev. Mr. Ogden conveyed by Edward's sister Elizabeth, to preach at Southington. We do know that he received but refused during this time an invitation by the Alumni Association of Hamilton College to deliver "a special oration" at his alma mater.[3] We also know that on September 8, 1830 he received word from Yale that he had been elected an honorary member of the Alpha Chapter of Phi Beta Kappa.[4]

Whether their trip to Connecticut took place immediately or after a month, the contrast between New York and Connecticut would have been quickly apparent to Therese. Hartford and New Haven, still sleepy towns of not much more than 5,000, were thoroughly Yankee and Congregational. New York already was beginning to receive many immigrants; Connecticut had very few. Those happy villages full of "Young Goodman Browns" were still there. So too was a lingering suspicion of the theater and European culture and a growing animus against Demon Rum and all other forms of alcoholic beverage.

If New York was full of the secular gusto of Jacksonian democracy, Connecticut bristled with rampant Whiggery. People generally deplored the decline of American values and the intrusion of new immigrants. "Papists" were of particular concern, for they were, obviously, a threat to all that right thinking people held dear. Connecticuters profoundly yearned to keep things as they were when everyone was Edwardsean and Sabbatarian, when the simple sober life of New England was in full bloom. Could they ever have imagined how provincial and foolish they looked to a German woman who had traveled the length and breadth of Europe, knew the most modern poets and philosophers of Germany, and corresponded with Johann Goethe and Jacob Grimm?

If Hartford and New Haven were provincial, Andover was certainly even more so. According to Steig,[5] Edward and Therese arrived there about

---

[3] Robinson papers, K-6, (August 28, 1830).
[4] Robinson papers, K-6.
[5] Steig, *op. cit.*, 361.

November 1 and took up residence in a house reserved for them by the institution. One can be sure that in their own way the faculty of Andover was cordial and genuine in their greeting of the Robinsons. After all, most of the faculty knew Edward as an old friend and wished him and his new bride well. But while Connecticut merely wanted to preserve the past, Andover was doctrinally committed to it. The faculty President Porter, Moses Stuart, Leonard Woods, Ralph Emerson—were well educated, intellectual leaders, but not one of them had been to Europe or even had much experience outside the confines of New England. They were committed to the old Andover creed and confession, to strict observance of the Sabbath, and now to a growing concern about the evils of drink. What would they think about a couple fresh from savoring the wines of Italy? How would they really understand a protégé of Goethe who loved the inspiration which nature brings more than stuffy churches?

New England was, of course, beautiful with its rolling hills and its picturesque towns and villages, but there was also a sort of ugliness quite evident to anyone used to the Gothic and Baroque churches of Halle. Rowe describes the Bartlet Chapel where faculty and students met on the Sabbath:

> In the summer soft breezes were wafted through the open windows, but in the winter the room was chilly. It was heated by a single wood stove, which the sexton stoked frequently from the woodbox which was on the other side of the pulpit. The heat radiated from the long pipes which ran around the chapel. The bare blue walls and the yellowish galleries did not give one the impression of the beauty of holiness. The stovepipes and the wood crackling in the stove were suggestive of unpleasant thoughts to sensitive souls which were conscious of faults that deserved eternal punishment, unless the divine mercy assured one a place among the elect. Bare floors matched the bare walls. Yellow pews added nothing attractive to the ensemble.[6]

To Therese, so used to the splendor of Medieval and Baroque churches and the rich intellectuality of her German circle of friends, some of the participants must have also seemed highly eccentric. Moses Stuart, Edward's own mentor and chief ally, ranked foremost among the peculiarities of the place. Stuart's own daughter describes him in the following way:

---

[6] Rowe, *op. cit.*, 63.

> Fourth-fifths of the year he carried his long blue cloak on his arm to church. Spreading it carefully over the back of the pew, and sitting on it, he was a most attentive but at the same time a most restless listener. To keep still seemed to be a physical impossibility for him. If the sermon was poor his impatience showed itself in shrugs, in opening and shutting his large white hands, in moving in his seat, and in a lengthened face pitiable to see. If it was good, no one doubted his appreciation, or the social feeling which made him wish to share his enjoyment. At the utterance of any especially pertinent remark, he would often rise in his seat, and turning round upon the young men, his students, draw his red silk handkerchief across his mouth several times, expressing in every feature the keenness of his pleasure. If he differed theologically from the sentiments uttered, no words could have expressed his dissent more strongly than did his looks and gestures.[7]

Steig tells us that in the face of Andover's ultraconservative sanctimoniousness Therese retreated into family life, woefully unhappy with her surroundings. Although he gives no evidence for this assertion, there is no reason to disbelieve him. Indeed, it would be difficult to imagine that she, a noted European intellectual and associate of Goethe and Grimm, would have been pleased with a situation in which her husband's livelihood and future entailed their both conforming to the orthodoxy and the piety of the place.

Moreover, Edward suddenly became enormously busy. The reputation of Andover had spread and students came from many parts of the country. Before 1840 the total student population had passed 160 while the faculty had remained more-or-less constant. Stuart and Robinson found themselves teaching languages to vast throngs of students and inspecting growing mountains of exercises. Furthermore, their labors were complicated by the fact that Andover's new rule that students were expected to have learned the rudiments of Hebrew before matriculating was observed in the breach. Those who were deficient tried to catch up once there, but that meant that they did not properly complete the regular course and, in fact, tended to move on to the study of theology without the regular Biblical education upon which to ground it.

---

[7] *Ibid.,* 64.

In a letter from Moses Stuart and Edward Robinson, the trustees and their curriculum committee were urged to allow them to divide the class, to enforce the regulations about preparation and time of matriculation and to appoint Leonard Woods Jr. to help carry the load. The trustees eventually relented. Classes were split in two and everyone worked hard to accommodate all the students who had been admitted. In the midst of all this, Moses Stuart became ill with some sort of affliction of the lungs—an ailment which apparently affected many students as well—which meant that he had to curtail his activities. One may be sure that it was Edward who was expected to take up the slack.

Robinson also served as the seminary librarian, a position, of course, not yet professionalized. Indeed, there was, at the time, no standardized cataloging system or training program for librarians. A librarian was someone who loved books and who provided general supervision of the development of the collection. Robinson was certainly fit for that role. His journal reveals that he not only visited many of the libraries of Europe but paid special attention to how they were organized and catalogued. He also spent many hours with book dealers, learning how they operated and which ones could be trusted. While in Europe he purchased a great variety of important books for the seminary library and thus had already taken responsibility for many of their new acquisitions. Most important, he had a wide knowledge of various fields and important authors and could be relied upon to keep the library up-to-date. But this did take time and energy, organizing the collection and ordering books. As the collection grew we may imagine that the work became more and more onerous.[8] It should be noted in passing that the library seems to have been for the faculty, not the students. Only the licentiates received "library privileges."

Whether E. R. did much preaching during this period, is an open question. He was admitted as a member of the Convention of Congregational Ministers in Boston on June 2, 1831 by a unanimous vote of the membership,[9] but the extent to which he exercised his talents as a

---

[8] In the Hamilton College library there is a printed listing of books in the Andover Library as of 1819 along with Robinson's hand-written additions to the collection penned in the appropriate places.

[9] Robinson papers, F-2 Letter from B. B. Wisner, Scribe of the Massachusetts Convention of Congregational ministers.

preacher is uncertain. It is probable that he was just too busy as a teacher and scholar to devote much time to the pulpit. One also may guess that his interests were now directed more to objective scholarship rather than to pious exhortation.

Certainly, Robinson was enormously busy and productive as a scholar. His translation of Wahl's Greek lexicon was very successful and needed a second edition. This he provided. Far more significant in terms of time and energy, was his editing of the journal advertised before his arrival by Moses Stuart. Robinson published it, however, not as the *Biblical Inquirer* but as *The Biblical Repository*. Moreover, he apparently did not have the editorial assistance which had been promised. In his letter to Robinson in Europe Stuart had commended to him C. E. Stowe, a young licentiate at the Seminary. By 1831, however, Stowe had taken a position teaching Greek at Dartmouth. In the journal, Robinson printed one of his articles, but otherwise did not benefit from his help. Parenthetically, Stowe became eventually the husband of Harriet Beecher, the daughter of Lyman Beecher and sister of the famous preacher Henry Ward Beecher. They returned to Andover in later life and acquired the old Mechanical Arts building as their home.

The Biblical Repository was, by anyone's standards, an extraordinary piece of work. In it, Robinson was able to draw together the best of German and American scholarship to create a rich blend of theological and Biblical study. The editor, relying upon his European contacts, included articles by Tholuck, Gesenius, Neander, Tittman of Leipzig, Planck of Göttingen, and Hengstenberg among others. There is also a smattering of English scholars represented and even an article by Eugene Burnouf of France. Among the Americans it is not surprising that, except for the editor, Moses Stuart himself is the most regularly represented. And then, of course, there are Robinson's own contributions.

In the first year of publication, Robinson contributed four articles concerning theological education in Germany which, even today, are of considerable value. He describes with care each university, its size, its strengths and sometimes its weaknesses. He outlines the curriculum and many of the educational techniques and attitudes of the Germans. The last article of this series is really not by Robinson but is a description by the faculty of Halle of the theological education there. In any event, for someone who wants to know about German higher education in the early nineteenth century these articles are invaluable.

Much of this information was republished by Robinson in Scotland in 1835 as *A Concise view of the Universities and the State of Theological Education in Germany*. Clearly he was touching upon a subject which was very much *au courant* in America. When New York University was being planned, Americans with educational experience in Germany were called together to discuss how that university could appropriate the German model. Whether Robinson attended that meeting or not is unknown, but he should have been invited, for more than virtually anyone else he was to write persuasively on the subject.[10] It is interesting to note that C. E. Stowe, mentioned above, also became well-known for his knowledge concerning the German educational system.

Beside translating many of the other articles from Germany, Robinson also offered for the 1831 issues of the journal an introductory essay on the language of Palestine in New Testament times and an exegetical article on the Song of Deborah in Judges 5. The latter is especially revealing of the techniques of the author. The article begins with a bibliographical essay and a short introduction to the passage, followed by a new translation and notes. The notes are very extensive and deal with problems of translation, word meaning, etc. The whole article is reminiscent of the format of *The Anchor Bible*. What is most significant is that he performs his task with seemingly little theological bias or commentary. There are herein no homiletical helps or theological asides. In other words, Robinson appears as a modern, rather objective Biblical translator and interpreter. Old Testament scholars today might quarrel with this philological assertion or that, but not with the general approach to the ancient literature.

The same may be said for his briefer article on the "Lament of David over Saul and Jonathan" published in the summer of 1834. In this study he includes the Hebrew text; otherwise, the format is the same. There are many occasions when he might have commented on the theology of Samuel, but he does not. He restricts himself to philological, historical, and literary analysis and leaves the theology to the theologians. Again, the modernness (but not post-modernness) of his approach seems quite apparent.

---

[10] Theodore Francis Jones, editor, *New York University: 1832-1932* (New York: New York University Press, 1933), 4, 22-25.

One of Robinson's more unusual articles entitled "On the Letter Attributed to Publius Lentulus, respecting the personal appearance of Christ" appeared in the April 1832 issue. Although a number of scholars as far back as the Renaissance critic Laurentius Valla had concluded that the letter's authenticity was very problematic, some people, even in Protestant America, continued to claim its probable antiquity. Robinson sets out to demonstrate once and for all that the text should be regarded as wholly spurious. The letter itself, which appeared in many forms, is of interest because it purports to give an eye-witness description of Jesus. It concludes in the following way:

> . . .there is something wonderfully charming in his face, with a mixture of gravity. He is never seen to laugh, but he has been observed to weep. He is very straight in stature, his hands are large and spreading, and his arms very beautiful. He talks little, but with great gravity, and is the handsomest man in the world.[11]

Robinson shows that there never was a proconsul or procurator by the name of the supposed author, that the manuscript was unknown in the ancient world and probably unheard of before the Renaissance, that the Latin style and idiom are simply wrong for the period, and that the epistle stands in contradiction to other established facts. Apparently, his arguments were widely accepted, for today the epistle is scarcely known at all, even by Biblical scholars.

The article about Publius Lentulus represents his one foray into what might be now called church history. For the most part, however, he concerns himself much more directly with Biblical matters. Robinson sets forth his basic attitude toward Biblical study in an article "Philology and Lexicography in the New Testament," which he had already published, in part, in 1826 in the *North American Review*. There are, however, important changes from the earlier essay. The title has been altered to include philology and the initial bibliography has been revised. Most important, the earlier version was published without mention of the author's identity! Although this was not uncommon in the *Review*, it may well be that Robinson was nervous about the article's theological implications and did

---

[11] Edward Robinson, "Letter of Publius Lentulus," *The Biblical Repository* (April 1832) I, 368.

not want his name included. This is particularly true since the journal had the reputation of being Unitarian. Whether his colleagues at Andover knew it was by him is unclear; the first version of the article saw the light of day after he had left for Europe.

The title is banal enough to avoid controversy, but the introduction to the article is not. He begins by commenting upon the fact that Biblical scholarship had greatly improved during the last twenty-five years. Before that time "knowledge of the Hebrew language was confined to a few individuals; and in those schools where it was professedly taught, it was practically accounted of secondary importance."[12] Now, he says, because of the efforts of scholars like Gesenius and many others, great advances have been made.

> The day, we trust has passed away, in which the body of our clergy will remain contented to receive their knowledge respecting our sacred books through the medium of mere translations, or on the authority of commentators. The spirit of the Reformation is again at work; the rights of private judgment, and the necessity of free and personal investigation, are beginning to be felt on this subject, as they long have been on all others; and if these be exercised with proper dispositions, the results cannot but be auspicious. We are not of the number of those, who fear the consequences of close scrutiny, or the most profound researches, into either the nature, or history, or interpretation of the records of our religion. We believe the truths, which these records reveal, will shine with purer lustre, when the veil of ignorance, by which they are yet in a measure shrouded, shall have been still farther removed. We know, indeed, that there are those, who are doubtless conscientious in the adoption of different views; and who regard with alarm all those efforts of critical acumen, that lead to results in any shape different from those received modes of interpretation, which, originally adopted perhaps without sufficient evidence, have been handed down from generation to generation, without question or examination. Such persons are, no doubt, conscientious in their motives; but it does appear to us, that they are alarmed at a shadow, which their own experience has not enabled them to distinguish from a substance; and that their motives, if traced to the ultimate source of them, will be found to rest on nothing better than the papal maxim, that "ignorance is the mother of devotion."

---

[12] Edward Robinson, "Philology and Lexicography of the New Testament," *The Biblical Repository*, (January 1834), 154.

> It was the glory of the Reformation, that it reversed this maxim, and strove to found a more enlightened system of faith and worship on the unlimited diffusion of knowledge; and we hope it will be the glory of this country to exhibit proof of the Protestant maxim in its fullest extent, as applied to the study of Scripture. [13]

He goes on to say that in order to understand Scripture, one must go beyond the mere words to paint a picture of how the ancient Jews experienced and understood their world. For him the Bible is not a collection of proof texts to be theologically reassembled, but a document of a living people whose faith was imbedded in their experience, in their very sense of the world.

> If we can, in a measure, transport ourselves back to the circumstances of the Jews; if we can speak as they spoke, and read as they read, and feel as they felt; we may raise our eyes and behold the painting, glowing with beauty and expression, and rich in graceful forms and brilliant coloring. Without such preparation, such a view; our eyes will rest only upon those outlines of the forms and scenes, which are suspended as a key beneath the picture, and which, of course, are destitute of coloring, of costume, of the minuter features and comparatively of expression. [14]

How this view played out at Andover is an interesting question. Clearly he is undermining those who believed that the Edwardseans spoke the last word theologically and that faith is simply hanging on to what has already been set forth by them. In fact, he is issuing a clarion call in the name of the Reformation for more and more research to follow the truth wherever it leads. His agenda has been and is the agenda of modern Biblical scholarship. To be sure, he covers himself a little by saying that the work of scholarship must be done with the "proper dispositions," but even here he leaves the phrase undefined.

In these paragraphs Robinson proves himself to be the father, not only of American Biblical archaeology—for to understand how the Jews "felt" one must recover a knowledge of their surroundings, their geography and civilization—but of Biblical criticism as well. Unlike the spokesmen for the Enlightenment, Robinson offers no appeal here to abstract reason nor does

---

[13] *Ibid.*, 156-157.
[14] *Ibid.*, 157-158.

he exhibit a desire to prove certain claims of the Bible true or false. The aim is to understand how the Jews and early Christians "sensed the world" and through that knowledge come to a clearer understanding and appreciation of what the texts written by them mean. Such an understanding involves not only careful philological and lexicographical work, but the exploration of the land where the Word was first heard.

Robinson's interest in the specifics of Palestinian geography is also made clear in his long, fifty-four page essay on the exodus of the Israelites out of Egypt. In this work, he avoids, for the most part, any attempt to deal with the miraculous features of the story, though he does point out that in the story of the crossing of the Red Sea, God employs natural forces to create the event which leads to Israel's freedom. His interest, however, is primarily in the geography; he wants to know what their route was rather than how Moses got water from the rock.

In order to discuss this matter, he refers to a variety of basic sources beside the Bible itself: Burkhardt, Niebuhr, deSacy, Cady, et al. It is clear that he has already become a master of the travel literature and has laid a very firm foundation for his own exploration of the Sinai and Negeb regions. He also mentions Eli Smith, his companion on his own trip, and Smith's earlier excursion in the region. In the journal he includes various excerpts from Burkhardt as well as a life of Carlsten Niebuhr. Clearly he had done an immense amount of reading to prepare himself for the great trip which is to make his fame secure. Scholars may forget many of his other great accomplishments—his lexicons and his grammars and his harmonies of the gospels—but no one can overlook his geographical and archaeological findings. They will remain for a long time to come the bell weather of his greatness.

Robinson includes this lengthy discourse on Exodus as a "teaser" for his new full length publication: his edition of *Calmet's Dictionary of the Bible*. Calmet, himself, was a French monk who published the first version of the *Historical and Critical Dictionary of the Bible* in 1722-1728 in four volumes. It was published in various translations during the 18th century until in 1797 Charles Taylor published a radically revised version in which Catholic and rabbinical based articles were dropped and additions were made in a separate volume. The fifth edition of this appeared in 1830 and

Robinson was invited to prepare an American edition of the old classic. His work was not made easier by the earlier editor. He writes:

> The character of Mr. Taylor as an editor, and the value of his additions to Calmet's work, may be given in a few words. Acquainted with oriental philology only through the meagre system of Masclef and Parkhurst; as an expounder of etymologies, outstripping even the extravagance of the latter; and as a theorist in the ancient history of nations, overstepping the limits which even Bryant had felt himself constrained to observe;—his remarks on these and many collateral topics, may be characterized as being in general fanciful, very often rash, and sometimes even involving absurdity. They must ever be received by the student with very great caution.[15]

Clearly Robinson's task was no minor one. He cut whole articles not directly concerned with Scripture, and collated with the main text the separate volume of additional material which Taylor had compiled. He drew copiously from German scholars of whom the English editors did not seem aware and struck out all that he considered crude and fanciful speculations, all that was "positively wrong and of injurious tendency." There was much left with which he still was not in full agreement, but since this was meant to be a new version of Calmet and not a wholly new work he left some of it intact. Still his editorial hand was evident on virtually every one of the 1000 pages which comprised the book. The plan he says "is neither doctrinal nor devotional. The object of it is simply to explain and illustrate the meaning of the Bible itself."[16] That, in a word, sums up the intent of all of Robinson's scholarship. He is not opposed to others offering doctrinal and devotional meanings, but he, in his work, will stick as closely as possible to the linguistic, historical, and geographical facts.

It should also be noted that he also produced a more simplified version of the dictionary for young people, a work which was to go through many editions.[17] This expresses a growing sense on his part that Bible study

---

[15] Edward Robinson, "Preface to the American Edition," *Calmet's Dictionary of the Holy Bible* (Boston: Crocker and Brewster, 1832), iii.

[16] *Ibid.*, iv.

[17] Edward Robinson, *A Dictionary of the Holy Bible, for the use of schools and young persons,* (Boston: Crocker and Brewster, 1833). This work went through at least ten editions (1856).

ought not be confined to the clergy but that ordinary people, even children, ought to have access to the good book. This was a theme which he emphasized when he accepted Union's call to become a professor there.

Nor were these dictionaries the last of his accomplishments. In 1833 he published *Buttmann's 'Larger Greek Grammar': translated from the German with Additions by Edward Robinson*,[18] a work which he had prepared in part while still in Germany. In the preface he gives an excellent overview of grammatical studies of classical Greek as well as personal reminiscences of Professor Buttman who died in 1829. He also adds many annotations and explications of his own. The work was so popular that a new edition was called for in 1839. It, and its successor in 1850, became a standard in schools and colleges.

E. R.'s many accomplishments did not go unheeded by the world at large. In 1832, long before his *magnum opus* on geography gave him international fame, Dartmouth College saw fit to honor him with an honorary degree. Significantly, Robinson only had one "earned" degree: an A.B. from tiny Hamilton. At neither Andover nor Halle was he a degree candidate. Happily, however, this was the age when eminent accomplishment counted for much more than credentials. A scholar was self-made, not university manufactured.

Although such honors are always cherished and to be heralded, there was another seemingly minor event which bore much more valuable fruit. In 1832 one of E. R.'s former students returned for a visit to Andover and enjoyed a reunion with his old teacher. Eli Smith (1801-1857) who, as we have already noted, was a distant relation of Robinson,[19] was born in Northford, Connecticut and graduated from Yale in 1821. After a stint teaching in Georgia he returned north to attend Andover Theological Seminary. Upon graduation in 1826 he was immediately sent by the American Board of Commissioners for Foreign Missions as associate editor of its publishing house on Malta. From there he had proceeded to Syria to study Arabic with the intent of translating the Bible into that language. His stay was cut short, however, because of the Battle of Navarino. In that battle squadrons of English, French and Russian ships destroyed the Egyptian navy

---

[18] Edward Robinson, *Buttmann's 'Larger Greek Grammar': translated from the German with Additions by Edward Robinson* (Andover: Gould Newman and Saxton: 1833).
[19] The relation was really by marriage.

as it lay in port. The Turks were furious and demanded reparations. Europeans—and by extension Americans—quickly became *persona non grata* in the Ottoman Empire.

Smith returned to Malta, but in March of 1830 he joined with Harrison Otis Dwight, a Hamilton College alumnus from Utica, to undertake an extended journey through Asia Minor, Armenia, and Georgia. Together they published a book entitled *Researches of the Rev. E. Smith and Rev. H.G.O. Dwight in Armenia: Including a Journey through Asia Minor and into Georgia and Persia, with a Visit to the Nestorian and Chaldean Christians of Oormiah and Salmas.*[20] From this investigation came the founding of a new mission station at Oormiah, but, perhaps more important, it also awakened Europeans and Americans to a part of the world which at the time was virtually unknown. Dwight became perhaps the first American to study the Armenian language in depth. Smith had just returned to America from this journey when he met E. R.

A glance at any yearly index for *The Missionary Herald* from 1826 until 1857 reveals that Eli Smith was one of America's leading missionaries. As head of the mission in Beirut he, of course, wrote annual reports, but he also contributed many articles and comments about the missionary venture and its difficulties.[21] These suggest that although he was thoroughly committed to the missionary venture, he also was a realist, recognizing the severe difficulties of any evangelization in a Moslem country. Although he used every opportunity available to preach and teach, he devoted much of his time to the translation of the Bible into Arabic.

Eli Smith, then, was a godsend to Robinson. He was extremely knowledgable in Arabic and, in fact, had become bilingual. He was a seasoned traveler in the Ottoman Empire and had contacts among both missionaries and Muslims. He was, in a word, exactly the contact and encouragement Robinson needed. E. R. had for a long time been considering a trip to Palestine; Smith, with his knowledge of Arabic and of the region

---

[20] Eli Smith, *Researches of the Rev. E. Smith and H. G. O. Dwight in Armenia etc.* (Boston: Crocker and Brewster, 1833).
[21] Some, but by no means all, of these are included in the bibliography.

was the person who could make that dream a possibility.[22] Robinson describes the meeting in his great work:

> In the year 1832, the Rev. Eli Smith, American Missionary at Beirut, made a visit to the United States; having recently returned from a long journey with the Rev. Mr. Dwight to Armenia and Persia. He had in former days been my pupil and friend; and a visit to the Holy Land naturally became a topic of conversation between us. It was agreed, that we would, if possible, make such a journey together at some future time; and the same general plan was then marked out, which we have since been permitted to execute . . . I count myself fortunate in having been thus early assured of the company of one, who, by his familiar and accurate knowledge of the Arabic language, by his acquaintance with the people of Syria, and by the experience gained in former extensive journeys, was so well qualified to alleviate the difficulties and overcome the obstacles which usually accompany oriental travel. Indeed, to these qualifications of my companion, combined with his taste for geographical and historical researches, and his tact in eliciting and sifting the information to be obtained from an Arab population, are mainly to be ascribed the more important and interesting results of our journey.[23]

The die was now cast. The question was only when. Although Robinson had been afflicted by various diseases throughout his life and was to become deathly ill in 1834, the hope of this new exploration doubtless helped to carry him through. Robinson was a scholar's scholar, able to devote endless hours to the minutiae of lexicons and grammars, but he was also, even more, an assiduous traveler and reporter whose keen eye, educated by his hours of tedious labor, prepared him to see as none before him had seen. He now needed only the right moment.

---

[22] Although it is impossible to do him justice in this work, Eli Smith surely deserves scholarly attention. It should be noted that, after he met with Robinson, he married the next year Sarah Lanman who was equally devoted to missionary work. She died, however, in September of 1836, just a year before Smith's and Robinson's famous journey. See: Edward W. Hooker, *Memoir of Mrs. Sarah Lanman Smith*, 2nd ed. (Boston: Perkins & Marvin, 1840).

[23] Edward Robinson, *Biblical Researches in Palestine, Mount Sinai and Arabia Petraea: A Journal of Travels in the Year 1838, by E. Robinson and E. Smith*. (Boston: Crocker and Brewster, 1841), 2.

On a more personal level, there was also some very good news. The property in Clinton which had for so many years remained unsaleable finally attracted some prospective buyers. The Robinson papers contain a number of letters from Othniel Williams and his successor describing the negotiation. Eventually, Robinson sold the property for $2,500. He was also able to negotiate long distance the sale of the property once owned by his father in Twinsburg, Ohio. Although the returns seem modest to us, the result was that he had some financial backing to sustain him during the lean years ahead. It is quite probable that the sale of these properties was also what made the Palestinian trip possible.

Although his scholarly work went exceedingly well as he produced one major work after another, his personal life was marked by difficulty. In February of 1832 his brother George's wife died and Edward in all likelihood went to New Haven to be with him. He does not specify exactly why the experience was "painful," but he wrote to Samuel Farrar in April, saying that because of the situation he could not return from New Haven to finish his courses or give examinations. Perhaps George had collapsed because of the shock of his wife's death and Edward had to remain to make sure that his several children were cared for. In any event, the usually conscientious and fastidious Robinson that year was unable to complete his duties at Andover.

In August of the same year, his own son, Maxmillian, who had been born on September 31, 1831, died. He was buried in the seminary cemetery where a marker still exists to memorialize him. On this marker the Robinsons included a quotation from II Kings 4:26: "'Is it well with the child?' And she said, 'It is well.'" Since the child in question was raised by Elisha from the dead, the quotation is an apt, if somewhat eerie, expression of faith in the resurrection.

Robinson's strenuous academic labor as well as his family tragedies apparently took their toll upon him. At least the usual theory is that he became so ill that he had to resign from his position at Andover. Whether that is what actually happened, however, is somewhat unclear. Resign he certainly did, for he says so himself, but whether it was entirely for reasons of ill health is really uncertain. We do know that in the October 1834 issue of the *Biblical Repository* he apologizes that that issue had been delayed by illness. We also know that at the end of that year, he decided to resign as editor because of his affliction and because he received no recompense from the journal. But it does seem unusual for him to have resigned from his position at Andover rather than to take a leave of absence. Perhaps ill health played a part in his decision, but it may also be that the unhappiness of Therese with the stifling nature of the Andover community as well as their new affluence from the sale of books and property tempted them simply to sever the ties at Andover and move to Boston.

No sooner had he left than he had another job offer. On March 11, 1834 he received a letter from Samuel Schumaker, J. F. MacFarlane and Robert G. Harper offering him the position of Professor of Biblical and Oriental Literature at the seminary in Gettysburg, Pennsylvania and President of its sister institution, Pennsylvania College. An appended note from Schumaker, an important leader in the Lutheran communion, commended Robinson for his valuable translation of Buttman's Greek Grammar. There were good reasons why Robinson might have been chosen for this position. Not only had he already made a name for himself as a scholar; he also spoke German and had a German wife, characteristics which would certainly have pleased the Lutherans. Either Robinson's poor health or his scholarly agenda or both decided him against the position. Instead he remained essentially unemployed, working feverishly on more publications.

It is uncertain what the returns on his books might have been, but clearly they were very successful, for they each went through several editions. Moreover, even more important publications were on the way. In 1834 E. R. offered to the world a new edition of *Newcome's Harmony of the Gospels*.[24] LeClerc was the first to produce the harmony, in 1699, in Amsterdam. Newcome then revised and edited the original, changing somewhat the general order and adding notes. Robinson reordered the text again so that the text would not be broken up into "minute clauses" and so that wasted space was eliminated. Unlike an 1814 edition published in Andover, his version uses Greek accents and is much more carefully edited. This work, with all these editorial and substantive improvements, became

---

[24] Edward Robinson, *A Harmony of the Gospels in Greek in the general order of Le Clerc and Newcombe with Newcombe's notes, printed from the text with various readings of Knapp. The whole revised and the Greek text newly arranged by Edward Robinson* (Andover: Gould & Newman, 1834).

the standard harmony of the gospels used by students until Robinson himself produced a new and better harmony to supplant it.

Two years later Robinson was to outdo himself with two works which alone would have made him a great scholarly reputation. First of all, he published a translation of Gesenius' Latin-Hebrew Lexicon, incorporating in it many of Gesenius' further studies found in his Thesaurus. This work, which went through many editions, became the standard lexicon for all serious work in Biblical Hebrew and eventually became the basis for the Brown-Driver-Briggs Lexicon which is still standard today.[25] It should be noted that his speed in preparing this work was all important. Over at Yale, Josiah Gibbs, a most meticulous scholar, was also preparing a translation of Gesenius, but was only one-third of the way through when Robinson's edition was published. Gibbs, needless to say, was depressed.

Second, E. R. also produced a lexicon of New Testament Greek which, unlike many of his other works, was entirely of his own creation. The lexicon has entries for every word in New Testament Greek and so many references to the text that it constitutes an almost complete concordance of the New Testament. The work was a great success in both America and England and, like Robinson's Gesenius, became a standard work for many years to come.

Thus, in a few brief years Robinson accomplished one of his major goals: to provide for American Biblical scholars the tools necessary for well-informed, up-to-date study. Between 1831 and 1836 he published a standard Greek grammar and standard lexicon, a revered Hebrew lexicon, a dictionary of the Bible, a harmony of the gospels, and a new and vital Biblical journal. With these publications, along with Stuart's Hebrew grammar, American Biblical scholarship came of age and gained a recognized preeminence which it has never relinquished. All that was left for him to do was to provide the basic facts about the land and its people—with maps—so that scholars could not only read the Bible accurately but visualize

---

[25] For a less than wholly enthusiastic review see: *The Biblical Repertory and Princeton Review* IX, no. 1 (Jan. 1837), 88-100. Although Charles Hodge and Robinson had been friends in Europe, there seems to have been very little admiration for Robinson among the Princeton Old Schoolers. It should be noted that the work was not just a translation as the reviewer says, but incorporated material from Gesenius' Thesaurus. As Roediger brought more of this work to the public, Robinson incorporated it into new editions. Thus the lexicon did not really reach its final form until 1855.

the scenes which its text depicts. That would be, as we have seen, his next goal.

We should not leave this epoch of publication without mentioning works of quite a different sort. In the last year of publication, *The Biblical Repository* contained two unsigned articles in the April and October issues entitled, "Historical View of the Slavic Language in its Various Dialects: with special reference to Theological Literature." The identity of the author is not difficult to guess. Clearly Therese, despite her domestic labors and the heart-break over the loss of their first two sons, was not intellectually idle. Her work, though only tangentially related to the subject matter emphasized in the rest of the journal, is in its own way epoch making. To this day she remains a major voice in the study of Slavic literature. Her first major efforts in America are essentially buried here in a journal otherwise concerned with the Bible. One may also guess that one of the reasons why Robinson could produce so much in so short a time is that he had the able assistance of a wife who could translate German and edit manuscripts with care. Her contribution to his "Biblical Studies Epoch" should in no way be underestimated.

Just when the Robinsons left Andover is nowhere stated, but it must have been before November 24 of 1833. This is the day when their second son, Arthur, who had been born on February 4 of that year also died. The heartache for Edward and Therese continued. Initially he was buried in Boston, an indication they had already moved. The next year, in October, the Robinsons received permission to move the body to Andover to be buried next to his brother. His grave stone remains in the old cemetery, not far from the burial places of Moses Stuart and Leonard Woods, but unlike his brother's, the inscription is virtually illegible.

In any event, it is very clear that after leaving Andover they moved to Boston and not New York as J. Andrew Dearman asserts.[26] Probably the reason why he makes this claim is that Robinson does tell us he spent some months in New York actually assessing the plans to create a seminary in New York and deciding whether he would teach there. That he lived in New York immediately after leaving Andover, however, is simply a mistake which can be easily disproved.

---

[26] J. Andrew Dearman, "Edward Robinson: Scholar and Presbyterian Educator," *The Journal of Presbyterian History* 96, no. 3 (Fall 1991).

Precisely where they resided in Boston is uncertain, but, since Arthur was baptized at the Old South Congregational Church, they probably lived in the heart of the city. It was there that Edward, recovering from an illness which he intimates could have been fatal, edited his last volume of the *Repository* and produced the two great lexicons for the Biblical languages.

Boston was still, by modern standards, a very small city, though it was growing rapidly and may have reached a population of 60,000 by this time. As one of America's oldest communities—it was founded in 1630—it had many old and established patrician families who, despite the tradition of town meetings, controlled most of what went on. The dwellings of these pillars of the community were substantial and sometimes even pretentious. Unlike New York, with its rather crass hustle and bustle, Boston was known for its more sedate, dignified air. It was a city of old money, of elegance, of intellectuality. Thomas Hamilton, a Scotsman describes the city in the following way:

> It is not that the streets of Boston are less crowded, the public places less frequented, or that the business of life is less energetically pursued. In all these matters, to the eye of the stranger there is little perceptible difference. But the population is more orderly; the conventional restrictions of society are more strictly drawn, and even the lower orders are distinguished by a solemnity of demeanour, not observable in their more southern neighbours. A shopkeeper weighs the coffee or measures tape with the air of a philosopher; makes observations on the price or quality with an air of sententious sagacity; subjects your coin to a sceptical scrutiny, and as you walk off with your parcel in your pocket, examines you from top to toe, in order to gain some probable conclusion as to your habits or profession.[27]

It was certainly not Berlin, but Therese doubtless felt a little more at home here. At least there were a few people who could speak German and who knew something of the culture which she remembered and prized so much. One thinks particularly of Karl Follen, the Harvard professor who led so many to love Germanic literature. Therese is described by one biographer as his "co-worker" in his attempt to introduce German popular poetry into

---

[27] Howard Mumford Jones and Bessie Zaban Jones, eds. *The Many Voices of Boston* (Boston: Little, Brown, and Company, 1975), 174.

America.²⁸ Edward also had the opportunity to make use of his Harvard contacts for both social and scholarly affairs. Although retired, John Thornton Kirkland, his brother-in-law, still lived in the area and doubtless they renewed old acquaintances. And Kirkland knew everyone, from Ralph Waldo Emerson to Oliver Wendell Holmes. Boston provided a range of contacts and excitement which Andover, located a few miles to the north, simply did not.

Boston, as a city, though perhaps a little socially stuffy, was certainly not stagnant. In 1834, the Boston and Worcester Railroad began to carry passengers as far as Needham. 1835 saw the opening of the Boston and Providence Railroad. Within fifteen years, Boston boasted no fewer that seven rail terminals. Before long people could ride all the way to Albany pulled by an iron horse. So enthusiastic were the Bostonians that they named streets "Troy" and "Oswego" and "Oneida" to commemorate the new passage to the west.²⁹

Moreover, in and around Boston there was a tremendous growth of industry. Lowell, Massachusetts, in fact, was founded at the confluence of the Concord and the Merrimack Rivers as a planned industrial town. All over the eastern part of the state knitting mills hummed and young men and women left the marginal farms of stony New England to seek their future among the machines of the new age. Although Boston itself was less industrialized, it was the hub of these new enterprises which were to reshape not only New England but the nation.

The city could also lay claim to being the intellectual capital of the nation. The Athenaeum, for which Robinson had a ticket in 1834,³⁰ sponsored a variety of lectures and presentations. Harvard University, in nearby Cambridge, was one of America's oldest and most prestigious institutions. E. R. acknowledges more than once in the prefaces to his works the help received from the Harvard Library for his research. In 1836 Henry Wadsworth Longfellow, Robinson's long-time acquaintance, returned from Europe to assume his professorship of modern languages and *belle lettres* at

---

[28] Irma Elizabeth Voigt, *The Life and Works of Mrs. Therese Robinson* (Chicago: Deutsche-Amerikanische Historische Gesellschaft von Illinois, 1914), 87.
[29] Walter Muir Whitehill, *Boston: A Topographical History*, second ed. (Cambridge: Belnap Press of Harvard University, 1968), 105.
[30] Robinson papers K-4, June 12, 1834.

that university and it is highly likely that the two met once again before Edward moved on.

The very same year, Oliver Wendell Holmes, having returned from study in Europe, received his M.D. from Harvard and began his career as a teacher of medicine, poet and essayist. Already in 1831 this author, who was to amuse so many nineteenth century readers, had published his first version of *The Autocrat at the Breakfast Table* in the *New England Magazine*. 1836 saw the publication of his first volume of *Poems*. Holmes, however, was a renegade from Calvinism, having had enough of that ideology from his father and from Phillips Andover Academy where he had studied. Doubtless he and Robinson would not have had much to say to each other. Or rather, Holmes probably would have kept right on talking while Robinson retreated into his customary silence.

In nearby Concord, Ralph Waldo Emerson, a distant relation of Andover's Ralph Emerson, recently returned from England and his conversations with Wordsworth and Coleridge, began to write, publishing his famous essay entitled "Nature" in 1836. A year later, he was invited to give the Phi Beta Kappa address at Harvard and produced for the occasion his justly famous and well-received "The American Scholar." Edward and Therese, however, were certainly not in the audience to hear him, for they had left for Europe before August 31, when he gave the address. Doubtless, Robinson would have taken issue with some things Emerson had to say, for it is doubtful that he would have liked the "metaphysical" talk about the "One Man" and the "Divine Soul," but there is also much with which he would have heartily concurred. In fact, he himself was making it possible for Emerson to say, "Our day of dependence, our long apprenticeship to the learning of other lands is drawing to a close"[31] and he surely would have liked most of Emerson's final words:

> We will walk on our own feet; we will work with our own hands; we will speak our own minds. The study of letters shall be no longer a name for pity, for doubt, and for sensual indulgence. The dread of man and the love of man shall be a wall of defense and a wreath of joy around all. A nation of men will for the first time

---

[31] Ralph Waldo Emerson, *The Complete Essays and other Writings of Ralph Waldo Emerson,* Brooks Atkinson, ed. with forward by Tremaine McDowell (New York: Random House, 1950), 45.

exist, because each believes himself inspired by the Divine Soul which also inspires all men.[32]

It is interesting to note that in 1878 Arthur Penrhyn Stanley, the Dean of Westminster and fellow student of the Holy Land, came to America and, among many other places, spoke at Union Theological Seminary. In a talk now entitled, "An American Scholar," he held up Edward Robinson as an example of what an American and a Christian scholar should be. He gleaned three lessons from him which he believed seminarians would benefit from: 1) Devote yourself to study without fear of the consequences. 2) Verify your facts and look the facts straight in the face, and 3) Express yourself simply and without exaggerated style.[33] In many ways, Robinson became the American scholar which Emerson envisioned: independent, down-to-earth, and attentive to the facts of existence.

Not all events in Boston in the 1830s were as optimistic and positive as Emerson's words. In fact, beneath the polished exterior of Boston society there was also a current of darkness and hate.[34] Boston was founded by the Puritans and though the strict Calvinism had to a considerable extent been eroded by financial prosperity and Unitarianism, many of the old biases remained. Jedediah Morse, the second great awakening preacher, had years before expressed almost paranoiac concern about the Masons and their plot to undermine pious America. Now, that paranoia was revived with the Anti-Masonic movement which, strangely enough, became a major political force.[35] Edward Everett, who had served his nation already in so many capacities, was elected Governor of Massachusetts in 1835 not only as a Whig but on the Anti-Masonic ticket. Although many of America's founders, including George Washington himself were Masons, numerous Americans were swept away by irrational fears of anything secret or esoteric.

---

[32] *Ibid.*, 63.
[33] Arthur Penrhyn Stanley, *Addresses and Sermons delivered during a visit to the United States and Canada in 1878* (London: Macmillan and Co., 1883, 23-33.
[34] See: Theodore M. Hammett, "Two Mobs of Jacksonian Boston: Ideology and Interest," *Journal of American History* 62, no. 4 (Mar. 1976), 845-868.
[35] For an interesting analysis see: Kathleen Smith Kuolowski, "Antimasonry Reexamined: Social Bases of the Grass-Roots Party." *Journal of American History* 71, no. 2 (Sept. 1984), 269-293.

At the same time, there still lurked throughout the Yankees of Boston a strong sentiment that this town is "for us" and not for "them." The Irish, though still relatively few in numbers—the great immigration was to get underway in the 1840s—were already moving into Boston and competing for work in the suburban industrial towns. They tended to be poor and live on "the wrong side of the tracks" and many people—even the supposedly "liberal" people—detested them and their Roman Catholic religion.

The Ursuline sisters had, as early as 1818, established a convent at nearby Charlestown and began a school which attracted both Catholic and Unitarian children whose parents did not like the influence of the strict Calvinists over other educational institutions. There was, however, resentment by many workers against the Irish who often competed with them for work. Their prejudices were fanned by rumors of dire papist plots and by the fiery anti-Catholic preaching of Lyman Beecher at the conservative Park Street Church in Boston. The result was a preconceived plan to destroy the nunnery and to drive out the offending Catholic sisters. In one of America's more shocking examples of bigotry, the whole establishment was torched and burned to the ground. The sisters sought to rebuild elsewhere but threats of further violence eventually forced the organization to move to Montreal.[36]

Another, equally shocking example of bigotry came on October 21, 1835 when William Lloyd Garrison (1805-79) was invited to speak to the Boston Female Anti-Slavery Society. Although by this time slavery was no longer common in the north, there were apparently plenty of people—many gentlemen of property and standing—who would hear nothing of abolitionism. It became clear from the time Garrison arrived that there would be trouble. A large gang of men had gathered threateningly and there was even talk of lynching the speaker. The mayor tried to step in but was ineffective and for a time it appeared that Garrison might actually be severely hurt or even killed. His clothes were largely ripped from his body, but he survived because some men took him in tow and virtually carried him to a nearby prison where he was incarcerated in order to save his life.[37]

---

[36] For an excellent description of the event, see: Howard Mumford Jones, ed., *op. cit.*, 177-183.
[37] For Garrison's own description of the event see: *Ibid.*, 184-189.

This event, which, of course, was **the** news of the day, must have profoundly affected both Therese and Edward, but it was Therese who was to become far more vocal about slavery and women's rights. It is difficult to believe, however, that it was not unsettling to a good churchman to realize that racial hatred was so deeply ingrained in a society which was still so piously disposed. There is reason to believe, in fact, that in all three instances (anti-Masonic fears, the burning of the convent and the attack upon Garrison) one of the chief causes **was** religion.

Religion, of course, stood on the other side as well. One of Garrison's supporters, who lived in nearby Haverhill and then Amesbury and who for a time edited *The American Manufacturer* in Boston, was the poet John Greenleaf Whittier (1807-1892). As an ardent Quaker and pacifist, he was thoroughly committed to the cause of abolitionism and wrote many poems directed to that end. Andrew Jackson and his followers, because of their willingness to tolerate slavery for the sake of the Union, were anathema to him. Although considered today by the intellectual establishment as a second rate poet, his role as a poet-radical should not be overlooked. Far from being the simple rural singer of "Snow Bound" and "Barefoot Boy," he might better be remembered as a leader of the opposition who, with Garrison and a host of others, attempted to turn a nation rife with prejudice onto a new path.

In any event, it would have been impossible for the Robinsons to have avoided the controversy about slavery which swirled about Boston as the first small, but virulent premonitions of the gathering storm which was to engulf the nation, became evident. It was really impossible to avoid taking some stand on the issue, so overwhelming did it become during the decades which followed. James Russell Lowell (1819-1891), another New England poet, wrote these lines in a poem called "The Present Crisis" to protest American involvement in the Mexican War, but they might just have well been written about the issue of slavery:

> Once to every man and nation comes the moment to decide,
> In the strife of Truth with Falsehood, for the good or evil side;
> Some great cause, God's new Messiah, offering each the bloom or blight,
> Parts the goats upon the left hand, and the sheep upon the right,
> And the choice goes by forever 'twixt that darkness and that light...
>
> Careless seems the great Avenger; history's pages but record

> One death-grapple in the darkness 'twixt old systems and the Word;
> Truth forever on the scaffold, Wrong forever on the throne,—
> Yet that scaffold sways the Future, and, behind the dim unknown,
> Standeth God within the shadow, keeping watch above his own.[38]

Where did the Robinsons stand? Therese eventually makes herself quite clear, but Edward's work is more circumspect. We shall have to read it most carefully to find any clues.

The last months of 1836 were critical ones in the lives of the Robinsons. On September 19, Therese gave birth to her third son, Edward, and there must have been great concern that as his two older brothers he would die in infancy. Happily, however, he survived the perils of childhood and lived to full maturity.

And then there was the great trip to Palestine. Therese had wanted to go with Edward on the venture, but clearly with two children that was now impossible. In any event, Smith and Robinson must have been in correspondence and decided upon 1837-38 as the propitious moment. Plans were discussed; dates were set.

It was just at that moment that Robinson received a communication from a newly formed theological institution in New York which was looking for a professor to teach the Bible. Would Edward be interested? Edward actually went to New York to survey the situation and talk to some of the founders. Then, in a long letter which is still extant, Edward accepted their offer with one important proviso: that he be allowed to postpone his arrival for a year until he had completed his already planned trip to Palestine. Fortuitously, the New York Theological Seminary agreed. The new institution, which would very soon change its name to Union Theological Seminary in the City of New York, hired a temporary replacement and E. R. prepared for the most important and most productive journey of his life.

---

[38] James Russell Lowell, "The Present Crisis," *The Poetical Works of James R. Lowell, Complete in Two Volumes* (Boston: Ticknor and Fields, 1864), I, 160-161. Garret Horder later excerpted lines from this poem to produce the famous hymn, "Once to every man and nation."

Chapter Seven

PALESTINE AND THE BOOK

Headlines and Notices: 1837-1840

1837   Victoria crowned queen of England.
             Samuel F. B. Morse demonstrates the telegraph.
             Daguerre invents an early form of photography.
             Martin Van Buren becomes President.
             Michigan becomes a state; Iowa, a territory.
             The Panic of 1837 sweeps the nation.
             New School and Old School Presbyterians split and remain separate until 1868.
             Grover Cleveland and Dwight L. Moody are born.
             Theodore Weld publishes *The Bible Against Slavery*.

1838   The first steamship crosses the Atlantic.
             The Underground Railroad is organized.
             Henry Adams and John Wilkes Booth are born.

1839   The first real bicycle is invented.
             Mahmud II, the Sultan of the Ottoman Empire, dies.
             The second Mohammed Ali crisis occurs.
             Matthias Jakob Schleiden formulates the cell theory in physiology.

1840   Samuel Cunard founds the first important transatlantic steamship line.
Sir William Grove invents the incandescent electric light.
The Treaty of London (England, Austria, Prussia, and Russia) attempts to impose a settlement on Mohammed Ali.
Finney publishes *Views of Sanctification*, a work which expresses his perfectionist views.

In the summer of 1837 the Robinson family set sail for Europe. They traveled with passports issued on June 21 and signed by John Forsyth, Secretary of State. One passport was issued in the name of Edward alone, presumably so that he could take it with him on his Near Eastern adventure. The second, enclosed within the first is for "Edward Robinson accompanied by his Lady, two children, and female servant." It is interesting that they were wealthy enough to employ a servant, though it must be admitted that at that time servants were not very rare for anyone of means.

They sailed on July 17, probably from New York. The word "sailed" is accurate, for regular steamship travel across the Atlantic did not begin until the next year. Up to that time there had been many steamships used for shorter runs, but steam required a great deal of fuel and before 1838, steamship travel over long distances was impossible because the amount of coal needed was larger than the ship's capacity. Only more efficient systems and the development of the screw propeller made steam travel across the Atlantic practical.

In any event, it must have seemed a very long and tiring trip, particularly with two children, including one infant. This time, however, the Robinsons did not have to wait for the right winds to land in France. Instead, they disembarked in Liverpool, England on August 18, thus crossing in but a month. While in England they spent their time in Leamington, Oxford, and then London. In the last stop he was able to contact "some veterans in oriental travel" from whom he received "many hints of information" which were of use to him on his trip to Palestine.[1]

---

[1] Robinson, *Biblical Researches,* I, 2.

Passport stamps on September 8 were issued in London for further travel to Belgium. From there the passports reveal that they journeyed to Aachen and then to Coblenz. According to his account in *Biblical Researches* he also went to Frankfort, though the passport stamp indicates Erfurt as the next stop. The Frankfort stop is significant because their itinerary thus allowed them time to dip down to Darmstadt, only a short distance from Frankfort, for a visit at the home of Leander Van Ess, who has already been mentioned briefly in connection with Edward's first trip to Germany.

Van Ess was, to say the least, an extraordinary character. At one time a monk in Marburg, he became concerned with the lack of Bibles translated into vernacular German for Roman Catholic lay people. As a result, he himself prepared his own translation and proceeded to distribute Bibles at a very minimal cost to thousands of German Christians. In this he was supported not only by some Catholics but even more by the British Foreign Bible Society. He, too, tried to foster Bible Societies in Germany among Catholics, but the Vatican curia strongly resisted such efforts and eventually even placed his translation on the Index of Prohibited Books. Protestant support continued for a time but this too withered away, largely because the British Foreign Bible Society did not want Bibles with the Apocrypha distributed in its name. Van Ess eventually moved to Darmstadt, a sick and somewhat bitter man.

Van Ess' other claim to fame was as a "bookman." Particularly because of the closing of the monasteries in Protestant sections of Germany, he was able to acquire, over the years, a vast collection of books and pamphlets from monastic and other libraries. Although he had already sold part of his collection to Sir Thomas Phillips in 1824, it was in 1829, particularly because of the illness of his sister, that he decided to sell the rest of his collection to acquire needed cash. The process of selling such a vast library was not quick or easy; several university libraries decided against purchase.

Finally, in 1838 the library of some 14,000 items—incunabula, Bibles, books, pamphlets—was crated and sent to the newly formed New York (Union) Theological Seminary in New York. Thus was created the first genuine research library for theology in the United States. Union's library has been at the forefront of theological collections ever since. President McAuley described the acquisition in the following way:

> This collection of books was commenced in the Monastery of Saint Mary, in Paderhorn, in Westphalia, during the time of the Reformation. At that time, the writings of the Reformers, and those of their opponents, were collected by the monastery, and kept in a room, the door of which bore the inscription, "PROHIBITED BOOKS," and the key of it being kept by the Superior of the Society of Monks. When the King of Prussia issued his edict for the suppression of the monasteries, the monks divided among themselves the moveable property of their institutions, and Dr. Van Ess, who had, in the Monastery of St. Mary, the charge of the "Prohibited books," took them as his share of the division. Thus there came into his possession this cabinet of rare works, containing, among them, at least 500 productions that bear the name of Luther. This was the commencement of our Library.[2]

Although there is no correspondence or other evidence to confirm Robinson's part in this acquisition, it appears not only possible but probable that E. R. played a major role in examining the collection and negotiating its purchase. Certainly he was the right man to be involved. He had been librarian at Andover and was responsible for extensive book purchases there. He knew the value of books and how to negotiate purchases. It is not surprising that he was also to serve as librarian for New York's fledgling institution.

According to George Lewis Prentiss who was, after 1851, Robinson's minister and who wrote the first full history of Union Seminary, the purchase came about in the following way:

> Prof. Calvin E. Stowe, just returned from Europe, was advised of the fact (that the Van Ess collection was for sale). In a letter from Lane Seminary, to Dr. Robinson, April 3, 1837, he advised the purchase of this unique collection by the New York Theological Seminary. Terrible as were the times, Dr. Robinson, on his departure for Europe and the Holy Land, in July, was instructed to obtain the refusal of the collection. After a careful examination of

---

[2] Milton McC. Gatch, ed., '*So precious a foundation': the library of Leander Van Ess at the Burke Library of Union Theological Seminary in the City of New York* (New York: Union Theological Seminary and the Grollier Club, 1996), 67.

the books by Mr. Phillip Wolff, of Erlangen University, (a brother of Mrs. Gurdon Buck of this city,) the purchase was effected, in April 1838, for 10,000 florins. It had cost Dr. Van Ess 50,000 florins. Its whole cost to the Seminary, when it arrived in October, all charges paid, was $5,078.08.[3]

The best guess, then, is that sometime in the middle of September 1837 E. R. visited Van Ess, inspected the collection, and began negotiation for purchase. If he had done nothing else for Union, he should still be remembered as one of the Seminary's primary benefactors. For $5,000 borrowed from President McAuley—which was a great deal of money for an institution that had scarcely opened its doors—Union became rich in what really matters to an academic institution. Medieval texts, rare Bibles, early Protestant writings and tracts taken from the "prohibited collection" of the monastery became available to generations of Union students. It was, as the first President of Union called it, a "precious foundation."

As the passport indicates, the Robinsons soon journeyed on through Erfurt to Berlin. In fact, it would appear that Edward and Therese spent considerable time in the latter city, undoubtedly with plans to consult with geographers like Carl Ritter and read ever more travel literature in preparation for his trip. Unfortunately, Ritter was away on a trip to Greece, but other scholars were certainly available. There Edward was to spend several weeks preparing for the exploration which was to come.

Surely it was a very happy time for Therese as she reunited with her family and her own Germanic culture. There was doubtless much satisfaction in being able to introduce her children to the world in which she herself was raised. Mary had survived her infancy there and so, in fact, would young Edward. Despite Robinson's promise to return to Union after a year in Palestine, they would not return to New York until 1840. Although the children were Americans, both came to regard, in many ways, Germany as their second home.

---

[3] George Lewis Prentiss, *The Union Theological Seminary in the City of New York: Historical and Biographical Sketches of its First Fifty years* (New York: Anson D. F. Randolph and Co., 1889), 75. Prentiss is actually quoting from an article by T. F. Crane so the information is second-hand. Because Prentiss knew Robinson, however, he probably had heard the story first-hand too. It is doubtful that he would have included this information had he known differently.

To Egypt

On the 13th of November 1837, E. R. left Berlin and his family and headed off to high adventure. His first stop was in Halle where he consulted with Gesenius, Tholuck, and Roediger who made many suggestions about topics to consider. From there, enduring storms of cold rain and snow, he traveled through Vienna to Trieste. Finally, the rains and winds stopped, the sky turned Mediterranean blue, and Robinson boarded a steamer for Alexandria.

Egypt was, of course, a part of the Ottoman Empire, a huge and ungainly collection of states stretching from what is now Iraq to Algeria, from the lower Nile to the Balkans. It had begun in the 14th century as a small tribal holding in Turkey but, through conquest, had spread rapidly until, by 1683 it was seriously threatening Vienna and the Holy Roman Empire. Happily for the Europeans, the Turkic offensive was turned back, but for a time the Ottomans controlled Hungary, Bulgaria, and the rest of the Balkans. The Black Sea became an Ottoman Lake.

During the 18th century the European powers made great advances militarily and politically and were gradually able to force the Ottomans out of much of southeastern Europe. In the 1830s the Greek revolt led to a freeing of that people from Turkic control. Ottoman diplomatic and military weakness, fostered by a failure to keep up with the times, led the Western powers to regard the Ottoman Empire as "the sick man of Europe." Russia, in particular, began to eye the eastern holdings of the Ottomans with the hope that she could win, through conquest, a corridor to the Arabian Sea. France, impelled by the victories of Napoleon in North Africa, also dreamed of diplomatic, if not military, control as a way of isolating British holdings in India. The French also, during this period, grabbed Algeria as their own, beginning a colonial story which is still not completed.

The English in their turn saw the dangers of a weakened Ottoman Empire and sought to prop it up in order to prevent Russian expansion and French hegemony. The Ottomans also began to see their own weaknesses and sought to modernize, but modernization meant for them primarily improved military training and armament. There was little sense that the whole state needed radical reorganization in order to survive.

The truth of the matter was that the Ottoman Empire had been gained by military conquest and political machination and had little more than military power to hold it together. Islam did help to unite some of the provinces, but it must be remembered that much of the Balkan area was Christian and hence quite averse to Islamic law. Moreover, ethnic and historical differences among Islamic countries were hardly destroyed by a common allegiance to Islam. The Ottoman Empire, then, was not a tightly unified reality, but a congeries of ethnic and political groups held together by a gradually weakening military force.

In 1808 Mahmud II, a reform-minded Sultan, came to the throne, intent upon modernizing the Empire. Although his power was theoretically supreme, his task was not easy, for he was opposed by the conservative aristocrats and by the Janissaries, a military organization which had once been the "new army" but which had since become the center of reactionary attitudes. Eventually, in 1826, Mahmud was able to destroy the Janissaries, but he never did build the strong military force he envisioned.

He found himself harassed by Balkan revolutionaries, European diplomats, and by major forces within his Empire and thus only partially completed the massive changes he envisioned. It is also the case that because of his isolation he probably never understood the motives of the several European powers which maneuvered him first one way and then another.

In Egypt, the governor was Mohammed Ali, an Albanian appointed to his position by the Sultan. He too sought reform and, because Napoleon's invasion had severely weakened the old aristocracy of Egypt, he was able to transform the army of Egypt into a much more modern fighting force modeled on the French system. Although he pledged his loyalty to the Sultan in Istanbul, clearly he was a force to be reckoned with, for he had done for his army what the Sultan intended but could never fully accomplish.

During the Greek War of Independence, the Sultan found himself militarily weak and called in Mohammed Ali and his Egyptian forces to aid in the struggle. The latter intervened successfully, putting down, for the moment, the revolt. As a reward, he asked for Greece to be placed under his aegis. When the Greeks ultimately gained their freedom, he demanded Syria instead. The Sultan temporized, fearing Mohammed Ali's power and the threat to the Sultanate were he to take over such a large area. Mohammed Ali, however, grew tired of the Sultan's delays and marched his army into

Syria anyway. A major battle ensued between the troops of the Sultan and those of Muhammed Ali. The result was disastrous for the Sultan. Had it not been for the intervention of the European powers, particularly Russia, the whole of the Ottoman Empire could have been Muhammed Ali's. That this did not happen proved to be a boon to the West, for the Ottomans remained militarily weak and hence subject to the various diplomatic and military pressures which the European States could exert.[4]

In any event, Robinson arrived in Egypt just at the time when Muhammed Ali controlled Syria-Palestine (1832-39) and wished to curry Western favor, particularly French support for his venture. As a result it was more possible than in times past to travel more or less freely in the Holy Land and to receive some modicum of Arab hospitality. This is not to say that such travel was simple or without danger. Clearly there were many more difficulties than Robinson even suggests in his book, but at least the momentary victory of Ali meant that the United States could have a Consul in Palestine and that missionaries had a little more freedom to operate in the Holy City. It is very doubtful whether Robinson could have done any excavating, even if he had wanted to, but at least he was able to travel the land with some sense that there was an American diplomatic presence to defend him.

Palestine, at the time, was a long neglected land. Lying between the two powers of Egypt and what is now called Turkey, the Holy Land, so precious to Christianity, Judaism, and Islam, was underpopulated and radically underdeveloped. There were probably only 300,000 people in the whole country. Most of the population was Sunni Muslim, but there were also significant Jewish, Christian, and Druze minorities. Jerusalem had about 14,000 inhabitants; Hebron, 5,000-10,000; Bethlehem and Nazareth about 3,000 each.[5] Cities which had kindled the imagination of western Christians for centuries were, in fact, small, impoverished villages devastated by disease, tribal feuding, and political oppression. International trade and commerce were almost nonexistent, because, among other things, Palestine

---

[4] Given the limited communication at the time, it is amazing how much Americans did know about Mohammed Ali. See, for instance, "Mehemet Ali and his Policy," *Christian Advocate and Journal* XX. 16 (Nov. 26, 1845) and XX. 17 (Dec. 3, 1845).

[5] Arnold Blumberg, *Zion Before Zionism: 1830-1880* (Syracuse: Syracuse University Press, 1985), 8.

had no seaports worthy of the name. The harbor at Jaffa was silted up and those who arrived by ship there had to clamber onto the Andromeda rocks in the harbor and then either wade in or be carried on the back of some burly Arab. The port at Acre, once the glory of the land, was almost as bad. On shore, matters did not improve. In 1838, when Robinson traveled the country, there were trails but not one true road![6] The first true road, from Jaffa to Jerusalem, was not constructed until 1867, along an old pilgrim trail.

Moreover, none of the trails was at all safe, for they were frequented by bandits and tribes which demanded whatever it was the traveler had. One is reminded of the street gangs of today and their "territory" which one enters at one's own peril.

> The stranger who came to Palestine as a pilgrim . . . was sharply reminded that he had better adjust to reality, or face the gravest danger. The newly arrived European, whether a pilgrim at Jaffa heading for Jerusalem or a merchant at Acre hoping to visit Nazareth or Safed, made it his business to buy protection.
>
> All of the principal towns of Ottoman Palestine were walled. These walls, manned by Turkish soldiers and by locally conscripted Arabs, were vital to the security of urban populations planted in the midst of an extremely dangerous countryside. The gates of the cities were locked at night, and no one entered or departed between sunset and dawn.
>
> Protection for the traveler who ventured outside the walls usually could be purchased from a number of sources, more or less trustworthy. The consuls of foreign powers were most dependable. Local merchants, who had learned the techniques required to ensure the safety of their own merchandise as it traveled inland, were almost as safe. Least dependable was the self-advertised dragoman, interpreter and guide, or cicerone. The latter was likely to be a thief who would strip the traveler of all he possessed and leave him to fate.[7]

Robinson does not overemphasize these dangers, though he must have been keenly aware of them. The modern reader, at any rate, should remember them as Robinson describes his journeys and his investigations. This was not

---

[6] *Ibid.*, 3.
[7] *Ibid.*, 6-7.

a place, like civilized Germany, where one could take long strolls around the countryside. It was not a place where one could really depend upon local officials or law enforcement agencies to take the part of the honest tourist. Although Mohammed Ali might have wished to curry the favor of the "Franks," many local leaders were far more suspicious and fearful of anyone from the outside world. Everyone wanted bribes; some desired only to express their own sadistic power. One must stand in awe of Robinson's sheer bravery in the face of a civilization which really did not have any sympathy for what he was doing and for Eli Smith's ability to arrange everything so that, in fact, there appear to have been few major problems anywhere.

Robinson and Smith, of course, were by no means the first travelers to record their observations and discoveries in the "land of the Book."[8] Since ancient times, Palestine has known innumerable pilgrims, crusaders, and merchants who have left for the world accounts of their journeys.[9] Frederick Bliss, in his Ely Lectures of 1903, describes in some detail the extensive travel literature from earliest times to the end of the nineteenth century.[10] In the course of the work he summarizes the works of many different travelers, but it is only to Robinson that he accords a full chapter. The reason seems clear, for Robinson was by far the best trained and most knowledgeable of any of the writers to visit the Holy Land.[11] Furthermore, while several others, such as Carsten Niebuhr,[12] Ulrich Seetzen[13] and Johannes Ludwig

---

[8] For a bibliography of late 18th and early 19th century books on Palestine see the appendix.

[9] Robinson, *Biblical researches,* III, First Appendix, pp. 3-28. In this appendix, E. R. provides a wonderful bibliography of Palestinian travel books from ancient times until 1838.

[10] Frederick Jones Bliss, *The Development of Palestine Exploration being the Ely Lecture for 1903* (New York: Charles Scribner's Sons, 1906).

[11] John Lloyd Stephens, who first wrote simply under the name "An American," is a good example of the typical writer. He followed, in 1835, much the same route as Robinson was to take and writes charmingly about his adventures, but with none of the precision or depth of analysis which E. R. was able to offer. See:[John Lloyd Stephens] *Incidents of Travel in Egypt, Arabia Petraea and the Holy Land* 2 Vols. (New York: Harper and Bros., 1837).

[12] Carsten Niebuhr, *Beschreibung von Arabien aus eigenen Beobachtunger und im Lande selbst gesammelten Nachrichten* (Koperhagen: Moller, 1772).

[13] Ulrich Jasper Seetzen, *Reisen durch Syrien, Palastina, Phonicia, die Trans-Jordan-Lander Arabia Petraea und Unter-Aegypten,* 3 Vols. (Berlin: G. Reimer, 1845-59).

Burckhardt,[14] really were in the Holy Land tangentially, i.e. for other purposes, Robinson was there specifically to study the land in order to illuminate his knowledge of the Bible.[15]

His plan was to study the physical and social geography of Palestine in order to understand more fully Biblical history. As a consequence, his investigations were much more thorough, often taking him off the usual pilgrim paths, and far better informed than even the best of his predecessors. He had read the works of earlier travelers with care and worked to confirm or deny their opinions. Those he had not read, he made a point to consult upon returning to Germany. He also took meticulous notes, often staying up late to record everything he had seen. To check on his accuracy, Eli Smith kept a separate record which they only compared with E. R.'s voluminous notes after the trip was over. The result was by far the most accurate description of the Palestinian landscape west of the Jordan ever recorded up to that time.

What he did not see and describe on his first trip, he made it a point to visit when he returned in 1852. His aim was not an easily skimmed work for the masses, but a specialized study for Biblical scholars who need to visualize the landscape when interpreting texts. That his work (which is in four volumes of 600+ pages)[16] also gained a measure of popularity among non-scholarly readers was always particularly surprising to him. That scholars and archaeologists still return to Robinson's work for details and insights in the 1990s would, I think, also be to him surprising but much more gratifying.

One should not infer from the remarks above, however, that E. R. started out intending to write the "great work" on Palestine. Indeed, he admits at the outset that his aim was far more limited:

> In respect to our further journey, it may be proper to remark, that I entered upon it without the slightest anticipation of the results to

---

[14] John Lewis Burkhardt, *Travels in Syria and the Holy Land* (London: J. Murray, 1822). See also Burkhardt, *Notes on the Bedouins and Wahabys* (London: H. Colburn, 1831).

[15] For a bibliography of books by Robinson's 19th century predecessors, see the appendix.

[16] The number of volumes is somewhat problematic, for sometimes volumes II and III are bound together. Volume IV is his account of his journey in 1852. Originally the supplement to his first volumes was also printed separately.

which we were providentially led. My first motive had been simply the gratification of personal feelings. As in the case of most of my countrymen, especially in New England, the scenes of the Bible had made a deep impression upon my mind from the earliest childhood; and afterward in riper years this feeling had grown into a strong desire to visit in person the places so remarkable in the history of the human race . . . With all this, in my own case, there had subsequently become connected a scientific motive. I have long meditated the preparation of a work on Biblical Geography; and wished to satisfy myself by personal observation, as to many points on which I could find no information in the books of travelers. This indeed, grew to be the main object of our journey—the nucleus around which all our inquiries and observations clustered. But I never thought of adding anything to the former stock of knowledge on these subjects; I never dreamed of anything like discoveries in this field.[17]

Because of his limited original aims, he took with him few instruments: an ordinary surveyor's and two pocket compasses, a thermometer, telescopes, and measuring tapes.[18] He also carried with him a limited number of books for reference. Most of his supporting references were simply in his memory; it was really that prodigious memory which made the trip successful. In any event, the real significance of the journey only began to unfold slowly to the travelers as they progressed. Gradually they came to see how inaccurate many of their predecessors had been and how little was really known about many areas they traversed. The travelers became, to their own surprise, explorers and discoverers.

Before E. R. entered the Sinai peninsula to begin his investigations, however, he spent several weeks as a sightseer. His first stop, after leaving Trieste was Greece, where he remained for seventeen days, touring Athens and a few other parts of Hellas—standing where Paul had stood on the Areopagus and imagining amid the poverty and desolation of contemporary Greece the glories of antiquity. Then he boarded another steamer and saw from shipboard several other Greek islands. Finally, on December 30, they docked in Alexandria. It was his first real encounter with a non-European culture. The culture shock was immediate:

---

[17] Robinson, *Biblical Researches*, I, 46-47.
[18] *Ibid.*, I, 47.

> The moment we set foot on shore, we needed no further conviction, that we had left Europe and were now in the oriental world. We found ourselves in the midst of a dense crowd, through which we made our way with difficulty,— Egyptians, Turks, Arabs, Copts, Negroes, Franks; complexions of white, black, olive, bronze, brown, and almost all other colours; long beards and no beards; all costumes and no costume; silks and rags; wide robes and no robes; women muffled in shapeless black mantles, their faces wholly covered except peep-holes for the eyes; endless confusion, and a clatter and medley of tongues, Arabic, Turkish, Greek, Italian, French, German, and English, as the case might be; strings of huge camels in single file with high loads; little donkeys, bridled and saddled, each guided by a sore-eyed Arab boy with a few words of Sailor-English, who thrusts his little animal *nolens volens* between your legs;—such is a faint picture of the scene in which we found ourselves on landing in Alexandria.[19]

One might think that E. R., good Connecticut Puritan that he was, might immediately begin to inveigh against Islam, the religion of Egypt. Such was the style of most writers of the time. John Wilson, writing a few years later, began his trip to the Holy Land from India and started his description of his adventure with some critical and intemperate remarks about the religion of the land where he began:

> INDIA has not been the scene of special communings of God with man; and its gigantic mountains and wide-spreading valleys have not been trodden by the feet of patriarchs, prophets, and apostles, and of God himself made manifest in the flesh. Though, for thousands of years, it has counted its numerous sages, renowned in the eastern world for the depth and subtlety of their inquiries and speculations, it has made no progress of itself in the attainment of that wisdom of greatest price, the beginning of which is the fear of the Lord. The prince of evil has reigned over its fair and luxuriant provinces, and amongst its countless inhabitants, with almost uncontrolled power and authority . . .[20]

---

[19] *Ibid.,* I, 20.
[20] John Wilson, *The Lands of the Bible Visited and Described* (Edinburgh: Wiliam Whyte and Co., 1847), I, 1-2. Actually, despite this diatribe, the book is quite useful and informative.

By way of contrast, E. R. says little about Islam. His first experience is of a festival to celebrate the end of Ramadan which he describes as a day of "joy and rejoicing." There is no judgment, only recognition that it exists.[21] This is not to say that he has no criticism of Egyptian life and culture which he describes as based upon the motto, "Do not do today what you can put off until tomorrow." He deplores the squalor of the cities and the horrors and abominations of the slave market. He saves some of his most critical remarks, however, for Mohammed Ali, Egypt's governor.

> This extraordinary man, with native talents which in other circumstances might have made him the Napoleon of the age, has accumulated in Egypt a large amount of wealth and power; but he has done it only for himself,—not for the country, nor even for his family. He has built up an army and fleet, not by husbanding and enlarging the resources of Egypt, but by draining them almost to exhaustion . . . With barbarian eagerness, he has overlooked the planting of the seed, and grasps only after the ripe fruit. Not a step has been taken for the education and improvement of the people at large; but all the schools established are intended solely to train up young men in his own service.[22]

In many respects, this comment is uncharacteristic of Robinson who generally avoids political judgments. Certainly, his journals reveal few critical remarks about the rulers of Germany. This particular bit of criticism is especially ironic, for Robinson himself admits that it is Mohammed Ali who has really made his investigations possible.

> In one respect, the energy of Muhammed Aly deserves all praise; although the severity by which it is attended may not always be the most justifiable. He has rendered the countries under his sway secure; so that travelers, whether Orientals or Franks, may pass in their own dress throughout Egypt and Syria, and also among the Bedawîn of the adjacent deserts, with the same degree of safety as in many parts of civilized Europe.[23]

---

[21] Robinson, *Biblical Researches*, I, 21.
[22] *Ibid.*, I, 41-42.
[23] *Ibid.*, I, 43. The peculiar diacritical marks are derived from John Pickering's system devised for native American languages. It should be noted that Therese Robinson translated Pickering's book on Indian languages into German.

After a brief stay in Alexandria, Robinson, on January 5, sailed on the canal to the Nile and Cairo. After a short sojourn there he took a boat up the Nile to view antiquities in Thebes. The plan was to sail on to Aswan, some 140 miles further, but bad winds so slowed the voyage that at Thebes they had to conclude their voyage upstream, stopping for a time to visit Luxor and Karnak and the Tombs of the Kings. On the way back they visited Dendera, the Tombs of Beni Hassan, etc., returning to Cairo on February 28. By this time Eli Smith had arrived and they began preparing seriously for the long trip ahead. Despite the demands of preparation, during their twelve days in Cairo they found time to visit many of the antiquities around Egypt's capital, including, of course, the pyramids and the sphinx as well as the sites of Heliopolis, Leontopolis, and Memphis.

Robinson's descriptions of all these places are rather brief, even perfunctory. He mentions various Biblical connections and describes ancient Egyptian architecture in general, but he also knows that all of this is merely introductory. The meat of the book lies elsewhere and so he provides only enough to encourage the reader to continue on. Soon the travelogue will be over and the serious business of careful description will begin.

It is interesting that throughout these volumes which chronicle his adventure, very little is said about his companion and co-author Eli Smith. He says nothing about the fact that Smith was recently bereaved, having lost his wife of only a few years to death. Neither does he spend much space describing what Smith himself may have discovered or opined. In fact, he devotes more space describing the bedouin guides than Smith's contribution to the expedition. For the most part, his eyes are on the landscape, not upon their very important and productive relationship.

To Suez and Beyond

After several days of preparation, buying a tent and water bags and provisions and engaging various Arabs with their camels and dromedaries, Robinson and Smith left Cairo on March 12. After three days journey, they arrived in Suez. This was a very important stop for Robinson because he was particularly interested in Israel's Red Sea crossing and examined the area with some care in order to determine just where such an event as is described in the Bible could have been possible.

It is interesting that he never considers questioning the Biblical story, even though he knows the problems involved. His intent throughout is to illuminate and not criticize the Bible. He simply looks for the most probable way to picture what the Bible describes. There is no intention to improve upon the Biblical story but only to visualize the narrative. For instance, because the Bible says Israel traveled three days before reaching the Red Sea, he eliminates Cairo as a point of departure and chooses instead the land of Goshen.

> The whole number therefore probably amounted to two and a half millions, and certainly to not less than two millions. Now the usual day's march of the best appointed armies, both in ancient and modern times, is not estimated higher than fourteen English, or twelve geographical miles, and it cannot be supposed that the Israelites, encumbered with women and children and flocks, would be able to accomplish much more.[24]

Hence they could not have come from Cairo, for that would have constituted at least a five day march. The preposterous nature of a picture of two and one half million people marching through the desert chased by an army of at most a few hundred is never mentioned by him.

He does see, however, that they must have crossed the Red Sea at a very narrow point, for that many people would have taken some time crossing any area and the Bible only allows them a few hours.

> As the Israelites numbered more than two million of persons, besides flocks and herds, they would of course be able to pass but slowly. If the part dry were broad enough to enable them to cross in a body one thousand abreast, which would require a space of more than half a mile in breadth, (and is perhaps the largest supposition admissible,) still the column would be more than two thousand persons in depth; and in all probability could not have extended less than two miles. It would then have occupied at least an hour passing over its own length, or in entering the sea, and deducting this from the largest time intervening before the Egyptians must also have entered the sea, there will remain only

---

[24] *Ibid.*, I, 75.

> time enough, under the circumstances, for the body of the Israelites to have passed at the most over a space of three or four miles. This circumstance is fatal to the hypothesis of their having crossed from Wady Tawârik; since the breadth of the sea at that point, according to Niebuhr's measurement, is three German or twelve geogr. miles, equal to a whole days' journey.[25]

This passage reveals both the great strength and great weakness of Robinson's method. On the one hand, he looks at the Biblical text with rational eyes, unwilling to accept easy solutions to difficult problems. And the reasoning is, of course, correct. No group of two and one half million people could cross a twelve mile stretch in a couple of hours. On the other hand, it never seems to have occurred to him that perhaps the Biblical figures are greatly inflated. He knows that under no conditions could that many people have found enough water in the Sinai desert to meet even their most basic needs, but he is still unwilling to doubt the Biblical story.

We must, however, remember that theological conditions were such that it may have been impossible for him to raise the question of Biblical inaccuracy. The most he could do, given the attitude of his church at the time, was to present the facts as he saw them and provide for the reader the most rational conclusion. He remained a literalist, but one has a feeling that he too was scratching his head about the apparent impossibility of it all. Two and one half million people drinking from twelve wells at Elim: one wonders. As Robinson says,

> But how they could have obtained a *sufficiency* of water during their whole stay in the peninsula and their subsequent wanderings in the desert, even where no want of water is mentioned, is a mystery which I am unable to solve; unless we admit the supposition, that water was anciently far more abundant in these regions, than at present. As we saw the peninsula, a body of two millions of men could not subsist there a week, without drawing their supplies of water, as well as of provisions, from a great distance.[26]

---

[25] *Ibid.,* I, 84. For a later assessment of the problem see: "Crossing the Red Sea," *New-York Observer* XXXIII, 18 (May 3, 1855), 141.
[26] *Ibid.,* I, 106.

On March 16th the party left Suez, destined for St. Catherine's Monastery at the traditional site of Mt. Sinai. The journey took seven days, with one day without travel for the observance of the Sabbath, a practice which they were able to maintain throughout their trip. On the way, Robinson visited a few ruins, inspected strange inscriptions, and speculated about the sites of Merabah and Elim, two watering places where the Israelites were said to have stopped. Most of the time, however, was spent enduring the desolate and arid landscape of the Sinai peninsula. Happily through the journey, the guides proved themselves to be not only trustworthy but immensely helpful. E. R. describes them as: "good-natured obliging fellows, ready and desirous to do for us every thing we wished, so far as it was in their power."[27] Robinson and Smith, in their turn, seem to have treated the guides with the utmost respect and kindness and hence won the same in return. There is no hint that the Arab guides were in any way looked down upon because they were not European Christians.

Finally, after a grueling week in which one camel "broke down" and eventually died, the party arrived at the famous monastery. As they approached Horeb, Robinson made, or thought he made, an important discovery:

> The front of Horeb rose like a wall before us; and one can approach quite to the foot and touch the mount. Directly before its base is the deep bed of a torrent, by which in the rainy season the waters of el-Leja and the mountains around the recess, pass down eastward across the plain, forming the commencement of Wady esh-Sheikh, which then issues by an opening through the cliffs of the eastern mountain,—a fine broad valley affording the only easy access to the plain and convent.—As we crossed the plain our feelings were strongly affected, at finding here so unexpected a spot so entirely adapted to the Scriptural account of the giving of the law. No traveller has described this plain, nor even mentioned it except in a slight and general manner . . .[28]

This is the sort of discovery which greatly pleased Robinson, for it allowed him the opportunity to visualize more clearly the ancient story. As he rode toward the monastery he could see in his mind's eye the Israelite multitudes

---

[27] *Ibid.*, I, 92.
[28] *Ibid.*, I, 131-132.

listening as the words of the commandments were delivered first in the voice of the thunder and then by Moses.

The next day he and Smith returned to the plain for measurements and discovered it to be about two miles long, varying in width from one third to two thirds of a mile. The more they examined the plain the more certain they became that this was the place where Israel received the law. When they climbed Jebel Musa, the traditional site of Sinai, however, they were disappointed that it did not really overlook the plain at all. Therefore, Robinson concludes:

> In the present case, there is not the slightest reason for supposing that Moses had any thing to do with the summit which now bears his name. It is three miles distant from the plain on which the Israelites must have stood; and hidden from it by the intervening peaks of the modern Horeb.[29]

If Jebal Musa was not the mountain of revelation, where was it? E. R. was determined to find out.

> While the monks were here employed in lighting tapers and burning incense, we determined to scale the almost inaccessible peak of es-Sufsâfeh before us, in order to look out upon the plain, and judge for ourselves as to the adaptedness of this part of the mount to the circumstances of Scriptural history. This cliff rises some five hundred feet above the basin; and the distance to the summit is more than half a mile. We first attempted to climb the side in a direct course; but found the rock so smooth and precipitous, that after some falls and more exposures, we were obliged to give it up, and clamber upward along a steep ravine by a more northern and circuitous course. . .
>
> The extreme difficulty and even danger of the ascent, was well rewarded by the prospect that now opened before us. The whole plain er-Râhah lay spread out beneath our feet, with the adjacent Wadys and mountains . . . Our conviction was strengthened, that here or on some one of the adjacent cliffs was the spot, where the Lord "descended in fire" and proclaimed the law . . . We gave ourselves up to the impressions of the aweful scene; and read with a feeling that will never be forgotten, the sublime account of the

---

[29] *Ibid.*, I, 154.

transaction and the commandments there promulgated, in the original words as recorded by the great Hebrew legislator.[30]

Robinson had, in a couple of days, discovered the great site of Israel's covenant! Or had he? He was well aware, of course, that there was a great gap in the ancient tradition between the original event and the identification of this area as the location of Sinai. He also knew that even the most generally accepted traditions connected with the monastery—such as its connection with Helena and Justinian—are entirely suspect.[31] But the temptation to imagine himself at the actual spot was just too great. With very little trouble he convinced himself that simply no other site would do.[32]

This opinion was to cause considerable controversy a few years later, for Miner Kellogg, an American painter of the Holy Land, disagreed with his conclusions about both the identification of Mt. Sinai and the plain where Israel camped. According to Kellogg, Robinson and many others had missed a much larger plain hidden on the other side of the traditional Mt. Sinai and hence had misidentified the sites involved. In a lecture before the Ethnological Society in New York in December of 1847, which Robinson may well have attended,[33] Kellogg argued that the plain where Israel camped was the overlooked valley Es-Saba'iyeh and not Wady Rahah as Robinson claimed. In an article to follow, which he published in *Literary World*, he included a map to illustrate his theory.

Robinson argued that Kellogg's map was exaggerated and misleading,[34] but other, less biased experts—who by and large had never been to the Sinai—were divided on the issue. Kellogg, for his part, eventually produced a painting of Mt. Sinai from Es-Sabiyeh, which stirred up considerable interest. In later life, Kellogg made a virtual career out of presenting his ideas about Sinai to the public.[35]

---

[30] *Ibid.*, I, 157-158.
[31] *Ibid.*, I, 175-184.
[32] Today great uncertainty exists as to the location of the original Mt. Sinai. See: G.I. Davies, "Mount Sinai," *Anchor Bible Dictionary* VI, 47-49.
[33] He was an active member of this society and, for many years, served as its President.
[34] For further discussion by E. R. see: *Bibliotheca Sacra* VII, 23 (Apr. 1849), 366-385.
[35] John Davis, *The Landscape of Belief: Encountering the Holy Land in Nineteenth-Century American Art and Culture* (Princeton: Princeton University Press, 1996), pp.101-126. See also Miner Kellogg, "The Position of Mount Sinai Examined," *Literary World* 55 (Feb. 19, 1848), 44-46. For another contemporary analysis of the problem see

If Robinson did nothing else, he at least raised questions about age-old identifications and engendered interest in site identification. What he did not quite anticipate was the result that some eventually began to question the historicity of the whole story. Did Moses and the people make a covenant at Sinai at all, or was this story a great "foundation myth" with little basis in fact? For Robinson, at least, such a conclusion is not even to be considered. To him, the story and the landscape meshed perfectly.[36]

To Elat and the Holy Land

After what they must have believed was a very productive six days at St. Catherine's monastery, Smith and Robinson decided to move on. On March 29, they were let down from the high window of the monastery (there was no door of access) and, after loading their camels, headed off in the general direction of the Gulf of Akabah. The trip to and stay in Akabah lasted until April 5 and is described in some detail by Robinson. In fact, however, there is little in this segment of the journey except the possible identification of the fountain el-Hudhera as the site of ancient Hazeroth[37] and the probable identification of ancient Elath which is of much interest to the modern reader. The author attempts to make the trek more interesting through personal anecdotes, but it is for the most part just one barren Wadi after another.

The same is true of their trip through the Negev, except that here they entered what Robinson calls *terra incognita*. Up until this point they had followed the same general route as Burckhardt, whom he frequently cites. Now they enter an area which no one up to this point had described in any detail at all. For the modern reader, however, the interminable Wadis and barren desolation are not nearly as interesting as the threat of bandits, which never materialized but may have been real enough, and the terrible sandstorm—a sirocco—the party had endure on April 11.

T.R.G.P., "The Sinai Controversy," *New-York Observer* XXXII, 1 (Jan. 6, 1854), 8.
[36] For a modern discussion of archaeological remains in the Sinai Peninsula see: Ofer Bar-Yosef *et al*, "Sinai" *NEAEHL*, IV, 1384-1403.
[37] Robinson, *Biblical Researches,* I, 223.

Later that day they were surprised to come across the ruins of an ancient city. It was on a level tract ten or twelve acres in extent which they estimated once housed from twelve to fifteen thousand inhabitants. The modern name associated with the area, Ruhaibeh, suggested to Robinson Rehoboth, but he rejected that association as probably incorrect and was content to leave the site unidentified.

They were more successful at el-Khulash, which Robinson identified as ancient Elusa, a city not mentioned in the Bible but referred to by Ptolemy.[38] Even more important, he identified the ruins not far from the wells of Bir es-Seba as ancient Beersheba.[39] Of course, much more proof was needed to establish his case. He found no tell-tale inscriptions; his investigation was only of the ruin covered surface. Essentially, he depended upon location as described by the Bible and other ancient sources and modern Arabic geographical nomenclature, which strangely often gave clues as to the ancient name. Nevertheless, because of his superior knowledge of the ancient sources and Eli Smith's fluency in Arabic, his guesses have proved to be right more often than not. To this day, his observations serve as a helpful guide to the modern archaeologist.

Before we begin to count Robinson's hits and misses, however, we must remind ourselves that the world of archaeology is constantly developing so that yesterday's "miss" may turn out to be tomorrow's "hit" and vice versa. Almost every year the consensus about one very important site changes. Moreover, concerning most sites there is at least some disagreement. Hence one should regard any remarks made here about modern consensus as provisional. There is no doubt that by the time this book is published some new discovery will have undermined some of the opinions expressed here.

As they entered at Beersheba within the bounds of the land of ancient Israel, the landscape became greener and the soil more fertile. By the time they arrived at Hebron, there were fruit trees and a well-settled population. The group, however, spent little time investigating this area for they knew they would return later. Instead, they hurried on, arriving on April 14, on

---

[38] For a modern archaeological description of Elusa see: "Elusa," *NEAEHL* I, 379-383. See also: Avraham Negev, "Elusa," *ABD* II, 484-487. Both sources credit Robinson with the discovery of Elusa.

[39] Jean Perrot *et al, NEAEHL* I, 167-173.

Easter eve in the holy city. With great joy and anticipation they entered the city of Christian dreams, Jerusalem the Golden.

Jerusalem

Jerusalem was, of course, by no means golden. Although not as miserable and poor as other writers had led him to believe, it still was not the glorious city so often pictured in Christian writings and illustrations. There were no hard and fast population figures, but, basing his estimates on tax data, he concluded that there were about 4,500 Muslims, 3,000 Jews, and 3,500 Christians (i.e. 11,000 *in toto*) residing in El Kuds.[40] Of the last, only a very few were Protestants; most were Arab speaking Orthodox Christians, though there were also Latins, Armenians, Copts, and Ethiopians. The Christian community, if one can call it that, was continually wracked by internal struggles over the use and control of the holy places. Protestants were new on the scene and hardly numerous enough even to be called a minority group. Certainly they were not there to convert Muslims, for such would not have been countenanced by the civil government. Nor were they really there to convert Orthodox Christians, for, although considered by the Protestants somewhat misguided in their rituals, were already believing Christians. As Robinson says,

> The object of the American Missions to Syria and other parts of the Levant, is not to draw off members of the Oriental churches to Protestantism; but to awaken them to a knowledge and belief of the Gospel-truth, in the purity and simplicity of its original scriptural form.[41]

In fact, however, what he describes as an awakening to a knowledge and belief in the gospel truth amounts really to conversion to Protestantism, for the missionaries regarded their own faith as expressing "the purity and simplicity of the original scriptural form." Still, there was some sense that conversion of Christians to Christianity might be slightly misguided. So why were they there? Clearly, although they sought to "improve" orthodoxy, it

---

[40] Robinson, *Biblical Researches,* II, 85.
[41] *Ibid.,* I, 332.

was apparently the Jews who were to be the main object of their evangelism.[42] In fact, plans were well under way to build a "Jewish-Christian" church in Jerusalem. Robinson admits, however, that "the efforts of the English Mission have as yet been attended with very slight success"[43] and wonders whether the new church building will do much to change their fortunes. Truth to tell, because the building was planned to be built on land not entirely owned by the Protestants, the whole project became embroiled in controversy and had to be suspended.

When Robinson arrived on Easter Eve, he was greeted by eight missionaries and their families who had come together for a conference on missions. Five of them were his former students, and so the meeting became a pleasant alumni reunion. Some of these missionaries went with Smith and Robinson as they explored the city and pointed out major sights. They also provided the explorers with a place to stay in what might otherwise have been a hostile environment. A few years earlier, Robinson and Smith would have had no one to greet them. A few months later, two of the principal missionaries were gone and the mission largely dissolved. Robinson arrived at just the right time.

Without the missionaries, Robinson and Smith would probably have had to stay in the Latin convent, a prospect they would not have relished. As it was, they never went near the Latin mission and only once, briefly, into the Church of the Holy Sepulcher, for Robinson clearly did not want to become corrupted by the old myths and legends about the holy city which the monks so enthusiastically accepted. He wanted to see, as much as possible, for himself. That, indeed, is the great strength of his research. While most other travelers had basically accepted the old traditions at face value, Robinson was unwilling to do this. As a good Protestant, he wanted to get back to the Bible itself without all the medieval overlay. Like medieval Christians he wanted to "envision" the Bible, to put the text into history, but to do that he needed to use modern, rational methods to find out, as accurately as possible, what "really" happened.

---

[42] For a discussion of British attitudes toward the conversion of the Jews see: R. H. Martin, "United Conversionist Activities among the Jews of Great Britain 1795-1815: Pan-Evangelicalism and the London Society for Promoting Christianity among Jews," *Church History* 46, no. 4 (Dec. 1977), 437-452.
[43] Robinson, *Biblical Researches*, II, 87.

His approach, as might be guessed, played very well at home where Protestants deeply resented the "invasion" of their country by Roman Catholic, especially Irish, immigrants and delighted in an objective, scientific scholar who could point out the superstition of their Catholic adversaries.[44] Thus, although Robinson intended to be rational and non-sectarian in his approach, his book served highly political purposes in Protestant America and Europe and, while lauded by most Protestants, was condemned by most Roman Catholics. This was one of those occasions when objectivity becomes the handmaiden of very partisan religious politics.

Because they spent several days in Jerusalem and returned to sites on more than one occasion, Robinson abandons his usual chronological narrative style in favor of a more topical arrangement of his findings. After a brief summary of his first walks about the city, he treats in order the topography, the present day walls and gates, the adjacent hills and valleys, the temple area, the ancient towers, the ancient walls and their location, the water supply, and cemeteries and tombs. Then, in volume II, he continues with a discussion of the history of Jerusalem and modern statistics concerning the city.

Much of the material covered is now common knowledge and need not be reviewed. For instance, after describing the topography of the modern city he compares it carefully with the topography as given by Josephus to be sure that modern Jerusalem is on the same general site as the ancient city. That he concludes positively should come as no great surprise. What is surprising, however, is how much he does discover or try to discover which still has relevance today.

Perhaps, the most difficult question which he raises concerns all those site identifications which had become "common knowledge" and which were (and are) passed on from one generation to the next as fact. For instance, The Church of the Holy Sepulcher is supposed to encompass within it both the site of Golgotha and the site of the original tomb of Jesus. For centuries—indeed, since the fourth century—pilgrims have risked life and limb to venerate these holy places. The problem is, however, that there is no evidence that any of these sites were identified as such before the time of Constantine who did so much to make Jerusalem into a pilgrimage city.

---

[44] See Leo P. Hirrel, *Children of Wrath*, 93-116.

Chateaubriand, whom Robinson discusses at length, had argued that there was a living tradition of Christianity in Jerusalem and that Constantine just continued that tradition by making public where the holy sites were. Thus all the traditional sites have a basis in fact. Robinson challenges this argument on two grounds. First, the stories about the discoveries made by Constantine's mother, Helena, do not mention continuing old traditions but rather emphasize the miraculous sources of such knowledge. What she learns from "real people," she learns from old Jews and not from the church's bishop.

Second, Robinson argues that if we can believe what Josephus and others say about the position of the second wall of the city, that wall would have encompassed the site of the church and hence excluded it as a possible location, for the gospels make clear that Jesus was crucified outside the city walls. Therefore, Robinson concludes that the site must be wrong.[45] Whether he is correct in that judgment is still a matter of some debate, but it seems clear now that he himself was probably wrong about the course of the second wall.[46] At least Kathleen Kenyon believed that she had discovered that the second wall followed a route which would have left the site of the church outside the walls and excavations by Lux tend to confirm this opinion.[47] Joan E. Taylor takes a still different approach, arguing that the church may be the correct site for the burial, but not for the crucifixion.[48] On the other hand, there are some who believe Robinson to be correct and even a few supporters of the Garden Tombs located to the north of the Damascus Gate as the site of the sepulcher.[49] Many more simply withhold

---

[45] This judgment led to considerable controversy. See, for instance, George Williams, *The Holy City. Historical, Topographical, and Antiquarian notices of Jerusalem*, 3 vols. (London: John W. Parker, 1845). Williams is an adamant supporter of traditional sites.

[46] For a recent view of the Second and Third walls see: Hillel Geva, "Jerusalem: Second Temple Period," *NEAEHL* II, 736, 744.

[47] See Dame Kathleen Kenyon, *Jerusalem, excavating 3000 years of History* (New York: McGraw-Hill, 1967). See also: Magen Broshi, "Along Jerusalem's Walls," *Biblical Archaeologist* 40, no. 1(March 1977), 11-17 and Emmet W. Hamrick, "The Third Wall of Agrippa," *Biblical Archaeologist* 40, no. 1 (March 1977), 18-23.

[48] Joan E. Taylor, "Golgotha: A Reconsideration of the Evidence of the Sites of Jesus' Crucifixion and Burial," *New Testament Studies* 44, 2 (April 1998), 180-203.

[49] See Jeffrey Chadwick, "In Defense of the Garden Tomb," *Biblical Archaeology Review* 12, 4 (July/August 1986), 16-17. Very few, if any archaeologists, however, hold this opinion.

final judgment. It should be noted, at any rate, that even if Robinson were wrong about the course of the second wall, there still is no proof that fourth century Christians were not just guessing when they located the church. That is, there is no clear evidence that they knew where Jesus was entombed.[50]

Robinson is clearly on safer grounds when he argues that the Church of the Ascension, located on the top of the Mount of Olives, is in the wrong place, because the Bible says very definitely that the disciples went with Jesus as far as Bethany before his ascension (Luke 24:50), and that village is considerably beyond the Mt. of Olives. The question today, however, is not whether Jesus ascended from the Mt. of Olives or beyond Bethany, but whether this event can be considered "fact" at all. In other words, it may be that the literal envisioning of certain parts of the Bible may itself have severe limitations. In any event, E. R. is certainly correct that the Bible makes clear that the ascension did not take place on the site ascribed to it by tradition.

On the whole, the Bible is rather vague about many, if not most topological and architectural details; readers are left to imagine the landscape and the appearance of buildings for themselves. Josephus, however, is much more explicit and at least intends to be factual. Therefore, it is frequently to him that Robinson turns for information and for him that he finds illustration. For instance, Josephus describes a bridge over the Tyropoean valley connecting the Temple and what came to be called Mount Zion. For years people believed that Robinson correctly identified a piece of the Western Wall which juts out as a part of that bridge. Ever after the abutment has been known as "Robinson's Arch." Today, however, the consensus is that the abutment was for a monumental stairway leading down into the valley.[51]

Moreover, a letter published in the *Christian Advocate and Journal* in 1845, indicates that E. R. may not have been wholly accurate about the way the discovery was made. He claims that he really discovered the arch for himself and marvels that no one before him had come to the same conclusion. H. A. Homes, a well-known missionary turned scholar and eventually head librarian of the New York State Library, however, claimed to have seen the arch earlier, guessed that it might have been the abutment

---

[50] For a recent survey of modern opinions about the second and third walls see: Hillel Geva, "Jereusalem: Second Temple Period," *NEAEHL* II. 698-804.
[51] Geva, *NEAEHL,* 740.

for the bridge mentioned by Josephus, and, in fact, pointed it out to E. R. during their tour of Jerusalem.

> One forenoon I eagerly told Dr. R. of the existence of this now famous arch, and from his surprise and awakened interest, it was evident he had never seen it before. And before he went to see it, I remarked to him on the probability that it was the bridge mentioned in history as going from the temple to Mount Zion . . . Ever after I had much personal satisfaction in reflecting that I had been the instrument in introducing Dr. R. to a ruin of so much importance. [52]

Homes also comments that no matter who saw it first—some people also say Frederick Catherwood also knew of its existence—it was Robinson who not only examined and measured to prove the point but made the identification public through his book. Thus, though his disingenuousness is troubling, the name "Robinson's Arch" has justification.

E. R. was also fascinated by the walls and fortifications of Jerusalem and attempted to rediscover the basic towers which Josephus describes. In this investigation, he was probably correct in identifying part of the so-called Tower of David as, in fact, the site of the ancient tower of Hippicus but incorrect in believing that it was here that there was a juncture with Josephus' "second wall." Whether he was also correct in identifying what he believed were the remains of the "Third Wall" some 450 meters north of the Damascus Gate near the tombs of the Kings, is still a matter of some debate. There are many who believe that the exact location of that hastily constructed barrier will never be known. On the other hand, a great array of scholars (Sukenik, Mayer, Avi-Yonah, Ben-Ariah, Netzer, Broslin, Bahat) tend to agree with Robinson's basic thesis.[53]

---

[52] Stephen Olin, "The Whole Matter Settled," *Christian Advocate and Journal* XIX. 44 (June 11, 1845), 173. Stephen Olin, later the president of Wesleyan, had traveled to Palestine almost exactly one year after Robinson and followed very much the same route. In his book he describes seeing the "Arch" and determining himself what it was. He was later criticized for "stealing" from Robinson and so produces this letter from Homes to justify himself. See Stephen Olin, *Travels in Egypt, Arabia Petraea, and the Holy Land* 2 vols. (New York: Harper and Brothers, 1843) II, 258-260.
[53] Philip J. King, "Jerusalem," *Anchor Bible Dictionary* III, 761.

Certainly more universally accepted is his identification of the so-called Tombs of the Kings as the Tomb of Helena.[54] And undoubtedly, he is correct in judging the tunnel which he crawled through under the Ophel as Hezekiah's Tunnel.[55] Parenthetically, it must be added that his willingness to slither through the silted up tunnel, obviously without flashlight—for such had not yet been invented—highlights Robinson's extraordinary courage and determination. It is also not surprising that, because of the lack of proper illumination, he missed the ancient inscriptions in the tunnel telling about the meeting of the original diggers.

Actually it took Robinson two tries to make it through the tunnel. The first time they started from the Pool of Siloam and proceeded up through the tunnel with torches about 800 feet until the passageway became very narrow and barely passable. They marked their point of progress with smoke from their torches and then retreated. A few days later they returned better dressed for the venture and entered at the other end. After a much longer crawl than they anticipated, they finally saw the place they had marked and knew they were near the end.

Robinson, of course, was severely limited in what he could discover. Aside from clearing the debris from the Tombs of the Kings, he did no digging, but even if he had, he had no knowledge of pottery types as a key to dating. Such knowledge has only developed over many years of painstaking observation and analysis. Had he tried to excavate, he undoubtedly would have destroyed much more than he would have discovered. It is a little surprising, however, that he seemed to have had no notion that Tells might contain the ruins of ancient cities. This idea, in principle, had been proved accurate at Nineveh and elsewhere and could easily have been applied to Israel. Somehow it does not seem to have occurred to him that not all ruins would be on the surface.

In any event, given the political situation, all he could really do was measure carefully, consult ancient descriptions of the land, pay attention to Arabic names—which often, though by no means always, preserved ancient

---

[54] Nahman Avigal, *NEAEHL* II,751.

[55] It is true that questions have been raised about this by John Rogerson and Philip R. Davies, "Was the Siloam Tunnel Built by Hezekiah," *Biblical Archaeologist* 59, no. 3 (September, 1996): 138-149. But see also Ronald S. Hendel, "The Date of the Siloam Inscription: A Rejoinder to Rogerson and Davies," *Biblical Archaeologist* 59, no. 4 (Dezember, 1996), 233-237.

nomenclature—observe as accurately as possible what was there and rely upon such intuitions as "those stones seem very ancient to me." He also tells us that part of his "method" was to get off the beaten path of pilgrims and travelers and to observe what no one else had yet described. All this he did with great skill.

Excursion to Bethel

After measuring, exploring, and describing Jerusalem for twenty days, E. R. and Smith and their missionary colleagues, Lanneau, Nicolayson, and Paxton set out, on May 4 to survey the central hill country north of Jerusalem. They rode on horses this time which Robinson describes as slender, active, and exceedingly hardy.[56] Their route took them off the main road north into areas which, as far as they knew, had never been visited by a "Frank" i.e. a Western traveler.[57]

Within the space of two days, they had identified ancient Anathoth, Michmash,[58] Bethel, Ophra, Gibeon, and Mizpeh and demonstrated that Neby Samwil was not really Ramah, the home of Samuel, at all. Results came so quickly because they had prepared for the journey so well. Not only was Robinson very knowledgeable about what the ancient texts said concerning various sites; it was also because Eli Smith had "taken great pains to collect from various quarters the native names of all the places in those parts which we hoped to visit."[59] He had begun his work much earlier, in 1834, but had continued it in Jerusalem, consulting with "intelligent Sheiks and other persons from the towns and villages of that and other districts"[60] Thus when they went out into the hinterlands they already had good knowledge of what they were looking for. By and large, their theory that ancient place names are hidden in traditional Arabic names proved to be a good one, though at times they seemed to be misled by it.

---

[56] Robinson, *Biblical Researches* II, 147.
[57] *Ibid.* II, 107.
[58] New evidence seems to show that Robinson's identification of Michmash, so long accepted, may not be accurate after all. Patrick M. Arnold, "Michmash," *ABD* IV, 814-815.
[59] Robinson, *Biblical Researches* II, 106.
[60] *Ibid.*

For instance, they initially passed over Tel El-Ful entirely, seeing nothing of significance there, even though this has come to be regarded as the site of Saul's ancient capital of Gibeah. Instead, because of the name Jeba, they connected Gibeah with that site. Then, on his second trip, Robinson changed his mind, identifying Tel El-Ful as Gibeah.[61] What is ironic is that although for years Tel El-Ful was regarded as Gibeah, today, some archaeologists have come to agree with his first identification rather than his second.[62] Many others, however, still equate Gibeath with Tell El-Ful.[63] Over all, however, one can only stand in awe of E. R.'s overwhelming successes. After centuries of misidentification or no identification, a map of ancient Israel which could be depended upon was beginning to take shape. Certainly Robinson was enthusiastic:

> This excursion was to us deeply interesting, and we returned from it highly gratified. It had led us through scenes associated with the names and historic incidents of Abraham and Jacob, of Samuel and Saul, of Jonathan and David and Solomon; and we had been able to trace out the places where they had lived and acted, and to tread almost in their very footsteps. True, in Jerusalem itself the associations of this kind are still more numerous and sacred; but they are there so blended together, as to become in a measure indistinct and less impressive; while here in the country, they stand forth before the soul in all their original freshness and individuality. It was like communing with these holy men themselves, to visit the places where their feet had trod, and where many of them had held converse with the Most High.[64]

The return to Jerusalem, though welcome, was only momentary, for the group now proposed to explore the region south of Jerusalem and east of Bethlehem and Hebron, an area still not widely frequented by tourists. Immediately, however, they began to hear stories about the dangers of that forsaken territory, for bands of thieves and robbers were common there. An armed guard was proposed as essential.

---

[61] E. Robinson, "Outlines of a Journey in Palestine in 1852 by E. Robinson, E. Smith and Others," *Journal of the Royal Geographical Society of London* XXIV (1854),17.
[62] Patrick M. Arnold, "Gibeah," *ABD* II, 1008.
[63] Nancy L. Lapp, "Tell El-Ful," *NEAEHL* II, 445-448.
[64] Robinson, *Biblical Researches* II, 148.

> We were urged to take with us a guard of soldiers from the governor of Jerusalem. For this we had no sort of inclination; partly because we must then have been in a measure under their control; and partly because, with such a guard, we could only expect to excite the ill-will and perhaps hostility of the Arabs we might fall in with; and thus frustrate in a degree the very object of our journey.[65]

As a result they acquired the services of the Sheikh of the Ta'amirah, a man with a price on his head for his part in the rebellion of 1834 who led one of the tribes known for their raiding. He was, of course, on excellent terms with all those outlaws of the desert and served the expedition very well. As a result, there never was a bit of trouble. Nevertheless, the modern reader must really respect Robinson's sheer bravery. Many lesser investigators would have stayed closer to the main routes under the protection of the military. It was to the great benefit of Biblical studies that Robinson did not.

The excursion, which lasted from May 8 until May 15, took them through the desert hill country of Judah where Robinson correctly identified "Frank Mountain" as the ancient Herodium[66] and discovered the ancient sites of such villages as Tekoa, Ziph, and Maon. Then they descended the very steep path to En-Gedi and the wonderful "fountain" near which David once hid from Saul. The path from this tropical paradise to the Dead Sea, however, was not traversible by horses, so they camped in En-Gedi and then walked down to the sea. They returned back up the slope to the desert once again. While resting, Robinson trained his telescope upon a nearby butte and spotted ancient ruins. Later, in consultation with Smith, he decided that what he had seen was the ancient fortress of Masada. Although they did not actually climb the butte for closer inspection, he was again correct in his identification.

The party then descended by means of another wadi to explore the northern end of the Dead Sea and the Jordan River before moving on to Ain Es-Sultan and the ancient site of Jericho. Robinson and his party went far enough up the Wadi Kelt to see and identify correctly the site of New

---

[65] *Ibid.* II, 153.
[66] Edwin M. Yamauchi credits him with the "final identification." See: Yamauchi, "Herodium," *ABD* III, 176-180. See also Ehud Netzer, "The Herodium," *NEAEHL* II, 618.

Testament Jericho and Herod's Winter Palace.[67] E. R. also identified what he describes as the pile of rubble across from the great spring as ancient Jericho, though it is doubtful that he had any idea just how ancient it really was. Hidden in that Tel was a tower dating back many millennia before Abraham ever entered the land. From the vantage point of Jericho's tower the ancient Israelites appear as almost modern conquerors of the land.

Finally they climbed up through another wadi, passing 'Ain Duk and the site of ancient Bethel[68] before returning via Tel El-Ful to Jerusalem. One of the places Robinson looked for on the way to Bethel, but failed to find, was ancient Ai, though he provisionally assigned it to "the place of ruins just south of Deir Dîwân."[69] Ironically, Robinson actually stood on top of Et-Tell, now regarded as the site of Ai by most, but, though he recognized it to be in the right area failed to connect it with the ancient site because he saw no ruins there.[70] His own identification, which is generally regarded as incorrect, may have been a failure, but the overall result of the exploratory trip was certainly not. Little by little, details were being added to the new map of ancient Israel which was coming into being, a map which archaeologists have been consulting and revising ever since.

The emphasis here upon the discovery of ancient sites may be a little misleading to those who have not actually read the book. The text is a rich blend of all kinds of ethnographic, historical, geological, and scriptural information. He describes the flora and fauna, the types of rocks and formations, the flow of waters in the Jordan and the rising and falling of the Dead Sea. He seems particularly intrigued by fountains and springs. He comments about how modern Bedouin practices illumine the Bible stories and how this ancient worthy or that was related to the place visited. With all this he weaves in references to Josephus' and Eusebius' descriptions, Benjamin of Tudela's pilgrimage, Crusader victories and losses, modern

---

[67] Ehud Netzer says that E. R. was the first to identify the Winter Palace. *NEAEHL* II, 682.
[68] Robinson was the first to discover this site. Kelso, "Bethel." *NEAEHL* I, 192-194.
[69] Robinson, *Biblical Researches* II, 313.
[70] The name should have given it away for Et-Tell (the Tell) is strikingly close to Ha'Ai (the Ruins). The Biblical name, however, raises serious questions about the historicity of the original story, for it is unlikely that anyone would name a city "the Ruins." It sounds, therefore, as though the site was already uninhabited when Joshua entered the land. See: Joseph Calloway, *NEAEHL* I, 39-45.

insurrections and oppressions. Throughout, he introduces the measurements he took and the results of compass readings. One comes away with a sense of having been there and seen as he has seen. One finishes each section with the vivid impression of a land vastly rich in life and history and of a great and meticulous intellect at work.

From Jerusalem to Gaza and Hebron

Robinson and his friends returned to Jerusalem to face an immediate problem. The plague which had been raging in Jaffa was spreading and there was a danger that Jerusalem would be put under quarantine. As a consequence there was a rapid change in plans. The whole group had thought they would spend several days in Jerusalem, taking relatively short trips to Bethlehem and the nearby monasteries, Mar Saba and St. John's in the desert, before proceeding to longer adventures. Instead, E. R. and Smith spent only a day in Jerusalem, leaving on the 17th of May for a journey which would take them through the southwestern district, to Gaza, and then back to Hebron. They traveled this time without other friends or armed guard, employing only one guide and mule drivers. To save the money for extra animals, they left much of their luggage behind, in Jerusalem, with friends.

The decision to leave quickly was propitious, for the next day Jerusalem was closed and did not reopen until July! Had they waited, much of their exploration would have had to be canceled and the world would have been much poorer for the loss. As it was, Robinson and Smith, without guards, did face danger at the hands of possible marauders. The southwest was safer than the southeast, but nothing was immune from the constant threat of bandits. Instead of attack, however, what they experienced was the considerable hospitality of the Muslims and Arab Christians whom they met.

Everywhere they camped there were local residents who kept guard over their tents at night without charge or even request for recompense. Granted, their constant story-telling sometimes kept Robinson awake, but their concern for guests is quite moving. Robinson and Smith were regularly offered meals and guide service and friendship without charge. As a result, E. R. has few critical remarks about the local inhabitants. Occasionally he finds a mule driver lazy or untrustworthy; there were certainly Arabs looking out for their own ends. Nevertheless, the words, "intelligent," "faithful," "dependable," "friendly," are most often used to describe their Palestinian hosts.

There were some reasons, beside the natural hospitality of the Palestinians, which made them particularly solicitous. First, the Egyptian government held villages responsible when foreigners were robbed within their boundaries. Second, many Palestinians believed that the Franks, as they called them, were coming to measure and repossess estates which they still claimed from Crusader days. Tired of both Ottoman and Egyptian rule, many looked forward to government by a European power. Hence they urged Robinson and Smith to return soon. Neither of these reasons should diminish, however, the importance or impressiveness of the helpfulness of those whom Robinson and Smith met. Frequently they went out of their way to feed them, to guide them to little known places, and to offer whatever information they could. One seriously doubts that Palestinians in the middle of Massachusetts would have fared as well.

All of this means that Robinson's *Biblical Researches* provides a very positive view of Palestinians. It is true that when Robinson refers to Islam (or as he calls it, Muhammedanism), he regularly speaks of the religion of the "false prophet," but there are few other demeaning remarks. Nor is he critical of the few Jews with whom he comes into contact. He concludes his description of his meeting with Jews in Hebron by saying, "We bade adieu to these kind friends with feelings of respect; and were highly gratified by our visit."[71] In other words, there are very few signs of religious bigotry or belief in Western superiority on the part of Robinson. He may make some snide remarks about the Romanish mummery of the Latin priests in Jerusalem, but in regard to the Muslims and Jews he shows genuine appreciation and respect.

The journey to Gaza passed by Soba which Robinson probably incorrectly identified as the Ramah where Samuel had his headquarters. He also concluded that Kuryet el-'Enab might well be the ancient Kiriath-Jearim and identified Shuweikeh as Socoh and Ain Shems, as Beth Shemesh.[72] His main concern throughout, however, was to find the ancient

---

[71] Robinson, *Biblical Researches.* II, 448.
[72] This last identification was accepted for some time but eventually archaeologists came

city of Eleutheropolis, for Eusebius located many other sites in relation to that episcopal city. When he first arrived at Beit Jibrin he suspected that he might have found the right place, but he was also very circumspect and did not jump to immediate conclusions. Instead he proceeded to Gaza, a city in those days somewhat larger than Jerusalem, and then rechecked his evidence on the way home. It was not until he measured the distance between Beit Jibrin and Idhana (ancient Jedna) by riding it and discovered that it took just the right amount of time, that he finally concluded that he had discovered Eleutheropolis. In this instance, he has proved to be absolutely correct.

In returning from Gaza he stopped briefly at Tell el-Hasy (Hesi) but saw no ruins and hence offered no guess as to its identity. In fact, he was not even sure that it was a city at all. Little did he know that a few years later Sir Flinders Petrie and then Frederick Bliss would find in the Tell great ruins and in so doing initiate the practice of archaeological excavation in the Holy Land. Whether the site really is ancient Eglon, one of the five Philistine cities, however, is still not absolutely certain.[73] Robinson proved himself wise in deferring judgment about this one.

This leg of their journey, like the preceding trip, lasted eight days, though in this case they returned to Hebron and not Jerusalem. There they studied the outside of the great mosque, but, because they were not Muslims, were not allowed within. Robinson also refused even to look at such traditional sites as the Tomb of Abner, for he had suspicions that they are the product of late season imaginings and have little to do with actual Biblical places. Rather he spent his time in Hebron, waiting impatiently for camels for the next stage of their journey and visiting various people in the area. Perhaps his most interesting experience was attendance at a meeting and dinner of the three governors of Gaza, Jerusalem, and Hebron. A brief vignette from his description of the occasion will give a sense of the whole:

> Sheikh Sa'îd was emphatically the great man, gave all the orders, and led the whole conversation; his colleagues sitting in such a

---

to prefer as the correct site, the nearby Tell-Rumeilah. See: G. Ernest Wright, "Beth-Shemesh," *EAEHL* I, 248-252. Today, however, Tel Beth Shemesh seems the preferred location. Shlomo Bunimovitz and Zvi Lederman, "Beth-Shemesh," *NEAEHL* I, 249-253.

[73] See: Valerie M. Fargo, "Tell El-Hesi," *NEAEHL*, 630-634. See also: Fargo and Kevin G. O'Connell, "Five Seasons of Excavation at Tell El-Hesi (1970-77)," *Biblical Archaeologist* (December 1978) 41.4, 165-182.

> position, that they could not address us, nor we them. A poor ragged peasant now came in with perfect unconcern, presented himself before Sheikh Sa'îd, uncovered his wounded shoulder, and begged charity. The Sheikh instantly sent him out; at the same time ordering a garment to be given him. This is one of the traits of oriental society and government, that the highest are thus entirely accessible to the lowest. Coffee was now brought, and presented first to the three Sheikhs, then to us, and afterwards to the rest.[74]

It was from Sheikh Sa'îd that Robinson received approval to proceed on the next phase of his journey, to the ancient city of Petra.

To Wadi Musa and Back

There were annoying delays getting camels and guides for this next phase of the journey and E. R. is not reluctant to express his frustration. Eventually, however, the camels did arrive, Sheikh Hussan, one of the leaders of the Jehalin, agreed to serve as chief guide and protector, and their small party set off on Saturday, May 26. Because the next day was Sunday, however, they only proceeded as far as the main camp of the Jehalin where they encamped and celebrated the "Sabbath." The journey, then, really began on the 28th as they headed in a southeasterly direction toward the Arabah.

On the first day, they passed Tell Arad, which E. R. correctly, though not surprisingly, identified as ancient Arad. No doubt he would have been amazed to know that next to the Tell were the scarcely hidden remains of an early bronze city (whose existence does not strictly fit with a literal Biblical chronology) and within the Tell the preserved structures of an impressive iron age fortress.

Shortly thereafter they passed Tell el Milh which he later identified tentatively as the ancient Moladah. Today, some archaeologists tend to place Moladah in a different location and identify Milh as another site for Arad,

---

[74] Robinson, *Biblical Researches* II, 451-452.

used when the traditional site was, for a time, abandoned. Exactly what ancient Milh was called is still, however, a matter of debate.[75]

Eventually, the party arrived at the southern end of the Dead Sea and explored the cavern in a "Salt Mountain" about which the Arab guides had spoken frequently. While Robinson and Smith were in the cave, the guides suddenly became aware of a party approaching and when Robinson came out of the cave he discovered his guides on alert with guns drawn. A scout, however, soon discovered that the party was not a group of raiders but a merchant returning with his purchases of sheep. In a moment, the once panicked defenders became themselves a raiding party and, much to Robinson's displeasure, robbed the merchant and his party of some of his merchandise.

Smith and Robinson were obviously upset by this turn of events and eventually convinced their guides that they must abide by their laws and give all the stolen property back. This they reluctantly did, although later it was discovered that they had retained a skin of butter which they enjoyed smeared upon their Bedouin bread. All of this serves to highlight how dangerous this whole venture really was. There were marauding Bedouins who preyed off caravans and even the friendly tribes, like the Jehalin, could very quickly become marauders themselves without feeling any particular compunctions about it. In the Negev, only the laws of the desert seemed to be in force. Political authorities were very far away.

One major question which the Dead Sea area raised and raises, of course, is the location of the "cities of the plain"—Sodom, Gomorrah, Zohar, etc.—which play such an important part in the Abraham and Lot stories in Genesis. Like many others, Robinson considered the matter carefully and decided that some radical natural disaster must have taken place which led to the destruction. His best guess was that these cities were located under what is now the southern end of the Dead Sea, south of the Lisan, that great tongue of land which extends into the sea from the east, across from Masada. An earthquake coupled with a lightning storm, he maintains, were the causes of the phenomena described in Genesis as the destruction of Sodom and Gomorrah. Of course, Robinson would ultimately

---

[75] See: Moshe Kochavi, "Tel Malhata," *ABD* IV, 487-488. It may be that Arad was the name of a district and not just one site. See also Miriam Aharoni, "Arad," *NEAEHL* I, 75-86.

ascribe the destruction to God, but it is interesting how quickly he resorts to "secondary causes" to explain the phenomena. It is also interesting that after returning to Europe he consulted with a professional geologist, Leopold von Buch, with whom he carried on significant correspondence. One letter from von Buch is quoted in the text[76] while the whole correspondence is included in Note XXXVIII.

In this appeal to geological science, Robinson parts from his mentor and friend, Moses Stuart. In fact, in both Stuart's *Hebrew Chrestomachy*[77] and his article in the January 1836 issue of the *Biblical Repository*,[78] Stuart argues against geological interpretations of the Bible. Geology is one thing, he says, philology another. Any attempt by geologists to interpret the Biblical text to make scripture and science cohere is ultimately suspect. Only someone expert in Hebrew philology should interpret the meaning of creation. If Moses said a "day," that, for Stuart, is what he meant.[79]

In a sense, of course, Stuart stood on firm ground. Textual interpretation must be done by experts, not by natural scientists vainly trying to "fit" religion and science together. Ultimately, however, this position, though in a way correct, led to the conflict between science and religion which, at the time, both sides wished to avoid. Robinson, in his deference to geological expertise, sought as much as possible to avoid the conflict. As geology developed, however, it became clearer that attempts to bridge the gap were becoming more and more difficult. Scholars are still divided, however, about whether the destruction of the cities of the plain should be understood as an historical event which needs natural explanation or a mythical event whose purport is spiritual rather than historical. Neither Stuart nor Robinson would have regarded the latter alternative as at all agreeable, for to them fact and truth are, if not synonymous, at least radically intertwined.

---

[76] *Ibid.* II, 606-8.

[77] Moses Stuart, *A Hebrew Chrestomachy Designed as the First Volume of a Course of Hebrew Study* (Andover: Flagg & Gould, 1829), 115.

[78] Moses Stuart, "A Critical Examination of Some Passages in Gen. 1; with Remarks on Difficulties That Attend Some of the Present Modes of Geological Reasoning," *Biblical Repository* 7 (January 1836), 46-106.

[79] For a good analysis of Stuart's position see: John H. Giltner, *Moses Stuart: The Father of Biblical Science in America* (Atlanta, Ga: Scholars Press, 1988), 66-74.

In certain respects, the trip to Wadi Musa was one of the most memorable parts of their journey. E. R. describes the night of May 29 in the following way:

> The evening was warm and still; we therefore did not pitch our tent, but spread our carpets on the sand, and lay down, not indeed at first to sleep, but to enjoy the scene and the associations which thronged upon our minds. It was truly one of the most romantic desert scenes we had yet met with; and I hardly remember another in all our wandering, of which I retain a more lively impression. Here was the deep broad valley in the midst of the 'Arabah, unknown to all the civilized world, shut in by high and singular cliffs; over against us were the mountains of Edom; in the distance rose Mount Hor in its lone majesty, the spot where the aged prophet-brothers took of each other their last farewell; while above our heads was the deep azure of an oriental sky, studded with innumerable stars and brilliant constellations, on which we gazed with a higher interest from the bottom of this deep chasm. Near at hand were the flashing fires of our party; the Arabs themselves in their wild attire, all nine at supper around one bowl; our Egyptian servants looking on; one after another rising and gliding through the glow of the fires; the Sheikh approaching and saluting us; the serving of coffee; and beyond all this circle, the patient camels lying at their ease, and lazily chewing the cud.[80]

Shortly after midnight they were on their way again, through the cool of the night and a desert stark and bare of all vegetation. Some wadis contained springs and fostered small oases with tamarisks, willows, and cane, but most was but sandy waste. By noon a pleasant morning had turned frightful:

> The South wind, which at early dawn was cool and pleasant, had already become a burning Sirocco . . . The violence and glow of the wind increased; so that at 12 o'clock the thermometer had risen to 102 F. It being difficult in such circumstances either to write or sleep, and our Arabs wishing to go on, we concluded to proceed . . .[81]

---

[80] Robinson, *Biblical Researches* II, 500.
[81] *Ibid.* II, 504.

The journey, so romantic and peaceful at one moment, could become wildly dangerous and threatening at the next. One must remember that Robinson, who was never in terribly good health, now, at age 44, endured not only strange and often unpalatable food, strenuous treks on very uncomfortable camels, but heat, sand storms, and constant danger in order to achieve his goals. One may question at times his theology or his geographical identifications, but one can never question his courage and sheer determination to finish his explorations.

Finally, after what can only be described as an especially long and grueling experience, they arrived, on May 31, in Wadi Musa. Although, in fact, many of the ruins here are post-Biblical and add little to our knowledge of Scripture, Robinson had been intrigued by reports of them ever since reading Burckhardt, their Western discoverer. Here his intent is not to give a complete description of the monuments—that would involve a whole book in itself—but simply to offer a general impression of the whole. In so doing he also clears up several misconceptions perpetrated particularly by Laborde.[82]

Robinson's own enthusiasm for Wadi Musa and Petra knows almost no bounds. He writes:

> The character of this wonderful spot, and the impression which it makes, are utterly indescribable; and I know of nothing which can present even a faint idea of them. I had visited the strange sandstone lanes and streets of Adersbach, and wandered with delight through the romantic dells of the Saxon Switzerland; both of which scenes might be supposed to afford the nearest parallel; yet they exhibit few points of comparison. All here is on a grander scale of savage, yet magnificent sublimity.[83]

Again he writes:

> All at once the beautiful facade of the Khuzneh in the western precipice, opposite the mouth of the Sîk, bursts upon our view, in all the delicacy of its first chiselling, and in all the freshness and beauty of its soft colouring. I had seen various engravings of it, and read all the descriptions; but this was one of the rare instances,

---

[82] Leon Laborde, *Journey through Arabia Petraea, to Mount Sinai and the excavated city of Petra,* 2nd Ed. (London: J. Murray, 1838).
[83] *Biblical Researches* II, 518.

where the truth of reality surpassed the ideal anticipation. It is indeed most exquisitely beautiful; and nothing I had seen of architectural effect in Rome, or Thebes, or even Athens, comes up to it in the first impression.[84]

It is no wonder then that so many great artists, from David Roberts[85] to Frederic Church and beyond, risked the long journey across the desert in order to depict with their brushes something of this old Nabatean splendor. It was a challenge which no artist, intent upon capturing the beauty of nature, could easily forego. One may suspect that Robinson's own descriptions helped to bring the area to their attention.

On June 1, Robinson continued to explore the ruins, entering some areas not described by preceding travelers, noting various features of each part of the great necropolis. What he did not know was that his party stood in grave danger and faced the most critical test of his whole journey. Suddenly, there arrived on the scene the Sheikh of the Bedun, Abu Zeitun, with several armed men in order to claim tribute, that is, protection money, for visiting the site. The amount asked was enormous, almost ludicrous. Robinson and Smith refused such payment but offered a small amount instead. This was, in turn, refused and the argument became intense.

During the discussion the party of the Sheikh grew to forty armed and threatening men, while Robinson and Smith eventually had to dismiss some of their men who had simply come with them but were not really guides and did not wish to become involved. Clearly, the situation looked grim. Abu Zeitun could easily have had the whole party killed and stolen all their property. Still, Robinson and Smith held their ground.

> The heads of our camels were seized and turned in the opposite direction, with orders to go by the way we came. Not a step, my

---

[84] *Ibid.*

[85] In 1842, Roberts, who was in Palestine only a short time after Robinson, published a volume subscribed to by Queen Victoria and many of the crown heads of Europe which contained his lithographs of the Holy Land, lithographs which were to shape the way "Franks" pictured the land ever after. The commentary was done by the Rev. George Croly who drew heavily on the work of Edward Robinson. See W. D. Davies et al, *Jerusalem and the Holy Land Rediscovered: The Prints of David Roberts (1796-1864)* with forward by M. P. Mazzatesta and preface by D. M. Campbell (Duke University Museum of Art, 1996).

> companion replied, except by force; and dismounting he stood up before them; We now knew them to be robbers, and were ready for them; let them rob and kill us if they chose, but not a para more of money should they get, than we have offered them. They replied, that not for a para less than a thousand Piastres should we go to Mount Hor.[86]

Smith and Robinson and their guides rode off with Abu Zeiten now calling for a compromise. They chose not to climb Mount Hor rather than satisfy the Bedouin extortioners. The danger, however, was not over. There was a genuine possibility that Abu Zeitin, frustrated at his attempt at extortion, would follow after and, in the night, set upon and rob them. To be sure, the Sheikh of Wadi Musa was afraid of reprisals from Muhammed Ali and the Sheikh of Hebron, but a sneak attack could be carried off anonymously and no one would be the wiser.

So Robinson and his party decided not to camp for the night but to engage in a "forced march" across the desert to safety. On June 2 they arrived at el-Weibeh in the middle of the 'Arabah. Since this was a meeting place for marauding tribes, they took great care before approaching. Happily, they just missed meeting a raiding party which had camped there and departed.

As usual, Robinson wanted to connect the site with some ancient location and offered for this group of springs an important identification, believing it to be Kadesh where the Israelites spent much time. Probably this identification is incorrect; today most maps show Kadesh (or Kadesh-Barnea) far to the west at Tell el-Qudeirat.[87] One reason for this is that the traditional site of Mount Hor, which Robinson did not get a chance to explore, is well within ancient Edomite territory. Since Israel, according to Scripture, was not allowed to enter the land of Edom, it would have been impossible for Moses and Aaron to have climbed the mountain called Mt. Hor. Nevertheless, Robinson's suggestion, though probably wrong, is intriguing.[88] Certainly he makes a good case for his identification. If, in fact,

---

[86] Robinson, *Biblical Researches* II, 544.
[87] See: Rudolph Cohen, "Excavation at Kadesh-Barnea 1976-78," *Biblical Archaeologist* 44, no. 2 (Spring, 1981), 93-105. See also: Rudolf Cohen, "Kadesh-barnes," *NEAEHL* III, 843-847.
[88] For further discussion by Robinson see: "Notes on Biblical Geography," *Bibliotheca Sacra* VII, no. 23 (Apr. 1849), 366-385.

Edom at the time was centered much further east—which admittedly seems highly unlikely—el-Weibeh might serve as the correct site. In any event, it should be noted that in no case could two million people have lived for any length of time at either oasis.

Happily, Abu Zeitun apparently did not pursue them further and they avoided all other bedouin tribes out for loot and plunder. On the way back, Robinson simply devoted himself to more possible identifications, connecting Themail with ancient Thamar, Ar'arah with Aroer, Milh with Moladah, Semu'a with Eshtemoa, and Yutta with Jutte. Except for Milh, most archaeologists tend to agree with these identifications.

Finally, after what must have been a most exhausting and exhilarating experience, the party arrived back in Hebron on June 5, ready to continue with the next segment of the journey. They discovered, however, that Jerusalem was still under quarantine and that they could not stop there at all for rest and recuperation. Instead, despite the forced marches which brought them back actually sooner than expected, they began immediately the next leg of the journey.

From Hebron to Jerusalem via Ramleh

On June 6th Robinson and Smith left by horse but without a guide on the next phase of their exploration. Perhaps because they could not find a good guide and had to rely on the less knowledgeable people whom they met on the way, this was to be the least productive and interesting segment of their journey. One also senses that they really did not have a particular objective in mind, like the viewing of Mount Sinai or Eleutheropolis or Petra, and hence did not focus their investigation very well.

On the trip, which led them through the hill country of Judah and the Shephelah[89] they did see several sites, some of which, like Dura (Adoraim) they identified correctly. The decision, to identify Bethshemesh with an area just west of Ain Shems "upon and around a low swell or mound,"[90] has also

---

[89] For a modern account of the area see: A.F. Rainey, "The Biblical Shephelah of Judah," *Bulletin of the American Schools of Oriental Research 251* (Summer 1983), 1-22.
[90] Robinson, *Biblical Researches* III, 17.

gained wide acceptance. Despite the clear connection between the name "Ain Shems" and "Heliopolis" (Beth Shemesh = house of the Sun), most archaeologists today believe nearby Tell er-Rumeileh to be the correct site. There still is disagreement, however, about whether 'Akir should be identified as ancient Ekron.[91] His identification of Yebna as ancient Yabneh and his discovery of Upper and Lower Beth Horon and Aijalon are generally approved.

On the way he stopped at Ramleh at the home of 'Abud Mûrkus, the American consular agent who was actually an Arab Christian. (It was not until 1850 that the United States insisted that all its consular agents be American.) The consular agent himself was away when they arrived but his son was most hospitable, offering a room for them to use and excellent food. The high point for Robinson, however, was the celebration of an ancient custom.

> Our youthful host now proposed, in the genuine style of ancient oriental hospitality, that a servant should wash our feet. This took me by surprise; for I was not aware that the custom still existed here . . . A female Nubian slave accordingly brought water, which she poured upon our feet over a large shallow basin of tinned copper; kneeling before us, and rubbing our feet with her hands, and wiping them with a napkin. It was one of the most gratifying minor incidents of our whole journey.[92]

Given the controversy about slavery in the United States, one wonders just why he would include this comment here. Was he a supporter of slavery or did he think that the fact that she was a slave irrelevant in this context? In any event, he offers no critique of the institution which, though as ancient as the Bible itself, was rapidly pulling his own country apart. One may suspect that for Robinson what mattered was not the contemporary problem of slavery but the "enscripturation" of events. The wheat and barley harvests which he observed transported him to the story of Ruth; his meeting with the Bedouins carried him into the desert with Israel. Now, as the woman washes

---

[91] Most scholars now identify Tel Miqne as the correct site for Ekron. See: Seymour Gitan and Trude Dothan, "The Rise and Fall of Ekron of the Philistines," *Biblical Archaeologist* 50, no. 4 (December 1987), 197-222. See also Dothan and Gitan, "Ekron," *ABD* II, 415-422.
[92] Robinson, *Biblical Researches* III, 26.

his feet, he sees in the ceremony Biblical events again reenacted. It was, despite the slavery, sacramental.

Robinson visited several other ancient sites, like Tell Beit Mirsim for which he offers no identification, but provides very useful summaries of the history of Ramleh and Ludd (ancient Lydda). For the most part, however, there is little here which is new or significant. He arrived back in Jerusalem on June 9th and camped in a field before the Damascus Gate for the next three days.

From Jerusalem to Mount Tabor

For modern travelers in Israel, motorized vehicles—taxis, busses, sheroots—are assumed for sight-seeing in Israel. The land is small, about the size of New Jersey, and one can today travel through many ecological and political zones in a few minutes. Robinson, however, journeyed by horse or camel and these averaged, he says, less than three miles an hour. It often took him days to traverse what today would be covered in a few hours. This lack of speed, however, provided the opportunity really to see the landscape and the people at first-hand. He could hear the birds, view the vegetation, talk to the people as he made his way. Inconvenience has its advantages after all.

In less than two months he had crisscrossed much of southern Palestine. Now on June 13, he moved north into the more fertile regions of ancient Israel, gradually heading toward Beirut, his ultimate point of disembarkation. Departure from Jerusalem, though necessary, was not without its nostalgic regrets.

> We passed on by the tomb of Sheikh Jerâfy at 6h 55'; and reaching the top of Scopus, stopped there for a quarter of an hour, to wait for our attendants, and to take our farewell view of the Holy City.
>
> The emotions which crowd upon the mind at such a moment, I leave for the reader to conceive. The historical associations connected with the city and the various objects around, cannot but be deeply interesting even to the infidel or heathen; how much more to the heart of the believer! What a multitude of wonderful

events have taken place upon that spot! . . . One long last look; and then turning away, I bade those sacred hills farewell forever.[93]

Southern Palestine had revealed to our travelers primarily the sandy desert wastes often associated with the Holy Land, but now they entered a different world. Although it was the dry season, vegetation was more lush; birds sang around them; there were more flowing brooks and fountains. The valleys and plains of the north were better watered and more fertile than the dry wadis of the south and Robinson notes the abundance of olive and fig trees and at least potentially productive agricultural lands.

The people, on the other hand, seemed less open and talkative, far less hospitable than in the south. Robinson and Smith had been warned ahead of time that Nablus might well be quite unfriendly. Here they had difficulty finding guides and those who were available were often uninformed and misleading. Nevertheless, the explorers were able to locate many of the places they were looking for in their attempt to remap the world of ancient Israel. The first major site for which they searched was Shiloh, where the ark was once kept and where Samuel first heard the Lord speak. Although the site had been lost for centuries, Robinson and Smith found it with relative ease, simply following the directions of Eusebius and Jerome. Seilûn was identified as Shiloh, not only because of its name, but because it is located at the correct distance from Nablus and Jerusalem. Today archaeologists still agree about this identification.[94]

About eighteen miles beyond Seilûn they came to Nablus (Neapolis), located in an area with so many associations with ancient Israel. They did not actually look for the remains of Biblical Shechem, for they incorrectly identified it with Nablus, but they did visit Jacob's Well, which Robinson considered quite possibly authentic, and climbed Mount Gerizim with a Samaritan guide. There, they saw the remains of Hadrian's Temple to Jupiter, but unaware of that construction, guessed it must have had something to do with the Samaritans. The latter group, however, denied any association with it.

In Nablus, Robinson seems to have been more interested in the Samaritans, themselves, than in archaeological remains. He and Smith met

---

[93] *Ibid.* III, 74-5.
[94] Israel Finklestein, "Shiloh," *NEAEHL* IV, 1364-1370. Apparently the site was well known in the Middle Ages.

some of the leaders of the tiny Samaritan community, viewed a few of their scrolls, which looked suspiciously modern to Robinson, and discussed their religious practices. All of this, of course, was of more than academic interest. E. R., as a conservative Christian, regarded the Bible as the Word of God and hence factually correct. The Samaritans, however, claim to have the authentic version of the Torah, the one written by Moses himself. Were it to differ decidedly from the Massoretic text, it could cause genuine theological problems. He was not, of course, in a position to do any textual analysis; in fact, copies of their Pentateuch had already been published in Europe anyway.[95] His visit with the Samaritans, however, would give great credence to his judgments about them. While others could only look at the text, he could say that he had examined Samaritanism directly.

After Nablus and the Samaritans, Robinson and Smith continued their journey northward, to the ancient site of Samaria itself, today Sebastieh (or Sebaste). There, he examined a church dedicated to John the Baptist which was said to be also his burial place. Robinson, as usual, traces the history of the site to show that that tradition is, in fact, based upon superstition. John was, according to Scripture, beheaded on the east side of the Dead Sea. To think that his disciples would have carried the body to this place is clearly counterintuitive, particularly because John did not come from Samaria in the first place. Most of what we know now as the remains of Samaria were then unexcavated and hence invisible to E. R., but he did see the ancient colonnade which he related to the time of Herod the Great.

By 10h 40' on June 15 they had left Sebaste and were heading north to Jenin which he correctly identified as the Ginaea of Josephus. From a distance he saw Ta'annuk which he equated with ancient Taanach and Lejjûn which he thought to be Megiddo.[96] Robinson, however, felt more and more pressed for time and visited neither site. Perhaps he had come to realize that, in fact, there was little for him to see. Only later excavators would uncover the riches which a site like Megiddo had to offer.[97]

The next three days were spent exploring the great plain of Esdraelon and Nazareth. He identified the village of Zer'in as ancient Jezreel and

---

[95] Robinson, *Biblical Researches* III, 129.
[96] Actually Megiddo is located 1.5 kilometers north of Lejjun. David Ussisikkin, "Megiddo," *ABD* IV, 669-679.
[97] Yigael Yadin, "Megiddo," *EAEHL* III, 830-856. **XXX**

Beisan as Bethshan. He questioned the location of Cana, where Jesus is said to have turned water into wine, at Kefr Kenna, proposing instead Kana el-Jelîl as a substitute.[98] He climbed Mt. Tabor and decided that it could not have been the mountain of transfiguration because, at the time of Jesus, there was a city on the top. About the location of Nazareth, however, he was more affirmative. He knew that neither the Hebrew Scriptures nor Josephus refer to the place and that, outside of the New Testament, no mention was made of it until the time of Eusebius. In other instances, this was a signal to him that we are dealing with a fabrication by fourth century enthusiasts. He could not quite bring himself, however, to question Nazareth's authenticity. Instead, he was overcome by a bout with enscripturation:

> Seating myself in the shade of the Wely, I remained for some hours upon this spot, lost in the contemplation of the wide prospect, and of the events connected with the scenes around. In the village below, the Saviour of the world had passed his childhood; and although we have few particulars of his life during those early years, yet there are certain features of nature which meet our eyes now, just as they once met his. He must often have visited the fountain near which we had pitched our tent; his feet must frequently have wandered over the adjacent hills; and his eyes doubtless have gazed upon the splendid prospect from this very spot. Here the Prince of peace looked down upon the great plain, where the din of battles so oft had rolled, and the garments of the warrior been dried in blood; and he looked out too upon that sea, over which the swift ships were to bear the tidings of his salvation to nations and to continents then unknown.[99]

Robinson was a keen, critical, and, for the most part, skeptical scholar. He seldom accepted any attribution without considerable scrutiny. Usually, as in the case of Mount Tabor, tradition was destroyed by reason. But occasionally, his religious sensibilities got the better of his stern critical reason. The name of Nazareth, the wonderful vistas, the glorious associations with the "Saviour of the World" became hypnotic. Like so

---

[98] Consensus today favors Khirbet Qana as the correct location, though no certainty exists. James E. Strange, "Cana," *ABD* I, 827.
[99] Robinson, *Biblical Researches* III, 190-191.

From Mount Tabor to Beirut

At about 7:30 a.m. Robinson and his party left their camp on the top of Mount Tabor and descended to the plain below, enjoying the "distinct and map-like" vistas as they went. Instead of following the "water route," down a wadi to the Jordan Valley, they set off through the hills to Hattin. Although the work is called "Biblical Researches," it is clear that E. R. was interested in more than the Bible. In fact, much of this vast work concerns the post-Biblical history of the land.

Robinson seems throughout particularly interested in the crusades and the 12th century crusader kingdom. Now, standing at the "Horns of Hattin" he describes how the crusader army lost its final, devastating battle to the forces of Saladin on this spot. After a brief inspection of the area and an assurance that this was probably not where the Sermon on the Mount was delivered, he headed off to Tiberias.

On the way, he received his first view of the Lake of Tiberias, i.e. the Sea of Galilee. Clearly, he was not overly impressed.

> The hills are rounded and tame, with little of the picturesque in their form; they are decked by no shrubs nor forests; and even the verdure of the grass and herbage, which earlier in the season might give them a pleasing aspect, was already gone; they were now only naked and dreary. Whoever looks here for the magnificence of the Swiss lakes, or the softer beauty of those of England and the United States, will be disappointed. My expectations had not been of that kind; yet from the romantic character of the scenery around the Dead Sea, and in other parts of Palestine, I certainly had anticipated something more striking than we found around the Lake of Tiberias.[101]

---

[100] It should be noted that today very few doubt the validity of the site. See: Vassilios Tzaferis and Bellarmino Bagatti, "Nazareth," NEAEHL III, 1103-1106.

[101] Robinson, *Biblical Researches* III, 253. It is noteworthy that the idea of the "picturesque" played an important role in 19th century aesthetics, especially among artists depicting scenes from Asia.

The village of Tiberias was also disappointing to the visitor. In January of 1837 a great earthquake had occurred and the whole village was still in ruins. Many people had died in the catastrophe and the village population which remained was small. Those who survived lived meagerly among the ruins. Robinson stopped to look briefly at the hot springs south of the city, but was not encouraged to remain there long. Instead, he set off along the shore to try to discover the site of ancient Capernaum.

According to Nahman Avigad, it was Robinson who first identified Tell Hum as the correct site,[102] but this is not the case at all. In fact, Tell Hum was already recognized as such when our party of explorers arrived.[103] Robinson accepted the ruins as obviously important, but he concluded they are not Capernaum.

> The considerations already adduced, which show with certainty that Capernaum was connected with the plain of Gennesareth, prove conclusively that these ruins, a hour distant from that plain, cannot mark its site.[104]

For once, it would appear, tradition was correct and Robinson was wrong. At least most archaeologists accept Tell Hum as the place where Jesus owned a house, healed, and taught. On the whole, however, the score remained very one-sided and in his favor. One also wonders whether, sometime in the future, archaeologists will not reconsider his argument that Tell Hum is neither located on the plains of Gennesareth nor near a large spring as Josephus describes.

Two events now occurred which were greatly to shape the rest of the investigations. First of all, Robinson began to feel ill with a fever and remained in camp while the rest explored the area around the lake east of the

---

[102] Avigad, "Capernaum," *EAEHL,* I, 286. See for a more modern view: Tzaferio, "Capernaum," *NEAEHL* I, 291-296.
[103] It is certainly not the case that "after having been abandoned and completely forgotten for centuries, Capernaum reemerged in 1894, when the ruins of the site were acquired by the Franciscan custody of the Holy Land." Virgilio C. Corbo "Capernaum," *ABD* I, 866. Tell Hum was identified as Capernaum before Robinson got there in 1838. It is interesting that Olin seems to have agreed with Robinson about the site. (Olin, *Travels, op. cit.* II, 404-405.)
[104] Robinson, *Biblical Researches* III, 300.

Jordan. He recovered after "abstinence and sleep," but this was a forewarning of things to come. The exertion of the trip had been enormous and now, as it neared its end, all the weariness and tension began to catch up with him.

Second, the party had received news in Tiberias of a Druze revolt which rendered much of the area north of them dangerous. Their plan had been to travel the Damascus road, stopping in Tell el-Qadi and Banias, before proceeding on to the ancient Syrian capital. Then they were to head back, by Baalbek and the Cedars of Lebanon, to Beirut.

Instead, they decided to stay off the Damascus Road which had become too dangerous for travelers and head up through the hills to Safed. This town, so important in crusader and Jewish history, was also a shambles because of the same earthquake which had destroyed Tiberias. Until that event, the old crusader castle in Safed had stood more-or-less intact; now it was in ruins. They wandered around the ruins, but in fact there was little to see. The best that the party could do was to travel to a nearby hill where they could view Lake Huleh and, in the distance, Tell El-Qadi (which Robinson correctly identified as Dan) and Banias.[105]

After a short stay, they headed off for Tyre, Sidon, and then Beirut. At this point Robinson says that he stopped making such detailed notes. In truth, however, the reader does not notice much difference, for the book is still full of exact references to the time at which they reached each of the many places along the route. One can tell, however, that E. R. is becoming more and more exhausted and is ready to go home. Most of this section is filled with historical notices about these towns, compiled after E. R. had returned to Germany.

When they arrived in Beirut, actually several days ahead of schedule, the plan was to press on to Baalbek and the Cedars of Lebanon, but Robinson was in no condition to do so:

> My own health too, which had been failing ever since we reached Tyre, now gave way; and on Friday (June 29th), and for the eight

---

[105] Today, of course, Lake Huleh, once a terrible source for malaria, has been drained and the area has become a rich agricultural region. Robinson may have been very lucky to have had to stay away from that mosquito-infested region.

following days, I was confined mostly to my room. I was thus cut off from visiting even Nahr el-Kelb and Deir el-Kul'ah.[106]

One might think that the journey was at an end. Today, we would fly from Beirut and be in Berlin in but a few hours. For Robinson, however, nothing was that easy. Because a sailing ship to Smyrna would have taken up to a month, he boarded a steamer to Alexandria on July 8, where he waited on board ship for a French steamer to Syria on July 17. Another ship carried him to Smyrna where he arrived on July 21. There he passed several days at the home of a Mr. Temple, eventually boarding another steamer to Constantinople, arriving on July 30. Finally, taking still one more ship up the Danube, Robinson and Smith arrived in Vienna on September 13.

Sometime on board ship, Robinson contracted or at least began to experience an "intermittent fever" which now grew seriously worse:

> Here my disorder, after a few days, assumed a new and alarming form, and brought me speedily to the borders of the grave. One day the physician left me, saying to my companion that I should probably expire in two or three hours. He afterwards returned, expecting to find me dead. Meantime, through the mercy of God, a crisis had taken place; I had slept, and was better. Two days later my family arrived by forced stages from Dresden; and from that time my recovery was as rapid, as had previously been the progress of the disease. For the preservation of my life, I regard myself as principally indebted, under God, to the judicious care and devoted attentions of the tried friend, who had been so long the companion of my wanderings in the East.[107]

So ends one of the greatest travel books and Biblical explorations of the nineteenth century.

But of course, the work had just begun. The trip had been made, the notes had been taken, but the monumental task of putting everything together in written form lay ahead. Union Theological Seminary expected him back, to begin teaching after a year's absence, but Robinson put them off and the seminary, to its good credit, exhibited supreme patience with its newly appointed but untried professor. For the rest of 1839 and most of 1840 he labored over the manuscript of this huge, three-volume masterwork.

---

[106] *Ibid.* III, 448.
[107] *Ibid.* III, 451.

One wonders, in fact, how he finished it so soon. For each major city and site he provided a rich "historical note" which traces the history of the site from Biblical times to the present. To do that he consulted a bewildering variety of sources from every stage of the place's existence. In this synopsis of the work we have emphasized Biblical site identification, for that has loomed large for the history of archaeology, but just as valuable is his ability to put together succinct historical summaries. Those interested in history of the crusades in Palestine, for instance, would do well to consult not only his vast bibliography but his notes which indicate where the major crusader castles were, when the battles were fought, and what the various crusaders were like.

His ethnographic descriptions of tribal life in the mid-nineteenth century are also very informative and important. Few travelers observed so carefully or understood so well the Bedouin and their customs. One comes away from his book with a fine appreciation of the various types of people who inhabited the land and how they lived. To be sure, there are no illustrations for visualization, but a glance at David Roberts' fine pictures can fill this lacuna easily. Together Robinson and Roberts present an irreplaceable picture of Palestine as yet largely untouched by the West.[108]

Perhaps, Robinson's most important accomplishment, however, was the drawing of new maps of the whole region. For this purpose he hired a young German map maker, Heinrich Kiepert, who provides in Appendix B of Volume III a "Memoir on the Maps Accompanying this Work." In this memoir he discusses the various sources used and how Robinson engaged himself in all the minute details of the work. It was an amazing and fruitful response to his teacher's cry for "Maps, Maps, Maps." Through his efforts the maps of ancient Israel were thoroughly revised and improved; modern cartography of the Holy Land had begun.

During this period he consulted not only his old teacher, Gesenius, but geographers like Carl Ritter and Alexander von Humboldt and philologists like Roediger. He also read before the Geographical Society of Berlin on December 8, 1838 and January 6, 1839 "A brief report of travels in Palestine and adjacent regions in 1838," a sort of "teaser" for the forthcoming huge volumes. This was subsequently published in English in the April 1839 edition of the *American Biblical Repository*.

---

[108] *Supra,* 248, n 85.

If he spent much time at the University of Halle, which he doubtless did, he very likely met George Lewis Prentiss, a fellow countryman destined eventually to teach at Union Theological Seminary, as well as the great Philip Schaff who was in Halle and Berlin in 1839-40 and who studied particularly with Tholuck and Neander. Schaff became one of the most important church historians of the 19th century and, some time after Robinson's death, was appointed to a professorship at Union. Henry Boynton Smith who later became Union's premier theologian was also there in Halle and Berlin at that time.

By 1840 *Biblical Researches* was virtually complete; in 1841 it was published simultaneously in Germany, England, and the United States. The German edition, corrected if not wholly translated by Therese, was dedicated to Carl Ritter, the great German scholar with whom Robinson often consulted after his return. In English, the work was dedicated, of course, to Moses Stuart. In a way, the whole work was an answer to his teacher's need for better geographical information. At the same time, it was this very work which propelled Robinson to a new level of fame beyond the reach of Stuart. Through it, the student overtook the teacher.

Chapter Eight

NEW YORK, NEW YORK

Headlines and Notices: 1840-1851

1840　　After a raucous campaign, William Henry Harrison (Tippacanoe) and John Tyler too are elected.
British and Austrian ships bombard the Palestinian coast, destroying much of Haifa, Acre, and Beirut.
At the Convention of Alexandria, Muhammed Ali agrees to give back Syria to the Ottomans but is recognized as hereditary ruler of Egypt.
Liberty Party runs on an abolitionist platform.
Frederick William IV becomes King of Prussia.
Thomas Cole exhibits *The Voyage of Life*.

1841　　Brook Farm is organized by the Transcendentalists.
Horace Greeley begins to publish the *New York Tribune*.
Charles A. Briggs, the Biblical scholar, is born.
The Amistad incident captures the headlines.

1842　　P. T. Barnum opens his American Museum in New York.
William James is born.
William Walford publishes the hymn, "Sweet Hour of Prayer."
Theodore Parker, a Unitarian strongly influenced by German scholarship, publishes *A Discourse on Matters pertaining to Religion*.

1843	Henry James and William McKinley are born. Jesus Christ does not return as William Miller had predicted. He does not come the next year either. John Nevin publishes *The Anxious Bench*, an attack on Finney.
1844	A mob kills Joseph Smith in Illinois. Morse sends the message "What hath God wrought?" on the new telegraph line between Washington and Baltimore. Charles Goodyear patents the vulcanization of rubber.
1845	James Polk becomes President after a close victory over Henry Clay. Texas is annexed and admitted as a slave state. Margaret Fuller publishes *Women in the 19th Century*. Edgar Allen Poe publishes *The Raven and other Poems*. Bruno Bauer publishes his radical book on Paul, the apostle.
1846	The Smithsonian Institution is founded. Melville publishes *Typee,* his first novel. Mendelssohn's oratorio *Elijah* is first performed. The international border between the U.S. and Canada is fixed at the 49th parallel. Elias Howe invents the sewing machine. The Mexican War begins; it ends formally in 1848 with the U.S. taking over the Southwest and California. The Christy Minstrels make their debut in New York City.
1847	Irish immigration reaches 105,000 for the year. Thomas Edison is born. Horace Bushnell publishes *Views of Christian Nurture.* Addison Alexander publishes his influential commentary on Isaiah.
1848	The Women's Rights Convention is held in Seneca Falls. John Humphrey Noyes establishes the Oneida Community, a radical perfectionist group, in Oneida, N.Y.

Asa Gray publishes his famous *Manual of Botany of the Northern United States*.
Hawthorne publishes *The Scarlet Letter*.
Louis Napoleon Bonaparte becomes President of the French Republic.
Revolutionary activity sweeps Germany and France.
Brigham Young leads the Mormons to the promised land in Utah.

1849   Luther Burbank is born.
Thoreau publishes "Civil Disobedience."
Poe dies.
The gold rush to California begins in earnest..

1850   Zachary Taylor, who had been elected President in 1848, dies and Millard Fillmore becomes President.
The Compromise of 1850, in which California was admitted as a free state, passes Congress.
Jenny Lind, the Swedish Nightingale, comes to America under the auspices of P. T. Barnum.

1851   The Erie Railroad, the first rail line to reach the Great Lakes, is constructed as far as Dunkirk N.Y.
Maine passes a prohibition law.
Herman Melville publishes *Moby Dick*.
Asher Durand paints "Kindred Spirits" in memory of Thomas Cole.
Finney becomes President of Oberlin College.

    The culture shock awaiting Edward and Therese when they returned to America must have been enormous. Edward, at least, had spent the better part of a year in the exotic world of the orient and then had sojourned in Germany, a land ruled by a king motivated by romantic notions about the mystic glories of a divinely consecrated and patriarchal monarchy. German society was hierarchical, nostalgic, aristocratic, but the intellectual mood was also revolutionary. Already, in 1835, David Strauss had published his *Das Leben Jesu* and had thrown down the gauntlet against all those literalists who wanted to accept the gospels as factually accurate. Bruno Bauer would soon follow to deepen even more the criticism. Ludwig Feuerbach was at that very time writing his *Wesen des Christentums,* (1841), one of the most telling philosophical critiques of Christianity ever published. In 1840, Karl Marx and Sören Kierkegaard turned twenty-five.

From this heady mix of royal romanticism and intellectual rebellion, the Robinsons returned to the world of "Tippecanoe and Tyler too." Happily, they missed most of the hoopla of the campaign which featured miniature log cabins and hard cider parties, mud slinging and gross appeal to the masses. Apparently, however, Edward's sister Elizabeth rather enjoyed the foolishness and brother Charles participated avidly as an ardent Whig supporter. By the time Edward and Therese arrived, the election, which the Whigs won, was almost at hand. Harrison, the old soldier hero, triumphed and was inaugurated in March of 1841. Almost immediately, however, he was taken ill and died and John Tyler, a southerner bent on preserving the status quo vis à vis slavery, came to inhabit the White House.[1]

In one sense nothing had changed politically. Calhoun, Clay, and Moses Stuart's old friend, Daniel Webster, dominated the scene with their rhetoric, while in the White House, a leader with a Whig label but with many Jacksonian views, still was in command. Martin Van Buren, the little Magician, waited in the wings, hoping to be renominated and elected the next time around.

Still, the more things stay the same, the more they change. While both politicians and theologians tried to keep the lid on the slavery issue, postponing discussion and resolution to some other day, preferably in the far future, the issue kept coming up, ever more vitriolicly. Not only did the abolitionists become more virulent in their attack. As the nation expanded ever westward, the inevitable question: "Slave or Free" would not go away. No rug was big enough to sweep the slavery question under.

It is not that people did not try. Discussion of the whole matter of slavery *per se* was virtually prohibited on the floor of Congress. Even the

---

[1] This was the first time a Vice President actually succeeded to a President in office. Whether he was to be considered "President" or merely a Vice President acting as President was a much debated issue at the time.

most eloquent of speakers—men like Daniel Webster—became mealy mouthed when faced by the issue. So did the churches. It is shocking to modern sensibilities to read the very bland statement about slavery offered to the General Assembly of the Old School Presbyterians. It is even more shocking to learn that the church could not even accept that.[2] Few wanted to rock the boat, for to condemn slavery was to attack the Union and to risk secession, and perhaps even worse.

Moses Stuart, himself, got into the fray. He was essentially opposed to slavery, but he favored the commonly accepted, but ultimately racist, plan to return slaves to Africa to be resettled in what was to become Liberia. In the meantime, he argued that the Bible itself offered no basis for condemning slavery as evil *per se*. After all, the Hebrew Scriptures accept slavery, offering *mishpotim* (ordinances) to regulate the practice. Even the New Testament, despite the emphasis upon love of neighbor, condones the institution. Stuart points, for instance, to Paul's letter to Philemon where the apostle encourages a slave to return to his master. As a result of this sort of attitude, Andover Theological School would not even allow its students to attend addresses by abolitionists.[3]

Whittier, the abolitionist-poet, was savage in his response. In a poem called "A Sabbath Scene," he pictures a fugitive woman fleeing from slavery to a church, only to be tripped up by the parson himself and turned over to the slave catcher. He includes these withering lines:

> My brain took fire: "Is this," I cried, "the end of prayer and preaching?"
> Then down with pulpit, down with priest, and give us Nature's teaching!
> I woke, and lo! the fitting cause of all my dream's vagaries—
> Two bulky pamphlets, Webster's text, with Stuart's commentaries!"[4]

---

[2] See: Samuel Miller, *The Life of Samuel Miller, D.D., LL.D* (Philadelphia: Claxton, Remsen, and Haffelfinger, 1869), 292-300.

[3] Giltner, *op.cit.,* 123-130.

[4] It is interesting that the last lines as quoted by Giltner (p. 130) concerning Webster and Stuart are to be found in the original pamphlet but not in subsequent editions. Cf. John Greenleaf Whittier, *The Poetical Works of John Greenleaf Whittier in 4 Volumes* (New York: Houghton, Mifflin and Company, 1892) III, 159-163.

It must be remembered, however, that Whittier did not represent the majority of citizens. There was a mild sense among many northerners that something was wrong with slavery, but basically slavery did not hurt them, so they did not worry about it. New Yorkers were, in fact, making good money exporting cotton. And where did the cotton come from? Abolitionists were considered by many, radicals and troublemakers, idealists with their heads in the clouds who did not understand reality. Some of them were. But there were also many moderates who began to feel more and more uneasy about the whole slavery issue. If churches as organizations could not bring themselves to take a stand, a growing number of churchmen and women did. A look at any one of a number of Christian newspapers and periodicals from the '40s and '50s shows an ever increasing number of articles on the subject.[5] And so the pot continued to simmer, heating slowly but surely to a boil. Edward Robinson lived the rest of his life in the midst of this tension.

The abolition of slavery, of course, was not the only issue on the nation's agenda. Because of the potato famine in Ireland and political turmoil in Germany, immigration from those countries mushroomed, increasingly rapidly both the work force and poverty. Moreover, since many of the immigrants were Catholic, new problems were presented to the Protestant majority which wished to maintain its control over the culture. Catholicism was blamed for all the social problems—poverty, crime, alcoholism, etc.—which began to plague American cities. The age of the Know Nothings was not far away.

Significantly, one of the primary spokesman for the immigrants and the oppressed of New York was the writer and editor and friend of the Robinsons, William Cullen Bryant, who used his newspaper to attack all those nativists who discriminated against immigrants and who wanted a twenty-one year waiting period before naturalization could take place. Using the *New York Evening Post* as his "bully pulpit" he poured contempt on all those who wanted to keep "America for Americans." For him, the Irish and Catholics in general had as much a place in America as anyone else.[6] For his

---

[5] *The New York Evangelist*, at least in origin a Finneyite publication, is full of anti-slavery articles.
[6] William Cullen Bryant II, "No Irish Need Apply: William Cullen Bryant Fights Nativism 1836-1845," *New York State History* 74, no. 1 (Jan. 1993), 29-46.

pains he was virtually drummed out of the Democratic Party. He became first a Free-Soiler and then a Republican, eventually introducing Abraham Lincoln for the first time to a New York audience.

Whether Bryant's enthusiasm for the cause of human rights affected Robinson is an open question. Presumably E. R. began with a position not unlike that of Moses Stuart. Henry Boynton Smith indicates, however, that by degrees E. R. changed his stance:

> Conservative by instinct, yet deeply sharing our national instinct—which is the love of an impartial liberty, he slowly but surely came to identify loyalty and liberty, and to see that our national cause is also freedom's cause.[7]

Perhaps it was Bryant who helped to change his mind.

Along with the ills of poverty and resultant discrimination, came economic bursts which produced a rich and fashionable moneyed class with an appetite for goods and services. These economic "ups" were followed by periods of panic, like the Panic of '37, which produced bankruptcy and ruin for those who had not hedged their bets properly. There was no safety net. To fall economically was to enter the terrible world of amoral, grinding poverty and crime.[8] Fear of that squalor heightened enormously the desire of the rich to stay that way. Haves and have-nots lived in different worlds.

Despite the panics and crises, however, America was expanding economically and geographically at a tremendous rate. This was true especially in the late 1840s when Oregon was secured by treaty with Britain and the whole southwest and California were wrested from Mexico by a war which many regarded as both unjust and unneeded. The gold rush initiated by the discovery at Sutter's Mill pulled the population westward and brought thousands of Europeans to the eastern shores in search of a new life and, if possible, wealth and excitement. Some never got beyond New York.

---

[7] Henry Boynton Smith, "Remarks of Henry B. Smith, D. D. pm the announcement of the Death of Dr. Robinson at a meeting of the New York Historical Society, February 3, 1863," in *The Life, Writings, and Character of Edward Robinson D D., LL.D.*(New York: Anson D.F. Randolph, 1863), 15.

[8] For a "ground's eye" view of the Panic of '37 see: William H. Siles, "Quiet Desperation: a Personal View of the Panic of 1837," *New York State History* 67, no. 1 (Jan. 1986), 89-92.

In many respects, New York City was simply a microcosm of the nation. Boasting in 1840 some 300,000 inhabitants living on the southern end of Manhattan Island,[9] New York was the largest city in the United States. It was the entrepôt of the nation, facilitating the exports from both the land of cotton in the south and the agricultural areas of the north and west. New York's natural harbor helped in this; so too did the Erie Canal. It is true that New York was particularly slow in developing rail transport and, therefore, was in danger of losing business to Boston which had been far more forward looking in this regard. Eventually, however, the Hudson River line was laid and New York, thanks in part to Cornelius "Commodore" Vanderbilt, became also a great rail center.

New York had already taken the lead as the nation's premier commercial center. Here were the influential banks and counting houses and financiers. One came to New York primarily, not for culture or intellectuality—you could find those in Boston—but to make money. The city was vibrant with activity and hard work as goods were shipped and received to and from all over the United States.

New York also became a focal point for manufacturing. Its ship builders outdistanced New England in the making of clipper ships which sped around the horn to San Francisco in record time. Soon it began to serve as a major center for the manufacture of ready-made clothes—Brooks Brothers had been founded in 1818—and musical instruments—Steinway pianos, for instance—as well as furniture, books, soap, cigars and a host of other products.[10] In New York there was money to be made and jobs to be found. It was a beehive of activity.

It was also a city of rapid change and improvement. In 1840, New York still had no water system; everyone depended on individual wells and septic systems. In 1842, however, with great fanfare, water from the new Croton reservoir in Westchester began spraying forth its fifty foot column in the city hall fountain. After the expenditure of some twelve million dollars, New York had a water system of which to be justly proud. Gas lights also

---

[9] Edward K. Spann, *The New Metropolis: New York City, 1840-1857*. (New York: Columbia University Press, 1981), 2.
[10] Oliver E. Allen, *New York, New York; A History of the World's Most Exhilarating and Challenging City* (New York: Atheneum, 1990), 118-119.

gradually replaced the old, dim oil lamps, though for sometime New York was illuminated half with one, half with the other.

Entertainments

Entertainments, some sophisticated, some not so sophisticated, began to emerge. In 1838, Frederick Catherwood's circular panorama of Jerusalem was brought from London to New York. The artist, who had lived in Jerusalem for several months in 1833, presented an in-the-round view of Jerusalem from a point overlooking the Dome of the Rock. Viewers could buy a key to identify all the sites presented and could attend lectures by the artist on what they were seeing.[11] Doubtless this was to spark great interest in Robinson's own work. So too did the various grand scale paintings of Holy Land scenes by, for instance, Thomas Cole, David Roberts, and later, John Bavard.

On a less religious note, in 1842, P. T. Barnum opened his very popular American Museum, featuring both freaks of nature and natural phenomena of a more scientific sort. There were also musical shows at the museum, including, for instance, the Prague Band of Musicians and Singers. One of Barnum's greatest successes was bringing Jenny Lind to America in 1850-51 to perform for $1,000 plus expenses for each concert. She became the darling of the evangelical Protestants because of her observance of the Sabbath and her promotion of the cause of temperance. The dwarf, Tom Thumb, also became one of Barnum's featured acts and was later taken to England with much publicity.

There were many other venues as well. Although New York's first true opera house had already come and gone, there was the Park Theater which frequently featured concerts of opera arias. Niblo's Garden, Apollo Hall, and eventually the Astor Place Opera House all featured opera. There were also the Bowery Theater which seemed to specialize in oriental romances, Castle Gardens, with band concerts as well as opera, and the New Chatham which sought to slake New York's insatiable appetite for black-face entertainment.[12]

---

[11] Davis, *The Landscape of Belief*, 59-64.
[12] "Places of Public Amusement," *Putnam's Magazine* III, no. 14 (Feb. 1854), 141-152.

After the Jenny Lind tour which had netted the performer at least $200,000 plus expenses, many other Europeans—Marietta Alboni, Henriette Sontag, Adeliona Patti, *et al*—decided to cash in on the bonanza. None of them, however, equaled the success of the Swedish Nightingale.[13] And then, of course, there were the sacred music concerts, by the Sacred Music Society and by Thomas Hastings' Academy of Sacred Music. In 1842 the New York Philharmonic Society was founded.

In 1845 the New York Knickerbockers, the City's first baseball team, was formed and the sporting world which now dominates so much of the American imagination began to come slowly into existence. "Professional" horse racing, and the gambling which went with it, was also becoming popular both in New York and around the nation

New York, it seems, was fast becoming what it was later to be: the musical and entertainment capital of America. Not all of the musical offerings were first-rate, by any stretch of the imagination. Henry Cood Watson, a young English reviewer on a mission to reform American music, frequently wrote scathing, even scandalous reviews of various performances. For instance, of a performance of the Sacred Music Society he reported that the chorus sang wretchedly and the orchestra "scarcely played six consecutive bars correctly."[14] Nevertheless, America was growing up musically. It would be years before the nation would match the sophistication of European ability and taste, but the hunger was there among the *nouveau riche* and the old Yankee aversion to the theater and opera was being eroded away. The Robinsons would not have to return to Europe to hear great music performed tolerably well.

---

[13] For a fine review of opera in Ante-bellum America see: John Dizikes, *Opera in America: A Cultural History* (New Haven, Conn.: Yale University Press, 1993) pp. 89-188.

[14] Vera Brodsky Lawrence, *Strong on Music: The New York Music Scene in the Days of George Templeton Strong, 1836-187*, 2 Vols. (New York: Oxford University Press, 1988) I, 97.

The Literary and Artistic World

As said above, it was Boston and not New York which was considered by many "the intellectual capital of America." One thinks of Emerson and Hawthorne, Whittier and Longfellow, the Bronsons and Thoreau. New York, however, was not without its writers and thinkers too. Indeed, Gaylord Clark, the editor of the well-known *Knickerbocker,* and his circle believed New York to be the center of everything literary. Although Clark had a great dislike for Emerson, he claimed responsibility, with at least some justification, for introducing the reading public to almost everyone else of note.[15] It is doubtful, however, that Clark, who was an Episcopalian by faith and a "Rabelaisian" by style, would have had much to do with Edward and Therese. He had a distinct dislike for things Puritan. Clark, however, was not the only literary figure to call New York home. William Cullen Bryant, the well-known poet and editor, worked in New York and made his home on adjacent Long Island. Another editor and writer, Evert A. Duyckinck, gathered about him the intelligentsia of the city, "holding court" at his home on Clinton Place. In nearby Tarrytown lived Washington Irving, America's first truly professional writer, who frequented New York often and who entertained regularly both literary and political figures at his home, Sunnyside. Fitz-Greene Hallek, the poet and satirist, and Herman Melville, the budding novelist, lived in the City.[16] Walt Whitman, still an unknown, was a native of nearby Brooklyn. And there were women writers like Caroline Kirkland who was well-known as both a novelist and an editor. One must also mention among the intellectuals Samuel F. B. Morse, quite a distinguished artist as well as the inventor of the telegraph. Since Edward knew his father through Andover and his brother Sidney who edited the *New York Observer* to which Edward regularly contributed, he probably had many contacts with Samuel as well. Among the artists known by Robinson was Daniel Huntington who painted E. R.'s portrait and Thomas Cole, a

---

[15] For a good picture of Clark and his friends see: Perry Miller, *The Raven and the Whale* (New York: Harcourt Brace and Co., 1956), chs. 1 and 2.

[16] For a look at New York from Melville's perspective see: Wyn Kelley, *Melville's City* (New York: Cambridge University Press, 1996).

very close friend of William Cullen Bryant and an acquaintance of E. R.'s sister Naomi who also lived in Catskill.

We know that the Robinsons became well acquainted with the Bryants and with Caroline Kirkland and it is not surprising that they also came to know and were, like so many others, entertained by Washington Irving, for they shared so much in common.[17] Irving and Therese had a mutual admiration for Sir Walter Scott who he knew intimately and whose work she had translated into German. Moreover, the Robinsons and Irving were both well acquainted with European intellectuals in general and shared many friends in common; Irving and Robinson also shared a passion for travel and the unknown.[18] According to Voigt, it was Irving who rekindled Therese's desire to write poetry.[19]

One small indication of their intellectual circle is found in the New York Public Library archives which contains an invitation sent by E. R. to Evart Duyckinck, the well-known editor, to meet at his home R. H. Dana, Bryant and two or three other literary friends. This could have been Dana Sr. who was a poet admired by Therese or his son, the author of *Two Years Before the Mast*.[20] In either case it indicates that Robinson's contacts and interests were literary as well as theological. Besides Bryant, Voigt also lists George Bancroft, Bayard Taylor,[21] Albert Gallatin, Frederick von Raumer, Frederick Olmstead, Margaret Fuller and J. C. Kohl among their friends.[22] It is clear that New York was a place where not only Edward but Therese could thrive intellectually. There were theatrical plays, much sacred and

---

[17] Voigt, *op. cit.,* 39. Voigt bases much of what she says upon Therese's papers which were, unfortunately, subsequently destroyed in a fire.

[18] Irving went on a two year tour of the American prairies and subsequently published *A Tour on the Prairies* (1835) which became quite popular in America.

[19] Voigt. *op. cit.,* 39.

[20] Among the Robinson papers (L.7) is a letter from R. H. Dana senior dated Oct. 6. 1841, thanking Robinson for his help in finding a publisher for his son's book. Ironically, J. Murray, E. R.'s London publisher, did not think that *Two Years before the Mast* would sell.

[21] There is an invitation which shows that the Robinsons knew Taylor well enough to invite him to their home, but it does seem strange that Taylor did not so much as mention E. R. in his *Cyclopedia of Modern Travel* (New York: Cincinnati, Moore, Wilstock, Keys and Co., 1861).

[22] *Ibid.*, 38-40.

secular music, a variety of writers and intellectuals, even a German newspaper.

And then there were the lectures.[23] America had, by this time, become inebriated with the public lecture. Some lecturers were local and drew small audiences but there were also the big names like Henry Ward Beecher and Ralph Waldo Emerson who attracted thousands. From 1840 until 1860 New York saw at least three thousand public lectures on virtually every conceivable subject, from astronomy to the Zulus. These were occasions which even the most fastidious and pious lady could attend without damage to her reputation. They were, in fact, a form of amusement especially for those who found music halls and the theater morally suspect. Undoubtedly Edward and Therese attended many of these presentations. Indeed, Edward offered a few himself, for there is evidence he gave more than one at the New York Historical Society.[24] There are also intimations, however, that his forte was writing and not speaking and it is doubtful that his lecture style would ever have drawn huge audiences.[25]

We must also mention the American Art-Union established in New York in the late 1830s as a way of fostering the arts in a country which had no aristocracy to serve as patrons.[26] This Art-Union, which was patterned after many similar institutions in England and the Continent, bought paintings from artists, showed them and sold them. In so doing, the Union

---

[23] Donald M. Scott, "The Popular Lecture and the Creation of a Public in Mid-Nineteenth century America" *Journal of American History* 66, no. 4 (Mar. 1980), 791ff.
[24] Records from the New York Historical Society indicate that he offered the following lectures: "The Druses" (April 4 and May 2, 1843), "Depression of the Dead Sea" (May 4, 1847), "The History and Recent Collation of the English Bible" (June 3, 1851), "Outlines of a Recent Journey in Palestine," (Dec. 7, 1852), "Historical Notices at Capernaum" (April 3, 1854). The record also says that on November 4, 1850 an Edward Robinson gave a lecture entitled: "Remarks with reference to the celebrated Ruin at Newport, R.I. known as the old Wind-Mill" and also "Upon the settlement at Riga, near the corner where the States of New York, Massachusetts and Connecticut meet- its name and history." These last topics seem so far from E. R.'s expertise or interest, however, that it is doubtful the presentations were by him. On March 4 and April 1, 1845 he did read a paper prepared by the recently deceased William L. Stone.
[25] Hitchcock, *op. cit.,* 86. See also the *New York Times* report of his presentation on Dec. 7, 1852 (*Infra* p. 295, n. 430).
[26] Rachel N. Klein, "Art and Authority in Ante-bellum New York City: The Rise and Fall of the American Art Union," *Journal of American History* 81, no. 4 (Mar. 1995), 1534-1561.

aimed to provide support for artists and spiritual inspiration to the public, for landscapes, in particular, were seen as of particular spiritual benefit.[27] Members who had joined the society for five dollars could participate in a yearly lottery with the chance of winning a work of art.[28] William Cullen Bryant and Evart Duyckinck, friends of the Robinsons, each served for a time as head of the Union and there is every reason to suspect that Edward and Therese may have been members.

Higher Education

New York also boasted of four academic institutions of higher learning.[29] The oldest was, of course, Columbia University which had been founded in 1754 as King's College. After an hiatus during the Revolutionary War it had been reopened in 1784 by the New York Board of Regents as Columbia University. "Kings" was thought to be no longer an acceptable part of an American's vocabulary. There was a medical school, which won the name "university" for the institution and Columbia College for undergraduates. The latter was classical in curriculum, aristocratic in clientele, and minuscule in size. As already noted, until the Civil War, Columbia's graduating classes were very small. In 1851, for instance, the student bodies of Union, Hamilton, and N.Y.U. were all larger.[30] Columbia was also considered sectarian because the President was required to be an Episcopalian.

---

[27] For interesting information about the Art Union see: *Literary World* (1847). Virtually every issue of that weekly literary newspaper during that particular year contains information about the Art-Union and its work. For a discussion of the spiritual values of Hudson River School Art see: Diane Apostolos-Cappadona, *The Spirit and the Vision* (Atlanta: Scholars Press, 1995).

[28] *The New-York Evangelist* reports that Thomas Cole's very famous series, "The Voyage of Life," was won by someone in Binghamton and then sold to the Spingler Institute. The fact that this set of paintings was the prize increased membership in the Institute enormously. These works by Cole are now housed in the Munson-Williams-Proctor Institute in Utica, N. Y.

[29] See: "Educational Institutions of New York," *Putnam's Magazine* II, no. 7 (July 1853), 1-16.

[30] *New-York Evangelist* March 13, 1851.

The second institution to be found on Manhattan Island was General Theological Seminary, another Episcopal institution. It was established by that church in 1817 to be the "general" seminary for the whole Episcopal communion. Clement Clark Moore, an ardent Hebraist and later author of "A Visit from St. Nicholas," gave the seminary building lots in Chelsea which was then outside the city. By 1836 the theological school had constructed two buildings on the site to house and instruct the 64 matriculants.

The third institution was the University of the City of New York, now New York University. It was founded in 1832 with the intention that it would provide a more practical education for the sons of businessmen than little Columbia offered. It was hoped that there would be modern languages and civil engineering and scientific courses. In fact, the university was badly undersubscribed financially when it opened its doors and during the first several years of existence was constantly in crisis. Determination prevailed and its doors stayed open on the east side of Washington Square, but its faculty seemed much less inventive than had originally been planned. There were professors of Greek, Latin, Mathematics, Chemistry, and Apologetic Theology, a variety not very different from Hamilton College at its inception. Other professors, like Samuel F. B. Morse in Art, taught courses on a fee per student basis, but, in fact, garnered few elections.[31]

In 1840, when the Robinsons arrived, N.Y.U. was a small, struggling institution with many more students in its Medical School than in its undergraduate program and with a faculty which was always underpaid and sometimes not paid at all. Part of the difficulty lay with the institution. Poor administration and constant squabbling made public in the press seldom attract big money. Then there was the great fire of 1835 which literally burned up a great deal of the city's wealth and the Panic of '37 which also made potential givers paupers. Moreover, there was that New York City mentality which did not value higher education all that much. Success in business at the time depended upon hard work, cleverness, and careful thinking but not upon a literary education. Sons went to work in the business to learn what they needed to know to succeed. Learning French did not help very much; learning Greek, even less.

---

[31] For a review of N. Y. U.'s early years see: Theodore Francis Jones, ed. *New York University: 1832: 1932* (New York: The New York University Press, 1933), 3-72.

The fourth academic institution of note was, of course, Union Theological Seminary which had been founded in 1836. Discussion of Union, however, will be postponed until we look further into the nature of New York City in 1840. It should be commented, though, that like N.Y.U., Union was founded at an exceedingly difficult time. The Fire, the Panic, the materialistic mood of commercial New York meant that endowment did not exactly flow freely into the fledgling institution. While Robinson prepared his *magnum opus* in Europe there were several occasions when it was not at all clear that the institution would survive. Perhaps there was good reason why the Directors accepted Robinson's request to stay in Germany longer. While he was there, they did not need to pay his salary.

Society and the Churches

The population of New York was growing at a rapid rate and as it did, the wealthy moved further and further uptown, building their "palaces" on the north side of Washington Square. It was still quite a ride from the city to the village of Harlem on the other end of the island and there was as yet no bridge to the small city of Brooklyn (30,000) across the East River. (Cornelius Vanderbilt made his money first providing ferry service and other nautical transportation around the busy harbor.) Nevertheless, Manhattan Island was gradually becoming one political entity and the suburbs were also being drawn into its orbit. The City, as we know it today, was coming into being. By the fifties, at the urging of William Cullen Bryant, a new, huge park called Central would be laid out in a largely uninhabited area north of 59th Street for the enjoyment of an ever increasing population.

As wealthier people moved uptown out of lower Manhattan, their places were rapidly taken over by a growing and impoverished lower class, made up largely but not exclusively of immigrants, mainly Irish and German, who inhabited the squalid slums of the lower east side, particularly around an area called "Five Points." Conditions were shockingly bad as all the evils of the modern metropolis emerged full force.[32] Gambling and prostitution and pornography were rampant.[33] So were the saloons—there

---

[32] Spann, *op. cit.,* 242-280.
[33] See: Elliott J. Gorn, "Good-Bye Boys, I Die a True American: Homicide, Nativism,

were more than 3000 of them—and other places of low entertainment where pickpockets and other criminals did their work. There were gangs and crime bosses; there were thousands of ragged children begging, stealing, pimping, dying. Venereal disease, tuberculosis, and other largely untreatable horrors ran rampant. Abortion mills were well known and frequented. New York was both the jewel and the nightmare of America. Even Charles Dickens, who knew something about slums, was shocked.

The horrors of the tenement slums quite naturally stimulated many people to think about reform. Although education was by no means universal, elementary schooling was improved and offered to many more children. There were children's aid programs and soup kitchens and temperance rallies. In many respects, American social progressivism got its start in New York as a response to the dreadful conditions. And there **was** improvement as many children and young women were rescued from disaster. Nevertheless, many problems seemed intractable and despite all the effort and best intentions, overall progress seemed minimal. There were always more immigrants and more country folk flooding into the city to seek their fortunes and there were always the unscrupulous to take advantage of them. These included not just the criminal bosses and flimflam artists but also the wealthy businessmen who hired workers for long hours at low wages and no benefits. Poverty was the long shadow that wealth cast across the island of Manhattan.[34]

In the midst of all this wealth and poverty, art and tawdriness, fashion and raggedness were the churches, still defining the skyline with their steeples and the moral tone of the city with their sermons. In 1846 Jonathan Greenleaf published a little book describing each of New York City's churches.[35] According to him, in that year there were:

> 16 Dutch Reform Churches with 4,773 members.
> 39 Episcopal Churches with 6,376 members.
> 39 Presbyterian Churches with 13,478 members.

---

and Working Class Culture in New York City," *Journal of American History* 74, no. 2 (Sept. 1987), 388-410.

[34] For an interesting, brief article on New York poverty see: "Life at Five Points," *New-York Observer* XXXIV, 4 (Jan. 24, 1856), 29.

[35] Jonathan Greenleaf, *A History of the Churches of All Denominations in the City of New York From the First Settlement to the Year 1846* (New York: E. French, 1846).

> 31 Baptist Churches with 8,744 members
> 48 Methodist Churches with 12,845 members
> 8 Congregational Churches with 1,087 members

Unfortunately, he does not give statistics for the sixteen Roman Catholic parishes or for the smaller denominations like the Lutherans, Unitarians, and Friends. Nevertheless, even if there were as many Catholics as Protestants, which is unlikely, only one third of New York was "churched" in the mid-1840s. The mainline Protestant denominations, numbering fewer than 48,000, accounted for less than one sixth of the population! Clearly from their point of view, there was much work to be done.[36]

This was the age of voluntary, interdenominational societies and New York was full of them: Bible, Home Missions, Children's, Temperance, etc.[37] All of this was sparked by a theological attitude which assumed that although humans are sinners, there are things which can be done by Christians to save the suffering and needy. God may be the ultimate source of salvation, but human will is not unimportant. Human beings are responsible for their own sins and for "turning toward the Lord." This was the message of the Calvinistic divines of New England, particularly Nathaniel Taylor, and Charles Granison Finney of New York and it was received with enthusiasm by many New York Protestants who knew they had to do something to change the terrible conditions so obvious in the city.

Although the theologians of New England still used the vocabulary of Calvinists, they did so with a difference. For Taylor and his many followers, moral law was almost as clear as the laws of nature and could be grasped by most people if it were presented rationally. The evils of alcohol were indisputable; so were the idolatries of Rome. About some things there was little room for debate.[38] Like the Seventeenth Century Cambridge Platonists, reason was identified as the "candle of the lord within," and, in some ways, virtually identical with the Holy Spirit.

Not all Presbyterians, however, agreed. At Princeton Seminary, across the river, there was much suspicion about the new divinity imported from

---

[36] These figures are in line with statistics offered by *The New York Evangelist* (Aug. 30, 1849), 140. In that year, only one out of five Americans was a member of a church.

[37] For a review of these institutions see: "The Benevolent Institutions of New-York," *Putnam's Magazine* I, no. 6 (June 1853), 673-686.

[38] Hiller, *op. cit.*, 26-40.

Connecticut. Adam's sin, said the old orthodox, is imputed to all humans from the beginning. We are born sinners and there is nothing **we** can do to rid ourselves of it. Only God can save; to think otherwise is to engage in the sin of pride. Certainly, morality is not just a matter of rationality. Only the Bible reveals what is right. At Andover, however, "imputed" was a word very much despised and the tendency was to find in the Bible what one already knew was right.

This debate, illustrated very well by the controversy between Moses Stuart and Charles Hodge concerning the meaning of St. Paul's remarks about sin in Romans 5, had become very heated by the 1830s.[39] It is important, however, to see that the debate was not purely philological or even theological. Old School Presbyterians tended to be Scottish or Scotch Irish who had settled in the middle Atlantic and southern states and who brought with them to America their long-standing dislike for the English and their descendants. *The Princeton Review*, the primary organ of Old School Presbyterianism, certainly reveals this attitude in the course of its rather vicious review of Robinson's *magnum opus*.

> Scotland and New England have been frequently compared, as to the shrewdness, industry, frugality, religious education, and good morals of her people; but even where other things are equal, there is a great difference between the dry metaphysical religion of one and the warm-hearted whole-souled devotion of the other.[40]

Just before that remark the anonymous reviewer offered his assessment of New England's religion:

> We have no hesitation in saying, that of all enlightened and religious countries, there is none in which the poetry, the oriental charm, of scriptural language and associations, seem to have so little power and to be so little cherished, as among our brethren of the eastern states. There is no part of Protestant Christianity in which even orthodox theology has shown so strong a tendency to substitute the barren forms and heartless phraseology of

---

[39] See Stephen J. Stein, "Stuart and Hodge on Romans 5:12-21: And Exegetical Controversy about Original Sin," *Journal of Presbyterian History* 47, no. 4 (Dec. 1969), 340-358.
[40] *The Biblical Repertory and Princeton Review* XIII, no. 3 (Oct. 1841), 591.

metaphysics for the lively figures and rousing, melting, soul-subduing eloquence of God's own word.[41]

It seems clear that that old struggle between the Scots and the English has been transferred to American soil and that to the New Englanders have been imputed all those English characteristics so scorned by the Scots.

While Old Schoolers disliked intensely the abstract and rationalistic nature of some New England theology, they also recognized that their own religious feelings and "social style" simply did not fit with the new measures of Finney's evangelism. It is not that they were not fervent in their beliefs, but they just did not like the enthusiasm, the emotionalism, and emphasis on works which went with the New School religion. The latter, they felt, had become like shouting Methodists. Real Presbyterians, that is Scottish Presbyterians, just wouldn't act that way. Again the *Princeton Review* minces no words:

> We tender him (Finney) our thanks for the substantial service he has done the church by exposing the naked deformities of the New School divinity. He can render her still another, and in rendering it perform only his plain duty, by leaving her communion and finding one within which he can preach and publish his opinions without making war upon the standards in which he has solemnly professed his faith.[42]

And again:

> We conclude this article as we did our former, by pointing out to Mr. Finney his duty to leave our church. It is an instructive illustration of the fact that fanaticism debilitates the conscience that this man can doubt the piety of any one who uses coffee . . . while he remains, apparently without remorse, with the sin of broken vows upon him. In this position we leave him before the public. Nor will we withdraw our charges against him, until he goes out from among us, for he is not of us.[43]

---

[41] *Ibid.*
[42] *Biblical Repertory and Princeton Review* VII, no. 3 (July 1835), 527.
[43] *Biblical Repertory and Princeton Review* VII, no. 4 (Oct. 1835), 674.

Moreover, that Finney emotionalism coupled with a strong strain of perfectionism had led, they thought, to an unwarranted belief in the ability of humans to change things. The Old School was very suspicious of interdenominational activity as an attack upon doctrinal purity. They did not like the Plan of Union of 1801 which had brought cooperation, if not union, between Congregationalists and Presbyterians. They were also quite aware of the connection between this volunteerism and social reform and those radical abolitionists and proponents of women's rights. Although it was not the only issue, behind the Old School-New School controversy was also, quite predictably, slavery. Because there were many slave-holding Presbyterians in the South, most members of the Old School wanted nothing to do with abolitionism which they regarded as, at best, a bad mistake perpetrated by radical extremists.

It should be noted, however, that there were both Old School and New School abolitionists and that the southern presbyteries were less interested in the squabble between Princeton and New England than they were in preserving the institution of slavery. Charles Hodges' attack upon William Channing's call for the abolishment of slavery and his defense of slavery on Biblical grounds in the 1836 *Biblical Repertory and Theological Review*, however, cemented the relations between Princeton and the South and made the denomination's schism inevitable.[44]

In all this one must not assume that this was a struggle between today's conservatives and liberals. In point of fact, the New School Presbyterians, with their emphasis upon revival and reform, were closer to modern evangelicals than Charles Hodge and the conservatives. Billy Graham doubtless would find Charles G. Finney and Joel Parker much more to his liking than the Alexanders of Princeton. The staid and sober attitude of old Princeton simply would not fit a great revival at Madison Square Garden.

This struggle within the Presbyterian Church came to a head in the mid-1830s. The Old School attempted unsuccessfully to try two major New School ministers—Lyman Beecher (1834) and Albert Barnes (1835)—for

---

[44] Elwyn A. Smith, "The Role of the South in the Presbyterian Schism of 1837-38," *Church History* 29, no. 1 (Mar. 1960), 44-63. See also [Charles Hodge] "Review of Slavery by William B. Channing," *Biblical Repertory and Theological Review* VIII, no. 2 (Apr. 1836), 268-305.

heresy. Neither was convicted, but the feelings engendered were cantankerous and nasty. It was inconceivable to New Schoolers that either one of these men could have been accused of heresy at all. Certainly no one could have been more fervently orthodox than Lyman Beecher! Few could have been milder and more pious than Barnes. To the Old Schoolers, however, these men represented a threat to the purity of doctrine and the stability of society. The trials which ended with acquittal left them frustrated and anxious to do battle again. Appeals to higher judicatories brought only more misunderstanding and recrimination.

In 1838, at the General Assembly of the Presbyterian Church, the great disruption occurred. The Old School proponents not only voted to dissolve the Plan of Union which had brought cooperation between Congregationalists and Presbyterians; in so doing, they severed from the rest of the church four synods—three in New York and one in Ohio—which had been directly involved with the Plan of Union.[45] From that time until 1868, there were two Presbyterian Churches officially divided over a subject which had bothered Christians at least since the fourth century: the nature of original sin,[46] but in fact separated as well by both ethnic and cultural considerations. Princeton looked to the South; Union Theological Seminary, toward New England.

Union Theological Seminary

Behind the founding of Union lay this whole dispute. When clergy and laymen met in 1835 to consider the establishment of a new theological seminary in New York, the impulse was not simply that New York, as America's largest city, ought to have a Presbyterian theological school of its

---

[45] The whole event is actually much more complex than this, but to explain the politics and the legal side of the matter would require a whole, separate book. New York and Ohio, in any event, had been populated quite heavily by Connecticut Yankees who may have become Presbyterian in denomination but had retained many of the attitudes of New England.

[46] For an Old School understanding of the schism see: James W. Alexander, *The Life of Archibald Alexander, D.D.,* Third Edition (New York: Charles Scribners' Sons, 1856),470-480 or Samuel Miller, *The Life of Samuel Miller* (Philadelphia: Claxton, Remsen, and Haffelfinger, 1869), 325-347.

own. It was also that many people in New York City and the northeast found the direction taken by the seminary at Princeton questionable if not abusive. They believed that there was room for another seminary beside Auburn upstate to stand for the New School position. They also believed that while Auburn was good at training ministers for the rural life in central and western New York, its program did not prepare young men to meet the challenges and opportunities of the big city. This desire was magnified when, but two years after its founding, Union found itself in a presbytery severed by the machinations of the Old Schoolers, from what Princeton proclaimed **the** Presbyterian Church .

Perhaps a word should be said about the name of Union Theological Seminary. When the trustees of the institution applied for a charter, they apparently assumed the name would be New York Theological Seminary. The usual theory is that the Board of Regents did not like that name because General Seminary was already in New York and the regents did not want to offend that older institution, so they changed the name to Union. It seems unlikely, however, that the Board would have chosen a new name without consultation. Other theories suggest that, when consulted, some of the founders who had been involved with Union Seminary in Virginia liked that name and chose it; or that in the face of schism they chose the new name to stand for the union of the church. Still another possibility, not often mentioned, is that the word Union refers to the Plan of Union against which the Old School stood. Whatever the reasons, by the time Robinson returned, New York Theological Seminary had become Union Theological Seminary in the City of New York and has remained so ever since.

Had Robinson begun his work with the seminary at the very beginning, he would have had to teach at home, for the institution in 1836 had no building to accommodate its students and their classes. Before his arrival, however, a site had been purchased on University Place, just up the street from New York University, between 6th and 8th Street, and there a modest seminary building had been erected. Four faculty homes were also constructed on the same plot, facing on Greene Street. The area was, at the time, very much "uptown," on the edge of the city, though before long many new residences were built to the north. The building was dedicated on December 12, 1838 and the institution itself incorporated by the legislature in March of 1839.

Even at the beginning, the building was too small, for it accommodated only thirty students and matriculation by the second year far surpassed expectations. By the fourth year they had taken in fifty-five new students and were the third largest seminary in America. Before long, two more stories were added to the building to accommodate the success. Much to the surprise of the founders, who believed they were building an institution to serve primarily the churches of New York and Brooklyn, most of the students came from elsewhere. Although the majority hailed from New School areas, there were always some from the south and midwest, and some from foreign countries.

The original faculty was drawn very largely from New York itself. The first President, Thomas McAuley[47] was an Irishman who, after several years of experience, was educated at Union College in Schenectady. He was called to be the pastor of the Rutgers Street Church in 1822. In 1827 he moved to Philadelphia but returned in 1833 to serve the Murray Street Presbyterian Church. He was, from the beginning, one of the founders of Union and served as its first President and Professor of Pastoral Theology. By the time Robinson came on the scene, however, he had already resigned from the faculty. He was replaced by Joel Parker,[48] a Hamilton College graduate, who had come to New York from Rochester and was known for his strong evangelical preaching. He lasted as President, however, only two years. Thereafter, there would not be another President for the institution until William Adams assumed the office in 1873. During the long interval, the Seminary was run by consensus of the faculty and the direction of the Board.

The other full-time faculty member, Henry White,[49] was from Durham N.Y. and, like McAuley, a Union College graduate. He had studied at Princeton Theological Seminary for two years and then, after a variety of positions, became minister at the Allen Street Church. Like McAuley he was a founder of the seminary and became the first Professor of Systematic Theology. He taught at Union until his death in 1850. Before Robinson

---

[47] George Lewis Prentiss, *The Union Theological Seminary in the City of New York: Historical and Biographical Sketches of its first fifty Years* (New York: Anson D. F. Randolph and Co., 1889), 149-151.
[48] *Ibid.*, 211-212.
[49] *Ibid.*, 251-254.

arrived, beside the President and White, there were only Professors Extraordinary, i.e. visiting lecturers, to teach the rest. Erskine Mason,[50] another founder and secretary of the Board, taught ecclesiastical history. Ichabod Spencer,[51] a Brooklyn pastor taught Biblical history, while Isaac Nordheimer, a devout Jew, taught Hebrew. The last appointment, even on a temporary basis, strikes one as particularly unusual. One wonders how many other Christian seminaries would have appointed a Jew, no matter what the credentials, to a position on the faculty. This appointment seems to show that from the start Union, though evangelical, was also quite open and broad-minded. Nordheimer also continued to teach Hebrew at Union for some time after Robinson joined the faculty. Perhaps it was the straitened circumstances, perhaps the city, but Union, for some reason, has always been more open to a variety of opinions than many other theological schools.[52]

From the outset, in any event, Robinson appears to have been the "star of the show." Even though he himself held only an earned A.B. degree, no one else on the faculty came close to having his credentials, his teaching record, his international experience. Parker, White, and Mason were doubtless good and enthusiastic men who worked very hard at the tasks before them, but they simply were not in his league. They had not published significantly; they had not even had much theological education. One can only wonder whether he did not feel some twinges of regret that he had decided to get into this.

What is ironic is that E. R. had not even been their first choice. According to Prentiss,[53] their offer went first to Addison Alexander of Princeton, a peculiar choice at best, for he was without a doubt from the Old School. He was a brilliant linguist and a considerable scholar, but he had no skills for dealing with people and seldom allowed for any genuine contact

---

[50] *Ibid.,* 14-16, 130-136.
[51] *Ibid.,* 152-153.
[52] It should be noted that Nordheimer was a consummate scholar, producing a well-reviewed *Critical Grammar of the Hebrew Language* (New York: Wiley and Putnam, 1838), *A Grammatical Analysis of Selections from the Hebrew Scriptures* (New York: Wiley and Putnam, 1838), and was working on *A Complete Hebrew and Chaldee Concordance of the Old Testament* (Part One only was published) at the time of his death. Even the hatchet men of the *Princeton Review* liked his work!
[53] Prentiss, *op.cit.,* 23-24.

with his students. As Moorhead says,

> Awkward in the presence of others, the adult Alexander was ill-disposed to social amenities . . . He professionalized contacts with his students, whom he usually avoided outside class lest they interfere with his demanding schedule of research.[54]

Undoubtedly, it was a fortuitous thing that Alexander said "no." Perhaps this is what the Directors expected anyway. Alexander was the son of Archibald Alexander, the first professor of Princeton Theological Seminary. He himself taught at the same institution. Therefore, since he had his roots in Princeton and was thoroughly in tune with Old School theology, it would have been highly unlikely that he would have left there for an untried and poorly financed New School institution. The invitation, so readily rejected, may have been simply a palm leaf to the Old School leaders. No one could say that Union had not tried to incorporate the Old School point of view.

Then they turned to Professor George Howe of the Theological Seminary in Columbia, South Carolina. He was a somewhat more likely choice, for he had been educated at Middlebury and Andover and had taught for a time at Dartmouth. Fear of tuberculosis led him, however, to move to South Carolina and it was to the South that he decided to devote his attention.[55] Only after he too turned the Directors down did they appeal to Robinson and receive a positive answer.

His reply has, happily, been preserved for us by George Prentiss in his biographical sketch of E. R.[56] In the letter, he begins by indicating that he had actually spent "some months" in New York in 1837 researching the plans and prospects for the Seminary and that he had concluded that he agreed with the substance of the project. He particularly liked the fact that "it is the nursling of the churches of the city and as such will, if deserving, be borne in their arms."[57]

He then goes on to emphasize how important and many-sided Biblical

---

[54] James H. Moorhead, "Joseph Addison Alexander: Common Sense, Romanticism and Biblical Criticism at Princeton," *Journal of Presbyterian History* 53, no. 1 (Spring 1975), 52.

[55] Dumas Malone, ed., "George Howe," *Dictionary of American Biography* (New York: Charles Scribners' Sons, 1932) IX, 286-287.

[56] Prentiss, *op.cit.*, 246-249.

[57] *Ibid.*, 246.

studies is and how no one person could really do it all. This, it appears, is to argue that from the outset the seminary ought to think about hiring more than one person for the task. Just to make the load even heavier he suggests that the Seminary engage in more popular forms of teaching too.

> Permit me to suggest whether it may not in due time be advisable to connect with the Seminary a popular class for Biblical instruction, intended particularly to prepare pious young men as teachers of Bible classes and in Sabbath schools.[58]

In other words, E. R. thought of a seminary as an educational institution for the whole church and not just for the clergy, an interesting and perhaps prophetic suggestion. Finally, he concludes his letter with an acceptance of the offer with the important provision that he be allowed to spend no more than a year in Europe and the Holy Land first.

Now, in 1840, he is at last, after long delays, to fulfill that promise. Everyone must have been exceedingly happy. The Robinsons moved into one of the faculty houses on Greene Street behind the seminary and began a new life, a life which, with a few interruptions, was to last until his death in 1863.[59] Mary was twelve; Edward, six. Therese, as usual, soon became involved in various social service projects as well as her own scholarly pursuits of which we will have more to say later.

The family chose to go to the Mercer Street Presbyterian Church which was located nearby. It was a new uptown church which had been started in 1834 with but a few members. It had grown rapidly, however, so that by 1846 the membership numbered more than 500. Greenleaf describes the building as elegant and the congregation as wealthy.[60] The pastor was Thomas Skinner whom Edward had known when they taught together at Andover a few years earlier. Skinner was a great supporter of Union and persuaded several of the most generous benefactors of his congregation to support the new seminary too. Later he would leave the pastorate to teach

---

[58] *Ibid.,* 247.
[59] According to *Trow's New York City Directory of 1863* (p. 737), the Robinsons were still living at 257 Greene St. at the time of his death. Edward Jr., then a lawyer, lived there too.
[60] Greenleaf, *op.cit.,* 194.

full time at the seminary.[61] He was replaced at the church in 1851 by George Prentiss who also eventually taught at Union and who was responsible for writing its fiftieth anniversary history. Prentiss too was instrumental in encouraging major benefactions for Union. It should be noted parenthetically that Prentiss' invalid wife was a hymn writer whose output included the famous, "More Love to Thee, O Christ."

Union Seminary officially required that all professors be Presbyterian, so Robinson, after a short delay transferred his membership and was ordained on November 15, 1841.[62] Throughout the rest of his life he remained a member of the Third Presbytery of New York, New School. Curiously, the historical office of the Presbyterian Church today claims to have no record of his transfer of membership, but General Assembly minutes clearly record his name. In any event, it is doubtful that his change of membership would have satisfied Princeton and the Old Schoolers. Charles Hodge insisted that Presbyterian clergy should be educated only by Presbyterians and it must have given him much pain to realize that many so-called Presbyterians at Union, Auburn, and Lane Seminaries were really Congregationalists "in disguise" with little experience in the "real" Presbyterian Church at all.

Given the heresy hunting that had gone on in Presbyterianism, Robinson must have felt somewhat relieved that he was at Union and not at an Old School Institution. Robinson was a quiet man who did not relish theological controversy. He was quite willing to accept, as Union professors were expected to do, the Westminster Confession, but would not engage in quibbling about precious doctrinal issues. His presence at Union indicated that this was, in truth, a "Plan of Union" seminary, not a sectarian one. It is noteworthy that Roswell Hitchcock, another Andover man who served on the faculty at Union and who offered to the world the first biography of Robinson, seems to have taught at the seminary as a Congregationalist. For Robinson, in any event, the change in denomination was no major matter. In his "autobiography" in the *Cyclopaedia of American Literature* he does not mention it at all.

---

[61] For an account of his life see: George L. Prentiss, *A Discourse in Memory of Thomas Harvey Skinner, D.D., LL.D.* (New York: Anson D. F. Randolph and Co., n.d.).

[62] S. D. Alexander, *The Presbytery of New York: 1738-1888* (New York: Anson D. F. Randolph, n.d.), 180.

Through this whole period, the basic problem for Union and the Robinsons was money. The seminary was badly under-financed and although many students matriculated, that did not help, for the students paid no tuition. The education was offered courtesy of the churches of New York and those institutions could not really afford the cost of the faculty. In a word, payment of salaries was intermittent and unpredictable. This situation was temporarily eased somewhat in 1842.

> At a period of the greatest darkness, on the 4th of January, 1842, the Directors were in session, and a communication came to them from Mr. James Boorman, in which he agreed to contribute the sum of two thousand dollars annually for three years, to support a Professor, and offered further immediately to pay two thousand dollars, which he desired, irrespective of the conditions imposed by his subscription, should be applied at once to the salary of Dr. Robinson, then largely in arrears.[63]

This grant lasted, however, only until 1845 at which point Robinson's salary seems to have ceased again. By 1846, E. R. had had enough—or perhaps we should say too little—and simply resigned.[64] Somehow, however, the difficulty was overcome, the salary paid more regularly and the resignation withdrawn. By the 1850s the seminary began to attract more sizable donations and moved financially on a more even keel. This was, in part, due to the appointment of Henry Boynton Smith in 1850.[65]

Like Robinson, Smith had studied in Germany under Tholuck and Neander and had, before he arrived at Union, already published a number of important works. Although educated at Andover, he brought a more flexible and modern form of theology which was attractive to students and to the church at large. No longer was Robinson the only star. With Smith, Union came into its own as a first-rate theological institution. Although finances were precarious even in the best days, Smith's presence after 1850 promoted confidence in the Seminary and bequests and donations, small and large,

---

[63] *Ibid.*, 32.
[64] Robert T. Handy, *A History of Union Theological Seminary,* (New York: Columbia University, 1987), 20.
[65] For a report of his inaugural address see: "Prof. Smith's Inaugural," *New-York Evangelist* XXVI, 19 (May 10, 1855), 74. See also *The New-York Observer* XXXIII, 19 (May 10, 1855), 146.

began to flow in. In the meantime, however, the seminary had to suffer through many days of only modest support.

On January 20th, 1841, Edward Robinson was officially inaugurated in his office as Professor of Christian Literature at Union Seminary. The event took place at the nearby Mercer Street Presbyterian Church. After what can only be described as an eloquent and moving charge to the inauguree delivered by the Rev. William Paton, pastor of the Spring Street Church,[66] Robinson offered his inaugural address entitled, "The Bible and its Literature." In it he outlined his view of theological education and the central place of the study of the Bible within it.

Protestantism, he says, is based upon the belief that the Bible is the source of God's Word.

> Where the Scriptures were translated and venerated as the only and sufficient rule of faith and practice, there the Reformation was established; and the limits within which this veneration of the Bible prevailed are to this day the boundaries of Protestantism. [67]

With that statement few Presbyterians of the day would have disagreed. *Sola Scriptura* has always been one of the hallmarks of Protestantism. Some probably would have taken issue, however, with his remarks about the heresy trials.

> Let me not be misunderstood. I am not calling in question the propriety, nor even the necessity of creeds and confessions. I hold that every religious community has the right to prescribe the system of doctrines, conscientiously drawn from the Bible which shall be the bond of its existence and the condition for membership. It follows as a matter of course, that when a member disregards, or acts contrary to, the profession he has made, such a community has the right to call him to an account, and even to exclude him from its pale. But it does not follow, nor can it ever be justified, that where there is merely a conscientious difference of opinion in respect to Scriptural doctrine, denunciation and persecution should be let loose upon their prey, or an individual be

---

[66] See Prentiss, *op. cit.,* 121-130 for a brief biography.
[67] Edward Robinson, *The Bible and Its Literature: An Inaugural Address with the Charge by the Rev. William Patton, D.D.* (New York: Office of the American Biblical Repository and the American Eclectic, 1841), 17-18.

injured in his good name, or deprived of social rights and privileges. This can never be otherwise than wrong in itself; directly opposed to the great and fundamental principle of Protestantism; and contrary to the whole spirit and tenor of the Gospel of Christ.[68]

Albert Barnes,[69] a Director of the Seminary and one of those so persecuted, must have been gratified by this remark. The seminary seemed to have wisely chosen a strong supporter of New School thinking. One wonders, however, whether that assessment of Robinson is wholly accurate. There is little in his lecture about the evangelical meaning of the Bible or about how the Bible stimulates people to change the world. He says nothing about those rational moral truths taught by the Bible nor about either temperance or the idolatry of Catholicism, themes which tended to dominate New School thinking. For Robinson, Biblical study, though presupposing the power of the Spirit, is about verb forms and ancient customs and chronologies and maps.

Given what he had already written in the *North American Review* and then in *The Biblical Repository,* E. R.'s remarks about Biblical study are quite predictable. He emphasizes, of course, the importance of Biblical languages, though he also believes that all the basic work should be done in undergraduate study. Moreover, since much of both Hebrew and Greek language has been lost—what we have left are literary documents which hardly represent the full range of ordinary speech and vocabulary—and we are left with many sentences which are difficult to translate, he stresses the importance of studying Rabbinical Hebrew, "noble" Arabic, Chaldee (i.e. Aramaic) and other ancient languages as well in order to translate difficult passages.

Clearly his approach to Scripture is a sophisticated one which sees the difficulty of ever achieving a literal translation or understanding. To grasp the meaning of the Bible, one must see as ancient people saw and feel as they felt and that means learning about a host of things—geography, botany, ethnography, history—in order to achieve this end. What he really points toward is the radical development of what we now know as

---

[68] *Ibid.,* 22.
[69] Barnes, who came from Rome, N.Y. and was a graduate of Hamilton College, had many close connections with Robinson.

archaeology and sociological history to reconstruct what life was like in Biblical times. He emphasizes far less, however, the literary analysis already well-known in Europe and destined to dominate the American scene by the end of the century. It apparently did not occur to him that ancient peoples may have thought in terms of myth, symbol, and metaphor rather than literal fact.

He does know that through the ages Christians have read the Bible in many different ways and hence encourages the study of the history of hermeneutics. Robinson, himself, however, shows little patience with those who ferret out "secret meanings" in Biblical texts. The Bible is, on the whole, straight-forward and simple in its message. Doubtless he would have had very critical comments to make about the message of William Miller who, by exploring the secret meanings of Daniel and Revelation, predicted that the second coming of Christ would occur on March 21, 1843. Such teaching "converts the Word of God into a book of riddles . . . and, more than all, it saps the fundamental principles, which regulate our conduct as beings capable of a mutual interchange of thoughts by means of language."[70] One might also guess that he was equally impatient with those who quibble about the fine points of theology. For him, it seems that it is the big picture that counts, not precious metaphysical or doctrinal logic chopping.

At the end of the lecture,[71] we discover part of the reason for its existence.

> It remains now for Christians to do their part. It is for the friends and benefactors of the Seminary,—it is for the churches of this city,—to determine, whether it shall grow up and become a fair and noble tree, whose roots shall strike deep in the hearts of the Christian community, and its leaves and fruits be for the healing of the nations; or whether, pining upon a barren soil, it shall again wither away, and its last state become worse than the first.[72]

Robinson lays out an ideal curriculum, but he knows that it still exists only in the realm of possibility. Offerings from benefactors are desperately

---

[70] *Ibid.*, 34.
[71] Horace Greeley, who reviewed the printed version of the address for the *New York Tribune* on April 22, 1841, indicates that he was in the audience and very much admired Robinson.
[72] *Ibid.*, 46.

needed to make the dream a reality. One wonders whether at the time he understood how true this was.

According to the Union Theological Seminary catalogue of 1840, E. R. and his Hebrew-teaching associate, Isaac Nordheimer, taught many of the same topics as were offered at Andover, but in a different sequence. At Andover virtually all of the Biblical materials were presented in the first (Junior) year, while at Union the Biblical program was spread out over the three years in the following way:

> Junior: Hebrew language—Exegetical Study of Greek and Hebrew Scriptures—Biblical Archaeology—the Sacred Canon—Sacred Chronology—Biblical History.
> Middler: Particular Introduction to the Study of Scripture - History of Biblical Criticism—Biblical History—Exegetical Study of Hebrew and Greek Scripture.
> Senior: Exegetical Study of Hebrew and Greek Scripture.

That year there were 55 Juniors, 41 Middlers, and 24 Seniors. It must have been assumed that all came with a knowledge of Greek, for no beginning course in that language was offered. There were three terms: the first, beginning the first Wednesday of October; the second, beginning the first Wednesday of January; the third, beginning the third Wednesday of May until the second Wednesday of July.

Robinson plunged into teaching with his usual vigor and enthusiasm. Hitchcock, who had access to testimonies from many of his formal pupils describes his teaching in the following way:

> He was likewise an able teacher: curt, blunt, and peremptory in manner, it is true; but always thoroughly master of his subject, and always best liked by the best scholars. He required no genius in his pupils, knowing well how rare that is; but he did require proper deference to his opinions, and, above all, fidelity and diligence in study; no man ever gave proof in his classroom of having slighted a lesson, without smarting from it.[73]

Robinson was a big man: six feet tall with broad shoulders and a muscular

---

[73] Henry B. Smith and Roswell D. Hitchcock, *The Life, Writings and Character of Edward Robinson, D.D., LL.D.* (New York: Anson D.F. Randolph, 1863), 91.

frame. He had been everywhere, knew everyone, and had written the most important work on many Biblical subjects. Add to this his coolness and reserve and one had a very formidable professor. One senses that many students were quite afraid of him. One student apparently prayed that God would give Robinson "better manners."

Beneath the surface, however, he was warm and concerned, sometimes anonymously supporting needy students, often developing cordial relations with graduates of the seminary.[74] Like many professors he valued "professorial distance" as a means of promoting diligence and hard work. He did not seek to be popular; he sought to communicate essential information which he believed any preacher of the gospel ought to have. Whether he ever knew that students, amused by his attention to geographical detail, nicknamed him "Old Wadi," is a question which remains unanswerable.

From 1841 until 1850, when Henry Boynton Smith succeeded him, E. R. also served as Union's librarian. He was certainly the most likely choice for the position. He not only had had experience as Andover's librarian but had purchased many books in Europe for that seminary and knew a great deal about the book business. The financial situation, however, was bleak. Union did not have money to pay its professors to say nothing of buying books for the library. The much prized Van Ess collection was, it is true, in place, but those manuscripts and books hardly comprised a very useful collection for beginners.[75]

Robinson had to work very hard to create even a minimal collection for the institution. He approached retired ministers or their widows to get them to donate their personal collections. He also gave many of his own books to the library. Most of all, he encouraged prospective donors to think about contributing funds to enhance the collection.[76]

E. R. prized books and envied the Europeans for their great library

---

[74] *Ibid.*, 92. See also his obituary in *The New-York Observer* Feb. 5, 1863.

[75] Nevertheless, the Van Ess collection made the Union library one of the largest on the North American continent. *The New York Evangelist* reports that in 1850 Harvard's library numbered 50,000 volumes while others tended to number 10,000 or fewer. The same newspaper also reports that as of May 29, 1845, McAuley had not yet been repaid the $5,000. (May 29, 1845), 85.

[76] It is something of a tribute to both Robinson and Smith that by 1856 Union had a library of 24,000 volumes. See: *The Evangelist* XXXVII, 25 (June 19, 1856), 48.

collections. In an essay entitled, "The Aspect of Literature and Science in the United States as Compared with Europe,"[77] he expresses his concern about the lack of good libraries in America and the dire need for them if science and literature are to prosper. In Europe the governments support libraries and research. In America we must depend upon private citizens for the most part.

> Let us exert our influence,—an influence strengthened by our example and by the fruits we may gather from science—upon the wealthy of our land; that so they may still further endow our seminaries, enlarge our libraries and our scientific lectures.[78]

This is not to say that government should do nothing. In fact he urges that "all those who take part in our public councils" should recognize that "knowledge is power" and that to attain supremacy and power among the nations America must develop all aspects of knowledge. Nevertheless, he sees that ultimately the solution will come through the influence of the private citizen and not big government:

> Let us prove to the world, that literature and science also can subsist and flourish, sustained by the public sentiment of an enlightened people,—without dependence on the state—without wearing the fetters of a slave, or the livery of kings.[79]

Doubtless, Robinson would be more than gratified to see how private funds built the great New York Public Library and how Union's own library became one of the finest theological libraries in the world through the power of private generosity.

Publications and Controversies

Later in 1841, his *Biblical Researches* was published simultaneously in Germany, England, and America. As one can see from the number of

---

[77] B. B. Edwards and E. A. Park, *Bibliotheca Sacra and Theological Review* I (1844), 1-38.
[78] *Ibid.*, 38.
[79] *Ibid.*, 39.

articles and extracts from the book he placed in various newspapers and journals, he knew how to pique the reading public's interest. It is also interesting that after publication the three volume set served as premium for anyone who could produce five paid annual subscriptions to *The New-York Evangelist*.[80] Perhaps that is a reason why such a huge and scholarly set of tomes was such an instant success. Robinson tells us that the publisher soon sold at least 5000 copies. Before long more editions followed. After his second trip in 1852, *Later Researches* was incorporated with the first three volumes in a new four volume edition.

Certainly it was more than good advertising which made the response from the international academic community immediate and almost entirely positive.[81] In November of that year, the University of Halle, while celebrating 300 years of Protestant Reformation in that city, conferred upon him *in absentia* an honorary doctorate.[82] In 1842, the Royal Geographical Society of London unanimously voted to award him a gold medal "placed at their disposal by the Queen" to honor his *magnum opus*. This was the recognition which E. R. most prized and he regretted being unable to accept it in person. As it was, Edward Everett, the famous political leader and orator who was then serving as Ambassador to Great Britain, received the medal from William Hamilton for Robinson in a ceremony on May 23, 1842 and responded to the honor with a fine piece of his own eloquence.[83] He then forwarded the medal to Robinson with a personal note. As a last great

---

[80] *The New-York Evangelist* (July 31, 1841).
[81] See *North American Review* LIII, no. 112, 175-211 for a very positive review. See also: Barnas Sears, ed. *The Christian Review* VI, no. 24 (Dec. 1841), 625-627.; "Robinson's Palestine," *New York Observer* (July 3, 1841), 106; *The Athenaeum* (1841), 550; *Methodist Quarterly Review* XXIV, Third Series II (Jan. 1842), 5-26. *The New-York Evangelist* (July 31, 1841) describes it as "the most full, complete, and accurate work on Palestine, that has ever been published." *The Quarterly Review* LXIX (Dec. 1841), 150-185 offered a lengthy and very favorable opinion. Less enthusiastic as usual was the *Biblical Repertory and Princeton Review* XIII, no. 4, 583-602. It would appear that the editors did not want to praise the star of the seminary across the river. They were equally nasty in their review of Henry Boynton Smith's inaugural address. See: "The Princeton Review and Prof. Smith's Inaugural," *New-York Evangelist* XXVI, 45 (Nov. 8, 1855).
[82] For a brief description of the event see: *New-York Observer* (March 12, 1842), 40.
[83] Robinson Papers I-1. For an American account of the ceremony see: "Compliment to American Authorship," *New York Observer* (July 2, 1842), 103. See also: "Geographical Society," *Athenaeum Journal* (1842), 508, 994. The official description is found in *The Journal of the Royal Society of London* XII (1842), xi-xvi.

hurrah, Yale College, E. R.'s father's old *alma mater,* also awarded him the honorary degree of Doctor of Laws on August 17, 1844.

It is ironic, if not tragic, that while he was receiving these honors and was corresponding with some of the great scholars and leaders of the world, he, like many other academics of the time, was not being regularly paid by the seminary. Somehow, through royalties on his books and the remainder of his inheritance he was able to survive, but life as a new professor was not easy. Given his growing reputation, it is very surprising that he was not snatched up by some other seminary or university.

It did not take long for E. R. to begin publishing again, although now much of what he produced was somewhat "derivative," that is, a further development of ideas presented in his *Biblical Researches.* Also, in 1841 a new edition of his Greek-English lexicon of the New Testament was published. This work, in a new and improved form, was issued again in 1844 and thereafter saw innumerable reprintings. In 1842, a set of appendices to his *Biblical Researches* appeared in a separate volume. These were later incorporated into volume three of the work.

1843 saw his return to journal publication with the first volume of *Bibliotheca Sacra or Tracts and Essays on Topics Connected with Biblical Literature and Theology.* In the first year of publication, Moses Stuart produced for it five essays, Eli Smith two, Francis Wayland, the President of Brown University, one and Robinson, seven. The journal was definitely a New School production and, in fact, after the first year, moved its headquarters to Andover under new editorship.

Much of the content of the first volume concerns further discussion of the geography of Palestine. Robinson edits and comments upon letters from Eli Smith and Samuel Wolcott who lived in Jerusalem in 1841-42 and who were able to observe some things not available to Robinson. In the article, there are strong indications that Robinson went at just the right time:

> Palestine is now in too disturbed a state to allow much travelling; and I have no hope of its being much better while this (Turkish) government remains. It is a most wretched system of fanaticism, corruption, oppression, and anarchy. [84]

---

[84] Edward Robinson, ed. *Bibliotheca Sacra or Tracts and Essays on Topics Concerned with Biblical Literature and Theology* (New York: Wiley and Putnam, 1843), 11.

Nevertheless, Eli Smith continued to travel and wrote about a temple on Mount Lebanon and about his visit to Antipatris.

Also of interest is another article containing Robinson's defense of his own position about the site of the Holy Sepulcher which had been attacked by John Henry Newman, in an "Essay on Ecclesiastical Miracles." The high churchman, who was later to become a Roman Catholic Cardinal, had tried to maintain the factuality of many ancient miracles, including St. Helena's discovery of the true cross, as well as the validity of traditional pilgrimage sites. E. R. lays out again his critique of that belief. He argues that his own position is not based upon his Protestantism—he finds himself beyond the Protestant-Catholic debate—but upon a rational assessment of the evidence. In a carefully developed argument he demonstrates that it is just not reasonable to believe that Helena's so-called discovery was anything more than a fourth century fanciful tale or that many of the traditional sites are rooted in historical fact.[85] Parenthetically, it is interesting that for opinions like this, *Biblical Researches* had already been banned in Catholic Austria.[86]

Robinson, in this journal, also entered into a rather amusing conflict with the Old School Presbyterians. The issue concerned one Rev. McQueen who had married his deceased wife's sister and had been adjudged guilty of incest by the General Assembly of the Old School Presbyterians in May of 1842.[87] Robinson's old friend, Charles Hodge, apparently had supported the decision. In April of that year and in January of 1843,[88] Robinson had published articles in the *New York Observer* attacking the whole idea. In *Bibliotheca Sacra* he now brings the two articles together as one in what he regards as a more permanent form.

The dispute hinged upon the interpretation of Leviticus 18:6-18 which, the author points out, may not be binding upon Christians anyway. In

---

[85] The *New-York Evangelist* (April 3, 1845) took note of the controversy in an article entitled "Dr. Robinson and the Relic Worshipers." An article in the new *North British Review* had attacked E. R. and the *Evangelist* responded in kind. It is clear that Robinson's attack upon "Medieval superstition" was very popular with the evangelicals.
[86] *Bibliotheca Sacra, op. cit.,* 157.
[87] For an account of the Old School General Assembly's action see: *New York Observer* (June 11, 1842). Apparently this was a controversy which raged in England and Scotland too. See: *New-York Observer* XXXIII, 16 (Apr. 19, 1855), 125.
[88] "Marriage of a Wife's Sister," *New York Observer* XXI, no. 2 (Jan. 15, 1843), 10. (The article in *Bibliotheca Sacra* seems very different from the original articles.)

fact, E. R. goes out of his way to explain that if Christians want to impose the sexual laws of the Hebrew Scriptures upon believers, they have to recognize that the ancient Hebrews regarded polygamy, concubinage, and easy divorce as quite acceptable. They should also recognize that in Hebrew marriages wives had few rights and were, in effect, the property of their husbands. Be that as it may, the point which he emphasizes is that the laws of incest are based, in the Bible, on blood relationships. One's wife's sister is not a blood relation and therefore marriage with her should not constitute incest at all. That, of course, seems quite obvious to the modern reader; one wonders why it was not to the Old School Presbyterians.[89]

A much more difficult and controversial question was tackled in E. R.'s essay, "The Coming of Christ." The question of millennial expectations had been raised full force by the Millerites who expected an immediate Second Coming in 1843 and then in 1844. Hence Moses Stuart wrote about "The Number of the Beast" and "The White Stone" of the Apocalypse. In 1845 he was to publish a two volume commentary on the book of Revelation. Robinson, in a way, takes on an even more difficult challenge, trying to understand Christ's own words about the imminent coming of the Son of Man. "Truly, I say to you, this generation will not pass away till all these things take place." (Matthew 24:34) In his essay he struggles bravely to avoid the conclusion either that the writers had misconveyed Jesus' thoughts, hence raising questions about the Bible's authority, or that Jesus himself had made a mistake and predicted incorrectly, which, of course, would be to give up everything theologically. He begins with the assumption that the Bible must be correct and then struggles to show how it is so. It is doubtful that many scholars today would agree with the details of his conclusions but one must admit his bravery and honesty in trying to face the problem head-on.

The other items which must be mentioned in connection with this volume of the journal are Robinson's obituaries for Wilhelm Gesenius, his great German mentor, and Isaac Nordheimer, his young Jewish assistant who, until the end, taught Hebrew at Union and N.Y.U. Robinson outlines

---

[89] For an Old School view see: J.J. Janeway, *Unlawful Marriage: An answer to "the Puritan" and "Omicron" who have advocated in a pamphlet, the Lawfulness of the Marriage of a man with his deceased wife's sister.* (New York: Robert Carter, 1844).

the lives and accomplishments of each in what must have been for him a very difficult article for him to write.

The next year the journal was transferred to Andover and merged with the *Biblical Repository* under the editorship of B. B. Edwards and E. A. Park. Just why this happened is intimated in a letter from Robinson to Edwards on January 12, 1844. E. R. describes his health as "feeble" and says that he has all he can do to teach his classes and write a few letters. The "paper" which Edwards wants to publish he says has not been looked at in two years and may need some rewriting, for which he has no time. Therefore he wants to "beg off" contributing to the first number. In fact, however, he must have relented because in the first issue from Andover there appears his essay on literature and science in America which will be discussed below.[90]

Robinson's name remains on the title page of the journal as a consultant and he continues to contribute major articles for some time, but the journal quietly changes as the years go by. New names—Henry Boynton Smith, Philip Schaff, Noah Porter, Enoch Pond, etc.—begin to appear more regularly. Stuart's contributions dwindle and Robinson's offerings become more and more confined to "Notes on Biblical Geography" until, after 1855, they disappear entirely. In fact, except for a few major articles, most of Robinson's contributions are on selected topics related to his first, and then his second, trip to Palestine.

The first article, "The Aspect of Literature and Science in the United States, as Compared with Europe,"[91] seems to have been first delivered in public in 1842, probably before some learned society in New York.[92] It has, as its title indicates, little to do with Biblical Studies *per se*, though Robinson does point out that one of the advantages that European scholars have is that their governments support research, like trips to the Holy Land, rather than leaving such expenses to be paid by the individual. Over all it is an interesting article assessing where America is in the realms of literature and science as it approaches mid century and what can be done to improve America's position. He assesses some of the reasons why American output

---

[90] See letter to B. B. Edwards from E. Robinson, Jan. 12, 1844 in Miscell. MSS. R., Library Archives, New York Historical Society.
[91] B. B. Edwards and E. A. Park, eds., *Bibliotheca Sacra and Theological Review* I, no. 1 (April 1844), 1-38.
[92] It was not the New York Historical Society, though that would have been an appropriate venue.

is not as great as that of Europe, but ends with the encouraging word that America has already accomplished much and that before long can overtake her much older competitor. One senses in Robinson both a bursting pride in America as well as an acknowledgment that there still is room for great development and improvement, particularly in support for the sciences.

A second article, published in 1845, is entitled, "The Resurrection and Ascension of our Lord."[93] In this piece, Robinson seeks to deal with the apparent discrepancies among the four gospels concerning the resurrection of Jesus. To many modern scholars, his aim to harmonize the four descriptions is impossible from the start, for there are just too many details which do not cohere. E. R., however, does his best to fit the different accounts into one consistent chronology to demonstrate to the world that the Bible can, after all, be considered consistent and believable. Again, many modern scholars, less concerned about consistency of detail, would probably not agree, but for the time this was certainly a theological *tour de force*.

Doubtless, in Robinson's mind this exercise was a teaser for his new harmony of the Gospels, published first with the Greek text in 1845 and then with the common (i.e. King James) version in 1846. These gospel harmonies did exceedingly well, with the former going through eight editions and the latter going through eighteen. Again in his publishing E. R. produced a best seller which must have helped to augment his rather small and sometimes unpaid salary.

Still a third article concerns the nature of the body of the risen Christ. Robinson entertains three possibilities: a body with "new substance," a glorified body, or a body like yours and mine, i.e. a real body. His essential argument is that the Biblical witnesses proclaim that it was a real body. Jesus came back "in the flesh" and not as an appearance only. Throughout, he reveals his own distaste for airy speculation and metaphysical theories. He concludes the article by saying that because the apostles thought the body real, if it was not, Jesus was then a deceiver and the whole faith, in effect, collapses.[94]

---

[93] *Ibid.* II, no. 1 (April 1845), 162-189.
[94] *The Christian Advocate and Journal*, in a review of that issue of *Bibliotheca Sacra*, proclaims Robinson's essay excellent. If Robinson does not convince the modern reader, it is clear he was cogent to contemporary readers. *Christian Advocate* (May 21, 1845), 163.

From a philosophical point of view, his problem, throughout, is that he accepts the obvious validity of "common sense." He assumes that we know what a real body is, that we know what matter is. All those questions raised by the British empiricists and by Kant about what we can know are swept aside. A real body is just that: what we can touch, feel, see. To inquire more deeply about the matter is to indulge in airy fantasies. But then you must somehow explain what happens at the ascension. If Jesus bodily ascends into heaven, then heaven must exist somewhere in time and space, for that is how bodies exist. Perhaps in the age of Ptolemy that was possible, but in the post-Copernican world the whole question of a "real" body in heaven becomes quite problematic. One might counter his dire conclusion with a remark that if he is correct, the whole account also becomes quite unbelievable.

Clearly Robinson was better at identifying sites than engaging in philosophical issues. Or perhaps it would be fairer to say that American Biblical scholarship, with its pronounced aversion to metaphysics, was bound to create as many problems as it solved, for certainly, despite all the claims to the contrary, American "common sense" is itself a metaphysical position. Given that difficulty, it must be added that Robinson addresses the problem in a non-partisan, careful, and rational way. Throughout, he aims, not at some preconceived, denominational conclusion, but at the truth.

Meanwhile, Therese had been monumentally active. Although this is not the place for a complete review of her work, one can hardly understand Robinson without realizing that his wife, while caring for their children and their home, was producing intellectually, in her own way, at least as much as he. In 1840 she published a book on German folk songs. In 1845 and then again in 1847 she published in Germany full length works on the history of colonial America. In 1850 was published a work on the languages and literature of the Slavic nations. Her several articles are found in a variety of journals, both in Germany and in America. In the 1850s she published no fewer than five novels.

Moreover, it was she who made lively contacts with all sorts of people outside the sheltered world of theology. Caroline Kirkland, the widow of William Kirkland, served as an editor for several journals and seems to have been instrumental in getting some of Therese's articles in print. Kirkland was a good friend of William Cullen Bryant and his wife and in fact lived in a small house on their estate. She and Therese and her daughter Mary spent much time at the Bryant home on Long Island and through them undoubtedly enjoyed a wide circle of friends in and around New York. It was Therese who translated John Pickering's book on Indian languages into German and carried on correspondence with Henry Schoolcraft, the anthropologist. To their home came George Bancroft, the American historian, and a host of other friends and guests. She also carried on an extensive correspondence with Jacob Grimm and other German intellectuals. While Robinson himself was rather shy and retiring, Therese loved conversation and intellectual stimulation.

We know from her articles that Edward and Therese also took trips to various parts of America. She returned with him to Mount Washington and writes about her visit to the Shakers. They traveled to Virginia where she observed first hand the dreadful reality of slavery. While he makes few comments about contemporary events, she is not afraid to write critically about what she sees. It was a wonderful combination: the cool, somewhat aloof scholar who attends to the most precise philological and geographical detail and the German intellectual who loves and hates America with a passion and who will say precisely what she thinks when she thinks it.

Throughout this whole period, Robinson had been contemplating another great work, a work describing and defining the physical, social, and historical geography of the Holy Land. It would be his last, great *magnum opus*. Unfortunately, however, such a study was impossible without further research in Palestine. In 1851, therefore, the Directors of Union, knowing his great dream and recognizing his eminence as a scholar granted him a leave to fulfill his life's labors by returning to the scene of his greatest discoveries and triumph.

In June of 1851, he and his family sailed to Germany where Therese and the children were to spend more than a year. Edward Sr., however, returned to America via Holland, England, and Scotland, arriving in October to teach the fall semester. This return apparently was the result of a plea from students that he finish the course he had started with them. To show their sincere appreciation for his accession to their request, Robinson's class presented him with a Bible as a good-bye present with their inscribed thanks for not leaving before finishing the course. Immediately after the end of the semester, in December of 1851, Edward set off for Europe and then, after a brief reunion with his family, for Palestine.

For Therese and the "children"—Mary was now 22 and Edward 15—the leave was a chance to return to their beloved Germany. For Edward Sr. it was the opportunity to fill in all those blanks left by the last trip and to further augment the knowledge for which he was so well-known. The land which he thought he had glimpsed for the last time, was to be seen again.

Chapter Nine

THE LAST YEARS

Headlines and Notices: 1852-1863

1852	Franklin Pierce becomes President. Harriet Beecher Stowe publishes *Uncle Tom's Cabin*. Cecil Alexander writes the hymn, "Jesus Calls us, o'er the tumult."
1853	Commodore Matthew Perry opens Japan to trade. Stephen Foster publishes "My Old Kentucky Home."
1854	The Crimean War begins. The Kansas-Nebraska Act is passed; Kansas soon becomes a battleground. Thoreau publishes *Walden*.
1855	Walt Whitman publishes the first edition of *Leaves of Grass*. Longfellow publishes "Song of Hiawatha." The Hymn, "What a Friend We Have in Jesus" is written by Joseph Scriven.
1856	The Hatti-i Humayan enacted in the Ottoman Empire: Christians thereby gain a modicum of freedom. Woodrow Wilson is born.

Elizabeth Prentiss writes "More Love to Thee, O Christ."

1857   James Buchanan becomes President.
A large New York bank closes, Wall Street panics.
The Dred Scott decision disturbs many.
The first baseball association is founded.
The Atlantic Monthly begins publication with James Russell Lowell as editor.
In India, the Sepoy Rebellion very nearly overthrows British rule.
Eli Smith dies.

1858   Transatlantic cable is laid for the telegraph.
Theodore Roosevelt is born.
Longfellow publishes "The Courtship of Miles Standish."

1859   Booker T. Washington and John Dewey are born.
The opening of Drake's oil well in Titusville, Pa. marks the beginning of the commercial exploitation of oil.
Frederic Church paints "Heart of the Andes."
Charles Darwin publishes *The Origin of Species*.

1860   Abraham Lincoln campaigns for President; Bryant introduces him to New York.
Winchester introduces the repeating rifle.
Stephen Foster publishes "Old Black Joe."

1861   Six southern states secede to be soon joined by Virginia, North Carolina and Tennessee.
Confederate forces fire on Fort Sumter.
The first battle of Bull Run is fought.
Abdul Aziz reigns in the Ottoman Empire.
Walter Rauschenbush, spokesman for the Social Gospel, is born.

1862   The Emancipation Proclamation is issued.

Billy Sunday is born.
"The Battle Hymn of the Republic" published by Julia Howe.
Gattling invents the machine gun.

1863   Henry Ford is born.
The Battle of Gettysburg is fought.
Lincoln proclaims Thanksgiving a national holiday.

1865   The Palestine Exploration Fund is established.

PALESTINIAN INTERLUDE

Robinson left New York on December 20, arriving in London on January 1. The improvement in the speed of ocean travel by this time is obvious and amazing: eleven days rather than a month. He spent two weeks in England, probably meeting with various scholars, and then joined his family who were already residing in Berlin. There he consulted with Ritter and Lepsius, Humboldt, Buch and "other veterans of science" before heading off to Trieste.[1] With Ritter, of course, he had had steady correspondence, for they were the two leading geographers of the region. Robinson's papers contain a number of Ritter's letters from the 1850s. With the death of Gesenius, Ritter became Robinson's major correspondent on the Continent.

The speed of the transatlantic crossing was a harbinger of the whole trip. Fourteen years had changed the world enormously in a variety of ways. Now as he set off from Berlin, he took the train, not the diligence, and arrived in Trieste far sooner than the first time. The trip to Beirut was by much improved steamship and, although there were delays, both speed and comfort were far greater.

Beirut had changed too. Although the shelling by English and Austrian ships in 1840 had caused much damage, everything had been rebuilt. Trade with the West had much increased and Beirut, a small town of 15,000 in 1838, had doubled its size. Eli Smith, who again was to accompany Robinson for much of his journey, now lived in a fine house in Beirut with

---

[1] Edward Robinson, *Later Biblical Researches in Palestine and in the Adjacent Regions: Journal of Travel in the Year 1852* (Boston: Crocker and Brewster, 1856), 2.

beautiful views of the mountains of Lebanon. The missionaries, though not very successful in making many converts, had settled down comfortably in their new surroundings.

Most important for the mood of the book, there were "Franks," i.e. Western Europeans and Americans, everywhere. In 1838, Robinson and company were explorers, like Lewis and Clark in Oregon territory. Their travel broke new ground. Sight of a European or American was unusual and worth mentioning. Now missionaries, traders and merchants, even sightseers were common. He tells of one British family on a sight-seeing trip across the desert, hiring an extra camel to carry water so that their son could have his daily bath!

Moreover, since his first trip there had been plenty of writers and artists visiting the Holy Land to record their impressions for the world. One thinks, for instance, of W. H. Bartlett,[2] George Thompson,[3] F. G. Hibbard[4] and David Roberts as prime examples. Robinson, in fact, lists no fewer than thirteen works about the Holy Land published in the 1840s.

Among these was a report from the expedition sponsored by the United States Navy which William Lynch (1801-1865) organized in 1848 to survey the Jordan River and the Dead Sea. For this purpose he had two boats, one of copper and one of galvanized iron, constructed at the Brooklyn Navy Yard. These boats were brought by ship to Acco and then hauled by camels to Tiberias where they were launched in the Sea of Galilee. The fifteen person team, including a botanist and a geologist, drew charts of the Jordan and the Dead Sea, collected minerals and plant specimens, and studied topography and ancient ruins.

Robinson had received a letter from Lynch in 1848 praising him for his map of the Dead Sea and confirming his observations about Sebbah.[5] The next month he also received a letter from J. Y. Mason, Secretary of the

---

[2] W. H. Bartlett, *Walks about the City and Environs of Jerusalem summer 1842* (1844), *The Christian in Palestine* (1847), *Forty Days in the Desert: On the Track of the Israelites* (1848), *Scripture Sites and Scenes from Actual Survey in Egypt, Arabia and Palestine,* (1851). Bartlett was an artist who included in his books illustrations of what he saw.

[3] George Thompson and others, *A View of the Holy Land: Its present Inhabitants, their manners, and customs, polity, and religion* (Wheeling, West Va.: John B. Wolff, 1850).

[4] F. G. Hibbard, *Palestine: Its Geography and Bible History,* ed. D. P. Kidder (New York: Land and Scott, 1851).

[5] Robinson Papers L-3, July 12, 1848.

Navy, asking for Robinson's help. Mason (and President Millard Fillmore) had received criticism for having authorized Lynch's expedition and asked E. R. for substantiation that this was a good and useful venture.[6] Presumably E. R. responded by underlining the significance of the expedition for science and for the nation.

From this point onward the trickle of books about and pictures of Palestine would become a great flood, with many famous American artists, like Frederic Church,[7] capitalizing upon the world's interest in Biblical sites and oriental scenes. Herman Melville went on a trip to Palestine but apparently hated every minute of it. By 1869, Mark Twain in *Innocents Abroad* could write amusingly about an extended sightseeing tour which included, among other places, the Holy Land in its itinerary. Parenthetically he refers in this work to Robinson as still a chief source of information about the area.[8]

In 1852, however, Palestine was not yet ready for the average sightseer. There still were only bridle paths, not roads, and dangers threatened from the ever rebellious Druze and from the Bedouins of the desert. Nevertheless, things were far more open and benign than in 1838. Robinson was no longer so much an explorer as a "geographical scientist" who was there to discover certain lost pieces in his geographical puzzle. As a result, he generally avoided the areas which he had seen before, heading even more off the beaten path into those areas which were still *terra incognita* to him. When he did go over old ground, as in Jerusalem, it was to confirm his old findings through further investigation.

The trip began frustratingly, for when he arrived in Beirut on March 2, Eli Smith soon fell sick with a fever and the spring rains continued for several days, literally washing out the possibility of travel. Much of the month was spent in local sightseeing and investigation and at a meeting of missionaries from the whole region. This delay must have really bothered Robinson who generally hated to waste the least moment doing something unproductive.

---

[6] Robinson Papers L-3, August 3, 1848.
[7] Church, who followed Alexander von Humboldt's route in South America, may well have taken Robinson's previous journey as a prototype of his own.
[8] Mark Twain (Samuel Clemens), *The Innocents Abroad or The New Pilgrims' Progress* in 2 Vols. (New York: Harper & Brothers, 1897), II, 271.

Even after they started on April 5 the rains continued and there were days when they were drenched to the skin and had to seek cover for considerable periods of time. Nevertheless, they made their way on somewhat new byways through Sidon and Tyre on their way to Palestine itself. Once in the land of ancient Israel, they took a route through the hill country seldom traversed even today by visitors to the land, ending up on the coast in Acco. From there they headed across the hill country east of Acco, visiting a great variety of tells. For many he does not even guess about their identity. He is intrigued, however, by Tell Jefat which he decides is surely the famous fortress of Jotapata which was commanded by Flavius Josephus himself. He also identifies Beit Lahm as the Bethlehem of Zebulon and Tell Kaimon as ancient Jokneam. About Tell Mutsellim, however, he has no opinion, perhaps because he had already placed Megiddo elsewhere and because he saw no trace of a city on the Tell at all.

Eventually, the party crossed the plain of Esdraelon and entered the hill country of Samaria, again avoiding the main routes to explore lesser known sites, such as Dothan, west of the main Jerusalem-Nablus road. After uneventful travel, they arrived in Nablus where they again visited the Samaritans and viewed a number of their ancient manuscripts. Eli Smith was even allowed to borrow one of their Arabic translations for his own work.

Finally, after twenty-four days of exploration they arrived in Jerusalem where they spent twelve days (from April 28 until May 10) revisiting sites to check out earlier conclusions about the Church of the Holy Sepulcher, the second and "third walls," the abutment now called "Robinson's Arch," etc. Not surprisingly he concluded that his earlier, much disputed critique of the site of the Holy Sepulcher was indeed correct. Indeed, he changed his mind very little about any of his earlier judgments. As the years have passed, many if not most of his opinions about Jerusalem have been proved problematic. Nevertheless, Robinson more than anyone else has set the agenda for argument about the ancient city. Without him the study of ancient Jerusalem would probably not have taken the course that it has.

The party also made a couple of short excursions outside the city to Bittir and to the area around Hebron. Because of time, however, a long excursion to climb Mount Hor was abandoned. E. R. went to Bittir to examine the possibility that it might be identified as Bether where the revolutionary Bar-Kochba was finally defeated. His conclusion was negative. Instead, he proposed that Bether is a corruption of Bethel and that the great battle and massacre took place there. On the trip toward Hebron, E. R. identified the ancient sites of Beth-Zur and Beth-Zacariah and opined that er-Râmeh might be the site of ancient Mamre. He also met some Seventh Day Baptists from Philadelphia who had come to Palestine to teach the Jews agriculture and eventually convert them to Christianity. Although Robinson surely was not opposed to missions, he also saw the foolishness of what they were doing. He writes:

> It is hardly necessary to remark, that the idea of speedily converting the Jews, living as strangers in Palestine, into an agricultural people, is altogether visionary.[9]

On May 10, after what Robinson believed a successful sojourn, the party set out again for the north. Their journey took them through Geba, Michmash, and Rimmon and then through relatively unexplored territory east of the Nablus road. After taking a route for which one needs a very detailed atlas to follow, they descended through a wadi to the *Ghôr,* i.e. the Jordan Valley. This they explored in a cursory fashion on both sides of the river, believing that they had discovered ancient Pella[10] and perhaps Jabesh Gilead.[11] Finally, they arrived on May 15th at Beisan, the site of ancient Bethshan, which, on the following Monday, they explored.

At this point Eli Smith went back to Beirut and was replaced by a Mr. Thomson. Although E. R. never mentions his first name this was undoubtedly William M. Thomson who, in 1858 was to publish a two volume work of his own on the Holy Land. *The Land and the Book*[12] was lavishly illustrated with drawings of famous sites and Palestinian life. He

---

[9] Robinson, *Later Biblical Researches*, 274.

[10] *Ibid.,* 321-323. See also: Robert Houston Smith, "Pella," *ABD* V, 219-221 and R. H. Smith, "Pella," *NEAEHL* III, 1174-1180.

[11] Robinson actually did not visit the site of ed-Deir which he thought was probably Jabesh-Gilead. Today archaeologists tend to place Jabesh-gilead at Tell Maqlub which E. R. also mentions but did not visit. Robinson, *Later Biblical Researches*, 319. See also: Diana V. Edelman. "Jabesh-Gilead," *ABD* III. 594-595.

[12] William M. Thomson, *The Land and the Book*, 2 Vols. (New York: Harper and Brothers, 1859).

also included many helpful maps. Unlike Robinson's work which was technical and ponderous in its detail, Thomson's work aimed at a much wider reading audience and, in fact, outsold *Biblical Researches* many times over. Because of his intimate knowledge of the land and its people, traveling with him must have been very informative for E. R.

As on the first trip, Robinson traveled around the Sea of Galilee looking for Capernaum, Bethsaida, and Chorazin. On his first venture he had concluded that the widely accepted site, Tell Hum, could not be Capernaum because Josephus said that the city was located on or very near the plains of Gennesaret and clearly Tell Hum is not. Tell Hum also has no fountain near it such as Josephus described. Therefore Robinson concluded again that Tell Hum could not be Capernaum and located it instead at Khân Minyeh. Modern archaeologists generally disagree, though it would appear to the uninformed that his argument still has much to commend it.[13]

The Druze remained in rebellion, threatening travelers, but this time Robinson's party ventured past Lake Huleh which they explored, before proceeding on to Hasbeiya. On their way they identified the probable site of Hazor[14] before proceeding to Kedes, probably ancient Kedesh. From there they went on to visit Tel el Qadi (Dan) and Banias (ancient Caesarea-Philippi). To the latter site Robinson accords considerable attention, describing in some detail what he saw there and offering an historical account of the place. Since Banias changed considerably between the time of his visit and modern archaeological excavations his precise descriptions are invaluable for those studying the area. In fact, for modern archaeologists his identifications are often not nearly as valuable as his descriptions of things which no longer exist.

The next stage was to travel east to Damascus, where they arrived on June 2, staying until June 7. There Thomson remained and was replaced by a Mr. Robson as Robinson's companion. After traveling to Baalbeck and by many other sights, including the Cedars of Lebanon, they arrived back in Beirut on June 19. On the 22nd Robinson took a steamer to Smyrna where he became very ill with a high fever. One wonders whether he contracted malaria while near Lake Huleh which was notoriously dangerous for that

---

[13] See also for a summary of his arguments: "The Site of Capernaum," *Bibliotheca Sacra* XII, no. 46 (April 1855), 263-282.
[14] See also *Bibliotheca Sacra* V, no. 14 (July 1847), 403.

disease. Parenthetically, one also wonders whether it was not malaria which returned to haunt Robinson during 1856-7 and '57-8. In any event, quinine was prescribed and he recovered enough to embark on July 5 on a steamer to Trieste. Finally he was reunited with his family in Salzburg where he stayed, recuperating from his ordeal. On October 8 they embarked from Bremen and by October 27, 1852 he was back in New York, ready to teach his courses.[15]

Unlike the first trip, there was no time or leisure to write up his experiences immediately. Instead he had to compose his new work whenever he could while carrying a full teaching load. This meant that the book, which numbers well over 600 pages, was not published until 1856 and had lost, by that time, a certain freshness of style and interest. In retrospect, volume four appears to have been a mistake. He adopts the same journal format which worked so well for the first volumes, but this time the excitement of new exploration and the severe rigors of desert travel are missing. He was, when he took the trip, 58 years old and not quite as able to endure physical challenges as he once had been. The first volumes, one can imagine, could be made into a T.V. event like the Lewis and Clark series; the last volume certainly could not. Moreover, for the most part, the places explored, with the obvious exception of Acco and Damascus, are historically less significant; hence the historical notices are fewer and of less interest. And finally, even with a modern atlas of the Holy Land at one's elbow, it is simply very difficult to follow his route. Perhaps someone who has traveled the length and breadth of Israel many times can imagine where he went, but the average reader simply gets lost as he moves from one wadi to another. Although there are many important and eminently readable sections, it is difficult to imagine much of this volume satisfying either a 19th or a 20th century reader. Perhaps the best way to approach it is to read first his article in the *Journal of the Royal Geographic Society of London* in which he summarizes briefly his findings and provides for the reader a very useful map indicating where he went.[16]

---

[15] It should be noted that shortly after his return, his good friend, William Cullen Bryant also left on a tour of Palestine which he later described in his *Journey to the East*. It would be very surprising if Robinson did not advise him about where he should go and what he should see.

[16] "Outlines of a Journey to Palestine in 1852 by E. Robinson, E. Smith, and Others," *Journal of the Royal Geographical Society of London* XXIV (1854), 1-35.

One can only lament, then, that instead of this volume E. R. did not immediately begin his projected geography of the Holy Land, incorporating his new findings into that. In truth, he produced a less than lively conclusion to a classic work and ultimately failed to complete the great work which was to have been the summation of his life.[17]

AMERICA IN THE 1850s: TRANQUILLITY AND CONFLAGRATION

The Robinsons always had a knack for avoiding periods of disaster and conflict. In 1830 they left for America just before revolution swept Europe. They returned in 1837, just in time to avoid the Panic of '37 in America. When they returned again to Europe the revolutions of 1848 had ebbed and in America the Panic of 1852 had not yet begun. By the time they returned the worst of the financial crisis had passed.

Now, however, their luck seemed to run out, for America appeared destined for disaster. By the 1850s the old statesmen who had dominated politics for so long were either dead or had lost their power to move the country. John Quincy Adams died in 1848; John C. Calhoun, in 1850; Henry Clay and Daniel Webster, in 1852.[18] In their place came politicians angling for victory rather than compromise and containment of the controversy: Stephen Douglas, James Buchanan, Charles Sumner, *et al*. There were few statesmen left. Presiding over the growing tension was the newly elected Franklin Pierce, a handsome, pleasant man, with a problem with drink and a bigger problem with backbone.

Actually, however, none of these participants should be blamed that the controversy, long simmering, finally came to a boil. The status of California as a free state had been bought at a price by the statesmen of an earlier generation. First of all, stricter Fugitive Slave laws made it more

---

[17] It is interesting that most reviews emphasize the whole work, i.e. *Biblical Researches* and *Later Biblical Researches*, combined and really say little definite about the last volume. I find it unaccountable, however, that the *Presbyterian Review* which was a New School journal and which even depended upon the Union faculty for editorial support did not choose to review *Later Biblical Researches* at all. It is also an interesting question whether any of the unsigned articles about the Bible in the *Review* were by Robinson.

[18] It should be noted that Daniel Webster's old friend, Moses Stuart, also died in 1852, on January 4, while Robinson was in Europe, on his way to Palestine.

difficult for slaves to find freedom by running to a free state; Northern citizens were required to return them to their owners.[19] Moreover, the agreement about Kansas and Nebraska not only violated the solemn treaty with native Americans according to which they were to have these territories "forever"; it also produced mayhem as both slave-holders and abolitionists rushed to fill Kansas with their representatives in order to assure that Kansas would vote for their side.

Perhaps those tougher Fugitive Slave laws which required northern complicity in returning runaway slaves to their owners and the compromise which produced Bleeding Kansas in the 50s—the final gifts of Henry Clay to his beloved nation—were necessary to polarize America and bring about the concluding conflict. The Dred Scott decision, which, in effect, seemed to make slavery legal everywhere, was just the proverbial last straw. Finally the abscess which had so pained the nation for so long had to be lanced. The events of the day made it clear that everyone was tarred by the brush of that peculiar institution, slavery, and that something had to be done. When a fugitive slave was recaptured and returned from Massachusetts while hundreds jeered in protest, the reality of the pervasiveness of sin became clear. The end was coming, one way or another. A nation, as Lincoln was to say, simply cannot remain half slave and half free.

All of this was reflected in subtle and not so subtle ways in literature and the arts. 1850 marked the publication of Nathaniel Hawthorne's first successful novel, *The Scarlet Letter,* a work which broods about human sin and self-righteousness until the moral line is totally blurred between the adulteress and those who condemn her. Who after all is without sin? This theme of sin was developed in new directions in 1852 in *The House of Seven Gables*, a work which explores how sin passes irrevocably from one generation to the next until some respite is, miraculously perhaps, found through the arrival of Phoebe, a young niece who brings light into an otherwise gloomy universe.[20]

---

[19] For an interesting discussion of Methodist reactions to the Fugitive Slave Law see: Ralph A. Keller, "Methodist Newspapers and the Fugitive Slave Law: A New Perspective for the Slavery Crisis in the North," *Church History* 34, no. 3 (Sept. 1974), 319-339.

[20] The narrator says, "It is implied that the weaknesses and defects, the bad passions, the mean tendencies, and the moral diseases which lead to crime are handed down from one generation to another, by a far surer process of transmission than human law has been

In 1852, Harriet, the daughter of Lyman Beecher and wife of Christian theologian, C. E. Stowe, who has already figured briefly in our story, produced *Uncle Tom's Cabin*. This work today is often regarded as both sentimental and racist, but in 1852 it was a brave attempt to say something germane about the issue which racked the conscience of the country and simply would not go away. While theologians hesitated and stuttered and demurred, she, at least, spoke with a voice which few could misunderstand.

More subtle, certainly, was the work of Herman Melville, *Moby Dick*, a seafaring novel about a half-mad Captain Ahab who is driven to kill the great white whale in order to avenge what that same whale had earlier done to his body.[21] Although one should never reduce a great work of art to one meaning or purpose, surely there are some parallels between Ahab and all those abolitionists—the Garrisons and John Browns and Gerrit Smiths—who would have destroyed the great monster, slavery, no matter what the cost. Melville reveals the cost, for in the end the Pequod and all its crew go down in the last great struggle to the death. The ship of state is capsized and destroyed. And yet, right out of the great eddy produced by the ship's sinking shoots up, like a miracle, a casket, a symbol of death, and in the casket is Ishmael, the hero of the story, still alive. Beyond death there is resurrection.

It was not a popular novel; few read it, few liked it. Perhaps readers, overwhelmed by that labyrinthine parable, did not get the point. Or perhaps they did and could not face the meaning: that like the Pequod, captained by the crazed Ahab, the American ship was racing toward disaster and could only hope against hope that somehow, after the carnage, there would be a "new birth of freedom."

Longfellow, Robinson's longtime friend, took a different route, writing, in several separate episodes the great American epic for the common man: "Evangeline," (1847) "The Song of Hiawatha" (1855), "The Courtship of Miles Standish" (1858), and right in the midst of our nation's

---

able to establish in respect to the riches and honors which it seeks to entail upon posterity." Nathaniel Hawthorne, *The Complete Novels and Selected Tales* (New York: Random House, 1937), 314.

[21] It is interesting that newspapers of the 1840s and 50s were full of stories about whaling and killer whales and their dangers. Clearly Melville chose a theme which fascinated his society.

most horrible conflict "Paul Revere's Ride" (1863). Today Longfellow is seldom read in classes in literature and is derided as a second-rate poet who pandered to common taste. He is not "deep." But that is to miss the point. Longfellow was surely intellectual enough. He taught for years at Harvard and was thoroughly acquainted with the best European literature. He had read Baudelaire and rejected for his purposes that style and malaise. *Les Fleurs des Mal* was not what Americans wanted to hear about or what he wanted to say.

What he desired to create was a folk epic for America, a "song" which ordinary folk could sing, words which they could recite which would bring a sense of unity and pride back to a nation which had gone mad in its political and moral division. Longfellow patterned his epics, not upon the sophisticated literature of the elite, but upon the *Kalevala,* the folk epic of Finland. It may be, in fact, that Therese's work on European folk literature played a role in his decision. And whether the *literateurs* like it or not he was magnificently successful. For the better part of a century his poems were prized, memorized, and recited in America as the best of our nation's literature.

It is interesting that the year after Longfellow published "The Courtship of Miles Standish" Robinson produced a memoir of his father which traced his own ancestry back to John Alden and the early Puritans. It was not an easy book to put together. He wrote to an extraordinary number of people and consulted many others personally in order to accumulate all the facts about the history of his family. His papers, indeed, contain a whole sheaf of letters in response to his various inquiries. Why would a great Biblical scholar, anxious to produce his last great work on Palestinian geography, divert his attention to his own family roots, to write his own Genesis? Perhaps that act tells us more about Robinson than anything else. Despite his years in Europe and his months exploring the secrets of the orient, he remained, at the last, a Connecticut Yankee who found sustenance in that family history which defined his life. In that way he proved himself Biblical to the core.

Another voice during this era found its way into the American heart. In 1848, Stephen Foster, a rather tragic figure addicted to drink and never very successful at anything else, wrote "Oh Suzanna," a tune popularized by the Christy Minstrels. It can be considered, in fact, the beginning of truly

American popular song. During the 1850s he continued to write one popular hit after another: "De Camptown Races" (1850), "Swanee River" (1851), "Massas in de Cold, Cold Ground (1852), "My Old Kentucky Home" (1853), "Old Dog Tray" (1855), and "Old Black Joe" (1860). The ironic thing is that he was from Pittsburgh and had never been in the South at all. Somehow, in the face of all the controversy and strife over slavery, he was able to write sentimental ballads which idealized Southern life and made everything seem all right after all. In the midst of the Civil War he produced the loveliest song of them all, "Beautiful Dreamer" . . . and then he died in 1864 of alcoholic nightmare.

There was still another movement in the American spirit which arose during this period in both literature and art. It is best typified by Henry David Thoreau's *Walden* which was published in 1854. While settlers raced to Kansas in order to assure that it would be a slave—or a free—state and killed each other off in the process;[22] while people in the North smoldered as they saw black men and women, escaped from their chains, sent back to bondage once again, Thoreau told of a better way, of living off the land beside a beautiful little lake in a cabin built for but a few dollars. The world had become too acquisitive, too civilized, too debauched. Thoreau called Americans to a simpler, more human life. It was not just escapism, though some have called it that. It was a reminder of the simplicity that life can have when all those power games and lust for things are put aside. It was a vision which has had amazing impact around the world.

A similar message was repeated over and over by the great artists of the Hudson River School which now, partly through the support of the American Art-Union, came into its own. Thomas Cole was dead, but his spirit was taken up by Asher Durand and George Innis and Frederick Church and a host of others who portrayed the world of nature and humanity as at peace. There are no starving people or marching armies or greedy politicians in their pictures. This is not the Ash Can school. There are trees and brooks and mountains and ordinary people going about their daily tasks. The American landscape for the Hudson River School was one of infinite serenity and sublimity. It reminds us that in nature one can sense the awe which is at the root of religious meaning. Perhaps this is the reason

---

[22] Lyman Beecher actually raised money to provide weapons for the proponents of a "free" state. His enemies dubbed the guns "Beecher Bibles."

why Edward and Therese journeyed back to the Mount Washington which he had climbed so many years before, to recapture that beauty and harmony which seemed to slip away with every passing day. New York City was simply not that "happy village" of his childhood where everyone went to church, observed the Sabbath, and drank deeply from the Biblical well. Perhaps this is the reason why the Robinsons maintained a retreat somewhere in the Catskills. The return to nature was not for him a rebellion against the Bible and the church; it was rather an attempt to rediscover in creation a sense of wonder before the creator of all.

Finally, in the midst of all this literary and artistic activity, there was published on July 4, 1855 by a newspaper editor over in Brooklyn a slight volume of verse entitled, *Leaves of Grass.* Most people never saw it or read it and of those who did, only a few liked it. Emerson admired the work, however, and his praise made its next edition. What can we say about this poem which ties together so much that had gone before, and, with great love for nature, for America, and with a transcendental sense of the unity of all life, points forward to the America of the future? The author, at least, tells us who he is:

> Walt Whitman, an American, one of the roughs, a kosmos,
> Disorderly fleshly and sensual . . . eating drinking and breeding,
> No sentimentalist . . . no stander above men and woman or apart
> from them . . . no more modest than immodest.[23]

Robinson doubtless would have preferred Longfellow. Most people did. Whitman was virtually banned in Boston because of his sexual language. It would have been difficult for any professor of Biblical Studies to accept someone who failed to distinguish the good and the evil but who literally loved all. Nevertheless, had E. R. listened carefully he would have found his own love for the freedom and democracy and equality in his nation expressed more vitally than had been done for a long time. Whitman was no sentimentalist; but he did believe deeply and fully in the United States which he calls in his introduction "essentially the greatest poem."[24] Longfellow

---

[23] Walt Whitman, *Leaves of Grass:* A facsimile of the first edition, introduced by Richard Bridgman (San Francisco: Chandler Publishing Co., 1968), 29.
[24] *Ibid.*, iii.

points to the past which has departed; Whitman sings of the day which is dawning and his song is America.

THE FINAL YEARS

It is in his *Later Biblical Researches*[25] that we learn that Robinson served on the American Board of Commissioners for Foreign Missions. This position is not surprising, for he was one of the few churchmen who was not a missionary but who had had direct experience on the missionary field. Moreover, it is clear from some of his published remarks that he was enthusiastic about the enterprise. In an article in *Bibliotheca Sacra*[26] entitled "The Druzes of Mount Lebanon," he concludes with the following passionate plea:

> The signs of the times are full of encouragement. The Spirit of the Lord is moving upon the minds of men; the fields are already white for the harvest. The East has for ages been the scene of external revolutions, but the oriental mind has long remained stationary and stagnant. That stagnant pool is beginning now to effervesce. The light and power of European civilization and science and art are rushing in with resistless force; and are borne on with the increasing energy by every steamer that foams through the Dardanelles and along the coasts of Syria and Egypt . . . How has the Musselman already cast off his prejudices; how changed already is the Druze to invite among his people the ministers of another religion! Soon the nothings of a nominal Christianity and the darkness and superstition of Islam, and the monstrous fables of the Druze, will be done away; but what shall come up in their place? For the answer to this question, the churches of Christendom, yea the churches of this land, are responsible. Before another half century shall have rolled away, in the providence of God, there will be seen revolutions in the oriental mind and oriental world, of which no one now has even a foreboding. Brethren, the time is short; the crisis rushes on; let us awake and be prepared.[27]

---

[25] Robinson, *Later Biblical Researches*, 22. Strangely, I have not found his name on any of the lists of Board members published in various newspapers.
[26] Robinson, ed., *Bibliotheca Sacra* (New-York: Wiley and Putman, 1843), II, 205-253.
[27] *Ibid.*, 251-252.

Actually, it is doubtful that Robinson himself could have guessed what West Asia would look like fifty or one hundred years later. Certainly, though science and technology had a major impact, Protestant missions hardly had the influence which he expected. What is particularly interesting is how closely Robinson relates the "light and power of European civilization, science and art" and the missionary movement. There is an implication that as soon as inhabitants of the region learn to think scientifically and get rid of their superstitions the old religions will dissolve and conversion to Protestantism will be an easy step to take, if the missionaries work diligently.

Not all of Robinson's missionary concerns involved Asia. In 1854, he received a letter from the Second Foreign Church in Honolulu which was looking for a new pastor.[28] A similar letter had been sent to the other two members of the committee chosen from Hawaii: Henry Ward Beecher, the beloved minister of the Plymouth Congregational Church of Brooklyn, and J. Spaulding, the Secretary of the Seaman's Friend Society of New York. Since the Hawaiian church, Beecher and Spaulding were all Congregational this seems to be a good indication that Robinson, though now a Presbyterian, still maintained connections with his old church. Just why the Hawaiians chose these men rather than their counterparts at Andover is, however, an interesting question.

The answer is found, in part, in the accompanying letter which makes clear that the church was looking for a minister who was flexible and open-minded and who could deal with a great variety of people: professionals, missionary children, visiting seamen, native Hawaiians. Although the church was founded to minister to "foreigners" living in Hawaii and was largely made up of physicians, lawyers, and government workers and officials, it also attracted a wide spectrum of other people. Doubtless they chose to work with a New York City committee because they believed that the mood of New York and Union Theological Seminary suited better their own situation than did the more provincial and doctrinaire Andover.

Whether the committee was successful in finding the right candidate is, at this time, unknown. Robinson, himself, must have been startled a little by the fact that the church offered to pay a new minister without particular

---

[28] Robinson Papers, L-10.

experience the same salary that Robinson had been getting at Union. Moreover, the letter indicated that it would not be difficult to increase that salary after a year. Doubtless, however, the temptation to apply was very brief. Robinson was devoted to civilization, to New York and Union and libraries and scholarship. Life on the beach in a Pacific paradise was not, by any stretch of the imagination, his cup of tea.

Although we should mention that as early as November 1841, he was a member of the Protestant Reformation Society,[29] it must also be observed that not all of Robinson's activities were directly related to the church. He was, for instance, an honorary member of the American Geographical and Statistical Society, and a regular member of both the American Ethnological Society and the New York Historical Society. Accounts of the American Ethnological Society contained in *The Literary World* reveal that he was at first Vice President under Albert Gallatin and then President. During 1847, when the journal regularly reported the activities of the society, E. R. was constantly involved, chairing meetings, reading important letters from other scholars, and laying before the society accounts of recent findings.[30] By the 1850s, however, the Society had apparently changed, taken over, charges *The New-York Observer*, by the infidels and free thinkers.

> Formerly, we recollect the presence at the Ethnological Society of the oriental scholar, Dr. Robinson, and the active and early archaeologist, Dr. Hawks, and some other well-known names of men who stood by Moses and the prophets. But these are decidedly to be classed among the antiquarian "old fogies" who are destined to put out their little lights. . .[31]

Clearly Sidney Morse was disturbed by new movements in science and the claims that human beings have been on earth at least 150,000 years. The

---

[29] *New-York Evangelist* Nov. 20, 1841. According to Hirrel this was a highly vituperative anti-Catholic Society. Hirrel, *op.cit.*, 114.

[30] See: *Literary World* Feb. 13, Apr. 3, 24, May 15, Nov. 20, for example. On April 24 the following tribute was paid to E. R. "To show what can be accomplished when such resources are afforded, one might instance *the History of Ferdinand and Isabella* and the *Biblical Researches in Palestine* which have probably done more to raise the character of American scholarship abroad than all else that has been published here for the last ten years." *Literary World* 12 (Apr. 24, 1847), 276.

[31] "American Ethnological Society," *New-York Observer* XXXII, 16 (April 20, 1854).

groundwork for the great Darwinian revolution was already being laid. With the authority of men like Louis Agassiz and Asa Gray becoming more and more recognized, it was increasingly difficult to be a scientist and a Biblical literalist at the same time.

Minutes of the New York Historical Society are to be found in 1840s issues of *The United States Magazine and Democratic Review* and reveal E. R. also to have been an active participant in that society, reporting for the Executive Committee, nominating honorary members, making resolutions. At some point he served the association as foreign corresponding secretary and offered public lectures on behalf of it.[32] For a man frequently described as somewhat withdrawn, almost antisocial, he certainly was surprisingly active!

Robinson's *Later Researches* also reveals another of his predominant interests, for he mentions in passing that he is an officer of the American Oriental Society, an organization founded by John Pickering in Boston in 1842. When one consults the *Journal of the American Oriental Society*, it is soon evident that E. R. was quite modest about his involvement in the society. When it was first founded in 1842, John Pickering, the lawyer-linguist from Boston was chosen as President with E. R. and Moses Stuart as Vice Presidents. Pickering, however, soon fell ill and died in 1846. Undoubtedly, E. R. as Vice President assumed the presidency in 1845 when Pickering could no longer function as head of the organization. When the fourth number of volume I of the journal was published in 1849 Robinson was already President and he remained in that office until he died in 1863.

Some of Robinson's correspondence indicates that he was active in recruiting new members for the New York branch of this society in the 1840s and 1850s. There were, in fact, meetings connected with the Society at his home at 257 Greene Street. Not surprisingly, it would appear that several other members of the organization were also clergy with an interest in Hebrew and other "oriental" languages. We must ask what the relation between missionary work and the Oriental Society was in the minds of

---

[32] A not-so successful example of this is mentioned in a report in the Dec. 9, 1852 edition of *The New York Daily Times*, p. 5. Robinson read a paper "of considerable length" which had been prepared for the Oriental Society. The *Times* is not reluctant to point out the lecture's excessive details and opaqueness, though it does go on to recap some its more lucid moments. See *Literary World,* Dec. 18, 1852, p. 395-96 for a much less critical review of the same lecture.

those so involved. How much did the Protestant impetus to missions affect the supposedly more "scientific" view of West Asia?

A look at the regular membership of the society reveals great variety: Edward Everett, Theodore Parker, William Lynch (who explored the Dead Sea), Edward Salisbury (Professor of Arabic and Sanskrit at Yale), etc. Nevertheless, the majority of the 80-90 members were Congregational and Baptist clergy from New England and New York. Rufus Anderson, who served as a director of the society, was also Secretary of the American Board of Commissioners for Foreign Missions and traveled regularly to the mission field. Corresponding members were, for the most part, missionaries from around the world. Indeed, this first attempt by Americans to study Asia and Africa quite consciously depended heavily on missionaries to supply information and articles.[33]

Nevertheless, the *Journal of the American Oriental Society* was not a new version of the old *Panoplist* but had serious pretensions to more objective scholarship. There are articles on African languages and translations of Buddhist texts. Edward Salisbury from Yale gave the society stature through his scholarly endeavors which he published frequently in the journal. Edward Robinson, in contrast, did not publish in the journal at all. In fact, despite the number of Hebraists among the members, little space is devoted to the eastern Mediterranean littoral or to anything Biblical. Eli Smith has an article on Islamic music, but, by and large, emphasis is upon south and east Asia and Africa. It is significant, in any event, that Robinson was not only aware of but presided over the development of America's consciousness of Asia. The attitude of the journal, though certainly not non-Christian, points toward a far more objective and open approach to non-Western phenomena. That E. R. had a part in this development is undoubted.

Edward Said, in his provocative and controversial book, *Orientalism,* argues that orientalism, from the beginning was a way for the West to dominate, restructure, and have authority over what Europeans and Americans designated the "orient."[34] It was and is a political act through which power and control are exerted over the "Other." Among those

---

[33] John Pickering, the first president of the society, emphasized this connection in his inaugural presidential address.
[34] Edward Said, *Orientalism* (New York: Random House, 1979), 3.

orientalists whom he examines and dissects is Silvestre de Sacy, a man well known to and admired by Robinson. Could Robinson be indicted in the same way?

One's first impulse is to say, no, of course not. Robinson had nothing to do with politics. He was not supported by any Western government but paid his own way. As a geographer he was most objective, often even quantitative in his analysis. Moreover, as a person he showed considerable respect for those native Egyptians and Palestinians and Bedouins whom he met. His praise or blame was based, not upon their religion or place of origin but whether they did the job he paid them to do, whether they were honest or dishonest, ambitious or lazy. Certainly, he did not "create" the oriental as an "Other." If the Palestinians appeared as "the Other" it is because they were, quite objectively, exotic to the European and American. The Cairo slave market was not Hartford. The armed Bedouins of Wady Musa were very different from the natives of Andover. Near Eastern and American cultures objectively differed in all kinds of ways and Robinson should not be blamed for seeing the differences.

Nevertheless, despite these objections there are strong reasons to regard Robinson's whole accomplishment as profoundly political. The Bible itself knows that to name something is to have control over it. That is why names are so important in the Bible and why Jews do not speak the name of God. To speak his name aloud is to claim control over him. To name the ancestors, by the same token, is to take control of time. To name Abraham, Isaac, and Jacob as forebears is to lay claim to the past.

When Robinson went to Palestine, several layers of names were already in use. Most important, there were the names Arabs used for places: Beisan, El Quds, Tell Qadi, etc. On top of these were the various ancient "Christian" and crusader names, used to indicate the sites of miracles or other Biblical events, names used by the "Greeks and Latins" for their own religious purposes. Robinson, in his explorations, reveals great skepticism concerning the latter, showing that they are frequently empty and without meaning. Even though many of the identifications came as early as the 4th century, they are adjudged by him "made up" and hence false. In other words, he destroys the traditional Roman Catholic and Eastern Orthodox landscapes in order to assert his own Biblical, that is, Protestant landscape. It is no wonder that John Henry Newman protested and Austria banned his book.

It is noteworthy that Robinson never asks whether any parts of the Bible itself could have been "made up." For him, the Bible is axiomatically true. If the Bible asserts that Jesus ascended into heaven somewhere "beyond Bethany" that is what occurred. If the Bible says that two million Israelites lived in the desert for forty years, it must have happened somehow. Now, in fact, there are many events in the Bible which are open to at least as much criticism as the position of the Holy Sepulcher in Jerusalem, but his skepticism does not extend that far. He claims that his conclusions are beyond any Protestant-Catholic controversy, and he may well have believed that, but, in fact, what he did was to undercut the Catholic and Orthodox presence in the Holy Land. His skepticism is aimed at Roman Catholic ideas so that the Protestant flag may be firmly planted in Palestine.

Robinson is, in a way, more positive about the Arabic names, for he guesses—often with good justification—that they hint at earlier, Biblical designations. He uses these names, however, in order to destroy them. Beisan is really Bethshan. The first is the corruption, the latter the reality. Biblical names (as, of course, corrupted in English transliterations) are the authentic names. Arabic names are only important as the gateway to something else. Contemporary history with its languages and places and people is set aside in favor of an antiquity which represents REALITY. And that REALITY is a Protestant reality, for it is the landscape upon which Protestants live and move. It is no wonder that his work was so heralded in Protestant Germany, England, and America.[35] One should not infer, however, that this was Robinson's intent. He certainly had no ability to force the Arabs to abandon their place names. He set the stage, however, for the mapmakers to do their work and when they did the power of Western imperialism over the region became effective.

This process works in the reverse in regard to Islam. For Robinson, present-day Muslims may be wise, honest, and helpful. He has no great quarrel with, indeed he admires, many of the individuals he comes to know. Those whom he dislikes he does not dislike because they are Muslim. Islam, however, he knows was founded by a false prophet and is "full of dark

---

[35] For an interesting study of this whole subject see: Keith W. Whitelam, *The Invention of Ancient Israel: the silencing of Palestinian history* (New York: Routledge: 1996).

superstition." Just as it never occurs to him that the Bible might be wrong in some respects, so it also never occurs to him that his own attitudes toward Islam ought to be treated with skeptical analysis. There is no evidence that he ever really sought to learn about Islam or what it teaches, even though his friend and contemporary, Washington Irving, did write a book on Mohammed and his successors.[36] His negative attitude toward Islam is as axiomatic as his positive attitude toward the Bible.[37]

This does not mean that Robinson accomplished nothing positive or that his labors should be regarded with disdain. On the contrary, his work is monumentally important for the study of the Bible and should be cherished as such. Nevertheless, it must also be seen as a major first step in the reconquest of the Holy Land by the West. It is not at all surprising that his investigations were eventually followed by the political control of Palestine by the British and then by those who many Arabs consider to be America's surrogates, the Israelis. Archaeology's attempt to "know the land" better than the inhabitants themselves has played a vital role in this new chapter of the crusades.

This is not to say that Robinson thought of himself as a conqueror. One can be sure that he would have responded that he had no desire to control any of the peoples of the area. He did, however, believe that Protestant missionaries could win over many of the Druze, nominal Christians, Jews, and Muslims of Syria-Palestine "to Christ." He also believed that a strong Protestant mission would serve the best interests of the British Empire in the area. So in the end, his political intents were not so veiled after all. Edward Said may sometimes overstate his case, but he is not far off the mark.

One other work from this period must also be mentioned. In 1856 the *Cyclopaedia of American Literature* edited by Evart and George Duyckinck was published.[38] In it are to be found biographies of both Edward and Therese Robinson. From unpublished papers in the New York Public

---

[36] Washington Irving, *Mahomet and His Successors* (New York: John B. Alden, 1884). First published: 1849.

[37] Given the information available about Islam, it was not difficult to take a very jaundiced view. For an example of biased Christian reporting see: "Mohammedanism," *Christian Advocate and Journal* IX, 40 (May 29, 1835), 157.

[38] Duyckinck, Evart and George Duyckinck, eds. *Cyclopaedia of American Literature*, 2 vols. (New York: Charles Scribner, 1866) II, 50-53.

Library it is clear that these biographies were written by the Robinsons themselves and hence provide the most reliable outline of their lives, at least as they wished them to be remembered. Although there is nothing very new in the accounts given, the biography of Edward confirms certain facts which otherwise would be historically debatable. Parenthetically, it should also be noted that unpublished letters in the same library suggest that the Robinsons also knew the Duyckincks on a more social basis and probably were members of their literary circle.

NUNC DIMITTIS

In 1856, while his *Later Researches* was being published, Robinson began work on his last great work on the geography of the Bible. Unlike his preceding volumes it was to be arranged topically rather than chronologically. The three main heads were to be I. Physical Geography, II. Historical Geography, III. Topographical Geography. It was to be, when finally written, his grandest achievement. Unfortunately, during the winter of 1856-7 he fell seriously ill with a "gastric fever" from which he only partially recovered by summer. On November 6, William Cullen Bryant wrote to his wife:

> I called on Mrs. Robinson last evening. Her husband has been ill with a remittant fever of the typhoid type, and is still quite weak, so that he scarcely goes out. Accordingly, neither she nor Mary can come out at present to Roslyn. I saw the young lady, and gave her a particular invitation, but her mother cannot dispense with her company yet.[39]

In the winter of 1857-8 the fever came back and he was "prostrated" for some time. Perhaps, as was suggested earlier, this was some form of malaria picked up in Palestine near Lake Huleh.

Eventually, he recovered, but somehow had lost the energy to work on the book. Instead, he devoted his time to the memoir of his father. As has already been suggested, this little work tells us a great deal about the

---

[39] William Cullen Bryant II and Thomas G. Voss, *The Letters of William Cullen Bryant*, 4 vols. (New York: Fordham Unversity Press, 1981), III, 397.

author both factually and psychologically. It was as though the force of his father's personality had loomed over Robinson for a long time. Now he gave that specter its due, but he did so by rooting himself in the history of New England, by revealing through his genealogy, his own sense of America and of himself.

Eventually he recovered enough energy to return to writing the Geography, but soon another difficulty emerged. Cataracts affected his sight until his ability to read and do research was severely impaired. He sought relief in an operation, but it seemed to do little good. The last page of his manuscript was written in June of 1861. Finally, in May 1862, as America was experiencing the most vicious and bloody war in her whole history, he set off for Europe to find more expert care. He visited Berlin and Vienna without effect. Time spent in an infirmary in Berlin helped his general health, but his eyesight did not return. After enjoying the company of old German friends, he returned to New York in November of 1862 and began teaching. Soon, however, another, perhaps fever-related affliction overtook him. On January 27, 1863, a few months short of his 69th birthday, he died peaceably in New York of Bright's Disease, an affliction of the kidneys.[40] A document preserved in the Robinson papers shows that during his last days he was no longer even able to sign his name. Only an "E" is vaguely legible; finally he had to be content to make a wavering X.

The funeral service was held at the Mercer Street Presbyterian Church at 2 p.m. on January 30.[41] The congregation was large, with members of several scholarly societies in attendance. Participating clergy included Gardiner Spring, Asa D. Smith, Henry B. Smith, Isaac Ferris, and Samuel Cox.[42] Thomas Skinner, Robinson's old friend and colleague, delivered the eulogy and described therein his last moments:

> The disease of which he died—one of the most distressing to which

---

[40] See: *New-York Tribune,* Jan 29, 1863 for an extended obituary. Other obituaries are listed separately in the bibliography.
[41] *New York Times* XII, 3541 (Jan. 29, 1863), 5.
[42] Obituary, *The Observer* XLI, 6 (Feb. 5, 1863), 42. Gardiner Spring was minister of Brick Church in N.Y.C.; A. D. Smith, the soon to become President of Dartmouth; H. B. Smith, a professor at Union; Isaac Ferris, the Chancellor of N. Y. U.; and Samuel Cox a well-known Brooklyn minister. It is noteworthy, perhaps, that Skinner, Spring, A. D. Smith, and H. B. Smith were all Andover men.

we are liable-though defiant of remedies and sure of its object, is usually lingering; but in his case its course was quick and gentle, and its termination was perfectly tranquil and easy . . . With no discomposure or agitation, he went softly to sleep; his pulse stopped, he ceased to breathe.[43]

Only a few days later, on February 8, a Dr. Osgood presented before the New York Historical Society a resolution offering tribute to E. R. for his great accomplishments. This resolution reads in part:

> Resolved, that with the decease of Rev. Dr. Robinson, the Society laments the loss of a cherished and faithful officer who has served it for twenty years and for a large portion of that time as Foreign Corresponding Secretary.
>
> Resolved, that his departure takes from our country the patriarch of sacred scholarship, an untiring student, a careful, learned and sagacious author whose works have enriched our own libraries, done honor to the American name abroad and written his own name with that of our Nation upon the land and language of the Bible.[44]

Robinson's colleague, Henry Boynton Smith, then offered before the assembly an often quoted tribute. This was followed by a longer essay read before a special meeting of the society on March 24 by Roswell D. Hitchcock, another colleague and fellow Andoverian.[45] Together these two accounts by Smith and Hitchcock of the life and work of Edward Robinson were published by the New York Historical Society and have remained until this time the most extensive single tribute to him.[46]

After his death Therese edited and published the part of his Geography which he had written, but it was only a fragment of what he intended. Many years would pass before another scholar had the knowledge and ability to confront the task anew. Subsequently, in 1864 his widow

---

[43] *The Evangelist* XXXIII, 6 (Feb. 5, 1863).

[44] Minutes of the New-York Historical Society, February 8, 1863. The final phrase is significant for assessing E. R.'s orientalism.

[45] The *American Presbyterian Review* II (Apr. 1863), 353, in a brief obituary, promised a longer article about Robinson by Hitchcock in the next issue, but curiously it never appeared.

[46] Henry B. Smith and Roswell D. Hitchcock, *The Life, Writings and Character of Edward Robinson, D.D., LL.D.* (New York: Anson D.F. Randolph, 1863).

returned to live in Germany with her daughter, Mary. There she died in 1870.[47] Her body was returned to America to be buried next to her husband in the Greenwood Cemetery in Brooklyn.

Edward, their son, served his country during the Civil War as a Lieutenant in the Eighth Regiment of New York Volunteers and as aide-de-camp for Major General Julius Shakel. He survived to practice law and become a diplomat serving the United States as American Consulate in Hamburg, Germany. Letters to him from persons such as William H. Seward, George Bancroft, and Henry Wadsworth Longfellow are also included in the Robinson Papers. Mary returned to America after the death of her mother and for a time was a guest of the Bryants at their summer home in Massachusetts. She never married but became known as a pianist and composer.

And so, as guns roar and thousands die in senseless but heroic battle, our story comes to an end. What finally shall we say about Edward Robinson? How shall we assess his life and work?

Certainly as a human being he had many virtues. It may be that he was cool and blunt on the outside and exceedingly retiring from social affairs. Still, many attest to his warm-heartedness and steadfastness in friendship. Although he never wrote about women's rights, he treated his wife as an equal and shared with her fully in a life of letters. As a husband and father he is described as especially gentle and loving. He was a stern taskmaster in the classroom, but then, quite anonymously, would give help to one of his students in need. He was also a very loyal brother, particularly close to his unmarried sister Elizabeth and very supportive of both George and Charles. On more than one occasion he was the source of funds to see them through a difficult period. At one time, he offered many of his books as collateral so that Charles could get a loan. On another occasion he bought from George his pew in a church in New Haven, not because he would ever use it, but in order to provide his brother with needed cash.

His scholarship was impeccable. Few, if any, from that whole era can rival the scope and high quality of his work: a superb translation and supplementation of Gesenius' Hebrew Lexicon, the best Greek-English

---

[47] An unpublished letter in the New York Public Library from Edward Robinson Jr. to William Cullen Bryant describes in some detail her last hours and her death. In it Edward expresses his mother's great admiration for the poetry and person of Bryant.

lexicon of the day, the best harmony of the Gospels, a fine dictionary of the Bible for scholars and another for students, an immense ground-breaking work on Biblical geography. In a few short years he provided the basic tools for Biblical study, tools which were published and republished long after his death.

He was a scholar's scholar: well-educated, objective, and open-minded. His presupposition was that of his church: that the Bible is true, but that seldom hampered his critical judgment. He seems to have had little interest in the religious passions of the day. We hear little from him about temperance, anti-Catholicism, the evils of chattel slavery. He may have felt strongly about some of these issues, but his publications are free of his own opinions. He is a geographer and a philologist, not a preacher. It is interesting that while most of his colleagues are represented in the Union Theological Seminary Library by many sermons, there are none by him in the collection.

There were, of course, things he did not do. He never, for instance, produced a commentary on any book of the Bible. The short commentaries he did write on the "Song of Deborah" and "David's Lament for Saul and Jonathan" reveal the work of a careful minimalist. He found the basic meaning of the text straightforward and simple. Much, he thought, could be summed up in a sentence or two. He was not a proponent of the vast elaboration of doctrine and certainly not of metaphysical interpretation.

As an undergraduate, we are told, he particularly liked mathematics and, in a way, that is how he treated the Bible. He began with the central axiom that the Bible is true and interpreted everything accordingly. As early as 1824, while Robinson was at Andover with Moses Stuart, the latter translated a little book on hermeneutics by J. A. Ernesti.[48] In that book the author provides basic rules for interpretation. Part II, Chapter VII contains the following:

> #176 If two passages contradict each other, the text of one must be faulty...
> #177 If the text of both be genuine, then conciliation is to be sought where apparent discrepancies exist. If the text of both passages plainly appears to be genuine, so that it cannot fairly be

---

[48] J. A. Ernesti, *Elements of Interpretation,* trans. and with notes by Moses Stuart (Andover: Flagg and Gould, 1824).

> questioned, then it must be understood that there is a mere appearance of inconsistency; which should be removed, and the passage conciliated by a proper interpretation.[49]

This is exactly Robinson's method in those articles on the resurrection, the body of Christ, and the second coming in which he faces apparent threats to the truth of the Bible. One never may consider that an inconsistency in the Bible might be genuine. All inconsistencies are apparent only. At the same time, he is not at all interested in putting words in the mouths of Biblical writers. He simply wants to discover what it is the Bible says.

This attitude, along with the identification of factuality and truth, was both the strength and Achilles heel of ante-bellum interpretation. On the one hand, it provided a certainty which could be very powerful. Many Christians are still drawn to a message which promises this sort of assurance. Even if something looks inconsistent, you can be sure that it is not. Somehow, some way two million Israelites did manage to survive around the tiny watering holes of the Negev.

But ultimately, like the "Wonderful One Hoss Shay" of Oliver Wendell Holmes, who was consciously satirizing the demise of Calvinism, such mighty systems are bound to break down and when they do they are likely to fall apart completely, leaving behind only worn out, useless components. Some jolt, some bump in the road can wake the reader up to the fact that the inconsistency really is there, that no amount of commentarial glue can prevent the parts from coming loose.

One big bump appeared in 1859 when Charles Darwin published *The Origin of Species*. For most of the 19th century, theologians had gone on the assumption that somehow, some way the Bible and science could be seen as saying the same thing. Not only the theologians but many scientists—the Edward Hitchcocks and the Benjamin Sillimans—believed that. Robinson, despite his literalism, was intrigued by the natural world and, in so far as he was a geographer, considered himself a scientist too. He was excited by Alexander Von Humboldt and consulted with Leopold von Buch, the best geologist Germany had to offer, about the Dead Sea. Throughout his adult career in New York, he seems to have devoted much more energy and interest to various secular and scientific societies—the

---

[49] *Ibid.*, 89-90.

American Oriental Society, the New York Historical Society, the American Ethnological Society—than he did to the Presbytery of New York. But Darwin really did not fit with Genesis; it had to be one way or the other and at that point the unity of Protestant culture began to break down.

Robinson, by that time, was probably too sick to care. Perhaps he believed that Darwin also could be made to fit somehow. But it could not be done and so, reluctantly, the theologians either attacked Darwin and all his successors as bad scientists or accepted the fact, and a "Shay" dissolving fact it was, that the Bible and science are inconsistent and that sometimes, science is correct and the Bible, at least on a factual level, is wrong.

Robinson had, throughout his life, been able to avoid all those German naysayers who questioned whether the Bible is even consistent with itself. It is interesting that one would never know, from reading Robinson, that David Strauss had ever written his *Life of Jesus* or that source criticism was moving ahead so rapidly among the German scholars. There is no foreshadowing of Julius Wellhausen and the documentary hypothesis. E. R. was content to "illustrate" the Bible through his discoveries about the Holy Land.

In many respects, as a Biblical scholar, Robinson was an island unto himself. Surely he had little sympathy for those German scholars such as Wilhelm De Wette, Johann Karl Vatke, and Bruno Bauer who wished to interpret the Bible through the categories of idealist philosophy. There is nothing of the radicalism or rationalism of someone like Gottlieb Kaiser or C. P. W. Gramberg about him either. Theoretically, I suppose, he was closer to conservatives such as Ernst Wilhelm Hengstenberg and Johann von Hoffman, but in fact he did not at all participate in their desire to restore Lutheran orthodoxy and, in fact, personally disliked Hengstenberg as something of a twit.[50]

Among American Biblical scholars, who, we must remember were really very few in number, he also stood very much alone. American Protestantism was fractured by both social upheaval and sectarian controversy. Most Biblical scholars wrote commentaries and theological treatises to defend their own church's theological position, not to develop

---

[50] For a good survey of 19th century German developments see: John H. Hayes and Frederick C. Prussner, *Old Testament Theology: Its History and Development* (Atlanta: John Knox Press, 1985). Unfortunately, little is included about American developments.

genuinely new ideas. When new ideas were developed, they were generally derived from reason and then read into the Bible. One thinks of, for instance, the "two wine theory" of the temperance movement.[51]

Even the Unitarians such as Andrews Norton and George Noyes, who did engage in Biblical criticism, generally rejected German scholarship as undercutting their own, preconceived theological position. Theodore Parker, who translated De Wette into English and both reviewed and came to appreciate the work of Strauss, was one of the few scholars to adopt the more critical attitude of the Germans and he was generally rejected even by most mainline Unitarians. Among the Trinitarians one might cite Horace Bushnell as one of the few to offer a genuinely different approach to the study of scripture. Although not a Biblical scholar *per se*, his emphasis, derived from Coleridge and his own teacher Josiah Gibbs, upon the subtleties of language had the potential to send Biblical studies in a new direction.[52]

Because theological education was directly under the control of the churches rather than, as in Germany, under the state, however, professors had to toe the theological line of their respective communions. Therefore neither the arguments of Parker nor the linguistic observations of Bushnell had longlasting effect. Robinson certainly had no inclination to revise theology or call old doctrines into question. Although a philologist, he showed no interest in Bushnell's observations about language. He was different because, for the most part, he was playing a different game. Basically he was not a theologian but a geographer and historian.

The attitude among American Biblical scholars that their calling was primarily to defend a pre-established position tended to dissolve, for the most part, after the Civil War.[53] It is perhaps ironic that one of E. R.'s

---

[51] Moses Stuart and many others, to deal with the Bible's apparent sanctioning of alcoholic beverages, argued that when the Bible spoke favorably about wine it was referring to unfermented drink. The wine it warns against is alcoholic.

[52] See Jerry Wayne Brown, *The Rise of Biblical Criticism in America, 1800-1870*. (Middletown, Conn.: Wesleyan University Press, 1969) for a good review of the period.

[53] For accounts of how religious life and perception had changed even in the 1850s see: Lori D. Ginsberg, "'Moral Suasion is Moral Balderdash': Women, Politics, and Social Action in the 1850s," *Journal of American History* 73, no. 3 (Dec. 1986), 601-622 and Clifford E. Clark, Jr. "The Changing Nature of Protestantism in Mid-Nineteenth century America: Henry Ward Beecher's Seven Lectures to Young Men," *Journal of American History* 57, no. 4 (Mar. 1971), 832-846.

successors, Charles Augustus Briggs, who held the Edward Robinson chair, became a not very radical proponent of some features of then modern German scholarship and found himself hauled up on heresy charges by the Presbyterian Church. The church still was living in ante-bellum times.

History was on the side of Briggs, however, and eventually even Princeton Theological Seminary came around to accepting the fruits of Biblical higher criticism. In any event, such developments were by no means an extension of Robinson's work. His work was carried on by the explorers and archaeologists, like Bliss and Albright, of the next generations.

In many ways, the death of Robinson marked the end of an era. After him very few of the truly great Biblical scholars could find a way to hold to the literalist position. The arguments of German critical scholarship and of natural science became just too persuasive. He was replaced at Union, not by another geographer and proto-archaelogist, but by William Greenough Thayer Shedd, a literary scholar and critic.

There is still one more topic which we must discuss, a topic alluded to in every chapter of this book. Throughout E. R.'s life, the United States had endured many crucial moral problems: the breaking of solemn treaties with native Americans and the destruction of tribal life on the flimsiest of pretexts, the "stealing" of the whole southwest and California from Mexico, the suppression of women, and, of course, the burning issue which finally produced the great conflagration: slavery. Robinson was a Christian and believed that his life should be guided by the Bible. He was a writer who put many words into print on a great variety of subjects. Nevertheless, in all the writings by him so far discovered—there are undoubtedly some newspaper articles as yet uncatalogued—there is no comment about any of these issues.

Certainly, it is not that he considered moral issues unimportant. In his essay on aspects of literature and science in America already mentioned, he writes:

> But while we thus urge that knowledge is power, let us also remember that, in itself and by itself, it is a power for evil as well as good. Knowledge in itself has nothing moral; it is the mere material on which the intellect works; it has no character of its own; and it becomes alike the instrument of good and evil according to the prompting of moral man . . . Let us then in all our efforts to

> increase knowledge, strive also to extend the influence of moral culture, to implant and cherish moral principles and religious feelings...[54]

One must ask then why the author himself, though he greatly increases knowledge, offers so little by way of moral guidance in a world which surely needed it.

One senses, in fact, a troubling blindness in Robinson which was characteristic not only of him but of his whole society. In describing America he writes:

> We know not among us the idea of rank; and the tendency doubtless is, to resist and spurn all adventitious claims, which in the diversified phases of society may be occasionally set up. Perhaps it is to this habitual feeling of equality and independence, imbibed in our earliest infancy and nursed through life by all external circumstances, that we look to the maintenance of our institutions.[55]

But wait, we are likely to say, surely you have forgotten some important facts. America **is** a nation with great emphasis upon rank, for some are immensely rich while others live in poverty and in America money does count. Even more important, some are free and some are bought and sold like cattle. Moreover, more than half the nation cannot vote or participate in various ways in civil and religious society because they are women, not men. One must also remember that the real native Americans have been lied to and cheated until they have no rights left at all.

One cannot place much of the blame on Robinson. When one looks at the Christian churches, in general, one finds few people who were willing to put themselves on the line for either native Americans or Blacks. Women remained second-class citizens within most churches until well into the twentieth century. Finally, we must ask of that era when people "knew their Bibles" whether those Bibles were very good guides after all. At least, Robinson had the good sense not to use the Bible to justify slavery and the patriarchal oppression of women as did many of his colleagues. There may be some virtue in his silence after all. Still, the modern reader would be far

---

[54] *Bibliotheca Sacra and Theological Review* (1844), I, 38-39.
[55] *Ibid.*, 7.

happier with a more articulate statement about the Bible's social teachings.

We must not end our discussion of Edward Robinson, however, on such a sour note. He was, after all, not only a great scholar but an intellectual hero who endured tremendous danger in his quest for truth. And, lest we forget, the Bible, though sometimes used as a justification for oppression, is also a clarion call for justice, for those who have ears to hear. Moreover, we should not stand in judgment of others while our own society is wracked with injustices of its own and we too stand idly by, letting oppression occur. In every age there is perception and there is blindness; hind-sight is always the clearest type of vision. Robinson's epic, which we now conclude, is, finally, a reminder to each of us that we should, after all, pay attention to our own inconsistencies and blind spots. Otherwise, the study of history is not worth anything at all.

APPENDIX

From Niebuhr to Robinson: A partial bibliography

This is a bibliography of books about Palestinian travel and geography drawn largely from Robinson's own library. In so far as it is possible the works have been ordered chronologically, though it must be noted that some expeditions taken before Robinson's were not reported until after his. Others, like Niebuhr's, were issued in several volumes over a long period of time. There are, besides books, many articles about travel in the Holy Land written in journals like *The Missionary Herald* and *Zack's Monatliche Correspondenz* and in newspapers. Some of these are included in the main bibliography.

1774-1799

Carsten Niebuhr (1733-1815). *Beschreibung von Arabien aus eigenen Beobachtuner und im Lande selbst gesammelten Nachrichten.* Kopenhagen: Moller, 1772.
_____. *Reisebeschreibung nach Arabien und andern umliegenden Landern.* 3 vols. Kopenhagen: N. Moller, 1774-1837.
    Robinson considered Niebuhr the prince to the explorers because of his precise descriptions, but unfortunately most of his exploration was in Arabia and not Palestine.

Eyles Irwin (1751?-1817). *A series of adventures in the course of a voyage up the Red-Sea, on the coasts of Arabia and Egypt: and of a route through the desarts of Thebais in the year 1777.* 2 vols. London: J. Dodsley, 1787.
    This is mainly about Egypt, but it has some relevance for E. R.'s explorations of the Sinai Penninsula.

Constantin-François Volney (1757-1820). *Voyage en Syrie et en Égypte.* 2 vols. Paris: Desenne, 1787.
    Much of this work is about Egypt and Syria in general, but volume II, Chs. XXX and XXXI deal with Palestine.

Giovanni Mariti (1736-1806). *Voyages dans l'isle de Chypre, la Syrie et la Palestine, avec l'histoire générale du Levant.* 2 vols. Paris: 1791.
    Vol. II contains an account of quite extensive travel in Palestine.

Ysbrand van Hamelsveld (1757-1812). *Biblische Geographie.* 3 vols. Hamburg: B. G. Hoffmann, 1796.
A major work with chapters on mountains, rivers, springs, lakes, seas, etc.

Ulrich Jasper Seetzen (1767-1811). *Ulrich Jasper Seetzen's Reisen durch Syrien, Palästina, Phönicien, die Transjordan-Länder, Arabia Petraea und Unter-Aegypten. Hrsg. un commentiert von Prof. Dr. Fr. Kruse.* 4 vols. Berlin: G. Reimer, 1854-59.
The author was a German physician who traveled widely in the Levant but who died of poison before his journals could be published. His travels were known, however, through *Zack's Monatliche Correspondenz.*

Heinrich E. G. Paulus (1761-1851). *Sammlung der merkwuerdigsten reisen in den Orient.* 7 vols. Jena: Christ. Heinr. Cuno's Erben, 1792-1799.
A vast collection of earlier travel writings which E. R. owned and used.

1800-1810

William Wittman. *Travels in Turkey, Asia-Minor, Syria, and across the desert into Egypt during the years 1799, 1800, and 1801, in company with the Turkish army, and the British military mission.* London: R. Phillips, 1803.

Charles Paultre des Ormes. *Kurze geographische nachrichten von Syrien.* Weimar, Landes-Industrie-Comptoire, 1804.
A small book done by an artillery officer for Napoleon's campaign in Syria. Includes a map of the region.

Johann Jahn (1750-1816). *Biblische Archäologie.* 5 vols. Wien: C. F. Beck, 1805-1825.
A vast compendium of the best information known at the time.

Edward Daniel Clark. *Travels in Various Countries of Europe, Asia, and Africa.* 5 vols. Cambridge: 1810-1823.
Clark was a British Protestant who looked for alternatives to traditional sites. See particularly II, 184-327.

François-René Chateaubriand (1768-1848). *Travels in Greece, Palestine, Egypt, and Barbary, during the years 1806 and 1807.* Trans. F. Shoberl. New York: Van Winkle and Wiley, 1814.
Chateaubriand was a defender of traditional site identifications. Robinson dismisses him abruptly.

Ali Bey (1766-1818). *The Travels of Ali Bey, in Morocco, Tripoli, Egypt, Arabia, Syria, and Turkey between the years 1803 and 1807.* 2 vols. Philadelphia: M. Carey, 1816.
The author is really a Spanish Christian and not a Muslim at all, though he does not reveal this fact in the book.

1811-1820

Elijah Parish (1762-1825). *Sacred geography, or a gazetteer of the Bible.* Boston: Samuel T. Armstrong, 1813.
   Information arranged alphabetically and drawn largely from Scripture. The map provided shows only the vaguest understanding of Palestinian geography.

Karl Friedrich Klöden (1786-1856). *Landeskunde von Palastina.* Berlin: Rucker, 1817.

Thomas Legh. *Narrative of a journey in Egypt and the country beyond the cataracts.* 2nd ed. London: J. Murray, 1817.
   This book is entirely about Egypt, but an appendix describes the itinerary for a proposed trip through Palestine which Legh did not take because of the plague.

Ern. Frid. Car. Rosenmüller (1768-1835). *Das alte und neue Morgenland: oder Erâuterungen der heiligen Schrift aus der natûrlichen Beschaffenheit, den Sagen, Sitten, und Gebrauchen des Morgenlandes.* 4 vols. Leipzig: Baumgartner, 1818-1820.
   A prime example of the vastness of German scholarship.

John Bramsen. *Bramsens Reise durch die Ionische Inseln, Aegypten, Syrien, Palästina und Griechenland, in den jahren 1814 and 1815.* Jena: Bransche buchhandlung, 1819.
   See particularly pp. 80-109.

William Turner (1792-1867). *Journal of a tour in the Levant.* 3 vols. London: J. Murray, 1820.
   Turner's trip began in 1812 and extended through much of 1813. The Holy Land is described in Volume II, 105-294.

1821-1830

James Silk Buckingham. *Travels in Palestine through the countries of Bashan and Gilead, east of the Jordan Rover including a visit to the cities of Geraza and Gamala in the Decapolis.* London: Longman, Hurst, Rees, Orme and Brown, 1821.
   A rather boastful account of his "new finds," which were not really new, but there are sections, on Gerasa and Gamala, for instance, which are useful.

Robert Richardson (1779-1847). *Travels along the Mediterranean and parts adjacent; in the company with the Earl of Delmore, during the years 1816-17-18.* 2 vols. London: T. Cadell, 1822.
   See Vol. II, 172-527. The book contains a very poor topographical map of Jerusalem.

John Lewis Burckhardt (1784-1817). *Travels in Syria and the Holy Land.* London: J. Murray, 1822.
   In 1823 Wilhelm Gesenius provided a German translation. Burckhardt was a Swiss explorer who was really preparing for travel in Africa. He describes primarily the area south of the Dead Sea, including Petra. Robinson cites him frequently.

J. Martin Augustin Scholz (1794-1852). *Reise in die gegend swischen Alexandrien und Parätonium, die libysche wüste, Siwa, Egypten, Palästina und Syrien in den jahren 1820 und 1821*.Leipzig: F. Fleischer, 1822.

The section on Palestine is fairly brief (pps. 127-305) but in it he treats not only contemporary conditions and population but antiquities.

Charles Leonard Irby (1789-1845) and James Mangles. *Travels in Egypt and Nubia, Syria, and Asia Minor: during the years 1817 & 1818*. London: T. White and Co, 1823.

Irby and Mangles were commanders of the Royal Navy who spent nine months in Palestine, exploring various areas including the area east of the Dead Sea.

F. W. Sieber. *Reise von Cairo nach Jerusalem und wieder zurück nebst Beleuchtung einiger heiligen Orte.* Prague: Martin Neureutter, 1823.

A fairly brief account by a pious Roman Catholic.

Ern. Frid. Car. Rosenmüller (1768-1835). *Handbuch der biblischen Alterthumskunde.* 4 vols. Leipzig: Baumgartnerschen Buchhandlung, 1823-1826.

A huge study of Biblical lands with some dependence upon recent travelers and discoveries.

Josiah Conder (1789-1855). *A popular description of Palestine, or the Holy Land: geographical, historical, and topographical.* London: J. Duncan, 1824.

A popular travel guide which quotes frequently Clarke, Pococke and Chateaubriand.

James Silk Buckingham (1786-1855). *Travels among the Arab tribes inhabiting the countries east of Syria and Palestine, including a journey from Nazareth to the mountains beyond the Dead Sea and from thence through the plains of the Hauran to Bozra, Damascus, Tripoly, etc.* London: Longman, Hurst, Rees, Orme, and Brown, 1825.

Jakob Berggren (1790-1868). *Reisen in Europe und im Morgenlande.* Trans. from Swedish by F.H. Ungewitter. 3 Vols. Leipzig und Darmstadt: C. W. Leske, 1828.

For his treatment of Palestine see: Vol II, 223-410 and Vol. III, 1-175.

Léon Laborde (1807-1869). *Voyage de la Syrie.* Paris: Firmin Didot, frères, 1827.

Johann Jahn (1750-1816). *The History of the Hebrew Commonwealth: from earliest times to the destruction of Jerusalem, A.D. 72.*, trans. C. E. Stowe. Oxford: Talboys, 1828.

This was the standard history of Israel used by Protestants in Europe and America, translated by Robinson's friend Calvin Stowe.

Alvan Bond (1793-1882). *Memoir of the Rev. Pliny Fisk, A.M.: late missionary to Palestine.* Boston: Crocker and Brewster, 1828.

Pliny Fisk was the first Protestant missionary to set up a mission in Jerusalem. In these memoirs there are interesting accounts of his first impressions.

Richard Robert Madden (1798-1886). *Travels in Turkey, Egypt, Nubia, and Palestine: in 1824, 1825, 1826, and 1827.* 2 vol. London: H. Colburn, 1829.
    See particularly volume II. Fascinating, dated letters written to a variety of people.

John Carne (1789-1844). *Recollections of travels in the east: forming a continuation of the letters from the east.* London: Colburn, 1830.
    Much of this chatty and personal reflection is about Palestine.

Joseph E. Worcester (1784-1865). *Outlines of Scripture geography with an atlas.* Boston: Hilliard, 1830.
    A tiny work of little significance, except to show the "state-of-the-art" in 1830.

Santino Daldini (fl. 1814). *Viaggio e visita di Terra Santa: Narrazione sincera e circostanziata.* 2nd Ed. Milano: Carrara, 1830.

Giovanni Finati (b. 1787). *Narrative of the life and adventures of Giovanni Finati, native of Ferrara; who, under the assumed name of Mahom made the campaigns against the Wahabees for the recovery of Mecca and Medina.* trans. William Bankes. 2 vols. London: J. Murray, 1830.
    He treats Palestine in Vol. II, Ch. III-V.

Léon Laborde (1807-1869). *Voyage de l'Arabie Petrée.* Paris: Girard, 1830.
    Robinson corrects many of Laborde's statements about Petra.

1831-1841

Josiah Conder (1789-1855). *A popular description of Syria and Asia Minor: geographical, historical, and topographical.* London: J. Duncan and T. Tegg, 183?.

William Rae Wilson (1772-1849). *Travels in the Holy Land, Egypt, etc.* London: Longman, Brown, Green, and Longmans, 1831.
    A very popular travel book which went through several editions.

John Lewis Burckhardt (1784-1817). *Notes on the Bedouins and Wahabys, collected during his travels in the East.* London: H. Colburn and R. Bentley, 1831.

Anton Prokesch von Osten (1795-1876). *Reise ins heilige Land: in Jahr 1829.* Wien: C. Gerold, 1831.
    A slender, personal volume.

Justus Olshausen (1800-1882). *Zur Topographie des alte Jerusalem.* Kiel: D.C.C. Schwers Wittwe, 1833.
    Deals with Josephus, the Bible and C. Niebuhr. The plans of Jerusalem offered are very inadequate.

Friedrich Gottlieb Crome. *Geographisch-historische beschreibung des landes Palastin.* Gottinger: Vanderhoeck und Ruprecht, 1834.

A fairly detailed description of the land with distances and topography.

Léon Laborde (1807-1869). *Carte de l'Arabie Pétrée levée et dressée: par Léon de Laborde en 1828 et gravée par Collin.* Paris: Giard, 1834.

A very rare linen map of Petra and the vicinity.

Thomas Tucker Smiley (d. 1879). *Scripture Geography or, A Companion to the Bible.* Philadelphia: T. K. Greenbank, 1834.

Another alphabetically arranged work drawn from the Bible.

Alphonse de Lamartine (1790-1869). *Souvenirs, impressions, pensées et paysages pendant un voyage en Orient 1832-1833.* 4 vols. Paris: Libraire de C. Gosselin, 1835.

Like Chateaubriand, Lamartine gives a very romantic account. Robinson pays no regard to him.

Edward Hogg. *Visit to Alexandria, Damascus, and Jerusalem, during the successful campaign of Ibrahim Pasha.* 2 vols. London: Saunders and Otley, 1835.

Volume II, Chs. 1-10 treats Damascus, Lebanon, and Jerusalem.

Vere Monro. *A summer ramble in Syria, with a Tartar trip from Aleppo to Stamboul.* 2 vols. London: R. Bentley, 1835.

Although the title doesn't indicate it, most of volume I concerns Palestine and Monro's experiences there in 1833.

Karl von Raumer (1783-1865). *Palâstina mit einem Plan von Jerusalem zure Zeit Zerstörung durch Titus und dem Grundriss der Kirche des heiligen Grabes.* Leipzig: F. A. Brockhaus, 1835.

A description of travel by a well-known German scholar.

Auguste Frederic Louis Viesse de Marmont. *Voyage dem. le maréchal duc de Raguse en Hongrie, en Transylvanie, dans la Russie meridionâle, en Crimeé, et sur les bords de la mer d'Azoff, à Constantinople, et sur quelques parties de l'Asia-Mineure, en Syrie, en Palestine et en Égypte.* 4 vols. Bruxelles: Meline, 1837-1859.

See particularly III, 1-87.

Thomas Skinner (1800?-1843). *Adventures during a journey over land to India, by way of Egypt, Syria, and the Holy Land.* Philadelphia: Waldie, 1837.

See Chs. 3-18 for treatment of Palestine.

Nathanael Burton. *Narrative of a voyage from Liverpool to Alexandria, touching at the island of Malta, and from thence to Beirout in Syria; with a journey to Jerusalem, voyage from Jaffe to Cyprus and Constantinople.* Dublin: J. Yates, 1838.

John Lloyd Stephens (1805-1852). *Incidents of travel in Egypt, Arabia Petraea, and the Holy Land.* New York: Harper, 1837.

Ascribed to "an American," this work contains a personal account of travels.

George Robinson. *Travels in Palestine and Syria.* London: H. Colburn, 1837.
George Robinson traveled in Palestine in 1831. Volume I deals with Palestine and contains a personal description of an extensive tour.

Karl von Raumer (1783-1865). *Der Zug der Israelites aus Aegypten nach Canaan: ein Versuch.* Leipzig: Brockhaus, 1837.
A monograph on the path of Israel's escape from Egypt relevant to E. R.'s travels in the Sinai.

Leon Laborde (1807-1869). *Journey through Arabia Petraea, to Mount Sinai, and the excavated city of Petra, the Edom of the prophecies.* 2nd ed., London: J. Murray, 1838.
Robinson corrects Laborde's descriptions at many points.

Gotthilf Heinrich von Schubert (1780-1860). *Reise in dar Morgenland in der jahren 1836 und 1837.* Erlangen: J. J. Palm und E. Enke, 1838-39.
This is an interesting work about the Levant from a German point of view but contains little about Palestine *per se.*

Marie-Joseph Geramb (1772-1848). *Pélerinage à Jérusalem et au mon Sinai en 1831, 1832 et 1833.* 3rd ed., Paris: Le Clere, 1836.
Geramb was a Roman Catholic priest and is very definitely on a pilgrimage to the traditional sites.

John D. Paxton (1784-1868). *Letters from Palestine; written during a residence in the years 1836, 7 and 8.* London: C. Tilt, 1839.
Paxton, an American Protestant clergyman, met Robinson during his first trip to Jerusalem. His letters tell of the mission there and about trips taken around the Holy Land.

(Anon). *Narrative of a Mission of Inquiry to the Jews from the Church of Scotland in 1839.* Philadelphia: Presbyterian Board of Publications, 1845.
This narrative contains a major section on Jews in the Holy Land.

Joseph Salzbacher (1790-1867). *Erinnerungen aus meiner Pilgerreise nach Rom und Jerusalem in jahre 1837.* Wien: Stephensplatz, 1839.
Definitely a Catholic pilgrimage book with an emphasis upon traditional holy sites.

Jean-Baptiste Morot (1797-?). *Journal de voyage, Paris à Jérusalem, 1839-1840.* 2nd ed. Paris: Claye, 1873.
Only chapters 8-10 (pp. 141-248) are about Palestine *per se.*

George Stokes (1789-1847). *The manners and customs of the Jews, and other nations mentioned in the Bible.* 2nd ed. Hartford: Benton, 1839.
A little book which reveals what people in the 1830's knew, or thought they knew, about ancient Jewish customs and life.

William Robert Wilde (1815-1876). *Narrative of a voyage to Madeira, Teneriffe and along the shores of the Mediterranean, including a visit to Algiers, Egypt, Palestine, Tyre, Rhodes, Telmessus, Cyprus, and Greece.* 2 vols. Dublin: W. Curry, Jr. and Co., 1840.
   Particularly II, 103-434. Wilde was an Irish physician who traveled from Sept. 1837 until June 1838.

Baptistin Poujoulat (1809-1864). *Voyage à Constantinople, dans l'Asie Mineure, en Mesopotamie, à Palmyre, en Syrie, en Palestine, et en Egypt.* 2 vols. Bruxelles: N. J. Gregoir, V. Wouters et cie, 1841.
   See Vol. II, 201-259. The author was in Jerusalem in Dec. 1837.

Harriet Catherine Ellesmere. *Journal of a tour in the Holy Land, in May and June 1840.* London: Harrison and Co., 1841.
   A brief, personal account of a trip which took place in 1840.

John Kitto (1804-1854). *Palestine: the Bible History of the Holy Land.* 2 vols. London: C. Knight, 1841.
   This large work treats both physical geography and history. It was the sort of work which Robinson meant to improve upon in his own physical geography.

John Gardiner Kinnear. *Cairo, Petra, and Damascus in 1839. With remarks on the government of Mehemet Ali and on the present prospects of Syria.* London: J. Murray, 1841.
   The author was in Palestine from Jan. to Sept 1839.

Ernst F.K. Rosenmüller (1768-1835). *The Biblical Geography of Asia Minor, Phoenicia, and Arabia.* trans. N. Morren with an appendix, containing an abstract of the more important geographical illustrations of Messrs. Robinson and Smith. Edinburgh: T. Clark, 1841.
   It is interesting how quickly scholars began to use Robinson's work!

Jean J.F. Poujoulet. *Histoire de Jérusalem.* 2 vols. Paris: L.F. Huiert, 1841-42.
   A much more Roman Catholic approach than Robinson would have approved of.

David Millard (1794-1873). *A journal of travels in Egypt, Arabia Petrae, and the Holy Land, during 1841-42.* Rochester, N.Y.: E. Shepard, 1843.
   Although "after Robinson," Millard traveled without benefit of his work.

John Carne (1789-1844). *Syria, the Holy Land, Asia Minor etc. illustrated in a series of views drawn from nature by W.H. Bartlett.* London, Paris and America: Fisher, Son and Co., 1842.
   This is mainly a series of plates done by Bartlett and William Purser with commentary for each. Only a few of the scenes are actually from the Holy Land. It is, however, a harbinger of things to come.

BIBLIOGRAPHY

General Reference Works

Allgemeine Deutsche Biographie. Leipzig: von Duncker & Humblott, 1875.
American Almanac and Repository of Useful Knowledge. New York: G. & C.& H. Carvell, 1830-1861.
Atlas of Israel, 3rd ed. New York: Macmillan Publishing Co., 1985.
Avi-Yonah, Michael, ed. *Encyclopedia of Archaeological Excavations in the Holy Land*, 4 vols. Englewood Cliffs, N.J.: Prentice-Hall, Inc., 1975-78. (EAEHL)
Balteau, J., M. Barrous, M. Prevost avec concours de nombreux collaborateurs. *Dictionnaire de Biographie Française*. Paris: Libraire Letouzy et ané, 1933.
Buttrick, George Arthur, ed. *The Interpreter's Dictionary of the Bible*, 4 vols. New York: Abington Press, 1962.
Duyckinck, Evert A. and George Duyckinck. *Cyclopaedia of American Literature*, 2 vols. New York: Charles Scribner, 1866.
Encyclopedia Americana, International Edition. Danbury, Conn.: Grolier Inc., 1996.
Freedman, David Noel, ed. *The Anchor Bible Dictionary*, 6 vols. New York: Doubleday, 1992. *(ABD)*
Fréres, Mme. Firmin Didot. *Novelle Biographie Universelle*. Paris: Imprimeurs-Libraires de L'Institut de France, 1852.
Garraty, John A. and Mark C. Carner. *American National Biography*, 24 vols. New York: Oxford University Press, 1999.
Jamieson, Robert. *Cyclopaedia of Religious Biography*. London: Richard Griffin and Company, 1853.
Johnson, Allen, ed. *Dictionary of American Biography*, 20 vols. New York: Charles Scribners' Sons, 1928-37.
Langer, William L., ed. *An Encyclopedia of World History*. Boston: Houghton Mifflin Co., 1948.
McClintock, John and James Strong. *Cyclopaedia of Biblical, Theological and Ecclesiastical Literature*. 12 vols. New York: Harper and Brothers, 1880.
National Cyclopedia of American Biography. New York: James T. White and Co., 1892.

National Union Catalogue, Pre-1956 Imprints. Chicago: American Library Association, 1977.
New Encyclopedia Britannica. Chicago: Encyclopedia Britannica, Inc., 1997.
Reid, Daniel G., ed. *Dictionary of Christianity in America.* Downer's Grove, Ill.: Intervarsity Press, 1990.
Schaff, Philip, ed., *A Religious Encyclopedia or Dictionary of Biblical, Historical, Doctrinal, and Practical Theology,* 4 vols. New York: The Christian Literature Company, 1888.
Stern, Ephraim, ed. *The New Encyclopedia of Archaeological Excavations in the Holy Land,* 4 vols. New York: Simon and Schuster, 1993.(NEAEHL)
Wilson, H., comp. *Trow's New York City Directory for the year ending May 1, 1863,* vol. LXXVI. New York: John F. Trow, 1862.

The Works of Edward Robinson
(in Chronological Order)

1822
Homeri Iliadis libri novem priores, librique XVIII, et ex XXII ex recensione C. G. Heyne, cum notis brevibus . . . adjecit E. Robinson. Catskill, N.Y.: N. Elliott, 1822.

1823
Prospectus of a Greek and English lexicon of the New Testament, trans. from the Latin and German work of Chr. Abr. Wahl. Andover: 1823.

1825
George Benedikt Winer, *A Greek Grammar of the New Testament,* trans. Moses Stuart and Edward Robinson. Andover: Flagg & Gould, 1825.

Greek and English Lexicon of the New Testament, from 'Clavis Philololgia' of Christ. Abr. Wahl, trans. Edward Robinson. Andover: Flagg and Gould, 1825.

1826
"Lexicography of the New Testament," *North American Review* 41, no. 27 (July 1826), 80-109. (unsigned article, later acknowledged)
"France: State of Protestant Religion," *The Missionary Herald* XXII, no. 10 (Oct. 1826), pp. 322-323.
"State of Missionary Exertions," *The Missionary Herald* XXII, no. 11 (Nov. 1826), pp. 361-362.

1831

"Theological Education in Germany I," *Biblical Repository* I, no. 1 (Jan. 1831), 1-51.

Translation: Prof. Tittmann, "Grammatical Accuracy of the Writers of the New Testament," *Biblical Repository* I, no. 1 (Jan. 1831),111-139.

Translation: Prof. Tholuck, "Theological Literature and Education in Italy," *Biblical Repository* 1, no. 1 (Jan. 1831), 177-186.

"Literary Notices," *Biblical Repository* 1.1 (Jan. 1831), 186-198.

"Theological Education in Germany II," *Biblical Repository* 1, no. 2 (Apr. 1831), 201-226.

"Language of Palestine in the Age of Christ and the Apostles," *Biblical Repository* I, no. 2 (Apr. 1831), 309-317.

"Literary Notices," *Biblical Repository* I, no. 2 (Apr. 1831), 407-408.

"Theological Education in Germany III," *Biblical Repository* I, no. 3 (July, 1831), 409-452.

Translation: Prof. Tittmann, "Simplicity of Interpretation in the New Testament," *Biblical Repository* I, no. 3 (July 1831), 452-464.

Translation: Prof. Tittmann, "Causes of Forced Interpretation of the New Testament," *Biblical Repository* I, no. 3 (July 1831), 464-491.

Translation: "Lexicography of the New Testament in a Critique of the Lexicons of Wahl and Bretschneider," *Biblical Repository* I, no. 3 (July 1831), 552-568.

"Interpretation of Judges, Chap. V. The Song of Deborah and Barak," *Biblical Repository* I, no. 3 (July 1831), 568-612.

Translation: "Theological Education in Germany: Directions for Theological Students entering the University of Halle. Published by the Theological Faculty of that University," *Biblical Repository* I, no.4 (Oct. 1831), 568-612.

Translation: Prof. H. Planck, "Nature and Character of the Greek Style of the New Testament," *Biblical Repository* I, no. 4 (July 1831), 638-691.

Translation: Prof. Buttmann, "General View of the Greek Language and its Dialects," *Biblical Repository* I, no. 4 (July 1831), 692-700.

Translation from Henstenberg's *Christologie des Alten Testaments*: "Genuineness of Isaiah, Chapters XL-LXVI," *Biblical Repository* I, no. 4 (July, 1831), 700-733.

1832

Prelimary remarks and translation by editor: Prof. Henstenberg, "On the Nature of Prophecy," *Biblical Repository* II, no. 5 (Jan. 1832), 138-173.

"Literary Notices," *Biblical Repository* 11, no. 5 (Jan. 1832), 210-216.

Preliminary remarks and translation by editor from Hengstenberg's *Christologie* "Interpretation of Isaiah 52:13-53." *Biblical Repository* II, no. 6 (Apr. 1832), 138-139.

"On the Letter Attributed to Publius Lentulus, respecting the Personal Appearance of Christ," *Biblical Repository* II, no. 6 (Apr. 1832), 367-393. [A correction of some details appears in the Oct. 1832 issue of the *Biblical Repository* II, no. 8, 797-798.]

Translation: Prof. Tholuck, "Theological Education in Italy," *Biblical Repository* II, no. 6 (Apr. 1832), 393-405.

"Literary Notices," *Biblical Repository* II, no. 6 (Apr. 1832), 407-408.

Translation: B. G. Niebuhr, "The Life of Carsten Niebuhr," *Biblical Repository* II, no. 8 (Oct. 1832), 593-656.

Translation: Abd-allotif, "Account of a Famine and Pestilence in Egypt A.D. 1200, 1201," *Biblical Repository* II, no. 8 (Oct. 1832), 657-680.

"Exodus of the Israelites out of Egypt and their Wanderings in the Desert," *Biblical Repository* II, no. 8 (Oct. 1832), 743-797.

Calmet's Dictionary of the Holy Bible, American Edition prepared by E. Robinson. Boston: Crocker and Brewster, 1832.

1833

A Dictionary of the Holy Bible, for the use of schools and young persons. Boston: Crocker and Brewster, 1833.

Translation with additions: Philip Buttmann. *A Greek Grammar for the use of High Schools and Universities.* Andover: Flagg and Gould, 1833.

Translation: Prof. Gesenius, "On the Sources of Hebrew Philology and Lexicography," *Biblical Repository* III, no. 9 (Jan. 1833), 1-44.

Translation: Prof. Tittmann, "On the Force of Greek Prepositions in Compound Verbs, as employed in the New Testament, *Biblical Repository* III, no. 9 (Jan. 1833), 45-66.

"Literary Notices," *Biblical Repository* III, no. 9 (Jan. 1833), 391-392.

Historical introduction to "Sketches of Idumea and its Present Inhabitants," from Travels of Burckhardt and Legh, *Biblical Repository* III, no. 10 (Apr. 1833), 247-288.

"Literary Notices," *Biblical Repository* III, no. 10 (Apr. 1833), 391-392.

Historical introduction to: Burkhardt, "Sketches of Idumea and its Present Inhabitants," *Biblical Repository* III, 12 (Oct. 1833), 613-652.

Translation: Prof. Tholuck, "On Want of Agreement among Interpreters of the New Testament with a critique on the various expositions of Matt. 5: 3-5," *Biblical Repository* III, no. 12 (Oct. 1833), 684-707.

Translation: Prof. Eugene Burnouf, "Discourse on the Sanscrit Language and Literature," *Biblical Repository* III, no. 12 (Oct. 1833), 707-721.

Translation: Hengstenberg, "On the Standing Still of the Sun and Moon, Joshua 10: 12-15," *Biblical Repository* III, no. 12 (Oct. 1833), 721-730.

"Literary Notices," *Biblical Repository* III, no. 12 (Oct. 1833), 755-760.

Translation: Tittmann, Johann August Heinrich, *Remarks on the synonymns of the New Testament.* Edinburgh: T. Clark, 1833-37.

1834

A Harmony of the Gospels in Greek, in the general order of Le Clerc and Newcome, with Newcome's notes. Revised and arranged by Edward Robinson. Andover: Gould and Newman, 1934.

Translation: "Outlines of a Course of Theological Study for use of Students, prepared by the Theological Faculty in the University of Leipsic," *Biblical Repository* IV, no. 13 (Jan. 1834), 127-138.

"Philology and Lexicography of the New Testament," *Biblical Repository* IV, no. 13 (Jan. 1834), 154-182. (First published, in part, in *The North Atlantic Review* July 1826.)

Translation from Hengstenberg's *Christologie II*: "On the Expression: 'He shall be called a Nazarene': Exposition of Matt. 2:23," *Biblical Repository* IV, no. 13 (Jan. 1834), 182-188.

"Literary Notices," *Biblical Repository* IV, no. 14 (Apr. 1834) 413-416.

Preliminary Note for "Greek and English Lexicography," *Biblical Repository* IV, no. 15 (July 1834), 556-557.

"The Lament of David over Saul and Jonathan; II Sam. 1: 19-27," *Biblical Repository* IV, no. 15 (July 1834), 594-605.

"Literary Notices," *Biblical Repository* IV, no. 15 (July 1834), 606-618.

Translation: C. G. Bretschneider, "On the Testimony of Josephus respecting Christ," *Biblical Repository* IV, no. 16 (Oct. 1834), 705-711.

"Literary Notices," *Biblical Repository* IV, no. 16 (Oct. 1834), 766-775.

1836

A Greek and English Lexicon of the New Testament. Boston: Crocker and Brewster, 1836. (This work became very popular and went through several editions. Robinson did a major revision of it in 1850.)

Wilhelm Gesenius, *A Hebrew and English Lexicon of the Old Testament, including the Biblical Chaldee*, trans. and ed. by Edward Robinson. Boston: Crocker and Brewster, 1836. (Robinson supplemented Gesenius' work with Gesenius' Thesaurus as it became available as well as with other information. He therefore was constantly bringing out new and revised editions until 1854. Even after that the work was frequently republished. In 1894 it saw its 29th edition.)

Translation: Berthold Georg Niebuhr, *The Life of Carsten Niebuhr, the Oriental Traveller*, with an appendix by J. D. Michaelis, trans. by Prof. Robinson. Edinburgh: T. Clark, 1836.

1838

"Kurzer bericht ueber eine reise nach Palastina und der ungegen im jahr 1838; in bezug auf die biblische geographie unternommen, von E. Robinson und Eli Smith" in *Zeitschrift fur die Kunde des Morganlandes*, B.2, H. 3, 325-383.

1839

"Extracts from a Journal of Travels in Palestine etc. in 1838," in *The Journal of the Royal Geographical Society of London* IX (1839), 295-310.

"A Brief Report of Travels in Palestine and Adjacent Regions in 1838; undertaken for the Illustration of Biblical Geography," *American Biblical Repository*, Second Series, no. 2 (April 1839), 400-430.

1840

"On the Dead Sea, and the Destruction of Sodom and Gomorrah," *American Biblical Repository*, New Series III, no. 5 (April 1840), 324-352.

"The Land of Goshen and the Exodus of the Israelites," *American Biblical Repository* III, no. 6 (July 1840), 306-324.

"The Jordan and its Valley," *American Biblical Repository*, Second Series, no. 8 (Oct. 1840), 265-277.

"Plan of Jerusalem," *New York Observer* XVIII, no. 50 (Dec. 12, 1840), 200.

1841

Biblical Researches in Palestine, Mt. Sinai and Arabia Petrae. A Journal of travels in the year 1838, by E. Robinson and E. Smith. Undertaken in reference to Biblical geography. Drawn up from the original diaries, with historical illustrations by Edward Robinson. Boston: Crocker and Brewster, 1841. (The work was published concurrently in Germany as *Palästina und die südlich angrenzenden Länder. Tagebuch eine Reise in Jahr 1838 in Bezug auf die biblishce Geographie unternommen von E. Robinson und E. Smith.* Halle: Verlag der Buchhandlung, 1841 and in England under the same English title by J. Murray. There are several subsequent editions. After 1856, his *Later Researches in Palestine and the adjacent regions* is incorporated as volume three of the newly titled *Biblical Researches of Palestine and the adjacent regions* which went through several editions.)

The Bible and its Literature; an inaugural address, delivered in the Mercer-Street Church in the City of New-York, January 29, 1841, with a charge by William Patton. New York: Office of the American Biblical Repository and the American Eclectic, 1841.

See also: "The Bible and its Literature," *American Biblical Repository* V., no. 10 (April 1841), 334-359.
Ernst Friederick Karl Rosenmüller, *The Biblical Geography of Asia Minor, Phoenicia, and Arabia. Trans. from German by Rev. N. Morris A.M. with an appendix, containing an abstract of the more important geographical illustrations of Messrs. Robinson and Smith, in their Biblical researches in Mount Sinai, Arabia Petraea and Phoenicia.* Edinburgh: T. Clark, 1841.
"Plan of Petra," *New York Observer* (Jan. 2, 1841), 2. (unsigned but see next item.)
"Visit to Jerusalem," *New York Observer* (Feb. 29, 1841), 29.
"Athens," *New-York Evangelist* (Feb. 13, 1841).
"Jerusalem and Vicinity," *New York Observer* (Mar. 20, 1841), 45-46.
"Tombs of the Kings and Judges," *New York Observer* (Apr. 3, 1841), 53-54.
"Jerusalem and Its Vicinity," *New York Observer* (Apr. 10, 1841), 57.
"Topography and Antiquities," *New York Observer* (Apr. 17, 1841), 62-63.
"Mountains Round About Jerusalem," *New York Observer* (May 22, 1841), 81.
"Farewell to Jerusalem," *New-York Evangelist* (Mar. 17, 1842), 44.
"The Nestorians: Review of Dr. Grant's Theory of the Lost Tribes, Part I," *American Biblical Repository,* Second Series, no. 12 (Oct. 1841), 454-482.
"Dr. Robinson's View of the Twelve Tribes," (An extract from the *American Biblical Repository* Jan. 1842) *New York Observer* 19, no. 48 (Nov. 27, 1841), 187.

1842
Biblical Researches in Palestine. First supplement. New York: Piercy and Reed, 1842.

Novum Testamentum Graece, post Aug. Henr. Tittmannum. Boston: Crocker and Brewster, 1842.

"The Nestorians. Review of Dr. Grant's Theory of the Lost Tribes. Concluded." *American Biblical Repository* VII, no. 13 (Jan. 1842), 26-68.
"Marriage of a Wife's sister," *New York Observer* (April 1842).
"Researches in Palestine," *New York Observer* (May 21, 1842), 82.
"Researches in Palestine, No. III," *New York Observer* (July 16, 1842), 114.
"Biblical Researches in Palestine," *American Biblical Repository* VIII, no. 15 (July 1842), 219-243.
"The Nestorians," *New York Observer* (Oct. 29, 1842), 174-175.
"The Nestorians, concluded," *New York Observer* (Nov. 5, 1842), 179.

1843
"Researches in Palestine. Compiled by the Editor from various communications received at different times from the Rev. Eli Smith and the Rev. S. Wolcott. With a Map of the country around the Sources of the Jordan," *Bibliotheca Sacra* I, no. 1, 4-88.

(This was also published as a booklet under the same title in Edinburgh by T. Clark in the same year.)

"Marriage of a Wife's Sister," *New York Observer* 21, no. 2 (Jan. 15, 1842).

"The Reputed Site of the Holy Sepulchre," *Bibliotheca Sacra* 1, no. 1, 154-202.

"The Druzes of Lebanon," *Bibliotheca Sacra* I, no. 2, 205-253. [This was presented first before the New York Historical Society in two segments: on April 4 and May 2, 1843.]

"Marriage of a Wife's Sister," *Bibliotheca Sacra* I, no. 2, 283-301.

"Biographical Notices of Gesenius and Nordheimer," *Bibliotheca Sacra* I, no. 2, 361-390.

"The Works of President Edwards: A Review," *Bibliotheca Sacra* I, 2, 391-392.

"The Coming of Christ, as announced in Matthew 24: 29-31," *Bibliotheca Sacra* I, no. 3, 531-557.

"Notes on Biblical Geography: the Exodus, Arimathea, Depression of the Dead Sea, etc." *Bibliotheca Sacra* I, no. 3, 564-566.

1844

"Letter from Dr. Robinson'" in *North American Review,* 59, no. 124 (1844), 253-258.

"The Aspect of Literature and Science in the United States, as Compared with Europe," *Bibliotheca Sacra* I, no. 1 (Jan. 1844), 1-38.

"Notes on Biblical Geography: Eleuteropolis, Legio, Megiddo, Maximianopolis," *Bibliotheca Sacra* I, no. 1 (Jan. 1844), 217-220.

"Notes on Biblical Geography: Gibeah of Saul, Rachel's Sepulchre, Ramah of Samuel," *Bibliotheca Sacra* I, no. 3 (May. 1844), 598-603.

"Cuneiform Inscriptions," translated from Ritter's 8th Volume, *New York Observer* 22, no. 27 (July 6, 1844). [Unsigned but probably by E. R.]

"Remains of the Ancient Bridge between the Jewish Temple and Mount Zion,"*Bibliotheca Sacra* I, no. 4 (Oct. 1844), pp. 794-800.

Introduction to: H. A. DeForest, "Contributions to the Climatology of Palestine," *Bibliotheca Sacra* I (Feb. 1844), 221-224.

1845

A Harmony of the four Gospels in Greek, according to the text of Hahn, newly arranged with notes by Edward Robinson. Boston: Crocker and Brewster, 1845.

"The Resurrection and Ascension of our Lord," *Bibliotheca Sacra* II, no. 5 (Jan 1845), 162-189.

"The Nature of our Lord's Resurrection Body," *Bibliotheca Sacra* II, 6 (May 1845), 292-311.

"Notes on Biblical Geography: The city of Ephraim," *Bibliotheca Sacra* II, no. 6 (May 1845), 398-399.

"Union Theological Seminary, New York," *New York Observer* 23. no. 29 (July 19, 1945), 114. (co-signed by H. White.) "Union Theological Seminary," *The New-York Evangelist* (July 17, 1845). (co-signed by H. White.)

"The Alleged Discrepancy Between John and the Other Evangelists respecting our Lord's Last Passover," *Bibliotheca Sacra* II, 79 (Aug. 1845). 405-436.

New Map of Palestine, from the latest authorities; chiefly from maps and drawings by Robinson and Smith, with corrections and additions furnished by Dr. Robinson. New York: J.H. Colton, 1845.

1846

A Harmony of the Gospels in English, according to the common version, newly arranged by Edward Robinson. Boston: Crocker and Brewster, 1846. (This was also published in London by the English Tract Society, n.d.)

"Topography of Jerusalem," *Bibliotheca Sacra* III, no. 11 (Feb. 1846), 413-460.

"Topography of Jerusalem II," *Bibliotheca Sacra* III, no. 12 (Nov. 1846), 605-642.

1847

"Notes on Biblical Geography: Hazor, Antiquities on the Route from Ba'albek to Hamath, The Sabbatical River, Raphanes," *Bibliotheca Sacra* V, no. 14 (July 1847), 403-409.

Neue untersuchungen über die topographie Jerusalems. Halle: Buchhandlung des Waisenhauses, 1847.

1848

"Notes on Biblical Geography: Lyranica, Chalcis, The Great Inscription of Apumea, Topography of Jerusalem," *Bibliotheca Sacra* VI, no. 17, 79-96.

"Depression of the Dead Sea and of the Jordan Valley," *Bibliotheca Sacra* VI, no. 19, 397-408. [This was first presented to the New York Historical Society on May 4, 1847.]

"Notes on Biblical Geography: Route from Beirut to Damascus, The Dead Sea Expedition," *Bibliotheca Sacra* VI, no. 20, 760-770.

1849

"Notes on Biblical Geography: A'waj, the second river of Damascus, The Natural Bridge over the Litany or Leontes, Kadesh of Naphtali and the Huleh, Kadesh Barnea, position of the Israelites at Sinai," *Bibliotheca Sacra* VII, no. 22, 366-385.

"Notes on the Words "All to" in Judges 9:53," *Bibliotheca Sacra* VII, no, 23, 607-609.

1850

A Greek and English Lexicon of the New Testament. A new ed., rev. and in great part rewritten. New York: Harper and Brothers, 1850.

Preface to: Talvi. Historical View of the Languages and Literature of the Slavic Nations. With a Preface by Edward Robinson. New York: George P. Putnam, 1850.

1852

Outline of a journey in Palestine in 1852. By the Rev. Dr. E. Robinson, E. Smith and others. (Read before the Royal Geographical Society of London on the 13th of December, 1852). London: W. Clowes and sons, 1852.

1853

"Outlines of a Journey in Palestine in 1852 by E. Robinson, E. Smith, and Others," *Bibliotheca Sacra* X, no. 37, 113-165.
"From Antipatris to Emmaeus," *Bibliotheca Sacra* X, no. 39, 528-543.

A Harmony of the four gospels in Greek: according to the text of Hahn/newly arranged, with explanatory notes by Edward Robinson, rev. ed. Boston: Crocker and Brewster, 1853.

1854

"Outlines of a Journey in Palestine in 1852 by E. Robinson, E. Smith, and Others," *The Journal of the Royal Geographical Society of London* XXIV (1854), 1-35. (This paper was read before the society on Dec. 13, 1852 by the Duke of Northumberland. It is accompanied by a very useful map of the journey through Palestine.

1855

"Excursion for the Identification of Pella," *Bibliotheca Sacra* XII, no. 45 (Jan. 1855), 131-144.
"The Site of Capernaum," *Bibliotheca Sacra* XII. no. 46, 263-282.

1856

Later Biblical Researches in Palestine, and in the adjacent regions. A journal of travels in the year 1852. Drawn up from the original diaries, with historical illustrations, with new maps and plans. Boston: Crocker and Brewster, 1856.

Four Maps to Accompany the Biblical Researches of E. Robinson and E. Smith, drawn by Heinrich Kiepert, 1856.

1857
"Synopsis of Robinson's Harmony of the Gospels" in *The New Testament with brief notes and instructions.* New York: American Tract Society, 1857. Also in: *The Family Bible.* New York, 1857.

Neuere biblische Forschungen in Palestina und in den angranzenden Landern. Tagebuch einer Reise in Jahre 1852. Berlin: G. Reimer, 1857.

1859
Memoir of the Rev. W. Robinson, former Pastor of the Congregational Church in Southington, Conn. Privately printed. New York: 1859.

1865
Physical Geography of the Holy Land, ed. Therese Robinson. Boston: Crocker and Brewster, 1865.

Selected Reviews of Robinson's Works

The Bible and Its Literature
New York Tribune I, 11 (April 22, 1841).

Biblical Researches in Palestine, Mount Sinai, and Arabia Petraea
The Athenaeum Journal (1841), 550.
Christian Review VI (Dec. 1841), 625-627.
North American Review LIII no. 112, 175-211.
Biblical Repertory and Princeton Review XIII, 4 (1841), 583-602.
Quarterly Review LXIX (Dec. 1841), 150-185.
Methodist Quarterly Review XXIV, Third Series, II (Jan. 1842), 5-26.

Bibliotheca Sacra
Methodist Quarterly Review XXV, Third Series, III (April 1843), 324.
Methodist Quarterly Review XXVI, Third Series, IV (April 1844), 324.

Buttmann's Greek Grammar
Methodist Quarterly Review XXXIII, Fourth Series, III (July 1851), 488-489.

Greek and English Lexicon of the New Testament
The Atheneum Journal (1837), 929.
Methodist Quarterly Review XXXIII. Fourth Series, III (1851) 156-163.
North American Review CLI (April 1851), 261-293.

Harmony of the Four Gospels in Greek
Athenaeum Journal (1846), 31-32.
Bibliotheca Sacra III, no. ix (Feb. 1846), 1-21.

Hebrew and English Lexicon of the Old Testament
Biblical Repertory and Princeton Review IX, 1 (Jan. 1837), 88-101.
Bibliotheca Sacra I (Aug. 1844), 607.
Journal of Sacred Literature VIII (Oct. 1849), 408-409.

Later Biblical Researches in Palestine and Adjacent Regions
Athenaeum Journal (1856), 1329-31.
Biblical Repertory and Princeton Review XXIX (Jan. 1857), 20-21.
Bibliotheca Sacra and American Biblical Repository XIV (Jan. 1857), 203-209.
The Evangelist XXVII, 43 (Oct. 23, 1856), 192.
Journal of Sacred Literature and Biblical Record VIII (Jan. 1857), 477-481.
The New-York Observer XXXIV, 43 (Oct. 23, 1856), 342.

Physical Geography of the Holy Land
Bibliotheca Sacra and American Biblical Repository XXII, no. lxxxviii (Oct. 1865), 689.
American Presbyterian Review XI (July 1865), 478.

Obituaries
American Presbyterian Review, II (April 1863), 353. (This brief obituary promises a longer article by R.D. Hitchcock in the next issue which curiously never appeared. but see below: Smith and Hitchcock, *The Life, Writings, and Character of Dr. Edward Robinson.*) *The Evangelist* XXXIII, 6 (Feb. 5, 1863).
Journal of the American Oriental Society, VIII (1863), iii-vii.
The Observer XLI, 6 (Feb. 5, 1863), 42.
New-York Evangelist XXVII, 43 (Oct. 23, 1856), 192.
New-York Daily Tribune XXII, 6,808 (Jan. 30, 1863), 2.
New York Times XII, 3542 (Jan. 30, 1863), 9. See also notice: XII, 3541(Jan. 29, 1863), 5.
Scientific American VIII, 7 (Feb. 14, 1863), 106.

Unpublished Materials of and about Edward Robinson
Andover Newton Theological Seminary Library
Hamilton College Library
Massachusetts Historical Society Library
New York Historical Society Library
New York Public Library
The Robinson Papers (privately held)
Union Theological Seminary Library

Books
Alexander, James W. *The Life of Archibald Alexander, D.D.* New York: Charles Scribner, 1854.
Albright, William Foxwell. *The Archaeology of Palestine and the Bible.* New York: Fleming H. Revell, 1932.
Allen, Oliver E. *New York, New York: A history of the World's Most Exhilarating and Challenging City.* New York: Atheneum, 1990.
Apostolos-Cappadona, Diane. *The Spirit and the Vision: The Influence of Christian Romanticism on the Development of 19th Century Art.* Atlanta, Ga.: Scholars Press, 1995.
Bartlett, S.C. *From Egypt to Palestine Through Sinai the Wilderness and the South Country.* New York: Harper and Brothers, 1879.
Bartlett, W.H. *Walks about the City and Environs of Jerusalem, Summer 1842* (reprint of the 1844 edition). Jerusalem: Canaan Publishing House, 1974.
Bliss, Frederick Jones. *The Development of Palestine Exploration: the Ely Lectures for 1903.* New York: Charles Scribners' Sons, 1906.
Blumberg, Arnold. *Zion Before Zionism 1838-1880.* Syracuse: Syracuse University Press, 1985.
Booth, Mary L. *History of the City of New York,* 2 Vols. New York: W. R. C. Clark. 1867, II, 723-881.
Bourbon, Fabio. *Yesterday and Today: The Holy Land. Lithographs and Diaries of David Roberts, R.A.* New York: Stewart, Tabori, and Chang, 1994.
Bowen, James. *A History of Western Education: The Modern West Europe and the New World,* Vol. 3. New York: St. Martin's Press, 1981.
Bozeman, Theodore Dwight. *Protestants in an Age of Science.* Chapel Hill, N. C.: University of North Carolina, 1977.
Brown, Charles H. *William Cullen Bryant.* New York: Charles Scribner's Sons, 1971.
Brown, Jerry Wayne. *The Rise of Biblical Criticism in America, 1800-1870.* Middletown, Conn.:Wesleyan University Press, 1969.
Brown, Richard D. *Massachusetts: A Bicentennial History.* New York: W. W. Norton & Company, Inc., 1975.
Bryant, William Cullen. *Letters from The East.* New York: G. P. Putnam and Sons, 1869.

_____. *The Letters of William Cullen Bryant*, ed. W. C. Bryant II and Thomas Voss. 4 vols. New York: Fordham University Press, 1977.

Buckingham, J. S. *Travels among the Arab Tribes inhabiting the countries east of Syria and Palestine.* London: Longman, Hurst, Rees, Orme, Brown, and Greene, 1825.

Burckhardt, John Lewis. *Notes on the Bedouins and Wahabys.* London: H. Colburn, 1831.

_____. *Travels in Syria and the Holy Land.* London: J. Murray, 1822.

Burg, B. R. *Richard Mather of Dorchester.* Lexington, Kentucky: The University Press of Kentucky, 1976.

Butts, R. Freeman. *Public Education in the United States: From Revolution to Reform.* New York: Holt Rinehart and Winston, 1978.

Carne, John. *Recollections of Travels in the East.* London: Henry Colburn and Richard Bentley, 1830.

Carpenter, W. H. and T. S Arthur. *The History of Connecticut From the Earliest Settlement to the Present Time.* Philadelphia: Lippincott, Grambo & Company, 1854.

Carr, William. *A History of Germany: 1815-1945.* New York: St. Martin's Press, 1969.

Channing, William Ellery. *Select Discourses and Essays.* ed. Copeland Bowie. London: Philip Green, 1895.

Cheeseman, Lewis. *Differences between Old and New School Presbyterians.* Intro. John C. Lord. Rochester: Erastus Darrow, 1848.

Cheyne, T. K. *Founders of Old Testament Criticism.* London: Methuen & Co., 1893.

Clemens, Samuel (Mark Twain). *A Connecticut Yankee in King Arthur's Court.* New York: Harper & Brothers, 1889.

_____. *Innocents Abroad.* New York: Harper & Brothers, 1889.

Cremin, Lawrence A. *American Education: The National Experience 1783-1876.* New York: Harper & Row Publishers, 1980.

Darliong, Arthur B. *Political Changes in Massachusetts 1824-1848.* New Haven: Yale University Press, 1925.

Davies, W. D., Eric M. Meyers and Sarah Walker Schroth. *Jerusalem and the Holy Land Rediscovered, The Prints of David Roberts (1796-1864),* with a forward by Michael P. Mazzatesta and a preface by Dennis M. Campbell. Duke University Museum of Art, 1996.

Davis, John. *The Landscape of Belief.* Princeton: Princeton University Press, 1996.

Dickens, Charles. *American Notes For General Circulation and Pictures from Italy.* New York: Charles Scribner's Sons, 1910.

Dizikes, John. *Opera in America: A Cultural History.* New Haven: Yale University Press, 1993.

Dwight, Benjamin W. *The History of the Descendents of Elder John Strong of Northampton, Mass.* Albany: J. Munsell, 1871.

Emerson, Ralph Waldo. *The Complete Essays and Other Writings of Ralph Waldo Emerson,* ed. Brooks Atkinson with forward by Tremaine McDowell. New York: Random House, 1950.

Ernesti, J. A. *Elements of Interpretation,* trans. and ed. by Moses Stuart. Andover: Flagg and Gould, 1824.

Fetterly, Clarence Aubrey. *Fifty Years Ago*. Clinton, N.Y.: 1947.
Formisano, Ronald P. and Constance K. Burns. eds. *Boston 1700-1980: the Evolution of Urban Politics.* Westport, Conn.: Greenwoord Press, 1984.
Frey, Hans. *The Eclipse of Biblical Narrative: A Study in Eighteenth and Nineteenth Century Hermeneutics.* New Haven: Yale University Press, 1974.
Frothingham, Paul Revere. *Edward Everett: Orator and Statesman.* New York: Houghton Mifflin Company, 1925.
Gatch, Milton McC., ed. *'so precious a foundation: 'the Library of Leander van Ess at the Burke Library at Union Theological Seminary in the City of New York.* New York: Union Theological Seminary and the Grollier Club, 1996.
Gaustad, Edwin Scott. *A Religious History of America.* New York: Harper & Row Publishers,1966.
Gillett, E.H. *History of the Presbyterian Church in the United States of America,* vol. II. Philadelphia: Presbyterian Publication Committee, 1864.
Giltner, John H. *Moses Stuart: The Father of Biblical Science.* Atlanta, Ga.: Scholars Press, 1988.
Godwin, Parke. *A Biography of William Cullen Bryant, with extracts from his private correspondence.* New York: D. Appleton and Co., 1883.
Grant, Robert with David Tracy. *A Short History of the Interpretation of the Bible,* second ed. Philadelphia: Fortress Press, 1984.
Greenleaf, Jonathan. *A History of the Churches of All Denominations in the City of New York.* New York: E. French, 1846.
Handy, Robert T. *A History of Union Theological Seminary.* New York: Columbia University Press, 1987.
_____. *The Holy Land in American Protestant Life, 1800-1948: A documentary history, edited with a commentary by Robert T. Handy.* New York: Arno Press, 1981.
Hart, Albert Bushnell. *Commonwealth History of Massachusetts: Colony of Massachusetts Bay*, Vol. I. New York: The States History Company, 1927.
Hawthorne, Nathaniel. *The Complete Novels and Selected Tales of Nathaniel Hawthorne*, ed. Norman Holmes Pearson. New York: Random House, 1937.
Hayes, John H. and Frederick C. Prussner. *Old Testament Theology: Its History and Development.* Atlanta: John Knox Press, 1985.
Hecht, Marie B. *Odd Destiny: The Life of Alexander Hamilton.* New York: Macmillan Publishing Co. Inc., 1982.
Hibbard, F. G. *Palestine: Its Geography and Bible History,* ed. D. P. Kidder. New-York: Land and Scott, 1851.
Hilprecht, H. V. *Explorations in Bible Lands During the 19th Century.* Philadelphia: A. J. Holman and Co., 1903.
Hirrel, Leo P. *Children of Wrath: New School Calvinism and Antebellum Reform.* Lexington, Ky.: University Press of Kentucky, 1998.
Hodge, Archibald Alexander. *The Life of Charles Hodge, D.D. LL.D. Professor in the Theological Seminary, Princeton, N.J.* New York: Scribners' Sons, 1880.

Hodge, Charles. "The Fugitive Slave Law" and "The Bible Argument for Slavery," in E. N. Elliott, ed. *Cotton is King, and Pro-Slavery Arguments*. Augusta, Ga.: Pritchard, Abbott, and Lewis, 1860, 810-877.
Holborn, Hajo. *A History of Modern Germany: 1648-1840*. New York: Alfred Knof, 1964.
Hooker, Edward W. *Memoir of Mrs. Sarah Lanman Smith.*, 2nd ed. Boston: Perkins & Marvin, 1840.
Howat, John K. *American Paradise: The World of the Hudson River School*. New York: Metropolitan Museum of Art, 1988.
Hudson, Winthrop S. *Religion in America*. New York: Charles Scribner's Sons, 1965.
Hutchison, William R. *Errand to the World: American Protestant Thought and Foreign Missions*. Chicago: University of Chicago Press, 1986.
Inalcik, Halil with Donald Quataert, ed. *An Economic and Social History of the Ottoman Empire, 1300-1914*. Cambridge: Cambridge University Press, 1994.
Ingersoll, Robert. *The Works of Robert Ingersoll* in 12 vols. New York: Dresden Publishing Co., 1908, Vol. I.
Irving, Washington. *Mahomet and His Successors*. New York: John B. Allen, 1884. (First published: 1849)
_____. *A Tour on the Prairies*, ed. with an introductory essay by John Francis McDermott. Norman: University of Oklahoma Press, 1956.
Janeway, J. J. *Unlawful Marriage: An answer to "the Puritan" and "Omicron" who have advocated in a pamphlet, the Lawfulness of the Marriage of a man with his deceased wife's sister*. New York: Robert Carter, 1844.
Johnston, Henry Phelps. *Nathan Hale: 1776*. New Haven: Yale University Press, 1914.
Jones, Howard Mumford and Bessie Zaban Jones. *The Many Voices of Boston*. Boston: Little, Brown and Company, 1975.
Jones, Theodore Francis, ed. *New York University 1832:1932*. New York: New York University Press, 1933.
Keller, Charles Roy. *The Second Great Awakening in Connecticut*. New Haven: Yale University Press, 1942.
Kelley, Wyn. *Melville's City*. New York: Cambridge University Press, 1996.
Kenyon, Kathleen. *Jerusalem, excavating 3000 years of History*. New York: McGraw-Hill, 1967.
Kiepert, Heinrich, *Atlas zu Robinson's Pälastina*. Halle: Verlag der Buchhandlung des Waisenhauses, 1841.
Kingsley, William L. *Contributions to the Ecclesiastical History of Connecticut*. New Haven: J.H. Bentham Printer, 1861.
Kling, David W. *A Field of Divine Wonders: The New Divinity and Village Revivals in Northwestern Connecticut 1792-1822*. University Park, Pennsylvania: Pennsylvania State University Press, 1993.
Kouwenhoven, John A. *The Columbia Historical Portrait of New York*. New York: Doubleday and Co., 1953.
Krafft, W. *Die Topographie Jerusalem's*. Bonn: H.B. König, 1846.

Laborde, Leon. *Journey through Arabia Petraea, to Mount Sinai and the excavated city of Petra,* 2nd ed. London: J. Murray, 1838.
Lawrence, Vera Brodsky. *Strong On Music: The New York Music Scene in the Days of George Templeton Strong, 1836-1975,* Vol. I. New York: Oxford University Press, 1988.
Leslie, R. F. *The Age of Transformation: 1789-1871.* New York: Harper & Row Publishers, 1964.
Lothrop, Thornton Kirkland, ed. *Some Reminiscences of the Life of Samuel Kirkland Lothrop.* Cambridge: John Wilson and Son, University Press, 1888.
Lowell, James Russell. *The Poetical Works of James R. Lowell, Complete in Two Volumes.* Boston: Ticknor and Fields, 1864.
Lynch, William Francis. *Narrative of the United States Expedition to the River Jordan and the Dead Sea.* Philadelphia: Lea and Blanchard, 1848.
_____. *Official Report of the United States Expedition to Explore the Dead Sea and the River Jordan.* Baltimore: John Murphy and Co., 1852.
Marsden, George M. *The Evangelical Mind and the New School Experience: A Case Study of Thought and Theology in the Nineteenth Century.* New Haven: Yale University Press, 1970.
Marty, Martin E. *Righteous Empire: The Protestant Experience in America.* New York: Dial Press, 1970.
Mead, Sidney Earl. *Nathaniel William Taylor: A Connecticut Liberal.* Chicago, Illinois: The University of Chicago Press, 1942.
Melville, Herman. *Journal of a visit to Europe and the Levant,* ed. Howard C. Horsford. Princeton, N. J.: Princeton University Press, 1955.
_____. *Moby-Dick or, the Whale,* intro. Viola Maynell. London: Milford, 1920.
_____. *Typee,* illus. Mead Schaeffer. New York: Dodd, Mead and Co., 1923.
Meyer, Adolphe E. *An Educational History of the Western World.* New York: McGraw-Hill Book Company, 1965.
Middlekauf, Robert. *The Mathers: Three Generations of Puritan Intellectuals 1596-1728.* New York: Oxford University Press, 1971.
Miller, Perry. *The Raven and the Whale: The War of Words and Wits in the Era of Poe and Melville.* New York: Harcourt Brace, 1956.
Miller, Samuel. *The Life of Samuel Miller.* Philadelphia: Claxton, Remsen, and Haffelfinger, 1869.
Montague, Edward P. (ed.) *Narrative of the late Expedition to the Dead Sea. From a diary of one of the party.* Philadelphia: 1849.
Morison, Samuel Eliot. *The Oxford History of The American People.* New York: Oxford University Press, 1965.
Morse, James King. *Jedediah Morse: A Champion of New England Orthodoxy.* New York: Columbia University Press, 1939.
Nichols, Robert Hastings. ed. and comp. by James Hastings Nichols. *Presbyterianism in New York State.* Philadelphia: Westminster Press, 1963.
Niebuhr, Carsten. *Beschreibung von Arabien aus eigenen Beobachtunger und im Lande selbst gesammelten Nachrichten.* Kopenhagen: Moller, 1772.

_____. *Reisebeschreibung nach Arabien und anderen umlegenden Landern*, 3 vols. Kopenhagen: N. Moller, 1774-1837.
Novalis. *Pollen and Fragments: Selected Poetry and Prose of Novalis*, trans. with an introduction by Arthur Versluis. Grand Rapids: Phanes Press, 1989.
Olin, Stephen. *Travels in Egypt, Arabia Petraea, and the Holy Land*, 2 vols. New York: Harper and Brothers, 1843.
Otto, Rudolph. *The Philosophy of Religion Based on Kant and Fries*, trans. E.B. Dicker. London: Williams and Norgate, 1931.
Parry, Ellwood C. *The Art of Thomas Cole: Ambition and Imagination*. Newark: University of Delaware Press, 1988.
Paulus, H. E. G. *Sammulung der werwurdigsten Reisen in den Orient*. Jena: Christ. Heine Cuno's Erden, 1792.
Pilkington, Walter. *Hamilton College: 1812/1962*. Clinton, New York, Hamilton College: 1962.
Poe, Edgar Allen. *The Complete Works of Edgar Allen Poe*, ed. James Harrison. New York: AMS Press, 1965, Vol. XV.
Pope, Maurice; *The Story of Decipherment*. London: Thames and Hudson, 1975.
Prentiss, George L. *A Discourse in Memory of Thomas Harvey Skinner*. New York: Anson D. F. Randolph and Co., n.d.
_____. *The Life and Letters of Elizabeth Prentiss*. New York: Anson D. F. Randolph & Co, 1882.
_____. *The Union Theological Seminary in New York City*. New York: Anson D. F. Randolph, 1889.
Purcell, Richard J. *Connecticut in Transition: 1775-1818*. Middletown, Connecticut: Wesleyan University Press, 1963.
Raff, Diether; *A History of Germany from the Medieval Empire to the Present*, trans. Bruce Little. New York: Berg, 1988.
Rapelje, George. *A Narrative of Excursions, Voyages and Travels performed at different Periods in America, Europe, Asia, and Africa*. New York: West and Trow, 1834.
Reisner, Edward H. *The Evolution of the Common School*. New York: The Macmillan Company: 1935.
Reisner, Edward H. *Nationalism and Education Since 1789: A Social and Political History of Modern Education*. New York: The Macmillan Company, 1922.
Remini, Robert V. *The Jacksonian Era*. Arlington Heights, Ill.: Harlan Davidson, Inc., 1989.
Robbins, Sarah Stuart. *Old Andover Days*. Boston: Pilgrim Press, 1908.
Roberts, David. *Yesterday and Today, The Holy Land: Lithographs and Diaries by David Roberts*. New York: Stewart, Tabori, and Chang, 1996. (See also above under Davies, W. D.)
Roth, David M. *Connecticut: A Bicentennial History*. New York: W. W. Norton & Company, Inc., 1979.
Rowe, Henry K. *History of Andover Theological Seminary*. Newton, Mass.: Andover, 1933.
Said, Edward W. *Orientalism*. New York: Random House, 1979.

Schlesinger, Arthur M. *The Age of Jackson.* Boston: Little, Brown and Co.: 1945.
Seetzen, Ulrich Jasper. *Reisen durch Syrien, Palastina, Phonicien, Die Transjordan-Lander, Arabia Petraea und Unter-Aegypten,* 3 vols. Berlin: G. Reimer, 1845-59.
Shaw, Stanford J. and Ezel Kural Shaw. *Reform, Revolution and Republic:The Rise of Modern Turkey, 1808-1975,* Volume II of *History of the Ottoman Empire and Modern Turkey.* Cambridge: Cambridge University Press, 1977.
Seymour, George Dudley. *Captain Nathan Hale, Major John Palsgrave Wyllys: A Digressive History.* New Haven: Tuttle, Morehouse, and Taylor Company, 1933.
Smith, Eli, *Researches of the Rev. E. Smith and Rev. H. G. O. Dwight in Armenia; Including a journey through Asia Minor, and into Georgia and Persia, with a visit to the Nestorian and Chaldean Christians of Oomiah and Salmas.* Boston: Crocker and Brewster, 1833.
Smith, Henry Boynton and Roswell D. Hitchcock. *The Life, Writings, and Character of Edward Robinson, D.D. LL.D.* New York: Anson D. F. Randolph and Co., 1863.
Spann, Edward K. *The New Metropolis: New York City 1840-1857.* New York: Columbia University Press, 1981.
Stanley, Arthur Penrhyn. "An American Scholar," in *Addresses and Sermons delivered during a visit to the United States and Canada in 1878.* London: Macmillan and Co., 1883, pp. 23-33.
Steig, Reinhold. "Briefwechsel zwischen Jacob Grimm und Therese von Jacob," in *Preussische Jahrbü cher* 76 (April-June 1894).
[Stephens, John Lloyd]. *Incidents of Travel in Egypt, Arabia Petraea and the Holy Land.* 2 vols. New York: Harper & Bros., 1837.
Stevens, Mary Anne, ed. *The Orientalists: Delacroix to Matisse.* Thames and Hudson and the National Gallery of Art, 1984.
Stuart, Moses. *A Commentary on the Apocalypse.* Andover: Allen, Morrill and Wardwell, 1845.
_____. *A Commentary on the Epistle to the Romans*, 2nd ed. Andover: Gould and Newman, 1835.
_____. *Conscience and Constitution, with remarks on the recent speech of the Hon. Daniel Webster in the Senate of the United States on the subject of slavery.* Boston: Crocker and Brewster, 1850.
_____. "A Critical Examination of Some Passages in Gen. 1, with Remarks on Difficulties that attend some of the Present Modes of Geological Reasoning," in *Biblical Repository* 7 (Jan. 1836): 46-106.
_____. *A Grammar of the Hebrew Language*, 5th ed. Andover: Gould and Newman, 1835.
_____. *A Hebrew Chrestomachy Designed as the First Volume of a Course in Hebrew Study.* Andover: Flagg and Gould, 1829.
Sweet, William Warren, *The Story of Religion in America*, enlarged edition. New York: Harper and Brothers, 1950.
Taylor, Bayard. *Cyclopedia of Modern Travel,* rev. and enl. ed., 2 vols. New York: Cincinnati, Moore, Wilstach, Keys, and Co., 1861.

Thompson, George and others. *A View of the Holy Land, Its Present Inhabitants, Their Manners and Customs, Polity and Religion.* Wheeling, West Virginia: John B. Wolff, 1850.

Thomson, William M. *The Land and the Book,* 2 vols. New York: Harper Brothers, 1859.

Thrupp, Joseph Francis. *Antient Jerusalem: A New Investigation into the History, Topography, and Plan of the City, Environs, and Temple.* Cambridge: Macmillan, 1855.

Tobler, Titus. *Topographie von Jerusalem und seinen Umgebungen.* Berlin: G. Reimer, 1853.

Trumbull, John. *The Autobiography of Colonel John Trumbull, patriot-artist (1756-1843).* ed. Theodore Sizer. New Haven: Yale University Press, 1953.

Tzaferis, Vassilios. *Excavations at Capernaum. Volume I: 1978-1982.* Winona, Ind.: Eisenbrauns, 1989.

Tyler, Bennet. *Memoir of the Life and Character of Reverend Asahel Nettleton, D.D.* Hartford: Robins and Smith, 1845.

Voigt, Irma Elizabeth. *The Life and Works of Mrs. Therese Robinson.* Chicago: Deutsche-Amerikanische Historische Gesellschaft von Illinois, 1914.

Whitehill, Walter Muir. *Boston: A Topographical History.* Cambridge, Mass.: The Belknap Press of Harvard University Press, 1975.

Whitman, Walt. *Leaves of Grass: A facsimile of the first edition,* ed. Richard Bridgman. San Francisco: Chandler Publishing Co., 1968.

Wayland, John Terrill. *The Theological Department in Yale College, 1822-1858.* Ann Arbor: University Microfilms, 1933.

Wette, Wilhelm Martin Leberrecht de. *Biblische Dogmatik Alten und Neues Testaments oder kritische Darstellung der religionslehre des Hebraismus, den Judenthums und Urchristenthums,* third edition. Berlin: G. Reiner, 1831.

_____. *Lehrbuch der Hebrä isch-jü dischen Archäologie nebst einem Grundrisse der hebrä isch-jü dischen Geschichte.* Leipzig: Friedr. Chr. Wilh. Vogel, 1830.

Whitelam, Keith W. *The Invention of Ancient Israel: the silencing of Palestinian history.* New York: Routledge, 1996.

Whiting, G.B. Letter from G.B. Whiting to E. Robinson in "American Ethographical Society," *Literary World* 44 (Dec. 4, 1847), 434.

Williams, George. *The Holy City: Historical, Topographical, and Antiquarian Notices of Jerusalem,* 2nd ed. London: John E. Parker,1849.

Williams, Hermine. *Talvj (Therese Albertine Luise von Jacob): an extraordinary faculty wife.* New York: Union Theological Seminary in the City of New York, 1997.

Williams, Jay G. *The Education of Edward Robinson.* New York: Union Theological Seminary in the City of New York, 1997.

Wilson, John. *The Lands of the Bible, Visited and Described.* Edinburgh: William Whyte and Co., 1846.

Winsor, Justin. *History of the Town of Duxbury, Massachusetts.* Boston: Crosby & Nichols, 1849.

Woods, Leonard. *Letters to Unitarians and Reply to Dr. Ward.* Andover: Mark Newman, 1822.

Wright, Conrad. *The Liberal Christians: Essays on American Unitarian History.* Boston: Beacon Press, 1970.

Articles

Abel, F.-M. "Edward Robinson on the Identification of Biblical Sites," trans. Ruth Norton Albright. *Journal of Biblical Literature* 53, no. 4 (Dec. 1939), 365-372.
Aharoni, Miriam. "Arad," in *NEAEHL* I, 75-86.
Aharoni, Yohanan. "Tel Beersheba," in *EAEHL* I, 160-68.
Albright, William Foxwell. "Edward Robinson," in Allen Johnson, ed., *Dictionary of American Biography, 20 Vols.* New York: Charles Scribners' Sons, 1927-37, XVI, 39-41.
Alt, Albrecht. "Edward Robinson and the Historical Geography of Palestine," *Journal of Biblical Literature,* 58, no. 4 (Dec. 1939), 373-377.
Anon. "The Benevolent Institutions of New-York," *Putnam's Magazine of American Literature, Science, and Art,* I, no. 6 (June 1853), 673-686.
_____. "Compliment to American Authorship," *New York Observer* (July 2, 1842), 103.
_____. "Dr. Robinson and the Relic Worshipers," *The New-York Evangelist* (Apr. 3, 1845).
_____. "Educational Institutions of New-York," *Putnam's Magazine* II, no. 7 (July 1853), 1-16.
_____. "Geographical Society," *Athenaeum Journal of Literature, Science and the Fine Arts* (1842), 508. See also p. 994.
_____. "Lot's Wife and the Salt Mountain of Uzdum," *New-York Evangelist* XXVI, 11 (Mar. 15, 1855).
_____. "Mehemet Ali and His Policy," *Christian Advocate and Journal* XX. 16 (Nov. 26, 1845) and XX.17 (Dec. 3, 1845).
_____. "Mohammed Ali," *Blackwood's Edinburgh Magazine, New American Edition,* XLIX (Jan. 1841), 65-82.
_____. "Mohammedanism," *Christian Advocate and Journal* IX (May 29, 1835), 157.
_____. "New-York Historical Society," *New-York Daily Times* 383 (Dec. 9, 1852), 5.
_____. "Obituary Notice of Eli Smith, D.D.," *The Missionary Herald* LIII, no. 7 (July, 1857), 224-229.
_____. "Places of Public Amusement," *Putnam's Magazine* III, no. 14 (Feb 1854), 141-152.
_____. "The Princeton Review and Prof. Smith's Inaugural," *New-York Evangelist* XXVI, 45 (Nov. 8, 1855).
_____. "Professor Smith's Inaugural," *New-York Evangelist* XXVI, 19 (May 10, 1855), 74.
_____. "Dr. Robinson's New Testament Lexicon," *Bibliotheca Sacra* VIII, no. 29 (Jan. 1851), 218-221.
_____. "Robinson's Palestine," *Christian Advocate and Journal* (July 3, 1851), 106.

_____. "Robinson's Palestine," *New York Observer* (July 3, 1841), 106.
_____. "Robinson's Researches in Palestine," *The New-York Evangelist* (Mar. 17, 1842 *et passim*), 51. (An advertisement of the book as a premium for paid subscriptions.)
_____. "The President's Address on presenting Medals," *The Journal of the Royal Geographical Society of London* XII (1842), xi-xvi.
Arnold, Patrick M. "Gibeah," *ABD* II, 1008.
_____. "Michmash," *ABD* IV, 814-815.
Avigad, N. "Capernaum," in *EAELD* I, 286-290.
Bar-Yosef, Ofer; Eliezer Oren, Avraham Negev, "Sinai," *NEAEHL* IV, 1384-1403.
Ben-Tor, Amnon. "Hazor," *NEAEHL* II, 594-605.
Bewer, Julius. "Edward Robinson as Biblical Scholar," *Journal of Biblical Literature* 58, no. 4 (Dec. 1939), 355-363.
Biran, Avraham. "Dan," *NEAEHL* I, 323-332.
Birdsall, Richard. "The Second Great Awakening and the New England Social Order," *Church History* 39, no. 3 (1970), 345-364.
Brandfon, Frederic, "Beth Shemesh," *ABD* I, 697.
Broshi, Magen. "Along Jerusalem's Walls," *Biblical Archaeologist* 40, no. 1 (March 1977): 11-17.
Bryant, William Cullen II. "No Irish Need Apply: William Cullen Bryant Fights Nativism 1836-1845," *New York State History* 74, no. 1 (Jan. 1993), 29-46.
Bunumovitz, Shlomo and Zvi Lederman. "Beth-Shemesh," *NEAEHL* I, 249-253.
Calloway, Joseph. "Ai," *NEAEHL* I, 39-45.
Carwardine, Richard. "The Second Great Awakening in the Urban Centers: An Examination of Methodism and the New Measures," *Journal of American History* 59, no. 1 (June 1972), 327-340.
Clark, Clifford E. Jr. "The Changing Nature of Protestantism in Mid-Nineteenth Century America: Henry Ward Beecher's Seven Lectures to Young Men," *Journal of American History* 57, no. 4 (Mar. 1971), 832-846.
Chadwick, Jeffrey. "In Defense of the Garden Tomb," *Biblical Archaeology Review* 12, 4 (July/August 1986), 16-17.
Cohen, Rudolph. "Excavation at Kadesh-Barnea," *Biblical Archaeologist* 44, no. 2 (Spring 1981):93-105.
_____. "Kadesh-Barnea," *NEAEHL* III, 843-847.
Corbo, Virgilio C. "Capernaum," *ABD* I, 866.
Davies, G. I. "Mt. Sinai," *ABD* VI, 47-49.
Dearman, J. Andrew. "Edward Robinson: Scholar and Presbyterian Educator," *Journal of Presbyterian History* 69, no. 3 (Fall, 1991): 163-174.
Dodge, Asa. "Journal of the late Dr. Dodge in Mount Lebanon and the Haouran," *The Missionary Herald* XXXII, nos. 3 and 4 (Mar. and Apr., 1836), 92-97, 124-130.
Dothan, Trude and Seymour Gitin. "Ekron," *ABD* II, 415-422.
_____. "The Rise and Fall of Ekron of the Philistines," *Biblical Archaeologist* 50, no. 4 (Dec. 1987), 197-222.
Edelman, Diana V. "Jabesh-Gilead," *ABD* III, 594-595.

Fargo, Valerie. "Tell El-Hesi," *NEAEHL* II, 630-634.
Fargo, Valerie M. and Kevin G. O'Connell. "Five Seasons of Excavation at Tell El-Hesi (1970-77)," *Biblical Archaeologist* 41, no. 4 (December 1978): 165-182.
Fellman, Michael. "Theodore Parker and the Abolitionist Role in the 1850s," *Journal of American History* 61, no. 3 (Dec. 1974), 666-684.
Finkelstein, Israel. "Shiloh," *NEAEHL* IV, 1364-1370.
Fisk, Pliny and Jonas King. "Journey of Messrs Fisk and King from Cairo to Jerusalem through the Desert," *The Missionary Herald* XX, no. 2 (Feb. 1824), 33-42.
_____. "Journal of Messrs Fisk and King at Jerusalem," no. 3 (Mar. 1824), 65-71.
_____. "Journal of Messrs Fisk and King," no. 4 (Apr. 1824), 97-101.
Fisk, Pliny, "Letter from Mr. Fisk," *The Missionary Herald* XXI no. 3 (Mar. 1825), 65-68.
Foster, Benjamin R. "Robinson, Edward," *American National Biography*. New York: Oxford University Press, 1999, XVIII, 647-649.
Ginsberg, Lori D. "'Moral Suasion Is Moral Balderdash:' Women, Politics, and Social Activism in the 1850's," *Journal of American History* 73, no. 3 (Dec. 1986), 601-622.
Gitan, Seymour and Trude Dothan, "The Rise and Fall of Ekron of the Philistines," *Biblical Archaeologist* 50, No. 4 (Dec. 1987), 197-222.
Gophna, Ram. "Petra," in *NEAEHL* IV, 1181-1193.
Gorn, Elliott J. "Good-bye Boys, I Die a True American": Homicide, Nativism, and Working Class Culture in New York City," *Journal of American History* 74, no. 2 (Sept. 1987), 388-410.
Hackett, H.B. "Synoptical Study of the Gospel, and Recent Literature related to it," *Bibliotheca Sacra* III, no. ix (Feb. 1846), 1-21.
Hammett, Theodore M. "Two Mobs of Jacksonian Boston: Ideology and Interest," *Journal of American History* 62, no. 4 (Mar. 1976), 845-868.
Hamrick, Emmet W. "The Third Wall of Agrippa," *Biblical Archaeologist* 40, no. 1 (March 1977), 18-23.
Hendel, Ronald S. "The Date of the Siloam Inscription: A Rejoinder to Rogerson and Davies," *Biblical Archaeologist* 59, no. 4 (Dec. 1996): 233-237.
[Hodge, Charles]. "Review of William B. Channing, *Slavery*," *Biblical Repertory and Theological Review.* VIII, no. 2 (Apr. 1836), 268-305.
Howe, Daniel Walker. "The Evangelical Movement and Political Culture in the North during the Second Party System," *Journal of American History* 77, no. 4 (Mar. 1991), 1216-1239.
Keller, Ralph A. "Methodist Newspapers and the Fugitive Slave Law: A New Perspective for the Slavery Crisis in the North," *Church History* 43, no. 3 (Sept. 1974), 319-339.
Kellogg, Miner. "The Position of Mount Sinai Examined," *Literary World* 55 (Feb. 19, 1848), 44-46.
Kelso, James Leon. "Bethel," *NEAEHL* I, 192-194.
Kempinski, A., "Shiloh," *EAEHL* IV, 1098-1100.
Kenyon, Kathleen; Ehud Netzer; Gideon Foerster. "Jericho," *NEAEHL* II, 674-697.

King, Jonas. "Extracts from the Journal of Mr. King," *The Missionary Herald* XXI (no. 4 (Apr. 1825), 105-109.
_____. "Journal of Mr. King," *The Missionary Herald* XXIII, no. 2 (Feb. 1827), 33-38; no. 3 (Mar. 1827), 65-70.
King, Philip J. "Edward Robinson: Biblical Scholar," *Biblical Archaeologist* 46, no.4 (Dec. 1983), 230-232.
King, Philip J. "Jerusalem," *ABD* III, 747-766.
Klein, Rachel N. "Art and Authority in Antebellum New York City: The Rise and Fall of the American Art-Union," *Journal of American History* 81, no.4 (Mar. 1995), 1534-1561.
Kochavi, Moshe. "Tel Malhata," *ABD* IV, 487-488.
Kutolowski, Kathleen Smith. "Antimasonry Reexamined: Social Bases of the Grass-roots Party," *Journal of American History* 71, no. 2 (Sept. 1984), 269-293.
Lapp, Nancy L. "Tell El-Ful," *NEAEHL* II, 445-448.
McFaul, John M. "Expediency vs. Morality: Jacksonian Politics and Slavery," *Journal of American History* 62, no. 1 (June 1975), 24-39.
Martin, R.H. "United Conversionist Activities among the Jews in Great Britain 1795-1815: Pan-Evangelicalism and the London Society for Promoting Christianity among Jews," *Church History* 46, no. 4 (Dec. 1977), 437-452.
Moorhead, James H. "Joseph Addison Alexander: Common Sense, Romanticism and Biblical Criticism at Princeton," *Journal of Presbyterian History* 53, no. 1 (Spring 1975), 51-66.
_____. "Social Reform and the Divided Conscience of Antebellum Protestantism," *Church History* 48, no. 4 (Dec. 1979), 416-430.
Morrison, Howard Alexander. "The Finney Takeover of the Second Great Awakening during the Oneida Revivals of 1825-1827," *New York State History* 58, no. 1 (Jan. 1978), 27-54.
Nicolayson, "Extracts from the Journal of Mr. Nicolayson, Missionary to the Jews," *The Missionary Herald* XXIV, no. 10 (Oct. 1828), 317-321.
Negev, Avraham. "Elusa." *EARHL I, 379-383.* See also: Negev, "Elusa," *ABD* II, 484-487.
_____. "Kurnub," *NEAEHL* II, 882-893.
Netzer, Elud. "The Herodium," *NEAEHL* II, 618-716.
_____. "Masada," *NEAEHL* III, 973-985.
Olin, Stephen. "The Whole Matter Settled," *Christian Advocate and Journal* XIX, 44 (June 11, 1845), 173.
Parsons, Levi. "Extracts from the Journal of Mr. Parsons," *The Missionary Herald* XVIII, no. 1 (Jan. 1822), 16-19; "Journal of Mr. Parsons, while at Jersualem," no. 2 (Feb. 1822), 33-44.
Patrick, Joseph. "Monasteries," *NEAEHL* III, 1063-66.
Pease, Jane H. and William H. "Confrontation and Abolition in the 1850s," *Journal of American History* 58, no. 4 (Mar. 1972), 923-937.
Peterson, John L. "Beth Horon," *ABD* I, 688-89.
Pritchard, James. "Gibeon," *NEAEHL* II, 511-514.

Rainey, A.F. "The Biblical Shephelah of Judah," *Bulletin of the American Schools of Oriental Research* 251 (Summer 1983), 1-22.

[Riggs]. "Journal of Mr. Riggs on a Tour in Syria," *The Missionary Herald* XXXVI, no. 9 (Sept. 1840), 337-345.

Ritter, Carl. Two Letters from Carl Ritter to E. Robinson in "American Ethnological Society," *Literary World* 42 (Nov. 20, 1847), 382.

Roediger, Prof. "German and American Scholar," *The New-York Evangelist* (May 22, 1845), 82. (A reprint of a letter from Roediger to Robinson.)

Rogerson, John and Philip R. Davies. "Was the Siloam Tunnel Built by Hezekiah?," *Biblical Archaeologist* 59, no.3 (Sept. 1996), 138-149.

Ruse, Michael. "The Relationship between Science and Religion in Britain, 1830-1870," *Church History* 44, no. 4 (Dec. 1975), 505-522.

Scott, Donald M. "The Popular Lecture and the Creation of a Public in Mid-Nineteenth Century America," *Journal of American History* 66, no. 4 (Mar. 1980), 791-809.

Schein, Bruce E. "The Second Wall of Jerusalem," *Biblical Archaeologist* 44, no. 1 (Winter, 1981).

Shiels, Richard D. "The Second Great Awakening in Connecticut: Critique of the Traditional Interpretation," *Church History* 49, no. 4 (Dec. 1980), 401-415.

Shiloh, Yigal *et al.* "Jerusalem," *NEAEHL* II, 698-804.

Siles, William H. "Quiet Desperation: A Personal View of the Panic of 1837," *New York State History* 67, no. 1 (Jan. 1986), 89-92.

Skinner, Thomas, "Eulogy for Edward Robinson," contained in "Death of Dr. Robinson," *The Evangelist* XXXIII, 6 (Feb. 5, 1863).

Smith, Eli. "Causes of Ecclesiastical Opposition to the Gospel," *The Missionary Herald* XXV, no. 1 (Jan. 1829), 18-20.

_____. "Discovery at Sidon," *New-York Evangelist* XXVI, 14 (April 5, 1855), 14. (From a letter from Eli Smith to Robinson.)

_____. "Extracts from Letters of Mr. Smith," *The Missionary Herald* XXXIV, no. 10 (Oct. 1838), 353-357.

_____. "Hints respecting the Political State of the Countries near Mount Lebanon," *The Missionary Herald* XXV, no. 9 (Sept. 1829), 279-280.

_____. "Notices by Mr. Smith of the Bedaween Tribes of the Arabs," *The Missionary Herald* XXXV, no. 9 (Sept. 1839), 81-91.

_____. "Peculiar Difficulties in the Way of Promoting Evangelical Piety in Syria," *The Missionary Herald* XXIV, no. 4 (April 1828), 111-114.

_____. "Present Attitude of Mohammedanism," *The Missionary Herald* XXIX, no. 10 (Oct. 1833), 383-387.

_____. "Recent Intelligence: Beyroot," *The Missionary Herald* XXXIV, no. 6 (June 1838), 237.

Smith, Elwyn A. "The Role of the South in the Presbyterian Schism of 1837-38," *Church History* 29, no. 1 (Mar. 1960), 44-63.

Smith, Ethan. "The Ten Tribes of Israel: a review of Dr. Robinson's View of the twelve tribes," *New York Observer* (Dec. 25, 1841), 205.

Smith, Robert Houston. "Pella," *ABD* V, 219-221. See also: "Pella," *NEAEHL* III, 1174-1180.
Stern, Stephen J. "Stuart and Hodge on Romans 5:12-21: An Exegetical Controversy about Original Sin," *Journal of Presbyterian History* 47 no. 4 (Dec. 1969): 340-358.
Stinesprug, W.F. "The Critical Faculty of Edward Robinson," *Journal of Biblical Literature*, 58, no. 4 (Dec. 1939), 379-387.
Strange, James E. "Cana of Galilee," *ABD* I, 827.
Taylor, Joan E. "Golgotha: A Reconsideration of the Evidence for the Site of Jesus' Crucifixion and Burial," *New Testament Studies* 44, 2 (April 1998), 180-203.
Tzaferis, Vassilos. "Capernaum," *NEAEHL* I, 291-296.
_____ and Bellarmino Bagatti. "Nazareth," *NEAEHL* III, 1103-1106.
Ussishkin, David. "Megiddo," *ABD* IV, 666-679.
Wilson, Major L. "Paradox Lost: Order and Progress in Evangelical Thought in Mid-Nineteenth Century America," *Church History* 44, no. 3 (Sept. 1975), 352-366.
Whiting, George B. "Extracts from the Journal of Mr. Whiting at Jerusalem," *The Missionary Herald* XXXII, no. 7 (July 1836), 251-255
Wright, G. Ernest. "Beth-Shemesh," *EAEHL* I, 248-252.
Wyatt-Brown, Bertram. "Prelude to Abolitionism: Sabbatarianism, Politics, and the Rise of the Second Party System," *Journal of American History* 58, no. 2 (Sept. 1971), 316-342.
Yadin, Yigael. "Megiddo," *EAEHL* III, 830-856.
Yamauchi, Edwin M. "Herodium," *ABD* III, 176-180.

Index of Persons

Abbott, Samuel 92
Abraham 237, 239, 244, 327
'Abud Mûrkus 251
Adams, John 37, 60, 80
Adams, John Quincy 3,80,114, 177, 178, 316.
Agassiz, Louis 325
Alboni, Marietta 272
Albright, William Foxwell 148, 162, 338
Alcott, Louisa May 175
Alden, John 23, 28, 29, 319
Alexander, Addison 264, 287-288
Alexander, Archibald 80, 289
Ali, Mohammed 296, 207, 213-216, 220, 249, 262
Amory, Frank 132-133
Anderson, Rufus 326
Andros, Sir Edmund 27
Arago, Dominique-Francois 120
Arago, Jacques 120
Audubon, James 113
Avigad, Nahman 256

Backus, Azel 64-66, 70, 97
Backus, Charles 96
Bacon, Leonard 97
Bancroft, George 3, 177, 274, 305, 333
Bardeleben, Frau de 163
Bar-Kochba 313
Barnes, Albert 283, 284, 293
Barnum, P.T. 262, 271
Bartlett, W. H. 310
Bartlet. William 92-94
Bauer, Bruno 264, 266, 336
Bavard, John 271
Beecher, Henry Ward 55, 185, 275, 323
Beecher, Harriet (See H. B. Stowe)
Beecher, Lyman 17, 83, 185, 203, 283, 318
Beethoven, Ludwig von 39, 113, 180
Bellamy, Joseph 14, 15, 32, 41, 66, 91
Ben Dor, Immanuel 1, 5
Benjamin of Tudela 239
Berkeley, George 13
Berlioz, Hector 175
Bialloblotsky, Dr. 134-135
Bingham, Dr. 169
Bliss, Frederick 242, 338
Blumenbach, Prof. 133
Blumhardt, Christian Gottlieb 125, 128
Boardman, Dana 97
Briggs, Charles A. 262, 338
Bristol, Eli 61
Bristol, Joel 61
Brown, Moses 92, 97

Bryant, William Cullen 10, 52, 113, 132, 178, 268, 269, 273,274,276, 278, 304, 305, 308, 315, 330, 333
Buch, Leopold von 245, 309, 335
Buchanan, James 307, 316
Buckminster, Joseph 32, 95, 135
Burckhardt, Johannes Ludwig 190, 216-217, 227, 247
Burnouf, Eugene 185
Burr, Aaron 39, 60
Bushnell, Horace 38, 264, 337
Buttmann, Philip Karl 171, 192, 196
Byron, George Gordon 52, 109

Cady, Mr. 190
Calhoun, Robert C. 178, 266, 316
Calmet, Augustin 190, 191
Calvin, John 13, 91
Catherwood, Frederick 234, 271
Caukins, Eleazar 61
Champollion, Jean Francois 79, 123, 147
Channing, William Ellery 90, 283
Charles X, 115
Chateaubriand, François René 232
Chauncy, Mr. 155, 156
Church, Frederic 52, 113, 248, 308, 311, 320
Clark, Gaylord 273
Clay, Henry 57, 114, 178, 264, 266, 316, 317
Clemens, Samuel (Mark Twain) 116, 176, 311
Cole, Thomas 38, 52, 80, 85, 262, 265, 271, 273, 320
Coleridge, Samuel Taylor 38, 80, 201, 337
Constantine 231, 232
Cooper, James Fenimore 12, 79, 80, 113, 118, 124, 167, 170, 177, 178
Cox, Samuel 331
Cunningham, Mr. 131, 133, 134, 140, 158, 169

Daguerre, L.J.M. 206
Dana, R.H. 274
Da Ponte, Lorenzo 122
Darwin, Charles 46, 163, 308, 335, 336
David 186, 234, 237, 238, 334
Davis, Henry 70, 83
Davis, Jefferson
Deborah 186, 334
Delacroix, Eugene 38, 52
DeWette, Wilhelm 101, 125-129, 143, 148, 336, 337
Dickens, Charles 279
Dickinson, Emily 175
Donnelly, Mary 71, 76
Durand, Asher 265, 320

Index of Persons

Duyckinck Evart 273-276, 329-330
Dwight, Harrison Otis 193
Dwight, Sereno 132
Dwight, Timothy 16, 32, 62, 66, 93, 95, 132

Edwards, B.B. 302
Edwards, Jonathan 13-15, 32, 41, 91
Eichhorn, Joachim 101, 135, 148, 155
Eliot, John 25, 26
Emerson, Ralph 182, 201, 275
Emerson, Ralph Waldo 38, 176, 178, 200, 201, 273
Ernesti, J.A. 334
Eusebius 144, 239, 242, 253, 255
Everett, Edward 3, 9, 72, 73, 98, 135, 202, 298, 326

Farrar, Samuel 92, 172, 195
Ferris, Isaac 331
Feuerbach, Ludwig 116, 266
Fillmore, Millard 265, 311
Finney, Charles Grannison 16, 17, 70, 80, 82, 83, 103, 1114, 178, 206, 264, 265, 280, 282, 283
Follen, Karl 199
Foster, Stephen 115, 307, 308, 319-320
Francke, Auguste Hermann 136-137
Franklin, Benjamin 48, 62
Frederick II, Elector of Saxony 137
French, Jonathan 93
Fries, Jacob Frederick 127
Fuller, Margaret 264, 274

Gallatin, Albert 274, 324
Garrison, William Lloyd 203, 204, 318
Genet, Citizen Edmond Charles 10, 15
Gesenius, Wilhelm 80, 138-146, 149, 152, 155, 165, 169, 185, 188, 197, 212, 260, 301, 309
Gibbs, Josiah 80, 197, 337
Goethe, Johann Wolfgang von 39, 113, 153, 154, 166, 175, 180-183
Gramberg, C.P.W. 336
Gray, Asa 265, 325
Greeley, Horace 39, 262, 294
Griffin, Edwin D. 20
Grillparzer, Franz 153
Grimm, Jacob 153,165, 181, 183, 305
Grotefend, George Frederick 38
Grotius, Hugo 97

Hale, Nathan 21, 32
Halleck, Fitz-Greene 178, 273
Hamilton, Alexander 9, 10, 33, 39, 60
Handel, George Frederick 163
Harrison, William Henry 39, 262, 266
Hastings, Thomas 65, 272

Hawthorne, Nathaniel 23, 176-179, 265, 273, 317
Hegel, George Wilhelm Frederich 6, 42, 126, 158, 161, 175
Hengstenberg, Ernest Wilhelm 160, 185, 336
Henry, Patrick 21
Hibbard, F. G. 310
Hillhouse, James 32
Hitchcock, Clarissa 44
Hitchcock, Roswell 4, 42, 290, 295, 332
Hodge, Charles 37, 149, 150, 158, 161, 165, 167, 170, 173, 179, 197, 281, 283, 290, 300
Hoffman, Johann von 336
Holmes, H.A. 233, 234
Holmes, Oliver Wendell 200, 201, 335
Hopkins, Samuel 14, 81, 91
Howe, George 288
Humboldt, Alexander von 119, 120, 123, 158, 159, 260, 309, 335
Huntington, Daniel 273
Hussan, Sheikh 243, 246
Hutchison, Ann 25

Ingersoll, Robert 120
Irving, Washington 79, 113, 177, 273, 274, 329
Isselen, Herr 128

Jackson, Andrew 56, 58, 80, 113, 114, 175-178, 180, 204
Jacob 237, 253, 327
Jacob, Ludwig Heinrich von 152, 155
Jauchnitz, Herr 146
Jay, John 10, 21
Jefferson, Thomas 9, 10, 38, 40, 56, 66, 80
Jerome, Saint 253
Jesus 22, 26, 90, 102, 145, 152, 187, 231-233, 255-257, 301, 303, 328
Jonathan 186, 237, 334
Josephus, Flavius 231-234, 239, 254, 255, 257, 312, 314

Kaiser, Gottlieb 336
Kant, Immanuel 37
Keats, John 37, 52
Kellogg, Miner 226
Kenyon, Kathleen 232
Kierkegaard, Soren 266
Kiepert, Heinrich 260
Kirkland, Caroline (Mrs. William Kirkland) 132, 273, 274, 304
Kirkland, Eliza (Mrs. Edward Robinson) 64, 70, 71, 73, 74, 77, 133
Kirkland, George Whitefield 61, 71
Kirkland, Jerusha 71
Kirkland, Joseph 131

Index of Persons

Kirkland, John Thornton 71, 73, 74, 76, 133, 200
Kirkland, Sally 133
Kirkland, Samuel 30, 59-63, 123
Kirkland, William 131-132, 304
Kohl, J. C. 274
Kotzebue, Auguste de 126

Lafayette, Gen. M.J. P. Y. R. G de M. 3, 80. 123. 167, 176
Lanneau, Mr. 236
LeClerc, Jean 196
Lee, Robert E. 39
Lentulus, Publius 185-186
Lepsius, Richard 309
Lewis and Clark 4, 22, 39, 51, 310, 315
Lincoln, Abraham 39, 269, 308, 309, 317
Lind, Jenny 265, 271, 272
Longfellow, Henry Wadsworth 3, 29, 39, 124, 200, 273, 307, 308, 318-319, 321, 333
Lowell, James Russell 204, 308
Luther, Martin 136, 137, 148, 210
Lynch, William 310, 311, 326

McAuley, Thomas 210, 211, 286, 296
MacDonough, Thomas 55, 58
McCormick, Cyrus 176, 178
McQueen, Rev. 300
Madison, James 39, 58, 80
Mahmud II 213
Marx, Karl 116, 266
Mason, Erskine 287
Mason, J. Y. 310, 311
Mather, Cotton 24, 27
Mather, Increase 24, 27
Mather, Richard 24, 25
Melancthon, Philip 137, 148
Melville, Herman 56, 177, 264, 265, 273, 311, 218
Michelangelo 170
Mills, Annie 34
Mills, Samuel J. jr. 34
Miller, William 175, 264, 294
Monroe, James 56, 80
Morse, Jedediah 93, 162, 202
Morse, Richard 93
Morse, Sidney 93, 273, 325
Morse, Samuel F.B. 93, 162, 178, 206, 264, 273, 276
Moore, Clement Clark 277
Mosely, Sophia 33
Moses 125, 135, 190, 225, 227, 245, 254
Mozart, Wolfgang Amadeus 122, 163
Murdoch, James 62, 97, 157, 172

Napoleon 38, 39, 51, 55-58, 137, 149, 212, 213, 220

Neander, Joachim 142, 144, 159, 160, 165, 185, 261, 291
Nettleton, Asahel 41
Nevin, John 264
Newcome, William 196
Newman, John Henry 300, 328
Nicolayson, Rev. 236
Niebuhr, Carsten 190, 216, 223
Niemeyer, August Hermann 150, 151
Niles, John 62
Nordheimer, Isaac 287, 295, 301
Norris, John 92
Norton, Amanda (Mrs. Seth Norton) 88
Norton, Andrew 337
Norton, Ashahel 35, 43, 61, 62, 74, 98
Norton, Elisabeth (Mrs. Elisabeth Robinson) 35, 36, 43, 88
Norton, Ruth (Mrs. Mark Hopkins) 35
Norton, Seth 35, 62, 63, 65, 66, 70, 73, 82
Norton, Thomas 35
Novalis (Frederick von Hardenberg) 115
Noyes, George 337
Noyes, Josiah 65

Ogden, David 88, 181
Olmstead, Frederick 274

Paine, Thomas 10
Park, E. A. 302
Parker, Joel 283, 286, 287
Parker, Theodore 262, 326, 337
Paton, William 292
Patti, Adeliona 273
Paulus, Heinrich Eberhard 129, 130
Paxton, Rev. 236
Pearson, Eliphalet 91, 93, 95
Percival, James Gates 49
Petrie, Sir Flinders 242
Philippe, Louis 114, 175
Phillips, John 91, 92
Phillips, Samuel 91, 92
Pickering, John 305, 325
Pierce, Franklin 307, 316
Pius VIII, Pope 170
Plato 102, 105
Plauck, Prof. G. J. 185
Plauck, Prof. Henry (the Younger) 133-134
Poe, Edgar Allen 39, 132, 264, 265
Polk, James K. 37, 264
Pond, Enoch 302
Porter, Ebenezer 20, 96, 97, 182
Porter, Noah 302
Porter, Robert 62
Pouillet, Claude-Servais Matthais 120
Prentiss, Elizabeth 307
Prentiss, George Lewis 210, 211, 261, 288, 290
Ptolemy 228, 304

Index of Persons

Raphael 170
Rauch, Frederick 163
Raumer, Frederick von 274
Rich, (Claudius J.?) 99
Ritter, Carl 162, 211, 260, 261, 309
Roberts, David 248, 260, 271, 310
Robespierre, Maxmilien 10
Robinson, Arthur 198, 199
Robinson, Charles 36, 42, 109, 181, 266, 333
Robinson, Edward (b 1794) education of 45-50, 59-69, 89-98, 136-165; death of 331-332; family of 22-36, 39-45, 50-51, 88, 195; as librarian and book buyer 130, 146-147, 184, 209-211, 296-297; as preacher 98-106, 184-185; as orientalist 5, 325-329; as publishing scholar 5, 98, 108-109, 185-192, 196-198, 259-261, 297-304, 315-316, 322-323, 330-221, 332; as teacher 107, 183-184, 292-296, 305-306; as traveler to Egypt 212-221;to Europe, 114-174, 208-211, 305-306, 309, 315; to Lebanon 258-259; to Mt. Washington 83-88; to Palestine 214-218, 227-258, 312-314; to the Sinai 221-237; to Syria 314; wives of 70-75, 152-155, 164-174, 180-183, 199, 274, 304-305
Robinson, Edward (b. 1836) 205, 211,289, 305, 333
Robinson, Elisabeth 36, 117, 141, 171, 180, 181, 266, 332
Robinson, George (b. 1798) 36, 88, 118, 181, 195, 333
Robinson, John (b. 1671) 27-29, 30
Robinson, John (of Leyden) 23
Robinson, Ichabod 30-31
Robinson, Mary Augusta 171, 174, 211, 289, 305, 306, 330. 333
Robinson, Maxmillian 195
Robinson, Naomi Sophia (See Mrs. James Woodruff)
Robinson, Samuel 26-27
Robinson, Therese (Mrs. Edward R.) 85, 152-154, 158, 164, 165-171, 198, 199, 211, 261, 265, 273, 274, 276, 289, 304-306, 318, 321, 330, 332
Robinson, William (17th C.) 23-26
Robinson, William (b 1754) 22,28, 31ff, 40-45, 49, 75, 88, 110-111
Robinson, William (b. 1784) 33, 43, 49, 50
Robson, Mr. 314
Roediger, Eugene 172, 197, 212, 260
Rossini, Gioachino 122
Rush, Benjamin 46

Sacy, Silvestre de 121, 123, 124, 147, 167, 190, 327
Said, Edward 5, 326, 329

Sa'îd, Sheikh 242-243
Salisbury, Edward 326
Sand, Karl 126
Saul 186, 237, 238, 334
Schaff, Philip 56, 261, 302
Schiller, Frederick 151, 163, 180
Schleiermacher, Frederick 38, 42, 126, 151, 152, 156, 158, 160, 161
Schoolcraft, Henry 305
Schopenhauer, Arthur 126, 158
Schweitzer, Albert 152
Scott, Sir Walter 39, 153, 274
Seetzen, Ulrich 216
Seward, William 333
Shedd, William Greenough Thayer 338
Schumaker, Samuel 196
Sheikh of the Ta'amirah 238
Silliman, Benjamin 23, 335
Skinner, Thomas 289, 331
Smalley, John 96
Smith, Adam 152
Smith, Asa D. 331
Smith, Eli 30, 190, 192-194, 205, 216, 217, 221, 224, 225, 227, 230, 235, 238, 240, 241, 244, 248, 250, 253, 254, 259, 299, 300, 308-312, 325
Smith, Gerrit 69, 318
Smith, Henry Boynton 56, 261, 269, 291, 296, 302, 331, 332
Smith, Joseph 39, 264
Socrates 102
Sontag, Henriette (also Sonntag) 121-122, 272
Spaulding, J. 333
Spencer, Ichabod 287
Spener, Philipp Jacob 136
Spring, Gardiner 92, 331
Spring, Samuel 92, 93, 95, 97
Stansbury, Caroline (See Caroline Kirkland)
Stanley, Arthur Penrhyn 202
Stier, Ewald Rudolf 128
Steuben, Frederick von 61
Stiles, Ezra 30, 35, 40, 41
Stowe, Calvin E. 94, 173, 185, 186, 210, 318
Stowe, Harriet Beecher 39, 94, 185, 307, 318
Strauss, David F. 152, 176, 266, 336
Strong, Cyprian 35
Strong, James 69
Strong, Theodore 65-66
Stuart, Moses 20, 77, 89, 95, 97, 98, 108, 123, 128, 130, 135, 147, 157, 163-165, 172, 173, 175, 182, 184, 185, 197, 198,245, 261, 266, 267,269, 281, 301, 302, 316, 325, 334

Tallmadge, Benjamin 32
TALVJ 153
Taylor, Bayard 274
Taylor, Charles 190, 191

Index of Persons

Taylor, Joan E. 232
Taylor, Nathaniel 16, 66, 162, 280
Taylor, Zachary 265
Tecumseh 57. 58
Tholuck, August 128, 137, 138, 140, 142, 150, 157, 160, 167, 169, 185, 212, 261, 291
Thomasius, Christian 136
Thompson, George 310
Thomson, William M. 313, 314, 315
Thoreau, Henry David 56, 265, 273, 307, 320
Tieck, Johann Ludwig 166
Tittman, Johann August 185
Tocqueville, Alexis de 175, 176
Trumbull, Faith 30
Trumbull, John 23, 30
Trumbull, Jonathan 23, 30
Tyler, John 262, 266

Valla, Laurentius 187
Van Buren, Martin 178, 206, 266
Vanderbilt, Cornelius 10, 270, 278
Van Ess, Leander 130, 147, 209-211, 296
Vatke, Johann Karl 336
Victoria, Queen 56, 206
Voltaire, François Marie Arouet de 17

Wahl, Christian Abraham 108, 147, 185
Ware, Henry 89
Washington, George 4, 9, 37, 38, 60, 202
Wayne, "Mad" Anthony 10, 21

Webster, Daniel 178, 266, 267, 316
Webster, Noah 45, 46, 113
Wellhausen, Julius 336
Wellington, Arthur Wellesley, Duke of 113
Wheelock, Eleazar 30, 59, 71
Whistler, James 176
White, Henry 286, 287
Whitefield, George 13
Whitman, Walt 56, 273, 307, 321-322
Whittier, John Greenleaf 39, 204, 267, 268, 273
Williams, Othniel 110, 195
Williams, Roger 25
Winer, Georg Benedikt 108, 164
Wolcott, Naomi 33
Wolcott, Samuel 299
Woodruff, James 51
Woodruff, Mrs. James (Naomi Sophia Robinson) 33, 43, 51, 64, 274
Woods, Leonard 89, 90, 92, 93, 95, 97, 182, 198
Woods, Leonard jr. 184
Wordsworth, William 37, 38, 109, 201

Yates, Andrew 165, 169

Zeitun, Abu 248, 249, 250

Index of Places

Acre (Acco) 38, 215, 262, 310, 312, 315
Adoraim 250
Aijalon 251
'Ain Duk 239
Ai 239
Ain Es-Sultan (Jericho) 238
Ain Shems 241, 250, 251
Akabah, Gulf of 227
'Akir 251
Alexandria, Egypt 212, 218, 219, 221 259, 262
Andover, Mass. 83, 84, 88, 91-93, 106, 150, 151, 171, 181, 302
Andover Theological Seminary 88-98, 181-184 *et passim*
Antipatris 300
'Arabah 246-249
Ar'arah 250
Armenia 193, 194
Aroer 250
Athens, Greece 102, 218, 248
Auburn Theological Seminary 56, 82, 285, 290
Austria 156, 157, 300, 328

Baalbeck 258, 314
Babylon 99
Baltimore, Md 264
Banias 258, 314
Beersheba 228
Beirut 193, 194, 252, 256, 258, 259, 262, 309, 311, 313
Beisan 255, 313, 328
Beit Jibrin 242
Beit Lahm 312
Belgium 209
Berlin, Conn. 96
Berlin, Germany 152, 154-158, 160-164, 199, 211, 212, 259, 261, 309, 331
Bethany 233
Bethel 236, 239, 313
Bether 313
Beth Horon (Upper and Lower) 251
Bethlehem 214, 237, 240
Bethlehem of Zebulon 312
Bethlehem, Conn. 66
Bethsaida 314
Bethshan (Beisan) 255, 313, 328
Beth Shemesh 241, 250, 251
Beth-Zacariah 313
Bir es-Seba 227
Beth Zur 313
Bittir 312

Boston, Mass. 11, 17, 23, 26, 29, 30, 82, 89, 90, 93, 104, 105, 133, 158, 175, 184, 196, 198, 199, 200, 202-204, 270, 273, 321, 324
Bremen, Germany 155, 174, 315
Brooklyn, N.Y. 279, 286, 321
Brunswick, Germany 155

Cairo, Egypt 221, 222
Cana 255
Canada 57, 264
Canterbury, N.H. 84
Capernaum 257, 314
Catskill, N.Y. 34, 51, 64, 274
Catskills, the 86, 321
Cedars of Lebanon 258, 314
Chorazin 314
Church of the Holy Sepulcure 230, 231, 300, 312, 328
Church of the Ascension 233
Clinton, N.Y. 2, 35, 51, 53, 62-64, 71, 74, 76, 77, 81-83, 88, 97, 109-111, 195
Colgate (Madison) University 176
Columbia University 63, 180, 276, 277
Connecticut 11-24 *et passim*
Constantinople 259
Cornwall, Conn. 18, 96
Crawford Notch 85

Damascus, Syria 22, 314, 315
Dan 258, 314
Darmstadt, Germany 130, 209
Dartmouth College 59, 71, 88, 96, 185, 192, 288
Dead Sea 238, 239, 244, 254, 256, 310, 326, 335
Deir Dîwân 239
Dendera, Egypt 220
Dorchester, Mass. 23, 24, 25, 28
Dornberg, Germany 166
Dothan 312
Dresden, Germany 164, 170, 259
Dura 250
Duxbury, Mass. 28, 29, 30

East Haven, Conn. 50
Edom 246
Eglon 242
Egypt 100, 190, 212, 213, 214, 219ff, 262, 322
Eisleben, Germany 136
Ekron 251
Elat 227
Elath 227
Eleutheropolis 242, 250

Index of Places

Elim 224, wells of 223
El Kuds 229
el-Weibeh 249, 250
Elusa (el-Khulash) 228
En-Gedi 238
England 125, 134, 201, 206, 208, 256, 297, 305, 309, 328
Erie Canal 80, 81, 110, 117, 270
er-Râmeh 313
Esdraelon, plains of 254, 312
Es-Saba'iyeh 226
et-Tell 239

Fairfield Academy 63, 65
Farmington, Conn. 35, 50
Five Points, N.Y.C. 278
Florence, Italy 169, 170
Florida 56, 57
Fort Niagara 57, 58
France 15, 37,38, 39, 51, 57, 114, 117, 119, 121, 123, 167, 175, 208, 265
Frankfort, Germany 130, 209
"Frank" Mountain 238

Gaza 240, 241, 242
Geba 313
Gennesareth 257, 314
Genoa, Italy 169
Germany 43, 108, 111, 117, 119, 124, 126, 128, 137, 140, 150-158, 162, 163, 167, 170, 192, 209, 211, 216, 217, 220, 258, 265, 268, 278, 297, 304, 306, 327, 333, 335
Gettysburg, Pa. 196
Gibeah 237
Gibeon 236
Ginaea 254
Gommorah 244
Goshen, land of 222
Göttingen 130-136, 138, 141, 150, 155
Greece 218

Haifa 268
Halle, Germany 136-138, 149, 150, 152, 154-158, 163, -167, 171, 172, 182, 185, 192, 212
Hamilton College 3, 16, 30, 35, 50, 53, 59-71, 94, 110, 131, 132, 181, 192, 193, 276, 277, 286, 293
Hamilton-Oneida Academy 35, 59, 60, 62, 65, 82, 97
Hannover, Germany 155
Hartford, Conn. 11, 32, 158, 181, 327
Harvard University 20, 25, 27, 50, 68, 71, 73, 89, 91, 94, 96, 97, 200, 201, 319
Hasbeiya 314
Hattin, horns of 256
Hazeroth 227

Hazor 314
Hebron 214, 228, 237, 240-242, 249, 250, 312, 313
Heidelberg, Germany 129-130, 166
Heliopolis, Egypt 220
Herodium 238
Heraculeum 169
Hezekiah's Tunnel 43, 52. 235
Hesse, Germany 130
Holland 125, 305
Holy Land 100, 210, 214, 260, 289, 305, 310, 313, 315, 329
Honolulu 323
Horeb 224, 225
Hudson River 12, 51, 87, 117, 270
Huleh, Lake 258, 314, 315, 330

Idhana 242
India 219
Ireland 268
Italy 167-171, 176

Jaffa 215, 240
Jebel Musa 225
Jericho 238
Jenin 254
Jerusalem 125, 148, 214, 215, 229-236, 237, 238, 240, 241, 242, 250, 252, 254, 271, 299, 311, 312, 328; Topography of 231; walls of 232, 234
Jezreel 254
Jokneam 312
Jordan River 100, 217, 238, 239, 258, 310
Jordan Valley (Ghôr) 256, 313
Jotapata 312
Judah 237, 250
Jutte 250

Kadesh (Kadesh-barnes) 249
Karnak, Egypt 220
Kanael-Jelîl 255
Kedesh (Kedes) 314
Kefr Kenna 255
Kensington, Conn. 98, 104
Khân Minyeh 314
Kharkov, Ukraine 152
Kiriath-Jearim 241
Kuryet el-'Enab 241

Lebanon, Conn. 30, 31, 32, 59
Le Havre, France 119
Leichester, Academy 96
Leipzig, Germany 136, 146, 147, 149
Lejjûn 254
Leontopolis, Egypt 220
London, England 298, 209, 309
Lowell, Mass. 200

Index of Places

Ludd (Lydda) 252
Luxor, Egypt 220

Magdeburg, Germany 155
Maine 81
Malta 192, 193
Mamre 313
Maon 238
Mar Saba 240
Masada 238, 244
Massachusetts 9, 12, 13, 15, 20, 24, 25, 27, 28, 29, 31, 33, 45, 50, 66, 71, 81, 83, 96, 103, 177, 202, 241, 317
Mediterranean Sea 100
Megiddo 254, 312
Memphis, Egypt 220
Merabah 224
Michmash 236, 313
Middlebury College 70, 94, 287
Missouri 81
Mizpeh 236
Mohawk River 117
Moladah 243, 250
Mount of Olives 233
Mount Gerizim 253
Mount Hor 246, 249, 312
Mount Lebanon 300, 322
Mt.Sinai 87, 224, 226, 250
Mount Tabor 252, 255, 256
Mt. Washington 52, 83, 85, 86, 305, 321
Nablus 253, 254, 312, 313
Naples, Italy 168, 169, 170
Nazareth 214, 254, 255
Neby Samwill 236
Negeb (Negev) 190, 227, 244, 335
Newburyport, Mass. 92, 97
New Haven, Conn. 11, 32, 53, 95, 104, 106, 155, 181, 195, 333
New York 11, 12, 16, 51, 56, 60, 81
New York City 23, 71, 79, 80, 82, 117, 180, 181, 198, 199, 205, 262-306, 309, 315, 321, 323, 331; churches of 278-284; public library 4, 297, 330; historical society 275, 324, 325, 332
New York University 180, 186, 276- 278, 285, 301
Nile River 212, 221
Nineveh 235
Northford, Conn. 192
Northhampton, Mass. 13, 25, 32

Oberlin College 176, 179
Oormiah, Armenia 193
Ophel 234
Ophra 236
Ottoman Empire 113, 193, 212-214
Palestine 19, 36, 52, 84, 145, 147, 148, 163, 186, 193, 205, 208, 211, 214-217, 252, 256, 259, 299, 302, 305, 306, 311, 312, 313, 327, 329, 330
Paris, France 115,118, 119-124, 133, 134, 149, 167, 170, 171
Pella 313
Petra 52, 243, 247, 250
Philadelphia, Pa. 60, 71, 82, 286, 313
Phillips Academy 91, 93, 94, 201
Plymouth, Mass. 28
Prague, C.R. 156
Princeton College 59, 149, 150
Princteon Theological Seminary 93, 197, 280, 283, 285, 286, 287, 290, 338
Prussia 137, 138

Ramah 236, 241
Ramleh 250, 251, 252
Red Sea 190, 221, 222
Rehoboth 221
Rhine River 129
Rimmon 313
Robinson's Arch 233-234, 312
Rome, Italy 169, 170, 248, 280
Rome, N.Y. 82
Ruhaibeh 221
Russia 55, 113, 153, 212, 214

Saale River 136, 154
Safed 215, 258
St. Catherine's Monastery 224, 225, 227
Samaria 254, 312
St. Petersburg, Russia 152
Sandwich Islands 18
Shechem 253
Scotland 281, 305
Sea of Galilee 22, 256, 310, 314
Sebastieh (Sebaste) 254
Sebbah 310
Seilûn 253
Shaker Village 84
Shephelah 250
Siloam, pool of 234
Shiloh 253
Shuweikeh 241
Sidon 258, 312
Sinai 145, 190, 225, 226, desert of 223, peninsula 218, 224
Sistine Chapel 170
Smyrna 259, 314
Soba 241
Socoh 241
Sodom 244
Somers, Conn. 96
Sorbonne 120, 123
South Carolina 176
Southington, Conn. 11, 31, 32-36, 40-53, 75, 77, 83, 88, 97, 103, 104, 106, 181
Stettin, Germany 155, 165

Index of Places

Stockbridge, Mass. 71
Strasbourg, France 167
Suez 221, 224
Switzerland 165, 166, 167
Syria 192, 194, 213, 214, 259, 262, 322

Ta'annuk (Taanach) 254
Tekoa 238
Tel Arad 1, 243
Tell Beit Mirsim 252
Tell el-Cadi (Qadi) 258, 314
Tel El-Ful
Tell el-Hasy (Hesi) 242
Tell el Milh 243, 244, 250
Tell el Qudeirat 249
Tell er-Rumeileh 251
Tell Hum 257, 314
Tell Jefat 312
Tell Kaimon 312
Tell Mutsellim 312
Thamar 250
Thebes, Egypt 248
Themail 250
Tiberias 257, 258, 310, lake of 256
Tomb of Abner 241
Tomb of Helena (Tomb of the Kings) 235
Trieste 212, 218, 309, 315
Tübingen 128
Turin, Italy 169, 170
Twinsburg, Ohio 110, 195
Tyre 258, 312

Union College 63, 94, 165, 276, 286

Union Theological Seminary 3, 130, 147, 176, 198, 202, 205, 209-211, 259, 261, 278, 284-297, 301, 323; library of 2, 130, 210, 334, 338
University of Basel 125
University of Berlin 125, 126, 138, 158
University of Halle 131, 136, 137, 140, 143, 150, 152, 164, 171, 261, 298
University of Jena 125, 127
University of Wittenberg 137
Utica, N.Y. 61, 63, 82, 117, 132, 193

Vienna, Austria 156, 212, 259, 231
Virginia 305, 307

Wadi Kelt 238
Wadi Musa 243, 246, 247, 327
Wady Rahah 226
Washington, Conn. 96
Washington, D.C. 55, 57, 264
Wilton, Conn. 95
Windsor, Conn. 32, 33
Winter Palace, Herod's 239
Wittenberg 147, 148

Yabneh 251
Yale University 15, 16, 28, 30-33, 35, 40, 50, 51, 62, 66, 68, 70, 76, 91, 94, 95, 97, 132, 181, 192, 197, 299, 326
Yale Divinity School 20
Yebna 251
Yutta 250

Zer'in 254
Ziph 238
Zohar 244

SOCIETY OF BIBLICAL LITERATURE
BIBLICAL SCHOLARSHIP IN NORTH AMERICA

Kent Harold Richards, Editor

Frank Chamberlain Porter: Pioneer in American Biblical Interpretation	Roy A. Harrisville
Benjamin Wisner Bacon: Pioneer in American Biblical Criticism	Roy A. Harrisville
A Fragile Craft: The Work of Amos Niven Wilder	John Dominic Crossan
Edgar Johnson Goodspeed: Articulate Scholar	James Cook
Shirley Jackson Case and the Chicago School: The Socio-Historical Method	William J. Hynes
Humanizing America's Iconic Book	Gene M. Tucker and Douglas A. Knight, editors
A History of Biblical Studies in Canada: A Sense of Proportion	John S. Moir
Searching the Scriptures: A History of the Society of Biblical Literature, 1880-1980	Ernest W. Saunders
Horace Bushnell: On the Vitality of Biblical Language	James O. Duke
Feminist Perspectives on Biblical Scholarship	Adela Yarbro Collins, editor
Erwin Ramsdell Goodenough: A Personal Pilgrimage	Robert S. Eccles
A Century of Greco-Roman Philology: Featuring the American Philological Association and the Society of Biblical Literature	Frederick William Danker
The Pennsylvania Tradition of Semitics: A Century of Near Eastern and Biblical Studies at the University of Pennsylvania	Cyrus Gordon
Moses Stuart	John H. Giltner
Max Leopold Margolis: A Scholar's Scholar	Leonard Greenspoon
The Bible and the University: The Messianic Vision of William Rainey Harper	James P. Wind
A History of Bible Translation and the North American Contribution	Harry M. Orlinsky and Robert G. Bratcher
Cadbury, Knox, and Talbert: American Contributions to the Study of Acts	Mikeal C. Parsons and Joseph B. Tyson, editors
The Times and Life of Edward Robinson: Connecticut Yankee in King Solomon's Court	Jay G. Williams